21世纪高等学校国际经济与贸易系列规划教材

U0663372

# 国际商务谈判：
## 理论·实务·案例分析

主　编　吴仁波　刘昌华
副主编　战岐林　刘　迅

ZHEJIANG UNIVERSITY PRESS
浙江大学出版社

**图书在版编目(CIP)数据**

国际商务谈判：理论·实务·案例分析/吴仁波，
刘昌华主编. —杭州：浙江大学出版社,2017.12（2025.8重印）

ISBN 978-7-308-17590-6

Ⅰ.①国… Ⅱ.①吴… ②刘… Ⅲ.①国际商务—商
务谈判 Ⅳ.①F740.41

中国版本图书馆 CIP 数据核字（2017）第 264954 号

**国际商务谈判：理论·实务·案例分析**

吴仁波 刘昌华 主编

| | |
|---|---|
| 责任编辑 | 陈丽勋 |
| 责任校对 | 董 唯 陆雅娟 |
| 封面设计 | 春天书装 |
| 出版发行 | 浙江大学出版社 |
| | （杭州市天目山路 148 号 邮政编码 310007） |
| | （网址：http://www.zjupress.com） |
| 排 版 | 杭州林智广告有限公司 |
| 印 刷 | 杭州钱江彩色印务有限公司 |
| 开 本 | 787mm×1092mm 1/16 |
| 印 张 | 21.5 |
| 字 数 | 512 千 |
| 版 印 次 | 2017 年 12 月第 1 版 2025 年 8 月第 5 次印刷 |
| 书 号 | ISBN 978-7-308-17590-6 |
| 定 价 | 59.00 元 |

# 前　言

中国经济特别是对外贸易的快速发展,需要大量既懂得国际商务知识又具备较强英语应用能力的高级复合型人才。国际商务谈判是国际经济与贸易及国际商务等专业的核心主干课程,是现代国际商务人员必备的一项基本技能;其内容涉及经济学、管理学、语言学、心理学、社会学、文化学、民俗学等诸多学科,是一门实践性很强的综合性应用课程。本书适合国际经济与贸易、国际商务、工商管理、电子商务及商务英语等专业的学生、外贸工作者及需要同外商进行沟通的从业人员参考使用,也可作为教学用书、公司培训以及自学参考用书。

本书分三篇,共9章,第一篇为理论篇(第1～2章),介绍了国际商务谈判的概况及主要理论;第二篇为实务篇(第3～6章),介绍了国际商务谈判的准备和过程(开局、报价与还价、磋商以及每个过程的策略);第三篇为知识篇(第7～9章),介绍了国际商务谈判的语言技巧、常用礼仪及主要国家商人的谈判风格。附录为模拟谈判资料和要求以及与谈判相关的常用术语。

本书主要有以下几个特点:

1. 知识的实用性。本书为双语教材,每章英语在前,汉语在后。适合于双语教学,也可用于单语教学,更有利于学生的自主学习。另外教材抓住"应用"二字,在编写风格上尽量淡化枯燥的谈判理论,重点介绍谈判实务中的一些做法以及策略和技巧。

2. 内容的时代性。本书内容取材真实,反映了当今国际商务谈判的现实状况与最新变化。书中很多内容都是编者通过实际工作经历和对外贸公司的调研,选自实际应用范例的第一手资料,能反映谈判的实际过程和真实情况,从而拓宽学生的视野。

3. 突出案例教学。书中列举了48个简短、典型且又通俗易懂的案例,紧扣每章所讲的内容，在为学生提供国际商务谈判真实情景的同时，以期培养学生分析问题、解决问题的能力。每章先以开篇案例引出主题，在主要内容中穿插相关案例佐以分析，结尾又以案例强化主题并附有思考题目。

本书基于编者多年的谈判工作和教学实践所积累的经验，由吴仁波和刘昌华两位老师与战岐林、刘迅等老师合作完成，全书由吴仁波设计、统稿，刘昌华负责翻译及文字润色。北京大学博士研究生吴唯伊参加了文字及格式的校对工作。本书的编写得到了浙江大学出版社的大力支持，编译过程中参考了多种同类教材，在此一并表示深深的谢意。由于编者水平有限，书中之不妥在所难免，敬请各位读者、同行及专家批评指正！

编　者
**2017 年 6 月**

CONTENTS 目 录

# 第二篇　实务篇

# 第三篇　知识篇

第一篇

理 论 篇

# Chapter 1

# An Overview of International Business Negotiation

☞ **Case study 1 – 1**   (**A prisoner and the guard**)

A prisoner was put into the jail alone and idled about all day. One day, he suddenly smelled out the flavor of Marlboro cigarette which he liked very much, the smell coming from the guard who was smoking. The prisoner knocked at the door gently. "What do you want?" the guard asked arrogantly. "Please give me one Marlboro cigarette," the prisoner answered. The guard felt surprised, "A prisoner even wants to smoke!" He hummed banteringly and left. The prisoner knocked at the door again, this time he knocked strongly. "What do you want again?" asked the guard. "Please give me one cigarette within 30 seconds, or I will knock at this concrete wall with my head till I am badly mutilated and lose consciousness, and when I wake up, I will say it's all because of you. Probably the authority will not believe me, but you simply have to attend every hearing to prove you are innocent. You will be asked to fill in all kinds of reports—all these are due to one inferior Marlboro cigarette. So only one cigarette, I'll make you no more trouble." At last the guard passed the prisoner one cigarette through the window and lighted for him.

Do you think the talk between the prisoner and the guard can be called a negotiation?

We live in a world of limited resources, but man's appetites are infinite, which has constantly given rise to conflicts with limited resources. There are two ways to resolve such conflicts: One is by force and the other is by negotiation, and it is no doubt that the latter is much better. In the field of international business, the era when one party manipulated the other by means of violence and force no longer exists. Instead, negotiation has become an effective approach to resolving conflicts and adjusting interests.

You probably think that negotiation is irrelevant to our lives, and that it is the matter concerning governments and large enterprises. As a matter of fact, it suits for not only matters of utmost concern, but also for any conflicts, contradiction and different opinions concerning our lives. There might be negotiations between governments, enterprises and even individuals. For each of us, everybody is a negotiator no matter whether you like it or not. You might be discussing with your classmates where to have your supper, debating with your parents which coat to buy, talking with your boss about your promotion, bargaining the price of buying a house, and handling the responsibility for a car incident, etc.

Therefore, every one of us is negotiating consciously or unconsciously. Negotiation is an indispensable part in our life, and exists in every aspect of our life. As long as there are conflicts in our society, there is negotiation. A successful negotiation can help us reach our expected goal.

An intelligent conversation can help a hopeless person to face up to his life again.

An open and frank negotiation can make a boy and a girl who are in an emotion crisis love each other again.

A right negotiation can make an enterprise which is in a dilemma turn for the better.

A successful diplomatic negotiation can change a bloody war into a peaceful situation.

A successful negotiator amounts to thousands of soldiers; he is not only a tactician who plays a vital importance, but also a strategic commander.

## Ⅰ. The Concept of International Business Negotiation

There are many kinds of negotiations. Negotiation might be formal or informal; it might be specialized or ordinary. According to the content, it can be divided into political negotiation, diplomatic negotiation, business negotiation and military negotiation. In this book, we mainly talk about business negotiation from the angle of international aspect.

### 1. The concept of negotiation

From the above case, we can see that a negotiation should at least include three factors: the negotiating subject, negotiating object and negotiating purpose. Negotiation, as a very general activity, can take place at any time in our daily life. It can happen between you and your counterparts, or in your family. When a person has a desire to be fulfilled, there is an incentive to lure people into negotiating process. As long as people exchange ideas for changing mutual relationship or negotiate for reaching a deal, they are actually negotiating.

In simple words, negotiation is a process of communication for reaching an agreement/or solving a problem or making an arrangement between two or more parties.

### 2. The concept of business negotiation

The so-called business negotiation refers to the process in which the two groups engaged in business activities conclude a deal by way of communication, interaction, discussion and compromise in order to meet the requirements of a transaction. Business negotiations are the most widespread and common activities under the circumstance of market economy.

So business negotiation is a process of communication by the participants of business activities to close a deal or achieve a proposed financial goal.

### 3. The concept of international business negotiation

International business negotiation refers to the process in which people from different countries or districts reach the goal of trade by way of communication, interaction, discussion and compromise to meet a certain need. It is the extension and development of business negotiation in the international field.

In other words, international business negotiation is a process of communication by the participants of business activities from different countries or districts so as to close a deal.

## Ⅱ. Characteristics of International Business Negotiation

### 1. Characteristics of negotiation

a. Every negotiation involves two or more than two parties. There are at least two participants in a negotiation.

b. The objective of a negotiation must be definite. Different from everyday talk, the purpose of a negotiation is to persuade someone else into accepting one's own ideas, and to maintain or achieve mutual interests.

c. Negotiation must be conducted on an equal basis. Both sides are independent and equal in dignity and legal status whether it is a high-level negotiation or a low-level negotiation. Neither side is subordinate to the other side or supposed to coerce the other side into giving in.

## 2. Characteristics of business negotiation

a. Its principle is equality and mutual benefit. Equality is the basis of any business negotiation. It is the only way to realize mutual benefit. Only the principle of equality and mutual benefit can lead to "win-win" or "multi-win."

b. Business is aimed at gaining economic interests and pursuing economic profits. Different negotiators have different economic goals. Without economic interests, business negotiation will lose its values and foundations. Therefore, business negotiations are negotiations intended to gain direct economic interests.

c. Price is the core of business negotiations, and all the other factors can be converted into price. Business negotiation involves many factors and negotiators' demands and interests can be manifested by many factors but price is always the core of all business negotiations.

## 3. The particular characteristics of international business negotiation

Besides the general characteristics of negotiation and business negotiation, international business negotiation also has the following particular characteristics.

a. There exists the obstacle of language. Different people speak different languages, so interpreter is of vital importance in international business negotiation. English is the most widely used language. Besides, Chinese, French, Russian, Arabic, Spanish, Japanese and German are also often used.

b. There exist cultural differences. Participants in international business negotiation come from different countries with different economic and cultural backgrounds, different values and ethics, different styles of thinking and manners and behaviors. Their language expressions or customs may vary a lot, too. Cultural difference is sure to make it more difficult for international business negotiations than domestic ones. This characteristic requires business negotiators not only to reconcile each other's economic relations, but also to respect and harmonize each other's cultural and religious aspects.

c. Negotiators must know both domestic and international law. Different negotiators come from different countries and regions, so apart from the domestic laws and regulations, they simply have to know the relevant international law and practices such as INCOTERMS, Uniform Rules for Collection, Uniform and Practice for

Documentary Credit, etc.

d. Negotiators must take many factors into account, such as international politics, international economics, diplomatic matters and religious belief. For example, because of the Financial Crisis of Southeast Asia in 1997, many business negotiations between Korean (R.O.K.) companies and domestic trading companies had to be stopped or delayed.

e. It is more complicated and difficult than domestic negotiations. Being transnational is the most prominent characteristic of international business negotiations, and it is also the foundation of other features. International business negotiations will result in international transaction, capital's transnational flow, international accounting, insurance, transportation, etc.

This characteristic requires negotiators to be familiar with international practices, the law in our counterparts' country, and all kinds of regulations of international economic organizations and international business law. The particular characteristics of international business negotiation determine its complexity and difficulty. Besides, the negotiators will simply have to take into account all kinds of factors, such as international politics, international economy and international culture.

## Ⅲ. Types of International Business Negotiation

According to different standards, international business negotiations can be divided into various types.

### 1. Classification by object or content of negotiation

(1) Product trade negotiation

Product trade negotiation is also called visible goods trade negotiation, the process in which importers and exporters from different countries confer with each other about the buying and selling of a product, the terms and conditions for the transaction, including the relevant quality, quantity, packing, price, shipment, insurance, payment terms, claim and arbitration. Import and export trade negotiations account for absolutely large part of international business negotiation and take on various forms.

(2) Technology trade negotiation

International technology trade negotiation refers to the conferring process in which the technology transferor and the transferee from different countries discuss about the features, price, payment terms and so on of a certain technology.

(3) Service trade negotiation

International service trade refers to the cross-border transfer of a service, including labor export，cross-border transportation，international communication，finance and insurance，tourism，advertising，medical care，film，auto-visual records，sports，technological instruction，designing，accounting，auditing，assessing，legal consultation and services，etc.

Besides，there are also compensation negotiations，leasing negotiations，etc.

## 2. Classification by scale or members of negotiation

According to the number of people，negotiations can be classified as individual negotiation and collective negotiation.

Individual negotiation refers to the pattern in which either side sends one representative to the negotiation table. The individual negotiators relatively have greater right to make decision and to deal with various situations independently，which facilitates negotiators solving different problems.

Collective negotiation refers to the negotiation in which two or more than two members participate. The team members have clear distinctive responsibilities. According to the usual practice，a negotiation with 4 – 12 negotiating members is called a medium-sized negotiation; a negotiation with 2 – 3 members is considered a small-sized negotiation; and a large-sized negotiation usually refers to the negotiation with more than 12 members.

## 3. Classification by attitudes and policies of negotiators

According to the attitudes and policies that both sides adopt，negotiations can be divided into compromise negotiation，ground negotiation（which means adopting a hard attitude）and principle negotiation.

Compromise negotiation can also be called friendly negotiation，in which negotiators are prepared to compromise to reach an agreement in order to avoid conflicts.

Ground negotiation refers to the situation in which negotiators regard negotiation as competition and struggle of minds，with the view that the firmer one holds his ground，the more benefits he can obtain.

Principle negotiation requires the two sides to treat each other as equals. That means paying attention to the cooperating relationship in the first place. Unlike compromise negotiation which stresses maintaining the relationship and ignoring the gain of interests，principle negotiation requires both sides to respect mutual basic needs and try their best to find the same interests，so it is more and more preferred and widely used.

## 4. Classification by procedure

（1）Horizontal negotiation

Horizontal negotiation refers to the conferring process in which all the issues concerned are presented first and then discussed one by one, and an issue which cannot be settled at once may be skipped and settled later until all the issues are settled properly. Horizontal negotiation is widely used in diverse international business negotiations as it shows the following advantages: Easy issues can be resolved first and then the tough ones; negotiators are allowed to conduct the negotiation flexibly and quickly; and at last the negotiation tends to be highly efficient.

☞  **Case study 1 – 2**    （**Horizontal negotiation**）

Dastech International Inc. in New York, US, negotiated with The Nissho Iwai Corporation in Japan over the transaction of beef export on March 15, 2017. American and Japanese sides first determined what clauses were expected to be in the contract for the beef transaction, such as the clause of beef quality, quantity, payment terms, shipment, price, packing, delivery, claim, force majeure, etc. Then they began to discuss about the quality,quantity of the product and the terms of payment. However, they had different views on price issues; and they decided to put it aside and confer about other clauses like packing, delivery. After they settled most of all clauses, they returned to the delayed issue of price terms to reach final agreement.

This kind of negotiation is called horizontal negotiation, which does not necessarily need to follow the sequence of the agreed contract clauses strictly.

（2）Vertical negotiation

Vertical negotiation refers to the process in which all the issues to be discussed are listed according to its logic and then settled one by one in its logical order. It is characterized by the fact that if the previous issues are not settled, the following issues cannot be conferred.

## 5. Classification by importance of negotiation

According to the importance or the degree how people have prepared for the negotiation,negotiations can be classified as formal negotiation and informal negotiation.

### 6. Classification by place

According to the place where the business negotiation takes place，negotiations can be classified as "host court" negotiation，"guest court" negotiation，"changing court" negotiation，and negotiation at a third place.

To make a comparison between "host court" and "guest court," both of them have advantages and disadvantages. Generally speaking，"host court" have the advantage of good timing，favorable geographical location and support from people all around. To be specific，"host court" have the following advantages：

a. Saving the traveling expenses；

b. Being familiar with the environment；

c. Being easy to get the necessary information；

d. Being able to take the initiative through relevant arrangements；

e. Choosing the most suitable occasion and site to hold the negotiation；

f. Creating pressure / obstacles for the other side. (Be careful if used.)

Every coin has two sides. Its disadvantages are also obvious：

a. Being easily distracted；

b. Having to make the relevant preparations；

c. In charge of guest-entertaining.

### 7. Classification by way of communication

According to the way of communication，negotiations can be divided into oral negotiation (face-to-face & telecommunication) and written negotiation (e-mail & fax). The negotiations presented above are almost oral ones. However，international business communication involves distance in time and space. To increase the efficiency and cut the cost，many negotiations are carried out in written forms. Oral negotiation and written negotiation are distinguished from each other in terms of the language used in communication.

Similar to "host court" and "guest court," both oral negotiation and written negotiation have advantages and disadvantages.

The advantages of an oral negotiation are as follows：

a. Negotiators can ask and answer questions in person directly and amply to decide whether to close a deal.

b. Negotiators can examine the facial expression，gestures，and psychology of the other side so as to adjust the techniques or strategies in the negotiation.

c. Seeing is believing. Oral negotiation can cultivate the mutual feelings and make the negotiation more fruitful.

The main advantages of a written negotiation can be summed up as follows:

a. It is with much low cost.

b. It is convenient. People can communicate with each other at any time anywhere.

c. There is no need to be in a hurry; you may have enough time to think over.

d. It is free from psychological pressure.

e. It is easy to keep as a record.

In reality, no hard and strict line can be drawn between "host court" and "guest court," and between the oral and written negotiation. In most of business negotiations, negotiators might have the necessity to be both a "host court" and a "guest court," and the two sides might conclude the business after both oral and written negotiations.

## IV. Principles of International Business Negotiation

The principles of international business negotiation are the basic rules or norms accepted in international business negotiation that all participating parties are obliged to observe. Understanding these principles help negotiators better apply and implement negotiating strategies and skills to increase the effectiveness and efficiency of their negotiations.

### 1. Equal and voluntary participation

Equal and voluntary participation are basic premises for international business negotiation. All parties should be equal, respect each other and cannot force other sides. They should negotiate on the basis of their free will and solve the discrepancies through friendly negotiation.

a. All parties, big or small, strong or weak, should be equal. In international business negotiation, all parties must be equal participants and be willing to participate in it, no matter how great the gaps are in their economic power and organizational scale.

This principle also reflects that participants in negotiations have the same option for choosing the trade items and terms. Only through equal talks and consensus may an agreement be reached and be followed by all the parties.

b. Veto power embodies equality. In international business negotiation, no situation exists in which one party is entitled to make the final decision or the minority must be subordinate to the majority. All parties have the power to veto any clause under negotiation, and so no agreement will be achieved if one party is not satisfied.

c. Respect embodies equality. All parties concerned should show respect for other sides regardless of their power and size, being careful to avoid showing discrimination against their counterparts. If any party abuses its power and bullies others, the negotiation will fail.

d. Voluntary agreement embodies equality. Voluntary agreement means that all parties can participate in the negotiation willingly and make their own decisions. They negotiate to pursue their own self-interest instead of doing so under external pressure or against their own will. Only if you are willing can you be equal, understand one another, make concessions, and finally reach a mutually beneficial agreement.

### 2. Abiding by the law and putting credibility first

International business negotiation is ongoing under certain legal environment, so negotiators must act according to the relevant domestic and international law and regulations.

a. The subject of the negotiation must be legal. It means that the negotiators should have the negotiation qualification. For example, a natural person should be legal in terms of his age; he should also have the ability of normal thinking and have the personal freedom. A legal person must negotiate within its business scope.

b. The content of the negotiation must be legal. It means the negotiation object or item should be legal. For example, negotiation on the buying or selling of gun is against the law.

c. The behavior of the negotiation must be legal. It means the way or measures used for the negotiation should be legitimate, you cannot force or threat the other party to conduct a negotiation.

Besides, negotiation should be conducted on the basis of credibility and honesty which is the commercial ethics. Being sincere and keeping one's words are the basis of mutual trust in international business negotiation. In short, putting credibility first means negotiators should be trustworthy and treat each other with all sincerity.

d. Understanding derives from credibility and trustworthiness. In international business negotiation, being credible and trustworthy does not necessarily mean revealing your objectives and plans directly and totally, but it does require saying frankly what the other party wants to know and ensuring his satisfaction, e.g., the quality of the product, the available quantity, time of delivery, etc. It is also essential to present your intentions in a proper way at a proper time.

e. Credibility enhances trustworthiness. Being honest and credible in international business negotiation is that a sincere attitude helps to remove psychological barriers and suspicion, laying a solid foundation for mutual trust.

f. Being aware of the level of the counterpart's credibility. All the parties should be reliable and trustworthy which is the basis of negotiation; there should be mutual personal trust among all the counterparts. If one side makes efforts to behave sincerely, but the other side does not, or breaks its promises all the time, then it will be suspected that the latter lacks sincerity. Therefore, you should understand quickly how sincere and trustworthy your counterpart in the negotiation is.

### 3. Reciprocity and mutual benefits

Mutual reciprocity and mutual benefit is the goal of international business negotiation. The optimal result for business negotiation is to realize a win-win outcome. The two sides should follow the principle of equality and mutual benefit and make necessary concessions according to the average price level in international market and the relevant pricing policy made by the government.

(1) Interests first, position second

An international business negotiation is centered on pursuing the interests of each party. However, you must be prepared to be flexible; do not hold your position doggedly and never give it up. No conflicting interests, no need for negotiation. Therefore, negotiation must be arranged around the central goal of gaining realistic interests. Focusing on interests rather than positions is a golden rule and precious precept in negotiation at all times and in all countries.

(2) Not bargaining over position

Since behind positions stand interests, gaining interests is not one-sided wishful thinking. Bargaining over positions will breach the following negotiation taboos.

A. Violating the equal negotiation game principle

In order to defend one's own position, negotiators may ignore the other side's actual situations and interests, and insist on fighting foes for every inch of land, resulting in a lengthy negotiation without results, and damaging the relationship. In such a situation, agreement is hard to reach.

B. Impairing the harmonious atmosphere

If all parties announce that their positions cannot be changed, the negotiation process will turn into a war of wills. As a result, one party or another would have to make a great sacrifice to reach an agreement, which will lead to the failure of the negotiation.

C. Hiding a snake in the grass

If one side is very calculating about its own profits, the other side may gain few of its interests and sign the contract reluctantly. In the future, they may breach the contract with numerous excuses. Only when all the concerned parties' interests are put into the negotiation plan and proper solutions are actively pursued can win-win or multi-win negotiation outcomes be achieved. This is what has come to be called the principle of mutual reciprocity and mutual benefit.

### 4. Maximizing commonalities and minimizing differences

Seeking common ground while reserving differences is a bridge to success in international business negotiation. The parties concerned should try to seek the common interest, solve the problems properly and ignore the minor discrepancies. Striving for the common ground for both or all parities is most important for business negotiations.

(1) Seeking common goals

In international business negotiation, conflicts of interests or discrepancies between the parties are unavoidable. Negotiators may follow the principle of "easy issues first, difficult ones later" and the principle of "be weak but win the negotiation with the powerful."

(2) Abandon minor points

Since all parties have chosen to sit together for negotiation, it means that they all have common interests. Therefore, negotiators should cling to the principle that the most important objectives and the negotiation criteria should be identical and the minor discrepancies and disagreements can be temporarily ignored. In other words, in order to advance the "shared interests," we should reconcile the differing interests and allow them to exist in the negotiation agreement.

(3) Compromise is the mother of success

Only through concessions can the discrepancies be eliminated. As the saying goes, "Necessary concession is the mother of successful negotiation and seeking commonalities while reserving differences is the vehicle for breaking up negotiation deadlocks." The process of negotiation is, in fact, a process of making concessions, but what can be compromised on should be decided first and concessions must be made at the right time, avoiding unnecessary sacrifices.

## 5. Speak on good grounds

Speaking on good grounds is a most powerful talisman in international business negotiation.

(1) Data and facts speak for themselves

In international business negotiation, you must list data and facts and convince people by sound reasoning if you want to ensure your benefits, eliminate your counterpart's doubts and refute their objections.

(2) Using objective criteria

When negotiators find themselves debating endlessly about one specific piece of data, they should consider bringing in an acceptable objective criterion, which should conform to the following three requirements:

a. It should have objectivity independent from the subjective will of all parties.

b. It should be legitimate and operable.

c. It should be authoritative and scientific.

For example, when two business people haggle over the price of a commodity, the criteria for the price are varied: its market price in the exporting country and/or the importing country, its price on the international market, the cost of production, trends on international market. These can all be viewed as objective criteria.

☞ **Case study 1 – 3**    (**Should the wind coat be sold**)

One day Madam Chen went shopping with her friend in a department store which started business several days ago. Before a row of fine-workmanship and particular-about-material choice wind coats, Madam Chen noticed the bid price on a tag for the wind coat was RMB600 which was obviously an error since the bid prices for all the wind coats were RMB1,600. The sales clerk made an apology to Madam Chen very friendly and told her that the bid price on that tag was the computer error and the first figure "1" was neglected. But Madam Chen insisted that she should buy the wind coat at RMB600 since the bid price on the tag was a promise to customers by the merchant. The sales clerk dared not make the decision and asked Madam Chen to leave her address and would give her a reply the following day. The relevant persons in charge held an immediate discussion and decided to sell Madam Chen the wind coat at RMB600.

This business conflict thus caught the attention of the news media and was reported by the local newspapers and periodicals, and there arose a discussion: Should Madam Chen buy the wind coat at RMB600? Most of the readers condemned Madam Chen's behavior and her motivation. This department store which started business several days ago won a high public praise since it kept its words very strictly and its popularity was enhanced. As a result, many visitors and potential buyers came to this store for shopping and the sales volume was increased greatly.

☞ **Case study 1 – 4**    (**How to divide the orange**)

This is a widely-known story in the field of negotiation.

A mother gave an orange to two kids of neighbors. The kids then discussed how to divide the orange. After quarrelling for a while, they reached an agreement that one child cut the orange into two and the other made the choice. At last, each of them got half of the orange as negotiated and went home happily.

One child threw away the orange peel and made orange juice out of the flesh. The other child threw away the flesh of the orange, ground the orange peel and put it in cake.

It can be seen that the division seems to be fair, however, both of the kids didn't make the best use of the orange. Obviously, they didn't communicate with each other beforehand, that is, each of them didn't state his benefit or interests, which led to the seeming fairness in form and position but their interests were not maximized in the negotiation.

If the kids had a good communication and stated their own interests, they could have more options. Apart from the one they already had, there might be another situation that one of them wanted both the flesh for juice and the peel for cake. Then the kid might propose to settle the issue together with other issues. He might say, "If you let me have the complete orange, you needn't give me the sweets you owed me."

The other kid would completely agree to this proposal because he just got some money from his parents to buy sweets he owed that kid. And now he could save the money for playing games. Who cared that sour orange!

The process of negotiation is, in fact, a process of continuous communication and creating value. While seeking the measures to maximize one's own interests, both sides also satisfy the needs of the other side.

☞ **Case study 1 - 5   〔Development of Matsushita Electric Corporation〕**

Matsushita Corporation was founded in March 1918. The corporation has grown from a small family enterprise into a well-known and one of the world largest electric producers. The corporation owns its success to its founder, Konosuke Matsushita, whose management philosophy and sound decision led the corporation growing healthily. A good example to illustrate the point is the negotiation between Matsushita Electric Corporation and Philip Corporation.

In the 1950s, Matsushita Corporation embarked on a business expansion, which required advanced technology to make the expansion possible. Philip Corporation at that time had already enjoyed the fame as a world celebrated electric producer with the most advanced technology and financial strength. Matsushita decided to seek alliance with Philip. Against such background, Matsushita started the negotiation with Philip on technical transfer.

There was a great discrepancy between the two corporations' negotiating power. Matsushita was a small and developing company while Philip was already a giant in the world of electric production. Matsushita depended heavily on Philip to have the technology it needed urgently. So from very beginning, Philip was demanding and pressing ahead. It required 7% of Matsushita's sales volume as payment for technical assistance, and the loyalty of $550,000 for the patent transaction must be paid in lump sum. The other provisions were also favorable to Philip, for example, the penalty for breach of contract on Matsushita side was strict and severe but the punitive clause for Philip's violation was obscure and indistinct.

Through hard negotiation, Matsushita was able to cut the payment for technical assistance from 7% to 4.5%; however, Philip resolutely refused to make any concession on patent payment. Konosuke faced a great challenge, which put him in a dilemma. Giving his consent and signing the agreement would mean great risk to him and the whole company because in the early 1950s, the total asset of the company was 500 million Japanese yen. $550,000 loyalty would be equal to 200 million yen, which was nearly half of the company's property. In case any unpredictable events happened, it would mean bankruptcy to the company. However, the company would miss a valuable opportunity and a good partner if he turned down the demand and saw the failure of the negotiation.

After careful deliberation between the present interests and the future development of the company, Konosuke was determined to take the risk. His consideration was that Philip owned sophisticated scientific equipment, research institute and 3,000 capable research fellows. If they could reach an agreement, Matsushita would have access to all the research resources which was possessed by Philip but lacked by Matsushita and which could not be measured merely in terms of $550,000. The sacrifice of the present interests would mean gaining of interests in the long run. It was worthwhile to take the risk.

The future development of Matsushita Corporation has proved that the decision was a risky one but also a brilliant one. The technical strength developed in the 1950s has built up a solid platform for future take-off of the corporation.

☞ **Questions for your consideration and discussion**

1. Do you have some experience of negotiation? Try to give us an example.

2. What is the meaning and characteristics of international business negotiation?

3. What are the main types of international business negotiation?

4. What are the principles of international business negotiation?

5. If you are a business negotiator,

(1) Do you want to be a host or a guest? Why?

(2) Do you like to adopt an oral or a written negotiation? Why?

(3) Would you like to conduct a compromise negotiation, a ground negotiation or a principle negotiation? Why?

# 第一章
# 国际商务谈判概述

☞ **案例分析 1—1**　（囚犯与卫兵）

　　一个被单独囚禁的囚犯整日无所事事。一天,他忽然闻到一股万宝路香烟的味道。他很喜欢这种牌子的烟。原来门廊的卫兵正在吸烟,勾起了他的烟瘾。他用手指轻轻地敲了敲门。卫兵走过来傲慢地说:"你要干什么?"囚犯答道:"请给我一支烟,就是你抽的那种万宝路香烟。"卫兵感到很惊异,囚犯还要抽烟,真是异想天开!他嘲弄地哼了一声,就转身走开了。囚犯又用手敲了敲门,这次他态度威严。那个卫兵吐出一口烟雾,恼怒地扭过头问:"你又想干什么?"囚犯回答:"对不起,请你在 30 秒之内给我一支烟;否则我就用头撞这混凝土墙,直到撞得自己血肉模糊,失去知觉为止。当我醒来时,我就说是你干的。也可能当局不相信我。但是,你必须出席每一次听证会,不断证明你是无辜的,你必须填写各种报告——所有这些都是因为你拒绝给我一支劣质的万宝路香烟!就一支烟,我保证不再给您添麻烦了。"最后,卫兵从小窗里给他递了一支烟,并替他点上。

　　你认为囚犯与卫兵的交流是否称得上是一次谈判?

　　我们生活在一个资源有限的世界,但是人类的欲望却是无限的。解决资源有限和欲望无限之间的矛盾无非有两种方式:即武力方式与和平方式。和平方式也就是通过谈判。毫无疑问,通过谈判解决冲突是更好的方式。在国际商务领域,一方通过武力操控另一方的时代早已成为历史;谈判已成为解决冲突、协调利益的有效途径。

　　你可能会认为谈判与我们的生活毫不相关,似乎那只是政府组织之间或者大公司之间的事。事实上,谈判不仅仅适用于重大的事件,它同样适用于人们生活的一切冲突、矛盾和不同的意见与观点。政府之间、企业之间、个人之间,随时都可能处于一个个大大小小的谈判过程中。对个人来说,无论你喜欢与否,每个人也都在生活中扮演着谈判者的角色。你可能与同学商量着晚饭在哪儿吃,与父母争论买哪一款服装,与上司谈论升迁问题,与陌生人商讨购买房子的价格,与另一个司机就一起车祸而进行的争辩,等等。

　　因此,我们每个人都在自觉或不自觉地进行着谈判。谈判是我们生活中的重要组成部分，它普遍存在于生活的各个方面，谈判无处不在。只要社会中存在着利益冲突，存在着追求目标的差异，就需要谈判。每个人都是一个谈判者，而且我们每个人都应当努力地充当一个成功的谈判者，因为成功的谈判可以使你达到预期的目的：

一次智慧的对话能使绝望的人重新正视生活；

一次推心置腹的谈话能使感情危机中的恋人重归于好；

一次恰到好处的谈判能使濒临困境的企业走出低谷；

一次成功的外交斡旋能使敌对双方化干戈为玉帛，避免一场血淋淋的战争；

一个成功的谈判高手，能抵得上千军万马，他既是叱咤风云的战术家，又是运筹帷幄的战略家。

## 一、国际商务谈判的概念

人类社会中有各种各样的谈判。谈判可以是正式的，也可以是非正式的；可以是专业的，也可以是普通的。根据不同的性质和内容，谈判可以分为政治谈判、外交谈判、军事谈判和商务谈判等。本书主要从国际层面对商务谈判进行探讨。

### 1. 谈判

通过上面的开篇案例，大家想一想，要构成一项谈判，是不是必须具备以下几个要素呢？

第一，谈判主体。谈判一定要有主体，即谈判的当事人。谈判的当事人可以是双方，也可以是多方。

第二，谈判客体。也就是谈判的标的、议题或内容。

第三，谈判目的。就是当事人进行谈判的动机或目标。没有目的的闲聊不是谈判。

因此，谈判就是参与各方基于某种需要，彼此进行信息交流、磋商协议，旨在协调其相互关系，赢得或维护各自利益的行为过程（刘园，2012）。说得更简单一些，谈判就是双方或各方为达成一致进行交流的过程。

### 2. 商务谈判

商务谈判是目前与人们日常生活联系最为紧密、在当前的经济环境下最为常见的一种谈判形式，存在于经济社会的整个过程当中。因此商务谈判指的是，在经济领域中，参与双方或各方为了满足自己的经济利益需求，协调彼此的经济关系，而进行信息交流、磋商并最终达成一致利益的行为过程。换句话说，商务谈判就是商人为成交进行交流说服的过程。

### 3. 国际商务谈判

国际商务谈判是经济社会发展到一定程度，在一个国家或地区内部进行的某些经济行为因受到较大限制而对外延伸的一种附属产物，是商务谈判的延伸和发展。在当今的经济社会,随着经济要素的增长,不同国家或地区之间的关系也越来越紧密,因此,国际商务谈判在促进经济发展上的作用也越来越明显。

国际商务谈判指的是居于不同国家或地区的商人,为了达成某种经济需求而进行交流、协商的行为过程。说得直白一点,就是不同国家或地区的商人为成交而进行交流沟通的过程。

## 二、国际商务谈判的特点

作为商务谈判的延伸和发展,国际商务谈判既有谈判和一般商务谈判的特点,同时还具有其独特的特点。

1. 谈判的特点

(1) 具有两个或多个当事人

双方或各方之间既有利益的相同点,又在追求最大利益上有偏差。

(2) 具有明确的目标

与闲聊不同,谈判的目的是说服他人接受自己的观点,例如,解决到哪儿吃晚饭的问题,买卖真丝衬衫,等等。

(3) 在平等的基础上进行

为达成协议,要相互沟通,进行信息交流、磋商,甚至让步,而不是一方听从另外一方的安排。

2. 商务谈判的特点

(1) 以平等互利为原则

平等互利是商务谈判的前提和基础,商务谈判的参与各方的目的是一致的,即通过商务谈判取得各方都可以接受的结果。只有在这种前提下,才能够坐在同一张谈判桌边。

(2) 商务谈判的目标是获取经济利益,也就是要赚取利润

一场商务谈判成功与否的标准就是能否满足各方的经济利益。换句话说,得不到经济利益的商务谈判是毫无价值的。

(3) 商务谈判以价格为谈判的核心,围绕经济利益展开

既然是商务谈判,就应该把经济利益放在首位。对企业来说,经济效益反映在商品的价格上。商务谈判所涉及的要素不只是价格,但价格永远在经济利益中居于核心地位,其他条款都能在价格上反映出来。

3. 国际商务谈判的特点

除具有谈判和一般商务谈判的特点外,国际商务谈判还具有以下特点。

(1) 双方的语言不同,必须解决语言的障碍

在国际商务谈判中,谈判双方首先遇到的障碍就是语言不同。因此,必须解决谈判当

中翻译的问题。英语是当今国际商务活动中最通用的语言,汉语、法语、俄语、阿拉伯语和西班牙语等联合国官方语言也都较多使用。除此以外,日语和德语也常当作谈判中的语言。

（2）文化不同,双方存在文化差异

在国际商务谈判中,谈判双方有着不同的历史背景,在文化、宗教信仰以及商业习俗等方面都存在着明显的差异。谈判人员如果不了解这些差异,就可能造成一些不必要的误解,甚至影响谈判的进行。例如,当你就同样的商品报出一个高价的时候,阿拉伯商人通常会很愉快地跟你讨价还价,而德国商人经常会感到不理解,甚至马上终止与你的谈判。

（3）谈判依据不同,谈判人员必须了解相关的国内和国际法

在国际商务谈判中,当事人来自不同的国家或地区,选择任何一国的法律作为谈判的适用法律对于另一方来说都是不公平的。因此,在谈判时双方既要受到国内法律的制约,又要受到国际惯例制约。例如,在国际贸易谈判中,我们的谈判人员首先要遵守中华人民共和国法律,还要按照有关国际法或者国际商会制订的《国际贸易术语解释通则》《托收统一规则》和《跟单信用证统一惯例》等国际贸易惯例谈判。

（4）谈判环境不同,必须考虑国际政治、经济和宗教等因素的影响

国际商务谈判是在不同国家商人之间进行的谈判,必然会要受到国际政治、经济、外交、宗教信仰、文化习俗等多种环境因素的影响。1997年东南亚金融危机发生后,韩国政府暂停一切美元支付,这也导致了众多国内出口企业对韩国的商务谈判被迫中止。

（5）谈判对象不同,比国内的商务谈判更难,成本更高

跨国性是国际商务谈判最显著的特点,也是其他特点的基础。国际商务谈判的结果是跨国贸易,跨国资金流动以及跨国会计、保险和运输等。

这个特点就要求谈判人员必须熟悉有关国际惯例、对方国家的法律以及相关国际经济组织和国际商法的各种规定。这就决定了国际商务谈判的困难性和复杂性。

### 三、国际商务谈判的种类

按照不同的标准,国际商务谈判可以划分为很多种类。

1. 按照谈判的客体或内容分类

（1）国际货物买卖谈判

国际货物买卖谈判就是国际贸易,包括货物进出口的贸易谈判。它指的是谈判双方就进出货物的品名、品质、数量、支付条款、包装、价格、运输条款、争议解决方法等内容进行的谈判,又称为一般商品的买卖谈判或一般贸易谈判。在当代国际贸易中,货物买卖仍然是最基本和最主要的内容。因此,在国际商务谈判中,国际货物买卖谈判所占的比重也是最大的。

（2）国际技术贸易谈判

国际技术贸易谈判是指来自不同国家的技术接收方（即买方）与技术转让方（即卖方）就转让技术的形式、内容、质量规定、使用范围、价格条件、支付方式及双方在转让中的一些权利、责任和义务关系问题所进行的谈判。

（3）国际服务贸易谈判

国际服务贸易谈判指的是谈判双方就建筑及相关工程服务、通信服务、金融服务、运输服务、旅游服务、环境服务、商业服务等内容所进行的跨国界谈判。从广义上讲，国际服务贸易谈判指的是国与国之间展开的有关服务部门市场准入、人员流动水平等内容的谈判。从狭义上讲，国际服务贸易谈判指的是企业与企业之间在以上服务领域就有关维护、维修、劳务等内容进行的谈判。

此外，按照谈判的客体或内容分类，还有索赔谈判、租赁业务谈判、"三来一补"谈判、国际资金借贷谈判和投资谈判等。

**2. 按照谈判规模分类**

按照谈判规模分，谈判可以分为大、中、小型谈判。通常，谈判所涉及的金额越大、内容越复杂，所参与的人数就越多。一场谈判各方参与的当事人数量超过 12 人，一般就认为是大型谈判；人数在 4～12 人，可以认为是中型谈判；人数少于 4 人，则属于小型谈判。

小型谈判，参与的人数较少，持续时间较短。特别是一对一的谈判，需要选择全能型的谈判人员，要求谈判者有独立掌控全局的知识和才干，需要知识广博、反应灵敏的人来充当谈判人员。而大、中型谈判，参加人数较多，因此需要强调内部成员之间的行为，既要有分工，又要讲究合作。

**3. 按照谈判主体所采用的态度和方针分类**

按照该分类方法，通常可分为让步型谈判、立场型谈判和原则型谈判。

让步型谈判是一种为了保持同对方的合作关系而做出退让、妥协的谈判；立场型谈判是指谈判者很少顾及或根本不顾及对方的利益，以取得己方胜利为目的的立场坚定、主张强硬的谈判；原则型谈判是指谈判者既重视经济利益，又重视人际关系，既不回避对立的一面，又更加重视合作的谈判。原则型谈判是一种激励性又富有人情味的谈判方式，因此在商界受到越来越多谈判者的青睐。

**4. 按照谈判程序分类**

按照该分类方法，通常可分为水平谈判和垂直谈判。

水平谈判是指谈判双方先列出双方要商谈的议题或条款，如果有哪个条款双方达不成一致意见，可先将其搁置一旁，等所有或其他条款都谈妥后再重新就这个条款进行谈判。这种谈判，双方不必严格遵循双方商定条款次序进行商谈，被称为水平谈判。水平谈判遵循的是先易后难的原则，因而被广泛采用。

☞ **案例分析 1—2** （水平谈判）

2017 年 3 月 15 日美国纽约的达斯特克国际公司与日本日商岩井株式会社就牛肉出口在纽约进行了谈判。美日双方首先商定了牛肉出口交易合同须确定的条款,比如产品质量、数量、支付方式、价格、包装、交货、索赔和不可抗力等。然后双方就按照顺序就产品质量、数量、支付方式进行了协商,然而当谈到价格时双方有不同的观点,于是双方决定将价格搁置一边,去探讨包装、交货等条款。等大多数条款都谈妥了以后,他们重新商讨价格问题,最后达成了一致。

垂直谈判是指谈判双方先列出双方要商谈的议题或条款,然后严格按照所商定的顺序进行谈判。如果有哪个条款双方达不成一致意见,双方的谈判就宣告失败。

5. 按照谈判的重要性或双方重视的程度分类

按照该分类方法,通常可分为正式谈判和非正式谈判。

6. 按照谈判地点分类

按照谈判在什么地方进行,可以把谈判分为主场谈判、客场谈判、主客场轮流谈判和中立地谈判四种。

主场谈判指的是当事人在自己的地方进行谈判。这里自己的地方可以狭义地理解为公司所在地、城市所在地,也可以广义地理解为国家所在地。而客场谈判指的是在谈判对方所在地进行的谈判,在国际谈判中通常理解为"海外或国外"。主客场轮流谈判则是谈判在主场、客场轮流进行。中立地谈判是在第三方中立国家进行。

主场谈判和客场谈判各有其优缺点。以主场为例,主要的优势为:谈判人员可节省差旅费,更熟悉谈判的环境,更易获取相关信息,还可通过相关安排争得主动,主要在谈判时间和地点的安排方面,可给对方制造障碍。当然事情都是一分为二的,作为主场的主要缺点是:必须花时间进行谈判的安排,谈判人员容易被本公司的员工干扰,不得不安排宴会、客人的观光等事宜从而增加成本。

7. 按照谈判主体接触的方式分类

按照谈判主体接触的方式,可以分为口头谈判和书面/函电谈判。口头谈判主要包括面对面谈判、电话谈判和视频谈判。

口头谈判和书面谈判各有优缺点。口头谈判的主要优点为:谈判人员可直接与对方交流,从而可当场决定是否与对方成交;可观察对方的面部表情、动作及心理并可猜测其下一步的行动或是策略从而调整己方谈判的技巧、策略;可培养相互的感情,使谈判更加富有成果。书面谈判的主要优点为:非常便捷,人们可随时随地与对方进行联系;谈判人员没有心理压力,有充分的考虑问题的时间,可从容应对;书面谈判还有成本低、易保存等优点。

在谈判实务中,很多谈判既需要口头谈判也需要书面谈判,既需要主场谈判也需要客场谈判。

此外,按照参加谈判的主体可分为政府间的谈判,企业间的谈判,政府与企业的谈判,企业与生产商之间的谈判,等等;按照参加谈判的主体数量不同,可以分为双边谈判、多边谈判,等等。

### 四、国际商务谈判的基本原则

国际商务谈判作为一项重要的商务活动,必须遵循一些重要的基本原则。国际商务谈判的基本原则就是在国际商务谈判中参与各方必须遵守的基本规则或规范。理解并实行这些原则有助于谈判人员更好地应用谈判的策略和技巧,提高他们谈判的效率。

#### 1.平等自愿的原则

平等自愿是国际商务谈判的基本前提。谈判各方相互间要求在尊重各自权利和国家主权的基础上,平等地进行贸易与经济合作事务。不论双方国家实力如何,也不论双方企业的规模如何,在谈判中,都应该是平等的,应相互尊重,不能逼迫对方。谈判各方都应尊重对方的愿望,根据彼此的需要和可能,在自愿的基础上进行谈判,谈判的结果也应当符合双方的共同利益。对于利益、意见分歧的问题,应通过友好协商加以妥善解决。

(1)谈判各方不论大小强弱,都是平等的

在国际商务谈判中,各方必须是平等的,而且是自愿参与,不论他们的经济实力或是其组织规模差异有多大。这个原则也要求参与各方拥有同样选择贸易术语和条款的权利,只有通过平等的交流与商谈,各方才能达成一致。

(2)拥有平等的否决权

在国际商务谈判中,不存在哪一方有权做最后的决定或是少数服从多数的情况。各方都有权否定谈判中的任何一个条款,如果哪一方不满意就不能达成协议。

(3)平等体现在尊重对方

有关各方,不管他们的实力和规模如何,都应尊重对方,避免歧视。任何一方如滥用职权,欺负对方,谈判就会注定失败。

(4)平等体现为自愿协议

自愿协议意味着谈判中各方能自愿参与,并且做出自己的决定。他们谈判的动机是他们追求己方的利益而不是违背己方的意愿或是迫于外界的压力。只有这样,各方才能平等,进而相互理解,做出妥协,最终达成一致。

#### 2.守法诚信的原则

(1)守法

任何的商务谈判都是在一定的法律环境下进行的,国际商务谈判也不例外,法律规范制约着国际商务谈判的内容和方法。在进行谈判时，必须按照参与方国家的法律及国际法的有关规定进行，以免徒劳无功，甚至造成无法估量的后果。具体而言，守法原则要求谈判主体必须合法，谈判内容必须合法，谈判行为必须合法，以及签订的合同必须合法。

①谈判主体合法指的是谈判者必须具备谈判资格。比如自然人必须年龄合法且有正常的思维能力和人身自由；法人必须在其经营范围以内进行谈判。

②谈判内容合法指的是谈判的标的或项目内容必须是合法的，比如买卖枪支的谈判就不合法。

③谈判行为合法指的是谈判所使用的手段是正当的，不能采用威胁或是胁迫对方进行谈判，或是强迫对方接受某个条款或协议。只有在满足上述条件的情况下，经过谈判签署的所有文件才是具有法律效力的。

（2）诚信

在遵守法律规定的同时，谈判者还必须在诚信的基础上进行交流。诚信作为商务谈判的前提与基础，是谈判者应当信守的商业道德准则，贯穿于商务谈判活动的全过程，对于谈判活动至关重要。商务谈判的目的与对象决定了谈判者必须讲诚信。有些企业在谈判过程中，不顾自己企业实际情况，盲目答应对方的苛刻要求，更有甚者，虚夸自己的生产能力、产品质量等关键因素，使合同订立在虚假甚至是欺诈之上，这种企业即使在一时能够取得谈判对象的信任，取得谈判的成功，签订商务合同，但在后续合同履约的过程中，也会因为不能够按照合同条款执行而被终止合作甚至被对方告上法庭。简单地说，诚信指的是谈判双方要讲信用，要以诚相待。

①理解的基础是诚信。在国际商务谈判中，诚信并不是说要把你的谈判目标和谈判计划完全直接地透露给对方，而是应当把对方想知道和应当知道的坦诚告诉对方，并且保证让对方满意，比如你的产品的质量、能供应的数量、交货期和包装等都应当向对方实话实说，不应欺瞒对方。还应当在合适的时间用合适的方式将你的意图告知对方。当然，价格是个例外。

②诚信可以增强相互信任。国际商务谈判中坦诚守信意味着坦诚的态度可以消除（对方的）心理障碍和猜疑，从而为相互信任打下坚实的基础。坦诚守信是国际商务谈判中相互信任的基础。

③留意对方诚信的程度。各方都应诚实可靠，这是谈判的基础。谈判成员之间应有相互的信任，如果一方表现诚恳，而另外一方总是不遵守诺言，那么后者就缺乏诚信。因此在谈判中，应尽快了解对方诚信的程度。

3. 互惠互利

互惠互利是国际商务谈判的目标。商务谈判最理想的结果是要达到"双赢"，谈判者应了解对方在谈判中的利益要求，尽量满足其需求，这样就会引起对方的积极响应，这是谈判双方能够迅速达成协议的有效途径。在国际商务谈判中，价格的高低是体现平等互利原则的一个重要方面。在进行价格谈判时,应遵循平等互利的原则,以国际市场平均价格水准和政府有关价格的政策为基础,结合所处环境,不固守己方立场,互惠互利,实现双赢。

（1）首先关注利益,将立场放在次要位置

国际商务谈判是围绕各方追求利益为核心展开的。然而谈判人员必须准备灵活,不固守己方的立场而从不让步。没有利益的冲突,就没有谈判的必要。因此谈判一定要围绕各方获取现实利益而开展。关注利益而非立场是所有国家商人在谈判中随时应遵循的黄金法则和宝贵箴言。

（2）不就立场问题而讨价还价

立场的背后是利益。谈判双方如果都坚持自己的立场,是难以取得一致的,只有关注利益,才有可能找到共同之处。追求利益并不是单方面的意愿。就立场问题而讨价还价违反了以下谈判的禁忌:

①违反了平等谈判的游戏规则。为了捍卫己方的立场,谈判人员可能会忽略对方的实际情况和利益,坚持寸土必争,导致了漫长拖拉的谈判,损害了双方的关系,在这种情况下是很难达成一致的。

②损害了和谐的气氛。如果各方都宣称其立场不能改变,那么谈判就变成了意志的较量。结果就是一方或另外一方不得不做出巨大的牺牲,因此谈判是不会成功的。

③留下后患。如果一方过于计较利益,那么另外一方就可能获利过少而勉强签订合同。将来他们就可能用很多借口违反合同。只有当谈判各方的利益都被充分考虑在谈判计划当中并积极解决,才可能获得双赢或共赢的结果,也就是所说的互惠互利的结果。

4. 求同存异的原则

求同存异是国际商务谈判通往成功的桥梁。求同存异原则,又称为相容原则,是指在符合本方总体目标的基础上,在某些方面能接受或容忍参与谈判的其他各方存在与本方利益不尽一致的要求。如果谈判各方的利益要求完全一致,就不需要谈判,正是因为各方意见、目标等存在着分歧,谈判才得以进行。国际商务谈判,就是通过协商使各方利益目标趋于一致而最后达成协议的过程。谈判各方应谋求共同利益,妥善解决和尽量忽略非实质性的差异。对双方来说,谋求共同利益是第一位的。在国际商务谈判中,"求同"是使谈判顺利进行和达到预期目的的基础。一项成功的商务谈判,并不是使对方一败涂地,而是各方达成互利的协议。谈判者都本着谋求共同利益的态度参与谈判,各方均能不同程度地达到自己的目的。

（1）寻求共同的目标

在国际商务谈判中,在各方之间总是存在着利益的分歧与冲突。谈判人员可以采用先易后难,搁置分歧,关注利益,努力寻求共同的利益目标。求同存异也是打破僵局的关键。

（2）放弃细微的分歧

既然各方坐在了谈判桌前，就是说他们有着共同的利益。因此谈判人员应坚持重要的目标和标准相一致的原则，细微的分歧或不同可暂时忽略。换句话说，为了共同的利益，应当允许分歧的存在。

（3）妥协是成功之母

谈判中只有通过妥协才能消除分歧，必要的妥协是成功的基础。"求大同、存小异"是打破谈判僵局的关键。"求大同、存小异"就需要对谈判中的分歧做出适当的妥协让步。这并不是指没有原则的妥协退让，而是做出一种姿态，互让互信。既要坚持、维护己方的利益，又要考虑、满足对方的利益，兼顾双方利益，谋求共同利益。当然妥协的内容要事先确定并在恰当的时间做出，避免不必要的牺牲。对于难以协调的非基本利益分歧，面临不妥协不利于达成谈判协议的局面，则要做出必要的让步，妥协让步的实质是以退为进，促进谈判的顺利进行并达成协议。

5. 言之有据的原则

言之有据是国际商务谈判中最有利的法宝。

在国际商务谈判中，要保障己方的利益，消除对方的疑虑或者应对对方的不同意见，就应当有合理的理由，用数据和事实说话。有理有据，除了用事实说话，还要使用客观的标准。当谈判人员之间就某一点陷入无休止的争论时，就应当找出一个双方可以接受的客观标准。这样的标准应符合以下要求：一是要独立于有关各方主观意志；二是必须合法且具可操作性；三是要有权威性和科学性。当双方就某一商品的价格吵得不可开交时，什么是合理的权威的令人信服的价格标准，就值得人们思考。比如，出口国的市场价格，进口国的市场价格，国际市场的价格，产品的成本价格，国际市场的价格走势，等等。

☞ **案例分析 1—3** （风衣该不该卖）

一天，陈女士携女友到一家刚开业不久的百货大楼购物。在一排做工精细、用料考究的女士风衣前，陈女士发现一件成衣的标签上赫然印着 600 元的标价。这是一起明显的标价错误，因为这排风衣的统一标价是 1600 元。售货员小姐非常友好地向陈女士道歉，并告之小标签上的价格是因为电脑的差错，600 元前面的 1 字没有标清楚。但陈女士认为，既然小标签上印着"600 元"，这就意味着商家对顾客的一种承诺，因此，她坚持要以"600 元"的价格买走该风衣。售货员小姐不敢做主，她让陈女士留下联系地址，告之次日将给她一个满意的答复。百货大楼的负责人连夜经过紧急磋商，最后决定以"600 元"的售价将该风衣卖给陈女士。

这起商业纠纷引起了新闻媒体的关注，一时，当地各大报刊纷纷报道了这则消息，并展开了一场讨论：陈女士该不该以 600 元的价钱买走这件风衣？大部分读者都支持百货大楼,纷纷谴责陈女士的行为是出于一种"占便宜"的动机。而这家刚开业不久的百货大楼由于严守信用、言出必行赢得了非常好的口碑,从而提高了知名度,一时间,该百货大楼门庭若市,生意火爆。

☞ **案例分析 1—4　（分橙子的谈判）**

这是一个在谈判界流传很广的经典故事。

有一个妈妈把一个橙子给了邻居家的两个孩子,这两个孩子便开始讨论如何分这个橙子。两个人吵来吵去,最终达成了一致意见:由一个孩子切橙子,另一个孩子选橙子。结果,这两个孩子按照商定的办法各自取得一半橙子,高高兴兴地拿回家去了。

第一个孩子把半个橙子拿到家,把皮剥掉扔进了垃圾桶,把果肉放到果汁机里打果汁喝。另一个孩子回到家把果肉挖掉扔进垃圾桶,把橙子皮磨碎了混在面粉里烤蛋糕吃。

从上面的情形可以看出,虽然两个孩子看似公平地各自拿到了一半,然而他们各自得到的东西却没有物尽其用。这说明他们在事先并没有做好沟通,也就是说两个孩子事先并未申明各自利益所在,导致了双方盲目追求形式上和立场上的公平,结果双方各自的利益并未在谈判中得到最大化。

试想如果两个孩子充分交流各自所需,或许会有多个方案和情况出现。可能的一种情况就是遵循上述情形,两个孩子想办法将皮和果肉分开,一个孩子拿到果肉去喝果汁,另一个孩子拿到果皮去做蛋糕。然而经过沟通后也可能是另外的情况,恰恰有一个孩子既想要果皮做蛋糕,又想要果肉喝果汁。这时,如何创造价值就非常重要了。

如果想要整个橙子的孩子提议可以将其他的问题拿出来一起谈,他说:"如果把这个橙子全给我,你上次欠我的棒棒糖就不用还了。"其实他的牙齿被蛀得一塌糊涂,父母上星期就不准许他吃糖了。

另一个孩子想了一想,很快就答应了,他刚刚从父母那儿要了五块钱,准备买糖还债。这次他可以用这五块钱去打游戏了,他才不在乎这酸溜溜的橙子呢。

两个孩子的谈判过程实际上就是不断沟通、创造价值的过程。双方都在寻求对自己最大利益方案的同时,满足了对方最大利益的需求。

☞ **案例分析 1—5　（松下公司的发展）**

日本松下公司成立于 1918 年 3 月,它从一个家庭式的小企业逐渐发展成世界 500 强的前 20 位。松下公司的成功得益于它的创始人松下幸之助。1952 年,日本松下公司与荷兰飞利浦公司就有关技术合作问题进行商务谈判。飞利浦公司提出技术转让费的提成率为销售额的 7％，松下幸之助经过艰苦的努力把提成率压价到 4.5％。但飞利浦公司又提出了新的要求作为提成率优惠的条件：专利转让费定为 55 万美元，并且必须一次付清。

当时的松下公司资本总额不过 5 亿日元，55 万美元相当于 2 亿日元！这笔专利转让费对松下公司来说的确是一个相当沉重的负担。对方的要求、条件能否接受呢？松下幸之助感到极度犹豫，合同文本由飞利浦公司拟就，其中的违约和处罚条款的订立也都有利于飞利浦公司。

为了保证技术合作项目的效益稳定，松下幸之助又对飞利浦公司做了深入细致的调查。他发现飞利浦公司拥有一个 3000 名研究人员的研究所，设备先进、人员精良，每天都在进行着世界上最新技术和最新产品的开发研究。松下幸之助暗自思量，如果创造一个同等规模、同等水平的研究所，要花上几十亿日元和几年的时间，而现在以 2 亿日元为代价，便可以充分利用飞利浦公司研究所的人员和设备，何乐而不为呢？于是，松下幸之助毅然同飞利浦公司签订了合作合同。从此，松下公司迅速发展，飞利浦公司派出了技术骨干前去赴任，他们把技术、知识和管理经验传授给松下公司。在双方的合作期间，松下公司迅速地获得了飞利浦公司最新的技术。双方的合作为松下公司驰名日本乃至全世界打下了坚实的基础。

本案例中，作为技术引进方的松下公司正是意识到飞利浦公司的新技术会给松下公司带来很大的效益，才愿意接受较高的引进价格。

☞ **思考题与讨论题**

1. 你是否有过谈判的经历？举例说明。
2. 国际商务谈判的概念与特点是什么？
3. 国际商务谈判的类型包括哪些？
4. 国际商务谈判的原则有哪些？
5. 如果你是一个谈判人员，请回答以下问题并说明理由：
（1）你愿意主场谈判还是客场谈判？
（2）你喜欢采用口头谈判还是书面谈判？
（3）你准备进行一场让步型谈判、立场型谈判，还是原则型谈判？

# Chapter 2

# Main Theories on International Business Negotiation

☞ **Case study 2 – 1**    (**Conflict on opening the window**)

Two men were quarreling in the reading room. One insisted on opening the window while the other insisted on closing the window. They argued away and neither of them compromised. The librarian came and asked about the reason for the quarrel. "With the window closed, there's no air in and out of the room. I just want to open the window to let fresh air in and stale air out," said one; "with the window open, the wind will blow books, which affects reading," said another. After thinking for a while, the librarian closed the window of the reading room and opened the window of the room next to it. In this way, there was not only fresh air, the wind also could not reach the books.

In the above-mentioned case, the conflict between the two parties appears to be the conflict of positions. But in the negotiation, the librarian did not focus on the different positions that the two parties held—opening the window or closing the window, but on the potential requirements of the two parties—fresh air and no wind. Thus, the agreement was reached. It can be seen that position and interests are not the same thing.

## Ⅰ. Win-win Theory

The development of negotiation can be traced back to the beginning of human civilization. In spite of its long history, studies on negotiation as a branch of social science are fairly late. However, great achievements have been made in the field as a result of a great deal of theoretical and empirical efforts so that the nature and the law of negotiations have been revealed beneath complex and bewildering superficiality of negotiations. The influential theories and principles stemmed from those studies and researches have served as guidelines for negotiation activities. One of the most popular and accepted theory is "Win-win Concept."

### 1. Traditional concept: Win-lose model

In the warring period, negotiation, although as a peaceful approach to conflicts, could be extremely risky for negotiators, who would prepare to risk their lives for talking with antagonistic side because the envoy would be beheaded if the talk failed. The outcomes of negotiations were no more than two kinds: Either negotiations were concluded successfully, avoiding military conflicts, or negotiations ended in failure, triggering blood battles and wars, and as a result one side would lose its territory and its people were submitted to slavery. It is due to such vital consequence of negotiations that both parties viewed negotiations either as overwhelming victory or disastrous defeat. Therefore negotiators would make every effort and sometimes even play tricks and use conspiracy to secure their own party's utmost gains. The traditional practice of win-lose concept became prevailing against such background.

There are usually four steps for traditional practice of win-lose model:

a. Determining each party's own interest and stance;

b. Defending one's own interest and stance;

c. Discussing the possibilities of making concession;

d. Reaching an agreement of making concession or declaring failure of negotiation.

Negotiators guided by win-lose concept would protect and defend habitually each party's utmost interests by taking firm stance in negotiations, therefore concessions often proved to be very difficult to make, which would inevitably lead negotiations into an impasse or failure. The two dimensional concept explains largely the failure of numerous negotiations. There are of course occasions in international society, business activities and daily life when one side is in a much more powerful position than the other side and the latter is forced into agreement. These sorts of negotiations are not real negotiations at all but rather a practice of hegemony or playing the bully.

In reality, the loser can hardly accept the fact of being defeated because no one is happy to be labeled as a loser. The defeated party would seek every opportunity to revolt the result, which buries the seeds of future disputes. It is true that negotiations need to produce winners, especially for specific issues and narrowly-based bilateral negotiations, but such negotiations have less chance for long-term success. People need something new to guide their dispute settlement.

## 2. Win-win concept

In the second half of the twentieth century, the rapid development of economic globalization and integration, by promises of great benefits from free flow of people, goods, services and capital, have mingled all countries and areas into one interdependent and interrelated body. Resolving political, especially economic disputes and conflicts by peaceful means based on equality and mutual benefit has prevailed in international affairs and also in domestic affairs since countries started to view each other as partners and cooperators rather than adversaries and antagonists.

Some scholars and social workers began advocating a brand new idea, which is win-win concept. Among those outstanding figures are American scholars Roger Fisher, William Ury, and British negotiator Bill Scott. The core of their thinking is mutual success and convergence of interests. By mutual success, they mean under the condition that one party tries to gain his utmost interests or at least takes action not detrimental to one's own interests, each party may find one way or another to satisfy more or less the counterpart's interests as well. Seeking convergence of parties is to conduct negotiations by exploring mutual benefits so that a better and bigger cake of common interests will be made jointly for mutual sharing. In the meantime, an American attorney, Gerard Nierenberg created his educational philosophy of "Everybody wins." Because of his success and popularity of his philosophy, he was recognized by *Forbes* magazine as "the Father of Negotiation Training." Based on the concept, a win-win negotiation model has been developed. Practices have demonstrated its high effectiveness in dealing with disagreement and conflicts in negotiations, therefore, it has become the most widely accepted negotiation principle.

The main steps for win-win model are as follows:

a. Determining each party's interests and needs;

b. Finding out the other party's interests and demands;

c. Offering constructive options and solutions;

d. Announcing success or failure of negotiation or negotiation in impasse.

A significant point that win-win model differs from win-lose model is that both parties will not only seek means to fulfill one's own interests but also hope the interests of the other party may be realized more or less. Negotiations guided by such concept are to be conducted in an atmosphere of mutual understanding and sincere cooperation and will be concluded with mutually accepted agreement to the satisfaction of both parties.

☞ **Case study 2 - 2**    (**Territory in exchange for peace**)

The negotiation between Egypt and Israel on Sinai Peninsula provides an excellent example contrasting the striking effects of win-lose and win-win concepts.

The Middle East War in 1967 ended with Israel's occupation of 60,000 square kilometers of Sinai Peninsula. As the mediators between the two countries, the US and some other countries had striven for 11 years to help the two countries settle the disputes through negotiations. However, all efforts failed since both parties adhered firmly to their own stance and showed no flexibility. For Egypt, the occupied Sinai was indisputable part of Egyptian territory. In view of the territorial integrity and national sovereignty, Egypt was entitled to recovering it without any conditions; for Israel, the occupation of Sinai was for the sake of Israel's security since several military attacks against Israel were launched from the Peninsula.

In 1978, the peaceful negotiation was reopened at the Camp Davis in the US, which was conducted, this time, by a completely new guideline of win-win concept. The two parties were encouraged to reexamine their own interests as well as interests of their counterparts. It was found out that Egyptian's primary interest lied in the recovery of its territory, not threatening Israel's security whereas Israel did not mean to expand its territory but rather to ensure its safety. Based on this mutual understanding, an acceptable accord was reached; Israel returned the occupied territory to Egypt, who in turn designated much part of Sinai as Nonmilitary Zone. A dispute dragging for 11 years was resolved in a matter of 12 days.

The success of negotiations between Egypt and Israel was a great breakthrough in settling conflicts through peaceful means guided by win-win concept in Middle East peaceful negotiations. Israel and Palestine followed suit and put forward the celebrated "territory in exchange for peace," a negotiation principle for Middle East Peace Talk. The principle has been working effectively in negotiations between Palestinian and Israel. It is inevitable that the "peace talk" in Middle East suffers from temporary setbacks, however, it is the wish of all people that win-win concept will eventually lead the two sides to final and permanent peace in the region sooner or later.

Win-win theory has proved to be successful and effective in many tough negotiations because it takes into full consideration of both sides' interests, which contribute greatly to the mutual understanding of the other parties, therefore, it can bring about positive results that both parties expect. However effective win-win model can be, not all people in all situations will be guided by win-win concept by virtue of the deep-rooted one-dimensional concept of win-lose, therefore there is still a long way to go since it is a formidable task for people to establish a new concept.

## II. Collaborative Principled Negotiation

Collaborative Principled Negotiation (CPN) is also commonly known as Harvard Principled Negotiation, which is developed by Roger Fisher and William Ury in the book *Getting to Yes*. The core of the principle is to reach a solution beneficial to both parties by way of stressing interests and valuing not by way of bargaining. The method of principled negotiation developed at the Harvard Negotiation Project is to decide issues on their merits rather than through a haggling process focusing on what each side says. Mutual gains are pursued whenever possible. The method of principled negotiation is hard on the merits, soft on the people. It employs no tricks and no posturing. Principled negotiation shows you how to obtain what you are entitled to and still be decent. It enables you to be fair while protecting you against those who would take advantage of your fairness. When the interests of the two parties are contradictory, an objective criterion should be applied to.

Collaborative Principled Negotiation consists of four basic components:

a. People—separating people from problem;

b. Interests—focusing on interests not positions;

c. Gaining—inventing options for mutual gain;

d. Criteria—introducing objective criteria.

The four components are interrelated with each other and should be applied to throughout the whole course of negotiations. The four components are explained as follows.

### 1. Separating people from problem

It is generally understood that in negotiations problems will be discussed and resolved if talks are going on in a friendly and sincere atmosphere. Unfortunately, more often than not high tension is built up due to negotiators' prejudice against the other party or poor impression on each other or misled interpretation of the other party's intention. It is conceivable that negotiations would be directed to personal disputes and both sides say something hurting each other when such prejudice or misunderstanding exists. As a result, negotiators' personal feelings are mingled with interests and events to be discussed. For example, you may feel very uncomfortable when your counterpart appears arrogant and superior, so you probably throw out something to knock off his arrogance, which may further irritate him and make him take retaliation action. The focus of negotiation is shifted from interests and issues of both parties to personal dignity and self-respect, thus the attacks and quarrels end up with nothing. In other cases, your counterpart may misunderstand your intention and openly show his emotion when you make comments on his opinions and events he has described. For situation as such, CPN develops three steps for both parties to follow.

(1) Developing empathy

a. We put ourselves in their shoes.

b. We avoid blaming them for our problems.

c. We help them participate in the process.

(2) Managing emotions

a. We allow them to let off stream.

b. We do not overreact to emotional outbursts.

(3) Communicating

a. We listen and summarize what we hear.

b. We avoid trying to score points on others and debating them as opponents.

c. We do not berate them about what they are doing wrong.

In general, to separate people from problem, the crucial point is to understand the other party, control one's own emotion and have more communication so that they can understand each other and solve the existing problems.

## 2. Focusing on interests instead of positions

Conflicts of interests bring people to a negotiation table. Negotiating parties hold on to their own positions for the purpose of having their interests realized or protecting their interests or gaining more interests. However, successful negotiations are the results of mutual giving and taking of interests rather than keeping firm on one's own positions. The method of focusing on the common interests of negotiating parties works well because firstly, there is always more than one way of fulfilling each other's interests, and secondly, both sides can always find out certain common interests, otherwise they will not sit together discussing and talking. Negotiating parties can try the following methods in order to concentrate on interests instead of positions.

(1) Identifying interests

a. We explore their interests which hinder in our way.

b. We examine the different interests of the other side from different angels.

c. We look at their human needs underlying their positions.

(2) Talking about interests

a. We summarize and accept their interests.

b. We describe our understanding or put forward a problem before proposing our solutions.

c. We try not to look backward and focus more on looking forward.

In negotiation it is often very difficult to focus on interests since the interests of one party are frequently not clearly identified and expressed outwardly, and comparatively speaking, positions are concrete and explicitly exposed to each other. One important task of negotiators is to overpass one's position and to look for solutions satisfying both parties' interests.

☞ **Case study 2 – 3**   (**Putting aside dispute, and engaging in joint exploration**)

The prolonged dispute over the South China Sea among neighboring countries has been a disturbing factor for the instability in the region. Some countries have demanded sea territory and some other countries have declared actual controlling right over some islands. Facing the dispute, China, being the real owner of the area, reiterates China's sovereignty over the territory, meanwhile exploring the real interests of the neighboring countries' demanding for the territory. It was found out that an important reason behind their claim is the rich fishing and mineral resources in the area. The Chinese government hence proposed in talks with relative countries to "put aside dispute, and engage in joint exploration." The proposal met with general acceptance and proved to be quite effective in lightening the tense atmosphere in the region. The instability would have been deteriorating if the disputing countries, particularly China, had held on to their positions and showed no flexibility on the issue.

### 3. Putting forward options for mutual gain

The first two components look at the relation between people and problems, interests and positions，which are conducive for negotiators to establishing an objective view on those important factors in negotiations. The third component of inventing options for mutual gain provides an approach to fulfillment of the two parties' demands.

Why are negotiators easily trapped by their own positions? The explanation is that many negotiations simply focus on a single event and the solution to the event is either win or lose，for example，price of a car，size of commission，or time limit of a loan. The distributive nature of interests gaining limits people's scope of thinking and causes people to insist on their own stance. In such case，there is one way out，which is to jointly make the cake of interests as large as possible before cutting it apart so that both sides may get what they desire for. To this end，negotiators should be able to provide creative options and alternatives to unaccepted solutions. There are，in fact，always alternative solutions to problems to be solved，which is，unfortunately，often not fully understood.

Generally speaking，there are three factors hindering people from seeking for alternative solutions. One is the fixed distributive plan. Both sides perceive the size of the cake is fixed，thus your gain is my loss and my gain is your loss. The rigid distributive concept retards creative thinking and options and hence results in the failure of negotiations.

The second is seeking for only one solution. Negotiators are inclined to rest on their laurels they have achieved and hope to arrive at the final solution without other nuisances. They are not aware of the fact that creative thinking and options are indispensable parts of a successful negotiation.

The third is considering only one's own options suiting one's own needs. A successful negotiation is a process of giving and taking which means options provided should be a consolidated body of both sides' interests. Keeping in mind not only one's own party's interests but also the other side's interests can stimulate creativeness which will bring about alternative options conducive to success of negotiations.

To get rid of the above-mentioned barriers and offer creative options，the following steps can be considered.

（1）Diagnose

a. We set aside the idea that their gains have to be at our expense.

b. We encourage each other to help solve problems.

c. We do not prematurely focus on an option before people are ready.

（2）Putting forward constructive options

a. We separate putting forward options from evaluating them.

b. We develop several options before determining on a solution.

c. We look for common and complimentary interests.

d. We look for options that would make the decision easier for them.

Options are provided and the next step is to determine and find out an option that will suit both sides best. Selecting an option requires a criterion to decide which option is better or the best among several options, and now it comes to the fourth component—introducing an objective criterion.

### 4. Introducing an objective criterion

The first three components advocate the benefits of considering both parties' interests and designing a distributive pattern that would satisfy both sides' demands. However, conflicts and disputes of the two parties over interests gaining will not disappear no matter how considerable the two parties try to be and how creative the options are. When the two sides cannot decide which option is reasonable and rational, looking for an objective criterion will be a way out.

（1）How to define an objective criterion

The following points will be considered when telling if a criterion is objective or not:

a. An objective criterion should be independent of wills of all parties and thus be free from sentimental influence of any one.

b. An objective criterion should be valid and realistic.

c. An objective criterion should be at least theoretically accepted by both sides.

One point is clear that different issues have different objective criteria. For example, criteria of price talking will include factors of cost, market situation, depreciation, price competition and other necessary factors. In other negotiations, experts' opinions, international conventions and legal documents will all serve as objective criteria.

（2）How to use an objective criterion

When an objective criterion is agreed upon, the other important thing to do is to choose a fair procedural standard, which means the procedure or way of carrying out the criterion. The procedure will be regarded as fair when one party cuts a cake and asks the other party to choose first. Other procedures which may be called fair can be "doing it in turns," "drawing lots" and "looking for an arbitrator."

The following steps sum up the fourth component:

a. We look for various objective criteria.

b. We discuss why different standards may be appropriate.

c. We look for fair procedural standard.

In Fisher and Ury's view, the three standards described below can be applied to judge the success or failure of a negotiation approach. First, if an agreement is possibly reached, it should satisfy the valid interests of both parties to the maximum and resolve their conflicts, meanwhile protecting public interests. Second, the agreement should be highly efficient. Third, the agreement will improve, or at least not hurt the relationship of the two parties.

Collaborative Principled Negotiation provides us with a way to reach a wise agreement for tough negotiations. CPN has proved to be suitable to almost all situations from international negotiations to domestic and private negotiations, from simple events to complex situations and from routine talks to urgent meetings. Principled negotiations can be used by diplomats of countries in nonproliferation of nuclear weapon talks with each other, by Wall Street lawyers representing Fortune 500 companies in antitrust cases, and by couples in deciding everything from where to go for vacation to how to divide their property if they get divorced. Anyone can use this method.

Every negotiation is different, but the basic elements do not change. Principled negotiations can be used whether there is one issue or several, two parties or many; whether there is a prescribed ritual, as in collective bargaining, or an impromptu free-for-all, as in talking with hijackers. The method applies whether the other side is more experienced or less, a hard bargainer or a friendly one. Principled negotiation is an all-purpose strategy. Unlike almost all other strategies, if the other side learns the strategy, it does not become more difficult to use, on the contrary, it becomes easier. The success of CPN does not rely on playing tricks or negotiators' resourcefulness but on fairness, objectiveness and mutual understanding.

### Ⅲ. The Basic Psychological Theories of International Business Negotiation

☞ **Case study 2 - 4**　(A clever Belgium carpet merchant)

The devout Muslims in Arab countries pray every day whether they are at home or travelling regardless of the weather. The characteristics of their pray is that all the prayers will face the Holy City Mekka. However, the problem is that when the Muslims are away from their home or at travelling, they often cannot recognize the direction, which is a barrier for their pray. One Belgium carpet merchant found this business opportunity and reformed the small piece of carpet and made it into a kind of specialized carpet for Muslims' praying: embedding a flat compass into the carpet, and the compass just points to the direction of Mekka. As long as the carpet is put on the ground, the direction of Mekka will be recognized immediately, which offers a great convenience for the Muslims. This product became hot in residential area of the Muslims. The Belgium carpet merchant thus made a lot of money.

The psychological principle of negotiation means the negotiators should make use of the opponent's psychological activities during the negotiations, make the best use of the situation, so as to make the transaction possible.

Due to the great influence of psychological activities on negotiations, researches on the negotiation psychology are becoming deeper and deeper, and the psychological analysis during the negotiation is gradually developing into a new branch of psychology.

### 1. People, in different demand levels, have different psychological activities

People who are in different demand levels have different levels of requirements for a satisfactory demand. Therefore, in business, to satisfy the other party according to his demand level will make it easier to make full use of the situation and make the transaction. Maslow's hierarchy of needs, one of the behavioral science theories, was proposed by Abraham Maslow, an American psychologist, in the thesis "Theory of Human Motivation" in 1943. He divided the human needs into five levels.

(1) Physiological needs

This is the basic needs for human to survive, including the needs of water, food, sleep, warmth, exercise and sex. If these basic needs cannot be satisfied, the survival of human will be a problem. In this sense, physiological requirement is the most powerful motivation to stimulate people to act. Maslow suggested that other needs cannot become the new motivator only when these most basic needs are satisfied, then, these requirements having been fulfilled are no longer motivators.

(2) Safety needs

This is the human's requirement to protect their own safety, free from the threats of unemployment and the loss of property, protect themselves from occupational disease or severe supervision. Maslow suggested that the whole organism is a mechanism which is in pursuit of security; the perceptive organs, effect organs, intelligence and other power of human are primarily tools of seeking safety, and we can even take the science and the conception of life as a part to meet the requirement for safety. Without doubt, once the need is satisfied to some certain degree, it is no longer a need.

(3) Needs of love, affection and belongingness

Requirement of this level includes two aspects. One is the need for friendship, that is, everyone needs a good relationship between partners and colleagues or keeps their friendship and loyalty; everyone desires to gain love, to love somebody as well as to be loved. The other one is the need for belonging. All human beings have the emotion to be a part of a group. We hope to be a member of it and care for each other. The requirement for emotion comes more meticulous than the physiology; it is related to one's physiological feature, education and religious belief.

(4) Needs for esteem

Everyone wishes to have a stable social status and gain the social acceptance towards their personal ability and achievements. The requirement for respect can be divided into internal respect and external respect. Internal respect means one wishes to be capable, competent, full of confidence and independent under different kinds of circumstances. In a word, internal respect is one's self-esteem. External respect means one hopes to have standing and prestige and to be respected, rusted and highly regarded. Maslow believes that the satisfaction of the requirement for respect can make people believe in themselves and feel enthusiastic about society, realize their value and uses for being alive.

☞ **Case study 2 – 5** **(The smile of US Hilton Hotel)**

US Hilton Hotel has been a well-known chain businesses in the world, which is famous for the smiling services. Conner Hilton, the Chairman of the board, believed that smiling will be contributed to the development of the hotel. He asked his subordinates constantly "There should be smiles on the faces of Hilton waiters and waitresses no matter what the hotel itself meets with," "Have you smiled to your customers today?" was often mentioned by Hilton. It turned out that the smiling faces of Hilton people make customers feel welcomed and respected, which are just like enchanting sunshine and make customers forget about their worries and troubles. In Hilton Hotel, customers feel they can be satisfied not only with the need of food and accommodation, but also with people's requirement for safety and respect. Under the unprecedented economic depression in the 1930s, 80% of the hotels in the US were closed down, but Hilton went through the depression and stepped in a golden age of its operation by smiling on the faces of the Hilton employees.

(5) Needs for self-actualization

This is the highest level of needs. It means the requirement to fulfill one's dream and ambition, show one's ability to the most and complete all things equal to one's ability. In another word, people do a job which is equal to his ability and only in this way can it make him feel great happy. Maslow proposed that the way to satisfy one's requirement for self-fulfillment varies from person to person. This requirement is to reach one's full potentialities and gradually become someone who lives up to his expectation.

Actually, all kinds of needs of a negotiator can be embodied in his negotiation. For example, to meet the physiological needs, it means negotiators should enjoy delicious and nutritious meals and a good sleep in comfortable hotels so that they can be in a good state of energy and mood. Safety needs is embodied in the negotiation that negotiators' personal safety and information safety should be guaranteed. Needs of love is embodied that members of one's own group can be united together and have a good cooperation, and they can establish a good and harmonious relations with their negotiating partners. Needs for esteem means not only members of one's own group can respect each other, but also they can get respect from their partners. Needs for self-actualization is embodied that the negotiation can be a complete success to his own expectation.

## 2. Some psychological factors should be paid attention to in negotiations

In a negotiation, if we find some common psychological factors, observe them consciously and make use of them, then adjust the negotiation strategy; this will have a positive effect on the negotiation.

Firstly, people who speak highly of the goods are not always the buyers, but the nit-pick is very likely the potential client.

Secondly, when the client ask many questions about the performance, quality, and specifications and so on, and discuss these carefully and actively, there must be a trading opportunity.

Thirdly，when the potential client begins to ask the details about before and after sales service，which means he is very likely to buy the products，the opportunity to make a deal is coming.

Fourthly，the main task for the seller in a transaction is to stimulate the buyer's desire to purchase and relieve his negative psychological effect of payment. Meantime，the buyer should make out the basic functions of the products and treat them rationally，and finally get the most utility satisfaction at the expense of the least input.

Fifthly，in our daily life，many products will become useless to the buyer after being bought. So buyers should treat the seller's instruction rationally，in case of buying unnecessary products.

Sixthly，once the transaction is made，we can disregard the request of increasing or decreasing of the price from the counterparty. Because it's the fluke mind of the buyer and seller，it won't change the transaction at all.

### Ⅳ. Negotiating Power and the Related Factors

Negotiation power is the overall ability that negotiators have at their command in a negotiation. It is the force to control the negotiation process and to affect the other party. No matter what kind of negotiation it is—a diplomatic negotiation，trade negotiation，technological or service negotiation—the gaps in negotiation ability (negotiation power) decide its outcomes to a great extent. In all the cases，negotiators hope their negotiation power can be stronger. Then what are the factors affecting the negotiation power?

Generally speaking，there are mainly eight aspects which are considered as eight abilities and decide the power of negotiation. These eight sources can be abbreviated as NO TRICKS which represents eight words by each letter. They are *need*，*options*，*time*，*relationships*，*investment*，*credibility*，*knowledge*，and *skills*.

#### 1. "N"—need

Generally，as far as the buyer and the seller are concerned，the one who has stronger need is less powerful. If the buyer needs the product badly，the seller has a stronger negotiation power. Conversely，if the seller urgently wants to sell the product，the buyer has the stronger position.

Note：Need or motivation of a negotiator can be mainly stimulated by the following means.

a. Offer inducements to the other party. For example，to offer a certain price discount or even buy one and take one free.

b. Demonstrate the attractiveness or the strong points. What are the advantages of your products? What are your selling points?

c. Get a third party's support, e.g. to ask a public figure or a famous person to advertise your product.

d. Place a time limit. Make a deadline for your favorable offer. For example, "This offer is valid for 5 days." or "This price is valid till the end of this month."

### 2. "O"—options

Should initial negotiations fail, the one who has more options or substitutions has greater negotiation power. Suppose the seller has more available markets, or his products and services are unique, the buyer has no options; in this case, the seller can capitalize better in the negotiation.

### 3. "T"—time

The more limited your time is, the weaker your position is in negotiation. If the seller is pressured by critical time constraints, the buyer's negotiation strength would be increased.

### 4. "R"—relationships

The better and stronger your relationship with your existing client is, the more powerful you are in your negotiation with other potential clients. If your existing clients maintain vigilant and do not want to develop further relations with you, your negotiation power will be weakened. These relationships reflect your reputation for morality and competence, and influence word-of-mouth within an industry.

### 5. "I"—investment

The more time, energy, and money you invest in the negotiation generally means the more adequate you prepare for it, which will increase your negotiating power. On the other hand, it means that you may be led by the nose, and easily manipulated, thus reducing your bargaining power since cost is very important to you.

### 6. "C"—credibility

Having reliable products that your potential clients are interested in can enhance your negotiation power. When the seller knows that his products have been used by the buyer, and his products have advantages in price, quality and service, there is no doubt that the seller may enjoy high credibility. However, this single merit alone cannot guarantee that the deal will be closed in the end.

### 7. "K"—knowledge

Knowledge is power. If the seller fully understands the buyer's problems and needs, and is confident that his products can satisfy the buyer's demand, his negotiation ability will be increased. On the other hand, if the buyer knows more about the product, he will have more power.

### 8. "S"—skills

Consummate skills directly and easily enhance negotiation power. Of course, negotiation skills are not innate; they are acquired by comprehensive learning, including extensive knowledge, speaking eloquence, acute thinking, and by experience.

In international business negotiation, we should skillfully use each source of negotiation power in the "NO TRICKS" principle, and should play no tricks.

☞ **Case study 2 – 6** **(China's status of entering the WTO)**

In the Sino-American negotiation that made China's entry into the WTO a success, the two parties had a fierce debate over the status China would have upon entering the WTO. If China entered the WTO as a developed country, it would not enjoy the beneficial treatment granted only to developing countries, including a generalized system of preferences, gradual opening of the market, and protection of infant industries. This was an important matter of principle, concerning the interests of a country. Therefore, China insisted on joining the WTO with the status of a developing country. However, in order to open the door to Chinese market quickly so as to gain more market entrant's opportunities and profits, the American negotiators insisted that China should enter with the status of a developed country. Their reason was that China's export industry was increasing rapidly, and its foreign exchange reserve was at top of the world list. China's technology for space satellite launches and returns had reached the level that only a few developed countries had reached. No other developing country was able to do so. One American representative even compared the situation of the poor areas in China with the situation in Africa and India. He said when he visited the poorest areas in the western China, he knocked at a door casually and asked the man of the house if they had had breakfast, the answer was yes. Then he went on asking if they had had lunch, the answer was that they were preparing it. Finally he was told that their dinner was no problem either. But in the poor areas in African countries, and even in India, the situation was totally different. When asked if they had had breakfast, their answer was no; when asked about lunch and dinner, they asked if he would give them relief food. The representative said that from these contrasting experiences, he felt that the situation of China's poor areas was not as serious as they reported it.

China and America had their own understanding and criteria on the issue of China's status when entering the WTO, and were unable to reach an agreement. The focus of this negotiation was which status really applied to China: a developing or developed country. In fact, the UN and the World Bank and some other international organizations had a prevailing criterion—the average GDP of a country. According to UN and World Bank's statistics, countries with an average GDP below USD785 (the criterion in 1996) were the poorest countries. And when this Sino-US negotiation was in process, the average GDP in China was only USD750. Actually, by this criterion China remained one of the poorest countries until the year 2000. Judged by the GDP criterion, the American opinion was obviously untenable.

## ☞ Questions for your consideration and discussion

1. How much do you know about the win-win theory?

2. Supposing you are the buyer in a negotiation, what will you pay your first attention to? Then how it will change if you are the seller?

3. In the process of your negotiation with others or solving a problem, have you ever taken other party's interests into consideration from another angle? If you have, what do you think of the effect?

4. What are the five different demand levels of people?

5. What are the factors affecting negotiating power?

6. How can you stimulate other people's motivation / How can you strengthen your negotiation power?

(1) You are working on a sales promotion plan to push sales of City Baby.

(2) You are running a bookstore and the business is not very encouraging.

7. You go to your boss for a raise in salary. He says OK by increasing your workload a little bit. Should you accept it or not? And why?

# 第二章

# 国际商务谈判理论

☞ **案例分析 2—1** （是否应当打开窗户）

两个人在阅览室争吵,一位坚持开窗,一位坚持关窗,他们为了是否打开窗户而争执不休。阅览室负责人走过来,向两人询问争吵的原因。一位说:"屋子封闭,空气不太好,我希望打开窗户通风,放进一些新鲜空气。"另一位说:"开窗户风太大,把书吹得乱飞,影响看书。"负责人考虑了一会儿,然后把阅览室的窗户关上,打开隔壁房间的窗户,既放进了新鲜空气,又不让风把书吹乱。

在上述案例中,双方的冲突看起来仿佛是立场的对立,但阅览室负责人并没有把谈判局限在双方陈述的立场——开窗和关窗,而是关注空气流通和没有风的潜在要求,从而达成和解。由此看来,立场和利益是不同的。

## 一、双赢理论

谈判是伴随着人类文明的发展而发展的。然而尽管谈判活动源远流长,但是直到第二次世界大战后的 20 世纪五六十年代人们才将谈判作为社会科学的一个分支来进行系统的研究。经过理论与实践工作者在这个领域进行的大量理论和实践的研究,人们透过纷繁复杂的谈判活动的表象,不断地揭示谈判活动的内在规律,取得了令人瞩目的成就。从谈判研究中产生的有影响的谈判理论和原则已成为指导人们谈判实践的重要理论依据。其中最有影响力和最广为接受的谈判原则即为双赢理念。

### 1. 传统的赢—输理念

战争年代,谈判是化解冲突的一种和平方式。对于谈判者来说,谈判是极其危险的任务。在中国被称为"说客"、在西方被称为"特使"的谈判代表在准备如何晓之以理,动之以情的同时,还必须准备一旦谈判不成功就要献出生命。对方在谈判失败后往往以砍掉使者的头表示宣战或者用使者的鲜血举行祭旗仪式,目的是激励士兵的斗志。谈判对于谈判各方来说不外乎两种结果:一种是谈判以各方达成协议而告终,这样就避免了冲突的进一步发展,避免了人头落地和大量的财产损失;另一种则是谈判以失败而告终,导致各方的武装冲突,结果常常是生灵涂炭,国家被侵占,人民沦为奴隶。

正是由于谈判的成功与失败所带来的后果如此严重,谈判各方都将谈判视为或者绝对的成功,或者绝对的失败。因此为了取得谈判的成功,谈判各方都尽一切努力,甚至包括使用阴谋诡计和欺骗的伎俩来确保自己一方利益得到最大的满足。

因此,人类也将商场视为战场,将同行视为冤家,于是就有了各种不正当的竞争手段。一些公司在与外商谈判中竞相压价,互相拆台,进行恶性竞争,以将自己的同行置于死地而后快。传统的输—赢模式遵循以下步骤:

①确定己方的利益和立场;

②捍卫己方的利益和立场;

③各方讨论做出让步的可能性;

④达成妥协方案或宣布谈判失败。

受输—赢理念的影响,谈判各方在谈判中习惯性地尽力维护自己的利益而保持坚定的立场,因此妥协就成为获取更大利益的砝码。各方都不会轻易让步,而妥协是各方达成协议的关键点,如果不能取得各方的妥协或一方的妥协,谈判就不可避免地会以失败告终。这种非赢即输的理念是造成众多谈判失败的原因。当然,在国际社会的经济活动中,有时由于一方的实力十分强大而迫使对方接受其条件,这样的谈判与其称之为谈判倒不如说是霸权的反映。

事实上,当一场谈判以某一方的胜利和另一方的失败而结束时,失败者一般很难接受作为失败者的事实,他会千方百计地寻找机会改变谈判的结果,这又为以后埋下了冲突的种子。有时谈判需要制造胜利者,这也是事实,特别是在特定的事件和有限的双边谈判中更是如此,但是这样的谈判所取得的成果常常难以为继。人们需要新的理念和原则来指导冲突的化解。

2. 双赢理念

20 世纪后半叶,随着经济全球化和一体化的不断发展和深化,世界各国和各地区之间的经济交往和经济协调不断密切,经济上相互联系和依存、相互渗透和扩张、相互竞争和制约的程度不断加深,形成了世界经济从资源配置、生产到流通和消费的多层次、多形式的交织和融合,使全球经济形成了一个不可分割的有机整体。这种你中有我、我中有你,一荣俱荣、一损俱损的局面使人们认识到,在经济相互依赖的世界里,不能简单地以输赢论英雄,而必须寻求通过合作来取得双赢的结果,这种认识使人们越来越多地通过和平的方式,在平等互利的基础上解决一切冲突,特别是经济领域内的冲突。

一些学者和社会工作者开始宣传和倡导解决冲突的全新理念,即双赢理念。其中比较著名的有美国学者罗杰·费希尔和威廉·尤里、英国谈判家比尔·斯科特等。他们的核心思想是强调共同的胜利和利益的一致性。所谓共同的胜利是指谈判一方在尽可能取得己方利益的前提下,或者至少在不危害己方利益的前提下,使对方的利益得到一定的满足。寻求各方利益的一致性是指在谈判中应努力挖掘各方利益相同的部分,再通过共同的努力将利益的蛋糕做大,如此各方都可获得更多的利益。美国律师格拉德·聂仁伯格于 20 世纪 60 年代中期在纽约创办了一所非营利性的谈判学院,在学院里他极力推销自己的谈判哲学——所有的人都是赢家。由于格拉德办学的成功和他的谈判哲学的推广,他被《福布斯》杂志誉为"谈判培训之父"。

以双赢理念为指导,一种全新的谈判模式形成了。大量的谈判实践证实了这一新的谈判模式在解决冲突的谈判中十分有效,成果卓著。在新的理念的指导下,许多长期无法解决的冲突得到了有效化解,许多可能升级的对抗得到了缓和。双赢理念极大地促进了合作,减少了对抗,提高了整个社会的共同福利。因此以双赢理念为基础的谈判指导思想已被全世界广泛接受。双赢模式遵循的步骤如下:

①确定己方的利益和需求;

②寻找对方的利益和需求;

③提出建设性的提议和解决方法;

④宣布谈判成功,宣布谈判失败或谈判陷入僵局。

比较双赢模式与输—赢模式可以看出,两种模式中最大的区别是在第二步和第三步。输—赢模式中捍卫己方的利益和立场被寻求对方的利益和需求所替代,这不是一个简单的文字游戏,而是一个思想观念的重大变化,是通过谈判取得双赢结果的第一步。在发现对方的利益和需求的过程中,谈判者可以更好地理解自己的谈判对手,并能够从对方的角度考虑一些问题,促使各方朝着相互理解与和解的方向发展。当各方建立了互相理解的关系后便可在此基础上提出各方都可能接受的建设性解决方案。由于这样的方案不仅仅是一方利益和意志的反映,而是结合了各方的观点,特别是各方共同的利益,因而谈判以各方满意的结果而告终的机会大大增加。

☞ **案例分析 2—2** （以土地换和平）

埃及和以色列为解决西奈半岛领土争端的谈判是一个著名的经典案例,这一案例常常被用来对比两种谈判理念的不同效果。

1967 年的"中东之战"结束之后,以色列占领了埃及西奈半岛 6 万平方千米的土地。战争虽然结束,但是两国之间的领土争端不断,成为这一地区一个重要的不安定因素。为协助各方解决争端,实现和平,一些国家特别是美国多次以协调人的身份督促各方通过谈判解决争端,然而各种努力均告失败,因为各方都坚持自己的利益和谈判立场,没有丝毫的妥协迹象。对于埃及来说,被占领的西奈半岛是埃及领土不可分割的一部分,鉴于国际上承认的领土完整和国家主权原则,埃及有权力要求以色列无条件地归还被占领土。对于以色列来说,占领西奈半岛是出于对以色列安全的考虑,因为几次针对以色列的武装攻击都是从这一区域开始的,所以以色列应当控制这一区域。由于各方分毫不让,谈判虽不断举行,但是一次次陷入僵局,持续11年也未取得任何实质性进展。

1978年埃以之间再次恢复谈判,地点是美国的戴维营。此次和谈不同于以往所有谈判的一点是,各方摒弃传统的思维模式而采用全新的双赢理念来指导谈判。双方在双赢理念的影响下重新审视各自的利益和要求,同时从对方的角度了解对方的利益和要求,各方有了新的认识和发现。埃及的主要利益在于恢复领土主权、保持领土完整而不是威胁以色列的安全;而以色列对于领土扩张并不感兴趣,它的主要利益在于保证国家的安全。基于这样的观念各方达成了共识,提出了一个各方都能接受的解决方案:以色列归还其占领的埃及领土,作为回报,埃及将西奈半岛的大部分领土划为非军事区域。这样,一场持续了11年的谈判,终于画上了圆满的句号,而这次谈判只用了短短的12天。

埃以之间的和平谈判结束了各方长时间的对抗,使两国实现了最终和平。埃以之间以双赢理念为指导,通过谈判解决冲突的成功为中东地区的和平谈判树立了一个可以遵循的榜样。以色列和巴勒斯坦之间的和平谈判受埃以谈判成功的鼓舞相应提出了著名的"以土地换和平"的方案。这一谈判原则在巴以谈判中一直发挥着重要的作用,是谈判的基石。当然,中东地区的和平谈判由于长期遗留下来的积怨,再加上外部势力的干扰,不可避免地出现各种挫折,但是,相信在双赢理念的引导下,通过世界热爱和平的人们的努力,中东地区永久的和平最终会实现。

双赢理念在解决许多难题时被证明是有效和成功的,这其中的主要原因是该理念强调从彼此的角度考虑问题,这大大地促进了各方的相互理解,因而就能产生事半功倍的效果。但是也必须意识到,双赢的理念尽管有效,但是并非所有的人在所有的场合都能自觉地运用这一理念,这是由于传统的非赢即输的观念还根深蒂固,再加上各方利益本质上的冲突性,因此,要使新理念成为人们的自觉行为还需长期的努力。

## 二、合作原则谈判法

合作原则谈判法的核心和精神实质是通过强调各方的利益和价值,而非讨价还价本身,以及通过提出寻求各方各有所获的方案来取得谈判的成功。从哈佛谈判项目发展起来的原则谈判法,通过强调事物的原则来确定事物的性质,而不是在各方曾经表示要做什么或不做什么的问题上讨价还价,争论不休。原则谈判法鼓励人们尽可能寻求使各方都获益的途径,在各方的利益发生冲突时应坚持以客观标准,也就是以独立于各方意志的标准为基础解决冲突。原则谈判法坚持对事不对人,在原则问题上毫不让步,但在对待谈判伙伴上应与人为善。原则谈判法强调在谈判中不用诡计,不故作姿态;它使谈判者既可得到理所应得,又不失风度;既能使谈判者保持公正,又不致使对方利用谈判者的公正。

合作原则谈判法具有广泛的适用性，学习应用合作原则谈判法对于各方取得双赢的结果具有十分积极的意义。它是对双赢理念的发展和理论化，由以下四个部分组成：

①对待谈判对手，对事不对人；

②对待各方利益，着眼于利益而非立场；

③对待利益获取，制定双赢方案；

④对待评判标准，引入客观评判标准。

合作原则谈判法的四个部分，互为依存，环环相扣，在谈判中贯穿始终，共同影响谈判的进程。下面就这四个组成部分做简要解释。

### 1. 对事不对人

谈判气氛是决定谈判各方关系的一个重要因素。众所周知，在诚挚友好的气氛中，谈判各方的心态比较平和，因而谈判中的难题也比较容易解决。但是遗憾的是，友好的谈判气氛时常由于各方互有偏见，或者在谈判过程中对对方形成的不良印象，或者是对对方意图的否定看法等而被破坏。当有此种情况发生时，谈判就无法围绕谈判议题展开，而成为了个人之间的攻击和对抗，相互之间的信任和感情被破坏，导致谈判无法正常进行。

谈判一方如果认为对方的行为举止显得傲慢无礼，说的某句话让他感到没面子，他反过来可能会抛出一两句话杀杀对方的傲气，这又会进一步激怒对方，促使其采取进一步的报复措施。例如，在各方相互争执的情况下，人们喜欢抛出这样一句话，"跟你这种人没法谈话"。当此句一出，可以想象，谈判的焦点只能从讨论各方的利益和问题转移到个人的脸面和尊严上来。谈判最终不欢而散，什么问题都得不到解决。

在另外一些情况下，谈判一方对另一方提出的理由和表述事件的目的存有疑虑，认为对方可能想利用谈判达到其险恶的目的时，一方常常会表现出情绪激动，出言不逊，使火气骤然上升而无法达到通过谈判解决问题的目的。针对以上这些情况，合作原则谈判法提出从以下三点来解决此类问题。

（1）发展移情法

①从对方的立场看待问题；

②避免因自己的问题而责备对方；

③协助对方参与到解决问题中去。

（2）正确看待情绪

①允许对方发火；

②恰当看待情绪的爆发。

（3）加强沟通

①注意倾听并总结听到的情况；

②避免给对方打分并将对方当作辩论的对手；

③不严厉指责对方的错误。

总的说来,要做到对事不对人,关键的是要使各方尽量相互理解,在气氛紧张时控制自己的情绪,并通过加强沟通和对话使各方相互了解从而达到解决问题的目的。

2. 着眼于利益而非立场

利益的冲突将人们带到谈判桌前。谈判各方为了实现各自的利益,或是维护自己的利益,或是通过谈判获取更多的利益,因而在谈判中常常坚持自己的立场,以此来达到上述目的。然而,由于各方的利益在大多数情况下是矛盾的,所以他们的谈判立场也常常是对立的。如果谈判各方都各自坚持自己的立场,则很容易出现僵持的局面,因为立场常常是难以调和的,而调和各方的利益则比较容易实现。成功的谈判是各方利益的给予和获取的结果,而不是通过坚持自己的立场来实现的。

着眼于利益而非立场就是为了克服因各方一味坚持自己的立场而使谈判陷入僵局的行为。着眼于利益不仅是指协调各方的不同利益,更为重要的是寻求各方的共同利益。谈判各方如果能够做到着眼于利益,他们就不会只坚持一种解决问题的方案。事实上,使各方利益得到满足的方法不止一个,当人们认识到这一点时就会变得富有灵活性和创建性。此外,谈判各方总是可以找到共同的利益,因为没有共同利益各方也没必要进行谈判。而找到各方的共同利益是取得双赢结果的一个关键点。为帮助各方做到着眼于利益而非立场,可以从以下两个方面着手。

(1) 明确利益

①探寻妨碍我方的对方利益;

②从不同的角度审视对方的不同利益;

③透过对方的立场看到对方的人性需求。

(2) 讨论利益

①总结并接受对方的利益;

②在提出解决方案前表达自己的见解或提出问题;

③在解决问题时尽量不追究过去的矛盾,应该向前看。

在谈判中要想做到以各方的利益为重,而不是在立场上争执往往不是一件轻而易举的事情。原因是谈判立场经常表现得具体而明确,但是隐藏在立场后面的利益却可能不明朗,不具体。有时人们出于策略的需要掩盖其真实的利益,这也增加了问题的复杂性。不过,即便如此,谈判各方只要努力就可以做到以利益为重,而避免在立场上讨价还价。下面的例子有力地说明了着眼于利益在谈判中的作用。

☞ **案例分析 2—3**　(搁置争议,共同开发)

中国南海的领海主权问题长期以来一直是中国与周边国家发生冲突的一个根源。一些国家宣称对中国南海的某块领域有领海主权,另有一些国家则提出专属经济区的要求。

面对周边国家的领土要求，中国一方面一再重申中国南海是中国领土不可分割的一部分，中国拥有绝对的主权立场；另一方面中国又在谈判中充分考虑冲突各方的利益所在，即南海蕴藏着巨大的海底矿藏和丰富的鱼类资源，并以此为出发点提出了著名的"搁置争议，共同开发"的谈判原则。这一原则充分体现了在谈判中应注重利益而非立场，向前看而不是纠缠过去的争议。由于提案考虑了各方的实际利益，因而被广泛接受，并成为缓解这一地区的紧张气氛、解决地区冲突的行之有效的原则。可以想象，如果冲突各方，特别是中国，坚持自己的立场，那么这个地区的冲突就会愈演愈烈，逐步升级，最终各方面利益都会受到重大损失。

事实上，在很多时候尽管冲突利益和共同利益是并存的，但是如果处理得当就可以使共同利益不断放大，使冲突利益不断缩小。例如，目前许多发达国家对从发展中国家进口的服装和纺织品都有配额限制，为此，发达国家和发展中国家之间不断有贸易摩擦发生，发达国家担心大量廉价的服装纺织品进入本国会对本国的同类产业构成威胁，损害本国同类就业人员的利益。这种摩擦看似不易调和，但是事实上，从发展中国家进口服装和纺织品既可以满足各个层次的消费者，特别是中低收入人群的穿衣需求，又可以将本国有限的资源配置到获利更高的行业，是各方都获益的交易。事实上，发达国家的纺织业早已成为夕阳产业，被边缘化了。这也就是为什么世界贸易组织不但要求成员国逐步取消配额，而且特别对发达国家在服装和纺织品进口配额上提出了明确的取消日期的原因。"乌拉圭回合"谈判中达成的《服装与纺织品贸易协议》要求在该行业已经失去竞争力的发达国家在十年内彻底取消对发展中国家进口纺织品和服装的配额制度。取消发达国家对服装和纺织品配额的要求从根本上说是一个对发达国家和发展中国家都有利的双赢措施。

### 3. 制定双赢方案

原则谈判法的前两部分主要是针对谈判中对事不对人、着眼于利益而非立场进行的论述，从而使谈判各方正确对待彼此间的利益，找准谈判的重点和立足点。而第三部分，制定双赢方案，则为各方实现自己的利益提供了一个可行的路径和方法。

在谈判中，人们为何极易陷入对自己的立场讨价还价之中？其原因有两个，一是由于谈判的内容属于非输即赢类型的，如汽车的价格、佣金的高低、房屋租期的长短等；或者人们遇到的问题是非此即彼的选择，如离婚谈判中对财产的分割、孩子的归属等。这种两分法类型的谈判限制了人们的思维，制约了人们的创造性，使谈判者的目光盯在谈判的结果是输还是赢这个问题上。二是人们往往把问题的解决方法限制在很窄的范围内，比较典型的做法是认为解决问题的办法只有一个，如果这个方案不能化解冲突，谈判只好陷于停顿。总的说来，阻止人们寻求建设性替代方案的原因有以下三个：

一是认为分配方案保持一成不变。各方都认为利益的蛋糕是固定不变的，因而你的胜利就是我的失败，或者我的胜利就是你的失败。这种僵化的分配观念制约了人们解决问题的创造力和谈判的灵活性,从而常常导致谈判的失败。解决这一问题的方法是转变观念,将固定不变转为灵活可变,即各方在利益分配之前共同将利益的蛋糕做大,这样各方都可以获得更大的利益。

二是只寻求一种答案。谈判者往往满足于已取得的成就和进展,并且希望谈判照此方式继续下去,不再出现其他麻烦,顺利达成最终协议。但是如果谈判中途出现其他问题使现有方案无法实施,他们又不愿意放弃在现有方案上已取得的进展,因此导致谈判失败。谈判各方应当认识到总有其他更好的办法来解决目前的困难,因此当一种方案行不通时应及时提出替代方案,避免谈判陷入僵局。

三是在提出方案时只考虑满足自己利益和需要的解决办法。谈判代表应当意识到谈判过程是给予与获取并行的过程,成功的谈判协议是权利与义务的结合体,因此谈判方案应充分体现各方共同的利益和要求。只有同时考虑自己的利益和对方的利益时,才能激发人们的创造力,提出富有建设性意义的提案。

针对以上问题,可以按以下步骤来制定双赢方案。

(1) 诊断

①放弃对方利益的满足一定是以我方的付出为代价的观念;

②鼓励各方共同解决问题;

③在对方未做好充分准备之前不预先锁定在一种方案上。

(2) 提出有建设性的方案

①将提出方案和评价方案分开;

②在确定最终解决方案之前先提出几个可供选择的方案;

③寻求各方的共同利益和互补利益;

④寻求使对方容易接受的方案。

这一部分的要点是构思多种选择方案并且在此基础上选择可行的方案。在谈判处于困难的关键阶段,最重要的就是能够拿出多种方法来,如:请有关方面的专家和专业人员共同讨论、集思广益,如果有可能也不妨与对方共同构思,通过共同探讨寻求一致。

在提出各种选择方案后,下一步就是选择一个切实可行的为各方所接受的方案。然而在选择方案时就存在着一个以什么标准来评价所选方案的问题,也就是说可以确定此方案优于彼方案,或者某一方案是几个方案中最好的方案的标准。由于各方的评判标准往往存在着很大的分歧,因而以谁的标准来衡量各种方案就成为一个关键的问题。

4. 引入客观评判标准

上述虽然强调从各方的利益为出发点来考虑分配方案,以求得令各方都满意的解决方法,然而无论各方如何从对方的角度考虑问题,理解对方的需求,争取提出具有创建性的方案,都无法抹杀各方利益冲突和对抗的一面。这种矛盾冲突在对待方案的评价标准上得到集中反映。当各方因评判标准不同而无法确定方案的合理性和公正性时,最好的解决方法就是寻求一个客观标准。

（1）如何规定客观标准

在判断一个标准是否属于客观标准时应从以下几个方面考虑：

①客观标准应当独立于所有各方的主观意志之外，因而它可以不受任何一方的感情影响。例如世界贸易组织所确定的各项原则如最惠国待遇原则、国民待遇原则、无歧视待遇原则、互惠原则、透明度原则、关税减让原则、取消数量限制原则等因为不代表任何个别国家或地区的利益，而是从全体成员的利益出发，因而被所有成员视为客观标准。

②客观标准应当具有合法性并且切合实际。上述世界贸易组织的各项规则已成为世贸组织宪章以及其他协定中的主要条款，成为各成员国普遍遵守的法律条约，同时这些原则通过多年的使用被证实是切合实际和可行的，所以被各成员在贸易争端中普遍用来作为解决争端的标准。

③客观标准应当具有科学性和权威性。例如麻省理工学院的经济学模式出自世界最著名的学府，并且该模式的建立是在科学理论基础上经过严格的计算而得出的结果，因而具有强大的说服力。显然，在确定客观标准时，对不同的事物有不同的客观标准，所考虑的因素也不尽相同。例如在与国外商人就产品的价格进行谈判时，对价格的衡量标准就应当包括产品的成本价、市场的变化、货币的稳定、竞争对手的情况以及其他必要的因素。此外，专家的意见、国家协议和国际惯例、一国的法律和规章制度都可以作为客观标准。

（2）如何应用客观标准

运用原则谈判法不仅涉及如何规定客观标准，而且涉及如何应用客观标准的问题。所以衡量客观标准是否公平，是否具有科学性和有效性应当从两个方面入手：一是从实质利益上看，二是从处理程序上看。从实质利益上看是以不损害各方各自的利益为原则；从处理程序上看就是解决方法本身是否公平，也就是要有公平的程序。例如从程序上看如果一方分割蛋糕，让另一方先挑选，这就是一个公平的程序。其他常用的被视为公平的程序还有"轮流坐庄""抓阄""寻找仲裁人"等。

下面的几个步骤是对第四部分的总结：

①寻求不同的客观标准；

②探讨不同客观标准的可行之处；

③寻求公正的处理程序。

人们可以采用不同的方法和途径来进行谈判。某种方法是成功还是失败，根据罗杰·费希尔和威廉·尤里的观点，可以从以下三个方面做出判断：一是一项可能达成的协议应当最大限度地满足各方的合法利益，解决他们之间的冲突，同时保证公众的利益不受损害。二是协议应当是高效的。三是协议应当改善，或至少不伤害各方的关系。

合作原则谈判法为我们提供了一个在艰苦的谈判中达成协议的方法。实践证明，合作原则谈判法适用于几乎所有的谈判场合：从国际谈判到国内谈判，从简单事件到复杂事件,从双边谈判到多边谈判,从日常商业交往到紧急突发情况。无论谈判场合如何变化,是在充分准备的场合中如集体辩论,还是在未经准备的突发场合如与劫持者的谈判都可以适用原则谈判法。合作原则谈判法还可服务于不同类型的谈判者以解决各种各样的问题,如各国外交官和政治家就限制核武器扩散进行的谈判,华尔街律师代表世界 500 强公司就反垄断进行的谈判;它还可以帮助夫妻在决定度假地、离婚时财产的分配等几乎所有问题上发挥作用。

人们每天进行着各种各样不同性质的谈判。可以说没有内容相同的两场谈判,但是无论谈判内容如何变化,谈判的基本要素都不变。在谈判中使用原则谈判法的策略十分安全,也就是说一旦被对方看穿,非但不会使谈判陷入困境反而更有利于谈判的进展,因为原则谈判法不依靠谈判者的计谋和随机应变,而是依靠公正、客观和相互理解。

## 三、国际商务谈判的心理理论

☞ **案例分析 2—4** （聪明的比利时地毯商）

在阿拉伯国家,虔诚的伊斯兰教徒每天都要进行祈祷,无论居家、旅行,风雨无阻。伊斯兰教徒祈祷的一大特点是祈祷者一定要面向圣城麦加。然而,困扰伊斯兰教徒的问题在于,当他们离家在外或在旅途中的时候,常常会辨别不清方向,为祈祷带来障碍。一个比利时地毯商发现了这个商机,他将小块的地毯进行了改造,制作出专门用于伊斯兰教徒祈祷的地毯,他聪明地将扁平的指南针嵌入祈祷地毯,指南针指的不是正南正北,而是麦加。这样,伊斯兰教徒不管走到哪里,只要把地毯往地上一铺,麦加方向顷刻之间便可准确地找到,为伊斯兰教徒提供了极大的便利。新产品一推出,在伊斯兰教徒居住的地方立即成了抢手货,这个比利时商人也因此赚了大钱。他成功的根本原因就在于他提供了满足他人需要的产品。

谈判的心理原则指的是谈判人员在谈判中应充分利用对手的心理活动因素,充分利用相关情势从而尽可能地成交。谈判人员的心理直接影响其谈判决策行为。对于谈判者来讲,掌握一定的心理分析技巧无疑有助于其谈判的成功。

由于心理活动对谈判的重大影响,因此对谈判心理的研究越来越深入,对谈判的心理分析逐步成为心理学的一个分支。

1. 人们处于不同需求阶段有着不同的心理活动

在不同的需求阶段,人们满意的需求层次也是不一样的。因此,做生意要根据对方的需求水平去满足对方,充分利用相关情势,使得交易成为可能。

美国心理学家亚布拉罕·马斯洛在 1943 年发表的《人类动机》一文中提出的"需求层

次论"现已发展为行为科学理论的一个分支。他将人类多种多样的需求归纳为五大类，并将它们分为五个层次。

（1）生理需要

这是人类最原始、最强烈的基本需要，包括对水、食物、睡眠、温暖、运动和性等基本生存要素的需要，是人类为维持和发展生命所必需的。这些需要如果不能得到满足，人类的生存就成了问题。因此，从这个意义上说，生理需要是推动人们行动最强大的动力。如果一个人最基础的需要都不能得到满足，这个人就会被生理需要所支配，其他需要都要退居次要的地位。

对于一个处于饥饿状态下的人来讲，食物需求将占据主导地位，除了食物，别的兴趣都退居其后：写诗的愿望、买汽车的愿望、对权力的欲望、买新衣服的需要，则统统被忘记或忽视。这时这个人想到的、梦见的只是食物，充饥成为这个人的首要目标。因此，人们在生存需要没有得到满足之前，不会去追求其他的社会需要。

（2）安全需要

当一个人的生理需要得到满足后，接着就要考虑安全和稳定的问题，安全需要就会被提到一个较为重要的地位上来，诸如人身安全，工作的稳定，要求在将来年老或生病时有所保障，要求避免职业病的侵袭，等等。为此，人们努力寻求舒适和安全的环境。

（3）社交需要（归属和爱的需要）

社交需要主要表现为对情感需求的渴望，包含两方面的内容：

一为爱的需要。即人都希望伙伴之间、同事之间关系融洽或保持友谊和忠诚，希望与他人有亲密的感情交往，希望得到爱情，组建家庭，交朋友等。人人都希望爱别人，也渴望得到别人的爱。

二为归属的需要。即人都有一种要求归属于一个集团或群体的感情，希望成为其中的一员。人们不仅希望得到群体成员的认可，也希望被社会所接受，并得到相互关心和照顾。

（4）尊重需要

人们对尊重的需要可分为两类：一方面为自尊，包括信心、能力、本领、成就等愿望。另一方面为来自他人尊重的需要，诸如，威望、接受、关心、地位、名誉和赏识等。

当人们的尊重需要得到满足时，能使其对自己充满信心，对社会满腔热情，体会到自己生活在世界上的用处和价值，积极地参与社会生活；当尊重需要受到挫折时，就会使人产生自卑感、软弱感、无能感，甚至会使人失去生活的信心。

☞ **案例分析 2—5** （希尔顿酒店的微笑）

美国希尔顿酒店是一家闻名全球的世界连锁企业，并且以微笑服务著称于世。董事长康纳·希尔顿确信微笑有助于酒店的发展。他时刻要求下属："无论酒店本身境遇如何,希尔顿酒店的服务员脸上都要带着微笑。"他对下属常说的一句话是:"你今天对顾客微笑了吗?"事实证明,希尔顿酒店服务员脸上的微笑使顾客感觉到自己受到了欢迎,受到了尊重,犹如明媚的阳光,使人忘却了烦恼与忧虑。人们感觉,在希尔顿酒店,不仅可以满足衣食住宿需要,而且可以满足人们对安全与尊重的需要。20世纪30年代,在空前的经济大萧条时期,全美国的酒店倒闭了80%,而希尔顿酒店则凭着服务人员脸上的微笑,渡过了萧条时期,跨入了经营的黄金时代。

（5）自我实现的需要

当人的生理、安全、社交、尊重需要得到满足之后,就是自我实现的需要了。这是需求的最高层次。自我实现的需要是指实现个人的理想、抱负,希望从事与自己的能力相适应的工作,实现自身的价值。也就是说,人必须干自己称职称心的工作。

因此,在谈判前,应该尽可能了解和掌握谈判对手的性格、特点、爱好、兴趣、专长,了解他们的职业、经历以及处理问题的风格、方式等。

一个谈判人员的各种需求在谈判中都会得到体现。例如,生理需求体现在为了确保谈判人员的精力和情绪处于最佳状态,需要饮食营养可口,住得舒服,保障睡眠,以便集中精力应对谈判;安全需要则体现在需要在谈判中保证谈判人员的人身安全、信息安全等;社交需要体现在,谈判人员希望在自己的团队内部成员之间团结合作,与谈判对方建立融洽良好的关系,能够在友好合作的气氛中进行协商;尊重需要不仅体现在来自谈判代表团内部成员的尊重,还体现在希望得到谈判对手的尊重;自我实现的需要表现为人们希望谈判取得圆满成功。谈判人员在谈判中所取得的利益越大,其自我实现的需要的满足程度越高。

2. 谈判中应注意的一些心理因素

谈判中如果我们能发现(对方)一些心理因素,有意识地去观察、利用这些因素并调整谈判策略,就会对谈判产生积极的效果。

首先,说货物好话的人一般不是买主,吹毛求疵的很可能是潜在的买主。

其次,当顾客就商品的性能、质量和规格等提出很多问题时,一定存在着商机。

第三,当潜在的顾客开始就产品的售前售后服务进行提问时,他很有可能要买这个商品,你与他交易的时机就要到了。

第四,交易中卖方的主要任务是激发买方的购买欲望,买方要认清产品的基本功能并理性处理,才能用最少的投入获得最大的满足。

第五,在我们的日常生活中,买方买的很多产品都毫无用处,因此对卖方的推销应理性对待。

第六,交易一旦达成,我们不用再去理会对方涨价或降价的要求,这纯粹是对方的侥幸心理,根本不会影响交易。

### 四、谈判力及其相关因素

谈判力是谈判人员能够控制谈判的总体能力。它是控制谈判进程、影响对方的一种力量。不管是什么谈判，外交谈判、贸易谈判、技术或是服务谈判，谈判力的差异在很大程度上决定了谈判的结果。在任何情况下，谈判人员都希望自己的谈判力能强于对方。那么影响谈判力的因素都有哪些？

一般来说，谈判力由八个方面决定，这八个方面的能力的英文可缩写为 NO TRICKS，其中每个字母代表一个词。这八个词分别是需求、替代、时间、关系、投入、信誉、知识和技巧。

1. 需求

在影响谈判力的诸多因素中，需求起决定性的作用。就买卖双方而言，谁对谈判需求更强烈，谁的谈判力就会越弱。如果买方急需某个产品，卖方的谈判力就会更强。相反，如果卖方急于出售某个产品，那买方的谈判力就会更强。

注：为了增加自己的谈判力，人们往往采用以下方法刺激对方的需求。

①诱导谈判对手或对手的支持者。如给予价格折扣，或买一送一。

②向对方展示你的方案/产品的诱人之处。你的卖点或优势是什么？

③获取第三方的好评或支持。例如，请公众人物或名人为你的产品做广告。

④限定所提供好处的时间。给你的优惠定个最终的时限，例如，"这个报价的有效期为5天""这个价格的有效期截至本月底"。

2. 替代

如果原来的谈判（方案）失败了，拥有替代方案的一方有着更强的谈判力。如果卖方有更多的市场，或是其产品/服务独特，而买方没有选择，那卖方在谈判中就会更加自如。

3. 时间

你的时间越是有限，你在谈判中的地位就会越弱。如果卖方受临界时间所限，买方的谈判力就会增强。

4. 关系

你与老客户的关系越牢固，你在与潜在客户的谈判中的谈判力就会越强。如果你的老客户不想与你发展业务关系，你的谈判力就会削弱。这种关系反映了你的能力和声誉，会影响你在一个行业的口碑。

5. 投入

在谈判中你投入的时间、精力和财力越多，一方面意味着你准备得越充分，从而提高了谈判力；另一方面，因为成本对你至关重要，你在谈判中可能会被牵鼻子，从而削弱你的议价能力,降低你的谈判力。

6. 信誉

拥有让顾客感兴趣的可靠的产品会提高你的谈判力。当卖方知道买方已用过他的产品,而且他的产品在价格、质量和服务方面都有优势,毫无疑问,卖方就会享有很高的声誉。当然,仅靠这一点还不足以最终达成交易。

7. 知识

知识就是力量。如果卖方完全知晓买方的问题与需求,并相信他的产品能满足买方的需求,那他的谈判力就会增强。如买方对产品了如指掌,买方就会拥有更强的谈判力。

8. 技巧

熟练的谈判策略和技巧很容易直接提高谈判力。当然谈判技巧不是天生就有的,需要通过广泛的学习和实践来获取,包括广博的知识、雄辩的口才、敏锐的思维能力。

在国际商务谈判中,我们应熟练运用这些方面的能力。

☞ **案例分析 2—6** 　（中国入世的身份）

在中美有关中国加入世贸组织的谈判中,双方就中国以什么身份加入世贸组织进行了激烈的辩论。如果作为发达国家加入,中国将享受不到给予发展中国家的一些优惠,包括普惠制、市场渐入、保护幼小工业等。这是涉及国家利益的原则性问题。因此,中国坚持以发展中国家的身份入世。然而,为了尽快打开中国的市场以便获得更多的进入市场及获利机会,美国代表坚持中国应以发达国家身份加入世贸。他们的理由是中国的出口增长迅速,外汇储备已居世界前列;中国发射和回收航天卫星的技术已经达到了只有少数发达国家能够达到的水平,其他发展中国家都不可能做到。一个美国代表甚至将中国贫困地区的情况与非洲和印度进行了对比。他说在他访问华西地区时,他随机敲了敲门,问主人吃过早饭没有,得到的答案是肯定的。然后又问是否准备了午饭,得知他们正在准备。主人还告诉他晚饭也没有问题。但是在非洲甚至印度的贫困地区,情况就完全不一样。当问到是否吃过早饭时,答案是否定的,当问到午饭和晚饭时,他们反问他是不是要提供救济粮。这个代表说,从这些鲜明的对比中,他感觉到中国贫困地区的情形并没有报道的那样糟糕。

中美代表对中国入世的身份的标准有着他们自己的理解,难以达成一致。这场谈判的焦点是哪种身份更适合于中国:发达国家还是发展中国家。事实上,联合国、世界银行以及其他的一些国际组织都有一个流行的标准,即一个国家的人均国内生产总值(简称人均 GDP)。根据联合国和世界银行的统计,人均 GDP 在 785 美元以下的国家(1996 年)属最贫穷的国家。而当中美进行这场谈判时中国的人均 GDP 仅为 750 美元。实际上,根据这个标准,直到 2000 年中国仍属于最贫穷的国家。根据人均 GDP 的标准,美国代表的观点显然是站不住脚的。

## ☞ 思考题与讨论题

1. 什么是双赢理论？

2. 如果你是谈判的买方，在谈判中你最关心的内容是什么？反之，如果你是谈判的卖方，你会注重哪些方面的东西？

3. 在与他人的谈判和解决问题的过程中，你是否曾经从另一方的角度考虑对方的利益？如果有过这样的经历，你感觉效果如何？

4. 人的五个不同的需求层次是什么？

5. 影响谈判力的因素有哪些？

6. 你认为如何做才能激发潜在消费者的购买欲望？

(1) 你正在拟订长安奥拓的促销计划

(2) 你经营一家小书店，但销售不景气

7. 假如你今天去找老板要求加工资。如果你的目的只是加工资，但是在谈判的过程中，老板提出给你再增加一点点工作量，就可以增加工资，那么你应不应该接受？为什么？

第二篇

实务篇

# Chapter 3

# Preparation of International Business Negotiation

☞ **Case study 3 – 1** （**Nixon's visit to China**）

In February 1972, US former President Nixon visited China, and there would be a historic negotiation between the United States and China. In order to create a friendly and harmonious atmosphere, the Chinese side, under the leadership of Premier Zhou Enlai, made an elaborate and careful arrangement for the whole process of the negotiation, even the choice of the music played at the banquet.

At the welcoming state banquet, when the military band skillfully played the music *The Beautiful America* deliberately chosen by Premier Zhou, President Nixon was greatly amazed, for it never occurred to him that he could hear the music that he was so familiar with in China! Furthermore, it was his favorite and assigned music played on his inauguration. When making a toast, he especially gave his thanks to the band and was affected by the warm and harmonious atmosphere at the banquet. A thoughtful arrangement won a harmonious atmosphere for the negotiation.

☞ **Case study 3 – 2** （**Tanaka's visit to Beijing**）

In September 1972, Japanese former Prime Minister Kakuei Tanaka came to Beijing for resuming the normalization of Sino-Japanese relations. He stayed at the guesthouse nervous about the coming summit talk between the two countries. The temperature in the guesthouse being comfortable, Kakuei Tanaka talked cheerfully with his accompanying personnel in a good mood. His secretary looked at the temperature of the room, it was exactly 17.8 Centigrade, the temperature that Kakuei Tanaka was used to. It was the temperature that made him feel at ease, and paved the way for the negotiations.

If you know yourself as well as your enemy, you will never be defeated. Whether an international business negotiation succeeds or not is not only determined by the strategies and skills used in formal negotiations, but also closely related to the careful preparations made before negotiations. Generally speaking, the more preparatory work is done, the more efficient the negotiation will be. The preparation for an international business negotiation consists of investigating background, collecting information, forming the negotiation team, developing negotiation plans, physical preparations and simulated negotiation.

## Ⅰ. Investigating Background

International business negotiation is conducted under certain environments of political, economic, cultural, social and law system which will directly or indirectly affect the negotiation. Thus, knowing and analyzing the background thoroughly will be helpful for negotiators to make right negotiation plan, so it is worthwhile and absolutely necessary to investigate objective environments. Background investigation usually includes political and economic status, laws, policies, religious beliefs, cultural customs, international conventions, infrastructures, natural resources, climate and geography.

### 1. Political status

(1) Political background and degree of stability of a country

Make clear whether the seller (buyer) has some relevance with his government. A turmoil political situation easily makes a negotiation interrupted or makes a signed agreement suspended. Political stability means whether there is any domestic turmoil or chaos caused by war.

(2) Relations between the two countries

If the relation between two countries is friendly or in a normal state, then the success of a negotiation completely relies on the two enterprises. If there is no foreign diplomatic relations between the two countries or they are hostile rivals, the negotiation might be interrupted by the government. For example, the trade might be restricted or banned, which will make the negotiation and the execution of a contract more difficult.

(3) The political and economic system of your counterpart's country

Negotiators must know something about the political and economic system of your counterpart's country, because under planned economy, contacts between enterprises are restricted by their government. Yet under the system of market economy, enterprises have much bigger autonomous rights, they can decide the contents of a deal themselves. So people can make correct analysis and judgment by knowing the economic system of the other country.

## 2. Economic status

Results of international business negotiations lead to the transnational flow of the capital. Different economic status will affect the efficiency of the capital flow.

(1) Foreign exchange reserve

Price is the core of international business negotiation, which manifests payment of certain currency. If one country has a poor foreign exchange reserve, there might be shortage of foreign exchange and breach of contract. In the international financial crisis in 2008, foreign exchange reserve of the Republic of Korea was in an emergency, which resulted in breach of many contracts, thus, many Chinese enterprises exporting to the Republic of Korea withdrew from negotiations with the Republic of Korea.

(2) Fluctuation of foreign exchange

Different countries use different currencies. There exists a rate of exchange between different currencies, whereas fluctuation of foreign exchange will affect the interests of enterprises. Since different countries adopt different exchange rate system, some countries adopting fixed system of foreign exchange, and some adopting floating system, fluctuation of foreign exchange will directly affect the economic benefits of enterprises.

(3) Payment credit

Different countries have different procedures when they make payment in foreign exchange. For example, when choosing letter of credits to settle account of international trade, some enterprises are faced with the risk of receiving no payment for goods because some banks with poor credit might delay the time of making payment when they open L/C. Thus, emphasis should be paid to the investigation of the paying ability of the bank in international business.

## 3. Laws, policies, religious beliefs and cultural customs

Before negotiations, we need to know whether the transacted items will be regulated or restricted by the laws and regulations of your own country or your partner's country, or by international laws; whether there is any trade control or restrictions or any measures to encourage trade; whether the cultures, customs, religious beliefs will affect the trade transactions or not. Besides, people should pay attention to the customs of greeting, clothing, daily topics and sending a gift.

**4. International conventions, infrastructures, natural resources, climates and geography**

People should know well about the relevant international conventions such as INCOTERMS, Warsaw-Oxford Rules and Uniform Rules of Documentary Letter of Credit, and know something about the understanding and the usual way of doing the business of the said country. Negotiators also should know whether there is modern equipment for loading and unloading in the port so as to meet the requirements of the future potential trade; whether the climate will affect the trade; what season is suitable for transportation of goods, etc.

☞ **Case study 3 – 3** **(A lesson a Suzhou company learned)**

A company in Suzhou heard that South Africa was a potential market, and hoped to find an access of its products to this market. In order to know more about their partner, the company decided to send a group to South Africa to have a field investigation.

Upon arrival, the partner immediately arranged a meeting with the general manager of the African company in a big, grand hotel. The delegation encountered a smiling receptionist at the elevator, who brought them to an updated, luxuriously decorated room. On a leather chair was the general manager, fat and with a cigar between his fingers, looking confident. He was full of passion when talking about the present situation, operating strategies and the future plan of the company. The delegation was deeply impressed and strongly believed that this company was a financially sound and reliable partner.

After the delegation returned to China, the Chinese side immediately delivered the goods amounting to more than USD1,000,000; however, there was no further news for the goods. The director had to send others to Africa for investigation. Until now they realized that they had fallen into a deliberately-plotted trap, the fat "general manager" turning out to be a local actor and the receptionist who greeted them at the elevator being the real general manager. And the well-decorated reception room was nothing but a temporarily rented room. When they knew the truth and located the company, they found that it had declared bankruptcy.

In this case, the main reason for the loss is that the company judged their partner from its superficial appearance, without making any investigation into its background. Such kind of loss could have been avoided if the delegation had managed to know the company from some reliable sources.

☞ **Case study 3 – 4**   （**Loss resulting from lack of knowledge of local law**）

A Chinese company which undertakes contracted projects had a project in Gabon. When the principal building of the project was completed, the company dismissed a large number of temporary workers employed in the local places. But this gave rise to strike by the dismissed workers which lasted for 40 days. The Chinese side had to have a hard negotiation with the local workers. The representatives of the dismissed workers proposed the Chinese side should compensate the dismissed workers a large sum of money according to the local law. At this moment, the Chinese members were aware that they knew about nothing about Gabon's law. As per Gabon's labor law, if a temporary worker works for over a week without being dismissed he will automatically become a permanent worker. And as a permanent worker, he has the right to obtain a wage which can support two wives and three children. Besides, he should get transportation fee and unemployment compensation fee. If an unskilled worker works for over a month, he will automatically become a skilled worker. If a skilled worker works successively for three months, he will be promoted to a technician, and the wage will be naturally raised. But the Chinese administrative staff dealt with the situation in Gabon as per the understanding in China for temporary workers, permanent workers, unskilled workers, skilled workers and technicians, which led to such a big trouble.

We can easily imagine the result of the negotiation. The Chinese company had to make a payment of a large sum of unemployment compensation for the dismissed workers. The amount is more or less the same with the wages which had been already paid to the workers. Since this expense falls within accidental payment which was not included in the project budget, the total loss would be on the account of the Chinese company.

## Ⅱ. Collecting Information

What has to be done during the preparatory period for international business negotiations is to collect, sort out and analyze the information and data in time about the negotiation counterparts, getting to know the purpose of their project and market prices as much as possible. Accurate and detailed information of the counterparts may ensure an advantage in the negotiation, which will be of great help to achieve success of a negotiation.

Information about the negotiation counterparts consists of the qualification and credit status of the partner company, their negotiators' profiles, domestic and international market trends, laws and regulations as well as cultural backgrounds in related countries and areas.

### 1. Market and quotations

Negotiators should make comprehensive comparisons concerning the technological specifications, use, purchasing cost, quantity available, freight charges, domestic market prices, patents, necessary accessories and after-services and the likes of negotiating item.

(1) Distribution, requirements and sales of the commodity

Collect information concerning the commodity, including distribution, location, radiation scope and potentials of the commodity in the market. You should also know the relevant requirements concerning the commodity in your counterpart's country, including the number of consumers and the composition, their habit, level, trend, preferences and any special service requirements of the consumption. You should pay attention to the sales of the commodity, like the channels, areas, prices, quantities, selling seasons and strategies.

(2) Market competition and price fluctuation of the commodity

Market competition mainly includes number of your competitors, their economic strength, marketing capability and their types, quantity, quality, reputation, performance and after-sale services of their commodities. Price fluctuation means the prevailing price in the market and the trend of the price.

### 2. Industry

(1) The industry scale and life cycle of the commodity

Try to get the information of the whole industry and analyze its developing trend, so that you will know the potential scale. Collect the information of life cycle of the commodity and the industry in different countries.

(2) Cost of the industry and factors deciding the success of the industry

Try to know whether there is any possibility to lower the cost or to increase the profit. Analyze the prospect of the negotiating products through collecting the experiences of the industry and analyzing the factors contributing to their success.

### 3. Product

Firstly, collect and master the information about the technology, packing and brand concerning the product. Secondly, know well about the performance, quality, advantages and disadvantages of your commodity. Thirdly, be familiar with the prospect, the life cycle of the commodity, etc.

### 4. Your counterpart

(1) Qualification and credit

The qualification and credit consist of the history and status quo, economic and political power, corporate reputation (its liabilities), capital quantity, operating capability, bank credit and such of the partner company.

The history and status quo of the partner company refers to the establishing time, registered office address, the number of the employees, main business scope, etc. Corporate reputation refers to its status of assets and liabilities, brand popularity and word-of-mouth in the market. Bank credit includes the names and numbers of contacting banks, credit it enjoys and whether it has bad accounts in banks, etc.

(2) Capability

Capital quantity refers to total assets, fixed assets, current assets, cash flow, etc. Operating capability refers to the status of operating profit and loss, contribution ratios of major products, the ability to develop new products, the business scope, the main marketing area of their products, their terms of payment, etc.

(3) Negotiating representatives

Information about negotiating representatives from the other side mainly include the number of the negotiating representatives, the composition of the negotiating team, limits of their authority, and their identity and status. The number and composition of the representatives refer to how many representatives have been chosen to participate in the negotiation and how the team is formed or what people it is composed of. Limits of the representatives' authority refer to whether the negotiation participants are the direct associates or their agents. Identity of representatives refers to their nationalities, birth places, diplomas, qualifications, family backgrounds, characters, hobbies, weakness, negotiation styles, experiences, etc.

☞ **Case study 3 - 5    (One success of Mr. Wang Guangying)**

In April 1983, Wang Guangying, the Director of China Everbright Industrial Co. LTD. Hong Kong, obtained a piece of important information. A copper mine in Chile went bankrupt. Before the bankruptcy, the owner of the mine had ordered varied types of large-tonnage trucks totaling 1,500, which were made in the US and Germany. Furthermore, all of them were brand new trucks. In order to pay the debt, the owner decided to sell these trucks by auction.

These new trucks were worth a lot, which had a great appeal to many entrepreneurs worldwide. Mr. Wang Guangying immediately sent the purchasing staff abroad for negotiation. After several rounds of bargaining, they concluded the business at 30% of the original price for those trucks, which saved $25 million.

The most important reasons for the success of the negotiation lie in the following factors: prompt and accurate information; immediate and correct decision and good timing for negotiation.

### Ⅲ. Forming the Negotiation Team

If you want to succeed in international business negotiations and achieve the expected economic goals, forming the negotiation team is of vital importance since all the jobs concerning the negotiation are to be fulfilled by negotiators. The organizational preparations for international business negotiations consist of deciding the size of the negotiation team, staffing the negotiation team and soliciting the coordination and support from the outside members.

#### 1. Size of the negotiation team

The size of the negotiation team refers to the number of staff taking part in the negotiation and should be decided by the principles of necessity and saving money. The following factors should be taken into consideration when we decide the size of a negotiation team.

（1）The number of the negotiation team members of your counterpart

A guideline is that both parties should have approximately the same number of negotiators in order to reflect equality. If possible, try to reduce the number of negotiators since there is no doubt that the more negotiators there are, the more cost it will be needed for the negotiation, which is especially the case for guest negotiators.

（2）The complexity of the negotiation

The number of negotiation staff should be proportional to the complexity of the negotiation, for the more complicated the negotiating project is, the more knowledge and experience it'll be involved and the more team members will be needed. The import and export trades usually don't need technical professionals, but the trades involving hi-tech products and patents require the participation of experts in that field; trades involving laws in one's own country or in the counterpart's country, or that relating to international or regional trade agreements have to include legal experts in the negotiation.

## 2. Staffing of the negotiation team

The composition of the negotiation team requires the consideration about the professional backgrounds, expertise and the status of the team members, and the role they play in the negotiation. When building a negotiation team, make sure of the specialized knowledge the negotiation requires. Generally, the specialized knowledge includes knowledge concerning technology, trade, law and language.

The structure of the team must be taken into consideration for the negotiation group that consists of two or more members. A relatively "standard" negotiation team should contain the following members.

（1）Leading personnel

Leading personnel should be an authoritative person with relatively high rank and more power, possess all-sided knowledge, and have an authoritative position and the ability to make a resolute decision. This person should be the core of the team and play a major role during the negotiation, in charge of controlling the process, adjusting the negotiation strategies and plans in emergencies and making the final decisions.

（2）Business/Commercial personnel

Business/Commercial personnel are usually the marketing personnel. They are usually quite familiar with the international trade practice, highly experienced in domestic and international marketing and negotiation, and well-informed in the situation of domestic and international markets of the project under the negotiation.

（3）Interpreters

Interpreters are usually good at foreign language and business，whose task is to do written or oral translation. Interpreters in international business negotiations are required to express precisely and make good use of language skills. Their translation skills will directly affect the effectiveness of communication and negotiation.

（4）Professional and technical personnel

Engineers or technical experts who are quite familiar with technological and product standards and the status quo of the technical know-how are responsible for negotiating production technology，product performance，quality standards，product acceptance，technological services as well as providing consultation and advice for making the decision concerning price bargain of the project.

（5）Financial personnel

Financial personnel who are familiar with accounting and finance and good at accounting are accountable for estimation of the prices，terms of payment，ways of payment，settlement currency and exchange rate for the project under negotiation.

（6）Legal personnel

The specially invited lawyers or enterprise law consultants who know trade laws，commercial practice agreements and law enforcement well are mainly responsible for the validity，completeness and preciseness of the contract terms. They also take part in the negotiation related to laws.

（7）Record-keeping personnel

Record-keeping personnel should usually know well about using computer，language，and so on.

In actual negotiation cases，the above-mentioned personnel can be increased or decreased in number according to the situation.

### 3. Qualities and abilities negotiators should possess

（1）A healthy body and a strong ability of using the relevant language and words

Only when negotiators have a healthy body and abundant energy can they meet the requirements of overloaded job for negotiations. An excellent negotiator can intensify the artistic effect through the appeal of language. Language used in negotiations should be not only accurate and strict but also vivid and attractive because how to apply a language affects the atmosphere of a negotiation and the effect of communication. A humorous person can attract more attention and easily resolve contradictions and make a negotiation successful.

(2) A good moral character

In the process of international business negotiation, negotiators should maintain benefits and images of their country, their enterprise and themselves. They should by no means reveal the business secrets of their country and their enterprise just for their own interest.

(3) A strong sense of responsibility and subjective initiative

Negotiators should adhere to their duty and the spirit of forging ahead from the beginning to the end, full of patience and confidence. In the practice of negotiation, negotiators should possess the abilities of flexibility, swift creative thinking, accurate analyzing and reasoning, strong operating and decision-making so that they can control the negotiation situation.

(4) A good personal cultivation and necessary knowledge concerning foreign affairs

Negotiators should lay emphasis on etiquette and interests of the whole. They should have an elegant behavior, a proper style of conversation, and be neither humble nor pushy. Besides, they should be good at listening and understand relevant policies, regulations and laws beforehand so as to avoid invalid or illegal negotiating actions.

### IV. Developing Negotiation Plans

Plan-making of international business negotiation refers to the managing intention for the import or export of a certain commodity, and the steps, strategies and measures for the goal. The purpose of making plans is to organize and control the negotiation activities effectively. The plans serve as the guidelines for the negotiation team, and play a very important role in the whole negotiation.

#### 1. Basic requirements for making negotiation plans

(1) To be concise and to the point

The first requirement for making negotiation plans is to be concise and to the point, which means negotiators can easily remember the contents and the principles so that they can follow the guidelines and control the situation of negotiation.

(2) To be specific and definite

Negotiation plans must be specific and definite in order to be operated easily. For example, the general objective or goal can be divided into several sub-goals. The plan should be reasonable and objective. Negotiation plans are usually made in words. They may be more than 10 pages long or as short as one page according to the importance of negotiations.

(3) To be flexible and practical

Negotiation plans are subjective assumptions and ideals of one side, so it must be flexible and practical in terms of the actual circumstances so as not to affect negotiations. It is absolutely necessary to make several negotiation plans so that negotiators can make a comparison and choose the best plan.

## 2. Contents of negotiation plans

(1) To fix negotiation strategics

Negotiation strategies refer to the tactics and techniques used in the actual process of a negotiation to meet the negotiation targets. The following are the factors that need to be considered in designing business negotiation strategies:

a. Will the negotiation take place at the host court, the guest court or a third place?

b. What are the advantages or strengths each party has?

c. Which party will be affected more greatly by the outcome of the negotiation?

d. What are the strengths (rank and composition) of the counterpart team and the characteristic of their chief negotiator?

e. Which party will be affected more greatly by the length of time the negotiation takes?

f. Is it necessary to build up long-term cooperative relationship?

In terms of negotiation process, negotiation strategies can be divided into opening strategies, offering strategies, bargaining strategies and concluding strategies. From the skills of negotiation, it falls into the categories of concession-making strategies, offensive strategies, defensive strategies and strategies of breaking a deadlock.

(2) To determine negotiation agenda

Negotiation agenda refers to the arrangement of the time and site for the negotiation, and issues discussed. The agenda is usually prepared by the host party or discussed by both parties in advance.

a. Schedule of the negotiation. Negotiation agenda should list when the negotiation is conducted, how long it lasts and what issues are to be discussed in each session.

b. Negotiation site. Negotiation sites are usually chosen by the host party and then informed to the visiting team. Such places as a negotiation hall, meeting room, manager's office of the host company are usually served as negotiation sites. A meeting room or an office of a third party can also be rented for use; the negotiation can also be arranged in a reception room or a bar in a hotel or a restaurant. Negotiation sites can be a fixed place or changed in order to adjust negotiation atmosphere.

c. Negotiation issues. Negotiation issues refer to the various problems that each side has proposed and planned to confer in the negotiation. Both sides can have communications beforehand to identify negotiation issues; or each side proposes different issues for discussion together. When issues are identified, they should be listed in terms of priority and logical order.

(3) Targets of a negotiation plan

Negotiation targets refer to the commercial goals that are expected to achieve through negotiation. Targets of an international business negotiation can be generally divided into three categories:

a. The highest target, or the maximum expectation or target. This is the best target that one party will seek to achieve and maximize its gains in the negotiation, and it is also the top limit that the other party can give up. This goal is very difficult to achieve. So it will be greatly appreciated if the negotiation personnel can achieve agreements at this critical point. The top target can be given up when it is quite impossible to achieve it.

b. Acceptable target, or expected target. This is an intermediate goal for one party and an acceptable one to the other as well. This goal has shown the sincerity of both parties.

c. The lowest target, or limited target, basic target or must-be-realized target. The lowest target is the least requirement of the negotiation. In other words, if the lowest goal can't be realized, the negotiation would rather be abandoned. The bottom line of the negotiation target must be strictly kept confidential. Generally, only the key personnel should be informed of it and other personnel do not need to know.

## Ⅴ. Physical Preparations

Physical preparations for international business negotiations mainly consist of the following five aspects: the arrangement of negotiation agenda, the choice of negotiation place, the decoration of the negotiation site, the arrangement for lodging and board, visiting and sightseeing. Carefully planned physical preparations can always have a direct or indirect impact on the whole negotiation process.

## 1. The arrangement of negotiation agenda

Negotiation agenda refers to the arrangement for the timing of the negotiation, and issues discussed and the order of issues.

(1) Arrangement for the timing

That is what time negotiation will begin and how long it will last and make sure that all negotiators can attend. Usually two important aspects should be considered: adequate preparations and the physical and mental state of negotiators.

(2) Negotiation issues and its orders

Negotiators make a list of all the issues first, and then discuss them one by one. The usual order is easy issues first and then the difficult ones. Surely people can act in the opposite way or a combined way according to specific situations.

## 2. The choice of negotiation places

The choice of negotiation place includes the choice of the country or region and the specific negotiation site.

(1) Negotiation location

Choosing different negotiation places will make a difference in the negotiation to some extent. However, wherever the negotiation takes place, there will be both pros and cons for both parties. (It has been explained in Chapter 1.)

(2) Negotiation site

Generally speaking, if conditions permit, a company will choose its own territory as the negotiation place. On the one hand, the host company can extend their hospitality and sincerity to the guests and show off its overall power or strengths as well; on the other hand, used as part of negotiation strategy, a well-decorated meeting room will exercise an active psychological impact on the other party. On the contrary, if a company often does not allow its clients to pay a visit to its headquarters, its overall strength is always doubtable.

## 3. Decoration of the negotiation site

(1) Setting of rectangular tables

Rectangular tables are usually used in business negotiations with both parties sitting on each side, the host party sitting behind the door or on the left of the door and all the guest members sitting on the right.

(2) Setting of round tables

The major negotiators sit face to face with the host party sitting behind the door or on the left of the door. All the other staff sit on the right or the left of the major negotiator of each party according to the ranks or they can sit in a circle.

Some international business negotiators often adopt a casual way of seating, even without a negotiating table, with only a coffee table in the middle, or both parties sitting in the same couch.

(3) Other facilities and equipment

Chairs should match the negotiation table in style and color, comfortable to sit in because too soft and sunken chairs will make people sleepy and distracted.

Demonstration boards can be used to demonstrate figures and explain cases directly.

Projectors can be used to demonstrate figures, pictures or other information.

Other devices: ashtrays, pads, ball pens, paper folders, tea, coffee, boiled water, iced water and so on.

### 4. Arrangement for lodging and board

Arrangement should be made for the accommodation of the guests beforehand. The host party should be considerate and careful, making the lodging convenient and comfortable for the visitors.

(1) Lodging

If the guests pay all the bills by themselves, it would be better if the host could communicate with them to make sure of the standard and the class of the hotel they want to stay in. If the host party pays the hotel bills, the host should have a careful consideration of the choice of the hotels (especially the luxurious hotels), which should be taken as a kind of investment, and thus needs to estimate its returns in future. The principle to arrange the lodging is to de-emphasize luxury, but to strive for convenient transportation and closeness to the negotiation site as much as possible; don't be too far away from shopping centers for the convenience for shopping.

(2) Board

Please leave some space to the guests. It is unnecessary to treat the guests for every meal or order expensive dishes for every meal.

### 5. Visiting and sightseeing

If time permits, especially when it is the first time the guests come to the host territory, the host party usually can arrange some visiting and sightseeing. The following places can be taken into consideration to visit:

a. Factories, equipment and places of origin related to the negotiation subject;

b. Famous and symbolic local scenic spots;

c. Worldly well-known restaurants and shopping centers with local characteristics;

d. Other places of interest or entertainment that guests get interested in.

Arranging the guests to have a visit will deepen the guests' knowledge of the host culture, remove the discomfort of the travel. It also provides an opportunity for the two parties to get in touch with each other so as to build up a harmonious relationship.

## Ⅵ. Simulated Negotiation

As for important international business negotiations, apart from the careful plans and arrangements made beforehand, we can carry out a simulated negotiation before formal negotiation begins in order to avoid various possible carelessness and mistakes, and see whether there still exist any problems and try to find as many countermeasures under emergencies as possible.

### 1. Necessity of simulated negotiations

Firstly, simulated negotiations can help negotiators to find out problems and faults, to test whether the negotiation plan is feasible or not. Since negotiation plans are mainly made according to the subjective experience, it is very hard to avoid any negligence, whereas simulated negotiations can help negotiators to think from the angle of the other side so as to improve the negotiation plans.

Secondly, simulated negotiations can help negotiators to obtain experience to meet the contingency so that they might have a better performance in the forthcoming negotiation.

Thirdly, simulated negotiations can offer exercise for cooperation and help negotiators to cooperate each other, train and improve the negotiators' ability for actual negotiation.

### 2. Assumptions

(1) Assumptions of objective existence

Assume that there appear any unfavorable factors in external environment, for example, if the negotiation time or place have changed, what would you do and how would you deal with it?

(2) Assumptions of the other side

Assumptions of the other side mainly include cooperative willingness and degree of accepting risks, etc. For example, what if the other side puts forward additional requirements in quality, price, payment terms or mode of transportation? The main purpose of the assumptions of the other side is to figure out the real intention of the counterpart.

(3) Assumptions of one's own side

Assumptions of one's own side mainly refer to self-testing and evaluation of one's own negotiation ability, psychological quality and negotiation plans. It also includes the countermeasures that might be taken in order to deal with new situations from the other side.

### 3. Forms of simulated negotiations

(1) Meeting simulated negotiation

This is also called one-to-many simulated negotiation. Negotiators can make a simulated negotiation by arranging the chief negotiator to play the role of the opposing negotiators and enabling them to ask questions against him. Or simply hold a meeting and have a full discussion in order to find out what problems still exist and how to solve them.

(2) Group simulated negotiation

This kind of simulated negotiation is fit for business negotiations that involve many staff. The staff can be divided into two groups, one is the host party and the other group acts as the counterpart. Group simulated negotiation is of great help to have a full check about the negotiation plans and to make the negotiation staff clearer about every step of the negotiation.

### 4. Summarization

The aim of summing up simulated negotiations is to find out as many problems as possible and to put forward and figure out countermeasures so as to take initiative in the negotiation.

☞ Case study 3 – 6　(**What do you think of the preparation of the Chinese party?**)

A giant of white electrical household appliances from European Union was invited by a well-known Chinese manufacturer of electrical household appliances to have a discussion about mutual co-operation. The European party sent an assistant, a fridge department manager and a washing machine department manager to attend the negotiation. After ten hours of flight, the European guests arrived in Beijing. Then they changed to another domestic flight to get to Zengcheng in Guangdong at 23:40 that night, where the electrical household appliances manufacturer was based. The senior managers and the related department managers were all present to meet them at the airport, which made the European guests very appreciative.

For the purpose of attaching importance to the meeting and showing kindness and hospitality, all the 12 Chinese senior managers, department managers and interpreters treated the three European guests in a five-star hotel on the 28th floor in the center of the city. During the dinner, the European guests accepted the toasts of Chinese representatives again and again, regardless of the strain from the flight and the discomfort due to the jet lag. Two of them were totally drunk by Chinese Maotai so that the negotiation planned on the following day was delayed till the third day. During the following week, Chinese party treated every meal. However, the European representatives had learned a lesson, controlling the amount of alcohol they drank, and did not make a show of themselves.

The Chinese negotiation team can be described as powerful: a president, two vice presidents, four department managers, a senior engineer, a CEO, a lawyer, an interpreter and a secretary. The Chinese party was quite familiar with the company's background and personal status of their negotiation counterpart. Additionally, they had made careful negotiation plans and physical preparations. All the expenses at the five-star hotel were charged to the account of the Chinese party.

Maybe in order to prove the feature of the air-conditioners displayed, the host party fixed the temperature at 16℃, which made the chief negotiator who had allergic rhinitis sneeze frequently. Fortunately, the host party realized the problem immediately and adjusted the temperature to the proper one. The European representatives noticed that Chinese party was very generous in all arrangements with the eagerness to cooperate with them. Therefore, they made proper adjustments in their offer.

In general, the whole negotiation went on quite smoothly. Both parties reached agreements on the introduction of the latest technology and equipment from the European factories. During the negotiation, the Chinese party specially arranged the European guests to visit several local places of interest. The European representatives were amazed at the Chinese traditional culture and attractive urban scenery in Southern China. Ideal investment environment and beautiful natural and cultural scenery made the European representatives quite pleased, which further contributed to the success of the negotiation.

☞ **Case study 3 - 7**    **（Japanese success in the negotiation on Daqing oil-field）**

In the 1960s, China began the exploration of Daqing oil-field, and all the information about it was almost confidential. Apart from a few people who were involved in this project, no one knew its location. However, the Japanese not only heard of that, but also got the accurate details of the oil-field. There were neither spies or agents nor bribery to the authorities or the masses. Instead, what they depended on was just the public information issued by our government and their comprehensive analysis. In July 1966, there was a photograph which had been signed out on the cover of the *China Pictorial*, describing how diligently the workers pioneered the Daqing oil-field, how they struggled for the exploration of the Daqing oil-field against the fluffy snow.

It was from this picture that the Japanese made a judgment that the oil-field might be located in northeast part of China. Then, the Japanese noticed a report in the *People*'s Daily. *In the report*, *Wang Jinxi*, *an oil-field worker*, *said loudly when he went to Majiayao*, "*How huge the oil-field is*！ *And we*'ll throw the bad name of Backward Country in oil development into the Pacific." Therefore, the Japanese got the old map of the puppet Manchukuo period, and found that Majiayao was a village located in southeast part of Hailun County, Heilongjiang Province, which was about 10 kilometers eastern away from a small railway station of Zhaoan.

Later, the Japanese version of *Chinese People* reported that the Chinese working class carried forward the spirit of fearing neither hardship nor death, and all the equipment had been carried by their shoulders to the site without any help of horses or carts. Accordingly, the Japanese decided that Daqing oil drilling was not very far from Majiayao, because those people could not bear so much equipment for that long distance. When the news that Wang Jinxi was invited to attend the Third National People's Congress hit the papers in 1964, the Japanese concluded that the Daqing oil-field had yielded much oil; otherwise, Wang Jinxi could not be the representative of the NPC.

After that, they made a further calculation, according to a photo of oil-field rigs in the People's Daily, to identify the diameter of the oil wells. All the data resulted from the handles of the racks on the drilling platforms. Meanwhile, by analyzing the statistics in the government work report issued by the State Council and subtracting the amount of oil in the past from that of the national gross production on oil, they estimated the average amount of oil production in the Daqing oil-field. Therefore, they designed proper equipment for exploration of that oil-field on the basis of surveys they had conducted. Thus, when the authority of Daqing oil-field announced that it would seek for the design of oil facilities from all over the world, Japanese had already prepared well for the plans of existing programs and equipment without being known by other countries. Eventually, they succeeded greatly in the negotiations with the representatives of Daqing oil-field.

☞ **Questions for your consideration and discussion**

1. What aspects should be covered when you prepare for a business negotiation?

2. How would you make your target levels for:

(1) Payment levels for exporters

(2) A job interview

3. What factors would you consider when you choose a negotiation site?

4. For Case Study 3－6, how would you comment on the preparation of the Chinese party? What are the good points and what are the weak points of their preparation?

5.Try to analyze Case Study 3－7, what are the main reasons why the Japanese could be very successful in the negotiations with Chinese representatives of Daqing oil-field, and what are the way the Japanese collected the relevant information?

6. What time do you think the preparation of a negotiation job should begin and when to end? How do you know preparations for a negotiation is enough?

# 第三章
# 国际商务谈判的准备

☞ **案例分析 3—1** （尼克松访华）

1972 年 2 月,美国总统尼克松访华,中美双方马上要展开一场具有重大历史意义的国际谈判。为了创造一种融洽和谐的谈判环境和气氛,中国方面在周恩来总理的亲自领导下,对谈判过程中的各个环节都做了精心周密的准备和安排,甚至对宴会上要演奏的中美两国民间乐曲都进行了精心的挑选。

在欢迎尼克松一行的国宴上,当军乐队熟练地演奏起由周总理亲自选定的《美丽的亚美利加》时,尼克松总统简直听呆了。他绝没有想到能在中国的北京听到他如此熟悉的乐曲,因为这是他平生最喜爱的,并且指定在他的就职典礼上演奏的家乡乐曲。敬酒时,他特地到乐队前表示感谢,此时,国宴达到了高潮,而这种融洽而热烈的气氛也同时感染了美国客人。一个小小的精心安排,赢得了和谐融洽的谈判气氛。

☞ **案例分析 3—2** （田中访问北京）

1972 年 9 月,日本首相田中角荣为恢复中日邦交正常化到达北京,他怀着等待中日间最高首脑会谈的紧张心情在迎宾馆休息。迎宾馆内气温舒适,田中角荣的心情也十分舒畅,与随从的陪同人员谈笑风生。他的秘书早坂茂三仔细看了一下房间的温度计,是"17.8℃"。这一田中角荣习惯的"17.8℃"使得他心情舒畅,也为谈判的顺利进行创造了条件。

知己知彼,百战不殆。准备工作是否充分对谈判的成功与否起着至关重要的作用。任何一场成功的谈判都是建立在充分的准备工作的基础之上的。一场谈判的准备工作越是充分、细致,其成功的概率就越大;相反,如果没有充分认真的准备工作,谈判是很难取得成功的。

国际商务谈判的准备工作一般包括谈判的背景调查、谈判资料的准备、谈判人员的组织、谈判方案的制定、谈判的具体准备工作与模拟谈判。

### 一、谈判的背景调查

国际商务谈判都是在一定的政治、经济、文化、社会制度和法律环境中进行的。这些背景将会直接或间接地影响谈判。因此，全面了解和分析谈判的背景将有助于谈判者制订出正确的谈判计划。对于参与国际商务的企业而言，谈判本身的成功并不是最终的，更重要的是合同的履行。因此在谈判之前，作为谈判者必须对客观存在的背景环境进行翔实的调查。

背景调查一般要包括政治状况、经济条件、政策法律、宗教信仰、文化习俗、国际惯例、基础设施和气候等。

#### 1. 政治状况

（1）政治背景和政局的稳定程度

政府与买卖双方之间是否存在某种关系。动荡的政局容易使谈判中止或者使已经达成的协议变成一纸空文，这样就会造成重大损失。政局的稳定指国内有无动乱或者战乱。

（2）两国的关系

如果两国关系友好或是处于正常状态，那么谈判的成功与否完全是买卖双方，即两个企业之间的事情。但是如果双方所在的国家之间没有建立外交关系，或者关系紧张，或是敌对国，谈判时交易双方就可能会受到政府的干扰，比如进行贸易限制或禁止等，这就增加了谈判的障碍。即使能够签约，履行合同的困难也会很大。

（3）对方国家的政治和经济体制

谈判者需要了解对方国家的政治体制和经济体制。因为在计划经济体制下，企业间的交往要受到国家计划的约束。如果在市场经济体制下，企业拥有较大的自主权，企业自身就可以决定交易的内容。因此，事先了解对方国家的经济体制有助于在谈判之前对对方的自主权做出准确的分析和判断。

#### 2. 经济条件

国际商务谈判的结果会使得双方的资本进行跨国流动。不同国家的经济状况会影响到资本流动的效率。

（1）外汇储备状况

国际商务谈判的核心是价格，而价格又表现为一定的货币支付。如果一个国家的外汇储备状况较差，则更可能出现外汇短缺、无法履约的情况。2008年国际金融危机中，韩国的外汇储备一度告急，导致很多合同不能按期履行，很多中国对韩出口企业撤出了与韩国的贸易谈判。

（2）汇率波动

由于不同国家使用不同的货币，货币之间的兑换又牵扯到汇率，汇率的波动必然会波及企业收益。不同国家汇率制度有所不同,有的实行的是固定汇率制,有的是浮动汇率制。汇率的波动情况会直接影响到谈判双方的经济利益。

（3）支付信誉

不同国家进行外汇付款的手续和环节都会有所不同。比如在选择信用证方式进行国际贸易结算时,信用较差的银行开立的信用证会延长企业的收款时间,甚至使企业面临收不到货款的风险。因此在国际商务中应该注重对银行支付能力的调查。

3. 政策法律、宗教信仰、文化习俗以及国际惯例等

（1）政策法律、宗教信仰

对方国家或地区有哪些与商务谈判相关的政策和法律制度,比如有没有贸易管制或是限制,有没有鼓励贸易的措施。宗教信仰对谈判有没有影响或是有多大影响。

（2）文化习俗

不同的国家有不同的文化和习俗,这些文化和习俗在一定程度上影响着谈判活动。对此,在谈判之前,必须充分了解下列因素:首先是合乎习俗的称呼,让对方感觉熟悉。其次是穿着,应该尽量合乎对方的社会规范。再次,人们习惯谈论的话题有哪些,业务洽谈时间的选择有什么特点。还有,见面是否应准备礼品,礼品的内容和包装有什么习俗,如何赠送。另外,该国商人做业务有什么商业习惯等。

（3）国际惯例

国际惯例是在长期经济交往中逐渐形成的一些有较为明确和固定内容的贸易习惯和一般做法。它对当事人没有普遍的强制性,但如果在合同中加以采用时,则对当事人有法律约束力。在国际贸易中有较大影响的国际惯例有《国际贸易术语解释通则》《华沙-牛津规则》《跟单信用证统一惯例》等。应了解对方国家商人对国际惯例的理解和做法。

4. 基础设施和气候等

（1）基础设施

交通状况、运输能力、通信能力、港口设施、建筑设备等会在一定程度上影响商务谈判活动。例如,在设施落后的港口进行装运,由于没有现代化的装卸设备,如果涉及装卸大型设备,就很难应对。

（2）气候

气候状况同样会对商务谈判产生影响。气候状况不仅会间接地影响商务谈判活动还可能影响到合同的履行,比如,哪个季节适合运输,哪个季节不适合运输,等等。

☞ **案例分析3—3**　（一个苏州公司的教训）

苏州某公司听说南非是一个诱人的市场,便希望将自己的产品打入南非市场。为了

摸清合作伙伴的情况,公司决定组团到南非进行实地考察。

到达南非后对方立即安排他们与南非公司的总经理会面,会面安排在一个富丽堂皇的大饭店里。考察团在电梯口遇到一位满面笑容的接待员,她将考察团引入一间装修豪华、设计现代化的房间。坐在皮椅上的总经理身材肥胖,手中夹着雪茄,脸上一副自信的表情,谈话时充满了激情。对公司的情况、经营方略及公司未来的打算侃侃而谈。总经理的介绍和他周围所有的一切都深深打动了考察团,他们深信这是一个可靠的财力雄厚的合作伙伴。考察团回国后,马上发去了一批价值100多万美元的货物。

然而,该批货物再也没有了音信。公司只好再派人去调查,此时才发现他们掉进了一个精心设计的圈套里。那位肥胖的"总经理"原来是当地的一个演员,在电梯口招呼他们的女招待才是真正的总经理,陈设精良的接待室不过是临时租来的房间。在真相大白之后再寻找这家公司,才知道它已宣告破产。

本案例中,苏州这家公司蒙受损失的重要原因,是仅从表面现象判断他们的合作伙伴的情况,而没有真正调查南非那家公司的背景。中方派去的考察团如果能从可靠的渠道调查了解情况,此类损失是完全可以避免的。

☞ **案例分析3—4** **（不了解当地法律导致的损失）**

中国某工程承包公司在加蓬承包了一项工程业务。当工程的主体建筑完工之后,中方由于不需要大量的劳动力,便将从当地雇佣的大批临时工解雇,谁知此举导致了被解雇工人持续40天的大罢工。中方不得不同当地工人进行了艰苦的谈判,被解雇的工人代表提出让中方按照当地的法律赔偿被解雇工人一大笔损失费。此时中方人员才意识到他们对加蓬的法律太无知了。根据加蓬的劳动法,一个临时工如果持续工作一周以上而未被解雇,则自动转成长期工。作为一个长期工,他有权获得足够维持两个妻子和三个孩子生活的工资。此外,还有交通费和失业补贴费用。一个非熟练工人如果连续工作一个月以上则自动转成熟练工,熟练工如果连续工作三个月以上则自动提升为技术工人。工人的工资也应随着技术的提升而提高。而中方公司的管理人员按照中国国内形成的对临时工、长期工、非熟练工、熟练工以及技工的理解来处理加蓬的情况,结果为自己招来了如此大的麻烦。谈判结果可想而知,中方公司不得不向被解雇的工人支付了一大笔失业补贴,总数目相当于已向工人支付的工资数额,而且这笔费用属于意外支付,并未包括在工程的预算中,全部损失由公司自行支付。

## 二、谈判资料的准备

谈判资料的准备就是在谈判的准备阶段尽可能收集、分析有关市场、商品和对方的情况,从而保证在谈判中处于有利的地位,有助于谈判的成功。谈判资料一般包括相关市场情况、对方公司及对方谈判人员资料。

**1.市场信息**

(1)商品的市场分布、需求与销售情况

收集国内外与交易商品相关的市场信息,包括商品市场的分布区域、地理位置、辐射范围、市场潜力,等等。了解商品在对方国家市场的消费需求信息,主要包括消费者的数量及其构成、消费习惯、消费水平、消费趋势、消费偏好、对该商品的消费有无特殊的服务要求,等等。了解商品的市场销售状况,主要包括商品在该市场的销售路径和销售区域、销售价格、销售量、销售的季节变化以及在该市场行之有效的销售策略,等等。

(2)商品的市场竞争情况与价格变动

市场竞争情况主要包括竞争对手的数量、经济实力、营销能力、商品的数量、种类、质量、特性、知名度、信誉度、商品的性能和提供售后服务的质量,等等。根据价格的变动信息就可以推测出价格的变动趋势,从而决定推销商品或采购商品的最佳时机。

**2.行业状况**

(1)行业规模和产品生命周期

了解同行业的相关情况,分析其发展趋势,是处于扩张、不变还是紧缩状态,得出该行业潜在的发展趋势和可能的规模,从而决定本企业的发展趋势和规模。收集不同国家不同阶段的该行业发展周期和同类产品的生命周期,以及在各个时期产品的竞争力。

(2)行业成本和决定行业成功的因素

对行业成本及其结构进行估算和调查,了解该行业的成本有无下降的可能,利润是否有上升的空间。要使产品在市场上占有一席之地,可通过收集行业成功案例的材料来分析其成功的因素,从而分析与谈判相关产品的前景。

**3.产品的资料**

首先,收集与产品本身有关的技术、工艺、包装、商标等信息;其次,要收集该产品在性能、质量以及其他方面与同类产品相比的优缺点;再次,该产品的发展前景、新技术所需要的费用、技术的先进性、寿命长短和生产周期,等等。

**4.谈判对手的资料**

(1)对方公司的资质及信用状况

对方公司的状况主要包括公司的成立时间,注册地址,员工数量,业务规模,经营状况,资信情况(品牌知名度和口碑),企业文化,商业信誉,高层管理者的特点,经营理念,目前和过去的经营战略,在管理、营销、财务、创新、服务等方面的优势与劣势等。这些有助于判断对方公司的实力,明确己方在谈判中想要获得的目标以及判断在合同签订之后对方的履约能力。

（2）对方公司的能力

对方公司的能力主要包括对方的财务状况（资产含固定资产和流动资产）、支付能力、经营范围、经营能力、销售能力、销售额、销售地区、销售方式、营业中的盈亏情况、增长率、主要产品的贡献率、新产品的开发能力及谈判商品在市场中的地位、支付方式和付款条件、银行有否坏账，等等。

（3）谈判对手的个人资料

对方谈判小组成员的有关资料包括对方谈判人员的人数、职务、年龄、分工以及各谈判人员的生活习惯、性格、专长、爱好、需求等，当然，如果可能的话，最好了解他们各自的弱点。除上述内容外，还应了解各谈判人员的谈判风格和情况，如是否参加过谈判、对方谈判人员之间是否有分歧等。

### ☞ 案例分析 3—5 （王光英的一次成功）

1983 年 4 月，中国香港光大实业公司董事长王光英先生收到一份重要情报：南美洲智利一家铜矿倒闭，矿主在矿山倒闭之前订购了美国的道奇、德国的奔驰等各种型号的大吨位载重车、翻斗车，共计 1500 辆，全是未曾启用的新车。为了偿还债务，矿主决定将这批新车进行拍卖。

1500 辆崭新的二手车，这是相当诱人的资产，可以想象此刻这份情报也被摆在世界各地许多企业家的办公桌上等待研究。王光英先生立即组织采购人员出国谈判，经过一番讨价还价，使 7 吨以上、30 吨以下的载重车以原价 30％ 的价格成交，节约了 2500 万美元。

本案例谈判成功的原因有很多，最主要的原因在于：①信息及时准确；②谈判决策迅速、正确；③谈判时机合适，正逢对手急于出售汽车还债。王光英先生对三个因素及时准确的把握促使谈判成功。由此可见，谈判前的准备工作是非常重要的。

### 三、谈判人员的组织

要做好国际商务谈判工作，无论是谈判前的准备工作，还是谈判中策略与技巧的运用都离不开谈判人员。而谈判者素质和能力的高低将会直接影响谈判的成败。因此，要使谈判成功，获得预期的经济效益，谈判人员的组成至关重要。

1. 谈判小组的规模

确定谈判小组的规模是谈判人员组织工作的首要问题。一般在确定小组的人员组成时，要依据需要与节俭原则。具体来说，可以从以下两个方面入手。

（1）根据对方参与谈判的人数，双方人数大致相等。这也是确定谈判人数的一个重要原则之一,以体现双方的平等。如果可行,应尽量减少参与谈判的人数,因为参与谈判的人数越多,企业的费用就会越高。因此,在组建谈判小组时,对谈判人员的数量决定上应该本着节俭原则,尽可能选择知识面广的专业人员或者一专多能者来减少人数,从而节约成本,提高效率。

(2) 根据谈判的复杂程度,比如具体内容、性质、规模以及谈判人员的知识、经验、能力等因素来确定谈判人数。如果谈判项目复杂,既要配备专业技术人员,又要配备具有相关商业知识、金融知识以及运输、财务、法律、国外民情等方面的专家。

**2. 谈判人员的组成**

组织谈判小组时,必须确定谈判所需的专业知识。一般所需的专业知识可以概括为下列几个方面:技术方面、贸易方面(包括价格、交货、支付条件和风险划分等)、法律方面(包括合同权利、义务等)和语言翻译方面等。因此,谈判小组通常由以下人员组成。

(1) 领导

谈判中一般称为谈判小组组长或谈判代表团团长,通常是公司的领导人员。领导一定是知识面很广的人士,更重要的是其必须拥有谈判的决策权。

(2) 商务人员

商务人员应该掌握洽谈交易过程中可能涉及的各种商务知识,如商品知识、市场知识、金融知识和运输、保险等方面的知识,熟悉贸易惯例和价格谈判条件,了解市场行情,熟悉合同条款,知晓各种支付方式。

(3) 翻译人员

翻译人员是谈判中的实际核心人员,要能洞察对方的心理和发言的实质,能改变谈判的气氛,善于与他人配合,还要懂得专业技术知识。在商务谈判中,即使所有的谈判人员都能够熟练地使用外语与对方进行交流,仍然需要配备高水平的翻译人员,以便谈判人员在翻译进行时有时间进行思考,并观察对方的反应,避免因考虑不周而出现失误。

(4) 技术人员

在谈判涉及比较复杂的项目时,需要有专门的技术人员或者工程师参加谈判。技术人员熟悉生产技术、产品性能、品种、规格、质量标准、工艺设计和技术发展趋势等问题,因此在谈判中可负责有关产品的性能、技术质量、产品验收和技术服务等问题的谈判。

(5) 财务人员

财务人员应熟悉成本情况、支付方式及金融知识。在谈判中,负责对谈判项目或商品的价格或成本进行核算。

(6) 法律人员

法律人员需要熟悉我国颁布的有关涉外法律、法令与规则,并了解有关国际贸易、国际技术转让和国际运输等方面的法律、惯例以及有关国家的政策措施、法规和管理制度等方面的知识,为谈判提供法律咨询或参考。

（7）记录人员

记录人员应熟悉计算机操作并能快速、准确地输入文字，记录谈判的内容，包括双方讨论的问题、提出的条件、达成的协议，等等。

3. 谈判人员应具备的素质和能力

决定商务谈判胜负的因素在于商务谈判人员的素质和能力。因此，选拔优秀的谈判人员是进行商务谈判的重要环节。优秀的谈判人员应具备下列素质和能力。

（1）健康的身体素质和较强的语言文字运用能力

谈判者必须有健康的身体素质。谈判者只有具备充沛的精力、健康的体魄才能适应谈判超负荷的工作需要。一个优秀的谈判者，应该能够通过语言的感染力强化谈判的艺术效果。谈判中的语言不仅应当准确、严密，而且应生动形象、富有感染力。因为语言运用能力还直接关系到交流的通畅和谈判的气氛。语言风趣幽默的人在谈判中往往更能吸引人的注意，能够活跃气氛，化解矛盾，促使谈判成功。

（2）良好的思想品德

谈判者在谈判的过程中，不仅要维护国家、企业和个人的经济利益，还要维护国家、企业和个人的形象。不能因贪图好处或个人的利益而出卖国家或企业的商业机密，损害国家或企业的利益。因此，良好的思想品德是挑选谈判人员的第一要素。

（3）强烈的责任感和主观能动性

参与谈判的人员在谈判过程中要始终坚守职责，不能轻言放弃，要有耐心和信心，同时具备积极开拓进取的精神。在谈判实践中要表现出灵活的应变能力、敏捷的创造性思维能力、准确的分析推理能力、较强的运筹能力和果断的决策能力。任何细致的谈判准备都不可能预料到谈判中可能发生的所有情况，因此谈判人员必须具备沉着、机智、灵活的应变能力，以控制谈判的局势。

（4）较高的个人修养和必备的涉外知识

谈判人员应注重礼仪，要做到举止优雅、谈吐大方、不卑不亢，凡事应顾全大局。同时还要能经受挫折的考验，保持自信的态度应对各种问题。另外，要善于倾听，无论对方的观点如何，应在听完之后再发表意见，不能断章取义。谈判者应事先了解所在国家和对方国家的相应政策、法规和法律，避免发生无效的谈判行为，更不能发生违法行为。

## 四、谈判方案的制定

国际商务谈判的方案，是指为了进口或出口某种商品而确定的经营意图、需要达到的最高或最低目标，以及为实现该目标所应采取的策略、步骤和做法。其目的就是做到能够有效地组织和控制贸易谈判活动，是整个谈判小组的行动纲领，在整个谈判中起着非常重要的作用。

1. 制定谈判方案的基本要求

（1）谈判方案要简明扼要

简明扼要就是让谈判人员能够容易记住其主要内容和基本原则。所以，谈判方案越简要，谈判人员在执行时就越容易记住，在错综复杂的谈判中更容易把握谈判的主题方向，从而掌控谈判的局势。

（2）谈判方案要具体

谈判方案要以谈判的具体内容为基础，具有可操作性。比如将谈判的总目标细化为若干个分目标或子目标。谈判方案要基于事实，具有可行性，要客观、理性。谈判方案一般以文字的形式出现，可以是长达十几页的书面文稿，也可以是一页纸的备忘录。

（3）谈判方案要灵活可行

谈判方案只是谈判前单方面的主观设想。但是在实际过程中，各种随机的因素都可能影响谈判，因此方案应该具有灵活性，以防出现一些无规律可循而又不可控制的因素影响谈判。在谈判方案的可行性研究阶段，还需要拟定出谈判的各种方案进行比较和选择。所以应制订几套替代方案，并从中选出最佳替代方案，以便自己有回旋的余地。能使己方获取最大利益的方案就是最佳谈判方案，在谈判时要尽可能按最佳方案执行。

2. 谈判方案的内容

（1）确定谈判的基本策略

谈判策略指的是为了实现谈判目标而采取的策略和技巧，是针对预期的谈判效果采取的进攻或防卫措施，是为达到谈判目标单方面采取的行动。谈判策略的采用注重的就是谈判结果。确定谈判策略应考虑以下的因素：

①是主场谈判，客场谈判还是第三方场地的谈判？

②双方的优势和实力如何？

③哪一方受到谈判结果的影响更大？

④对方的实力（成员的职务和组成情况）以及主谈人员的性格和特点如何？

⑤哪一方更易受谈判用时长短的影响？

⑥是否有必要建立长期合作的关系？

从谈判的过程来看，谈判的基本策略可以分为开局策略、报价策略、磋商策略、成交策略；从谈判的技巧来看可以分为让步策略、进攻策略、防守策略、打破僵局策略，等等。

（2）确定谈判的议程或项目

谈判的议程指的是谈判的时间与地点的安排以及要讨论的内容，一般由主场准备或由双方商定。要明确谈判需持续多久，何时开始，何时结束；谈判的地点所在。通常，谈判地点可设在谈判大厅、会议室、经理办公室，也可租用第三方或酒店的会议室、接待室或办公室。一场谈判的地点可以固定也可以变换。谈判的议题是双方在谈判中要商讨的事宜，确定了哪些事宜后，一般要列出先后次序。

### 3. 谈判目标的确定

（1）确定谈判目标应该遵循的原则

①实用性。确定谈判目标时，首先要考虑实用性，也就是合同达成之后可以预见的收益。可预见的经济效益或社会效益会督促谈判双方认真履行合同，从而减少损失的发生。

②合理性。在确定谈判目标时，不能将目标设定得太高或太低。太高对方不会接受，直接导致谈判失败；太低，对己方来说利益太少，即使达成协议，在履约时也不会认真。因此，一个合理的目标非常重要，会使双方各取所需，这就是通常所说的"双赢"，是谈判目标的最高境界。

（2）确定谈判目标时主要考虑的因素

在确定谈判目标的过程中，要全面地考虑相关的因素。这些因素包括谈判的性质及其领域、谈判的对象及其环境、项目所涉及的业务要求、各种条件变化的可能性、变化方向、对谈判的影响等。另外，还要考虑长期目标和短期目标的问题。以简单的商品贸易为例，在确定目标时不能仅仅考虑价格水平，只考虑价格就会牺牲质量；也不能只考虑质量，以高价购入高质量的商品，期望再以高价销售保证利润；而是要把各种因素结合起来，综合考虑确定谈判的目标。

（3）谈判目标的层次

通常，谈判者常常会将自己的目标划分为三个层次：最低限度目标、可接受目标、最优期望目标。

①最低限度目标。最低限度目标是谈判必须达到的最基本的目标。对己方来说，宁愿谈判破裂，放弃商贸合作项目，也不愿接受比最低限度更低的条件。在谈判中，对最低限度目标要严格保密，否则会使对方主动出击，使己方陷入困境。最低限度目标是要坚守的底线，毫无讨价还价的余地。这样，就给谈判划定了一个明确的界限。

②可接受目标。可接受目标是指谈判人员根据各种主要客观因素，通过考察种种情况，经过科学论证、预测和核算之后所确定的谈判目标，介于最优期望目标与最低限度目标之间。这个目标是一个区域范围，谈判中的讨价还价就是在争取实现可接受的目标，所以可接受目标的实现，往往意味着谈判的成功。可接受目标是己方力保的实际需求目标，只有在万不得已的情况下才考虑放弃。

③最优期望目标。最优期望目标是对谈判者最有利的一种理想目标。它在满足己方实际需求利益之外，还有一个"额外的增加值"。这个目标虽然很难实现，但它激励谈判人员尽最大努力去实现，也可以很清楚地评价出谈判最终结果与最高期望目标之间存在多大差距。在谈判开始时，以最高期望目标作为报价起点，有利于在讨论还价中使己方处于主动地位。当然，在谈判中，不能盲目追求最高期望目标而忽视谈判过程中出现的困难，

这样容易造成束手无策的被动局面。在这三个目标中,己方争取的最优期望目标是最高目标,但在必要时可以放弃这一目标。

## 五、谈判的具体准备工作

谈判的具体准备工作主要指谈判议程的安排、地点的选择和座次的排列、客人膳宿安排及参观游览等。谈判的具体准备工作对谈判的整个过程有着重要的影响。

1. 谈判议程的确定和安排

谈判议程主要指谈判时间的安排、谈判的议题及顺序安排。

(1)谈判时间的安排

时间安排就是要确定谈判在何时举行,持续多久并确保谈判人员能参与谈判。谈判的时间安排有时会对谈判结果产生很大的影响。所以,谈判者应该对谈判时间的选择给予足够的重视。谈判时间的安排要考虑下列因素:一是资料的准备状况。谈判人员要有充足的准备时间,只有准备充分,才能事半功倍;二是谈判人员的状态。谈判是一项精神高度集中的工作,对体力和脑力的消耗较大,同时,谈判时需要思维敏捷、反应迅速、灵活地处理问题,所以谈判人员应在精神和情绪良好的状态下进行谈判,才有可能达到预期的目标;如果谈判者在旅途之后未经休整立即投入谈判,劳累、精力不足就容易导致精神难以集中,记忆力下降,反应迟钝等,进而影响谈判的进程。

(2)谈判议题和顺序

谈判的议题和顺序是指谈判的项目内容以及各谈判项目的先后次序和分别占用的时间。首先列出与本次谈判有关的所有问题,因为每个问题都关系着双方的利益。议题的顺序通常可以先易后难,也可以先难后易。前者指先安排双方容易达成共识的议题,这样可以为整个谈判创造友好的气氛。后者指先讨论复杂的重要的问题,双方集中精力解决重点难点。还可以采用混合型的方法,不管重点还是非重点的议题,一揽子解决。谈判的议程一般不会由谈判一方单方面决定,而是由双方进行协商。

2. 谈判地点的选择和安排

(1)谈判地点的选择

谈判地点的选择包括在哪个国家或地区进行谈判以及具体谈判场地的确定。

①在哪个国家进行谈判

选择不同的国家进行谈判,在一定程度上会影响谈判的结果。然而,不管是主场还是客场,对谈判双方都各有利弊。(这一点在第一章已有介绍。)

②具体谈判场地的确定

一般而言,只要条件许可,应当选择自己的领地。一方面,主人可以向客人展示自己的好客与真诚,还可以向对方展示己方的总体实力。另一方面,作为谈判的一种策略,装饰豪华的会议室能给对方带来心理上的积极影响。相反,如果一个公司总不让客人拜访其总部,而是在外租借地方谈判,那么其公司的实力则令人怀疑。

3.谈判场地与座次安排

(1)谈判场地

谈判场地指谈判的具体场所和环境。谈判场地应选择在宽敞舒适、布置幽雅、相对安静、交通便利、通信方便、设备比较齐全的环境和场所。不利的环境会使人心烦意乱,精力不易集中,影响谈判效果。因此我们在进行商务谈判时一定要选择一个明亮、通风、使人心情愉快、精力集中的场地,避免对谈判产生不利影响。

(2)座次安排

谈判时的座位次序也是一个比较突出、敏感的问题。正式的商务谈判,按照礼仪要求,一般谈判者双方代表各坐在桌子的一侧,双方主谈者居中相向而坐。主方谈判人员背对正门而坐。双方均以首席谈判员为首,其右手为上,左手为下,近位为上,远位为下。译员一般在首席谈判人员的右侧。双方人员分别坐在谈判桌的一边,容易使谈判成员产生安全感和自信感,也便于查找一些不愿意让对方知道的资料,还方便与己方人员交换意见。

(3)其他设施

椅子:椅子在风格和颜色等方面应与谈判桌相匹配,应舒适方便。

展示板:用来直接展示数字解释案例。

投影仪:用于展示图片、短片等信息。

另外还有烟灰缸、便笺、圆珠笔、文件夹、茶、咖啡、开水或冰水等。

4.客人膳宿安排

客人膳宿事宜应提前安排,主人应考虑周到,让客人感到方便、舒适。

(1)住宿

如果是客人买单,主人最好征求客人的意见,看他们想住什么档次的酒店;如果是主人买单,应认真考虑酒店的选择,特别是豪华酒店,因为这是主人的一种投资,要考虑将来的回报。安排酒店的原则是不求奢华但求方便,不要与购物中心相隔太远。

(2)膳食

请给客人留一定的空间,没有必要每顿饭都安排好或是每餐都点昂贵的菜肴。

5.参观游览

如果时间许可,当接待的是第一次拜访的客人时,主人通常可安排一些参观游览。比如,与谈判项目相关的工厂,当地的风景名胜,具有地方特色的知名饭店、购物中心,其他名胜古迹或客人感兴趣的娱乐场所都可考虑。安排参观游览可加深客人对主人文化的了解,消除旅途的不适,有助于双方建立和谐友好的关系。

### 六、模拟谈判

模拟谈判一般在谈判方案确定之后和正式谈判开始之前进行,根据具体情况提出各种假设,进行谈判演习。主要是用于改进和完善谈判的准备工作,检查谈判方案中可能存在的漏洞和问题,对谈判方案进行改进和完善。

#### 1. 模拟谈判的必要性

首先,模拟谈判能够使谈判者发现谈判方案中的问题或准备工作不充分的地方,有利于谈判者及时纠正这些不足。谈判方案通常是谈判人员根据主观经验规划的,难免有疏忽的地方。而模拟谈判有助于谈判者从对方的角度思考问题,使谈判者能够及早发现问题,及时查漏补缺。

其次,模拟谈判能够使谈判者获得谈判经验,在谈判练习中提高谈判能力。模拟谈判可以训练和提高谈判人员的应变能力,为实际的临场发挥做好铺垫。

再次,模拟谈判为谈判人员之间的分工配合提供练习,磨合谈判队伍,提高己方谈判小组整体的默契程度和谈判能力。谈判人员在实际谈判中需要做到配合默契,提高整体的谈判能力。

#### 2. 拟定假设

（1）对外界客观存在的事物的假设

对外界客观存在的事物的假设包括对环境、时间、空间的假设。通常假设外界环境出现了不利的因素,应如何处理？比如谈判时间、谈判场所等。谈判者根据这些假设,做好充分的应对准备。

（2）对谈判对手的假设

对谈判对手的假设,主要包括对方的合作意愿、愿意接受的风险的程度、在谈判具体内容上的态度,如在商品的质量、价格、支付方式、运输方式等方面可能提出的要求。目的就是揣摩对方的真实意图,明确在遇到谈判对手坚持己见时如何处理,轻易让步时如何处理,加快或拖延谈判时如何处理。

（3）对己方的假设

对己方的假设主要是对己方谈判能力、心理素质、谈判方案等方面的自测与评价。除此以外,对己方的假设还有建立在对对方假设的基础上所采取的对策。通过对外界因素和对方的假设,根据自身的实力来假设对策,以用于实际的谈判。

#### 3. 模拟谈判的两种方式

（1）会议式模拟

就是把谈判者聚集在一起,以会议的形式,充分讨论,自由发表意见。谈判者根据自己的理解,发表自己的看法,互相启发,共同提高谈判水平。这种方法可以让所有的谈判人员开动脑筋,积极进行创造性思维,通过集体思考发现问题、解决问题。

（2）实战模拟

实战模拟是将谈判人员一分为二，或在谈判小组之外再建立一个实力相当的谈判小组，一方实施己方的谈判方案，另一方站在对方的立场，根据假设实施对手的谈判方案。这种实战练习可以更换不同的人员来扮演对方的角色，想出不同的问题，从而让己方对对方有充分的了解，进一步完善谈判方案，提高己方谈判人员的谈判能力。

4. 模拟谈判总结

进行模拟谈判的目的就是为了及早地发现谈判方案中存在的问题，提出解决问题的对策，掌握谈判的主动权。因此在实施模拟谈判之后，需要及时进行总结，有针对性地进行改进，从而制定出一份完善的谈判方案。

☞ **案例分析 3—6** （中方的准备工作怎么样？）

欧盟的一个白色家电巨头应中国一家知名家电制造商的邀请进行双边合作的谈判。欧洲方面派出了一名助理以及冰箱部和洗衣机部的经理参加谈判。经过 10 个小时的飞行，欧洲客人抵达北京，然后又换乘国内航班于当晚 23：40 飞抵家电制造商所在的广东增城。所有的高级经理和相关部门的经理都到机场迎接，这使得欧洲客人很感动。

为了表示对会谈的重视和热情友好，他们在市中心的一家五星级酒店的 28 楼款待欧洲客人。中方的高级经理、部门经理和翻译员总共 12 人全部出席。尽管有长途飞行的紧张和时差带来的不适，但是，在宴会期间欧洲客人频频地接受中方的敬酒。两个欧洲客人喝茅台都喝醉了，以至于原计划在第二天进行的谈判不得不延迟到第三天。在随后的一个礼拜，他们的餐饮全由中方买单。然而，欧洲代表吸取了教训，控制了酒量。

中方谈判阵容可以说是十分强大：董事长，两名副董事长，一名执行总裁，四名部门经理，一名高级工程师，一名律师，一位翻译员和一个秘书。中方对对方公司的背景了如指掌，对谈判代表的个人情况也很熟悉。另外，他们认真地制订了谈判计划，进行了具体的准备。五星级酒店所有的费用都由中方负担。

也许是为了展示空调良好的性能，主人将空调的温度设定在 16 摄氏度，使得欧洲的主谈人员得了过敏性鼻炎，不断地打喷嚏。好在主人马上意识到这个问题并调到了正常的温度。欧洲代表注意到中方急于与他们合作，所有的安排都很慷慨，因此，他们适当地调整了报价。

总之，整个谈判进展得很顺利，双方就中方从欧洲工厂引进最新的技术和设备达成了一致。在谈判过程中，中方特别安排欧洲客人参观了当地的几个风景名胜。欧洲代表对中国的传统文化和中国南方的具有魅力的城市景观感到震惊。理想的投资环境、美丽的自然和文化环境使得欧洲客人非常满意，所有这些都促进了谈判的成功。

☞ **案例分析 3—7** （日本人在大庆油田谈判中的成功）

20 世纪 60 年代，中国开始探测大庆油田，有关这方面的所有消息几乎都是保密的。除了参与这个项目的几个人外，谁也不知道它的位置。然而，日本人不仅知道这件事，而且还得到了油田准确的详情。这既不是间谍或代理人所为，也不是向当局或群众行贿所得。相反，他们所依赖的恰恰是我们的政府发布的信息以及他们的综合性分析。1966 年 7 月，《中国画报》的封面刊登了一幅照片，描述了大庆油田首批勤劳的工人冒着鹅毛大雪如何为了开采大庆油田而奋斗。

正是根据这张照片，日本人判断，该油田可能位于中国的东北地区。然后，日本人注意到《中国日报》上的一篇报道。报道中，王进喜——油田的一个工人——去马家窑时大声地说，"好大的油海！我们要把中国石油工业落后的帽子抛到太平洋去！"因此，日本人找到了伪满洲国时期的旧地图，并且发现马家窑是位于黑龙江省海伦县（今海伦市）东南部的一个村子，该村位于距离诏安火车站以东大约 10 千米的地方。

后来，日本版的《中国人民》报道，中国工人阶级发扬一不怕苦二不怕死的精神，所有的设备都是工人在没有马和车的情况下用肩膀扛来的。因此，日本人判断大庆石油钻井就在距马家窑不远的地方，因为靠那些人扛设备，距离不可能太远。1964 年当报纸上发表王进喜被邀请参加第三次全国人民代表大会的消息时，日本人断定大庆油田已经生产了很多石油，不然王进喜不可能成为全国人大代表。

此后，他们又做出了进一步的推算，根据《人民日报》上的油井无线电惯性制导系统的照片，确定了油井的直径。所有的数据都来源于钻探平台设备机框的了解。同时，通过分析国务院发表的政府工作报告的统计，再减去过去全国总的石油产量，他们就估算出大庆油田平均年产量。因此，他们根据所调查的情况设计出开采大庆油田的合适的设备。当大庆油田宣布将在全世界范围内寻找石油设施的设计时，日本人已经准备好了项目的计划，而其他国家却一无所知。最终，他们和大庆油田代表的谈判取得了巨大的成功。

☞ **思考题与讨论题**

1. 谈判的准备工作包括哪些方面？
2. 你将如何确定谈判目标？
   (1) 作为出口商考虑支付方式时
   (2) 应聘一项工作

3.在商务谈判中,谈判者在选择谈判场合时要考虑哪些因素?

4.在案例分析3—6中,你认为中方的准备工作做得怎样? 有什么优点和不足?

5.在案例分析3—7中,日本代表在与大庆油代表的谈判中能够取得成功的主要原因是什么? 日本人收集相关信息的途径是什么?

6.谈判的准备工作从何时开始,从哪里结束? 怎样才能知道准备工作已经足够了?

# Chapter 4

# Opening of International Business Negotiation

☞ **Case study 4 – 1**    (Regan's opening speech)

US former President Regan once paid a visit to Fudan University and delivered a speech in the school auditorium. In his opening remark, he deliberately mentioned his "close" relationship with the university:"In fact I have a close relationship with the university. Mr. Xie Xide, president of the university, is my wife's schoolmate in American Smiths College. Accordingly, you and I are friends!" His remarks were rewarded with warm applause and made the students at present regard this blue-eyed, big-nosed foreign President as their close friend. There was a warm and harmonious air in the subsequent talk.

International business negotiation usually involves 4 stages: opening stage, quoting stage, bargaining stage and the stage of concluding business and signing contracts.

The opening stage of a negotiation refers to the process soon after the two sides meet and before the formal negotiation begins. In this stage, negotiators greet each other, introduce each other, have a prologue and state their positions and explore the counterpart's intention in order to influence and manipulate the process of negotiation and obtain an advantageous position.

"Well begun is half done." Opening stage is the starting point of negotiation and the first step for the two sides to meet each other. Whether for trading or investing, buying or selling, the opening approach and atmosphere are of great importance to the development of the negotiation. At the beginning of a negotiation, experienced negotiators tend to read the signals released from what the other party says and does to explore their attitude and sincerity and decide whether the other party is willing to reach an agreement. Therefore, the opening decides the tone and direction of the whole negotiation.

## Ⅰ. Types of Opening Atmosphere for Negotiation

International business negotiation atmosphere refers to the atmosphere and the surroundings that one or both parties create before a negotiation gets started. A good negotiation atmosphere will help the negotiation proceed smoothly; on the contrary, a bad negotiation atmosphere will hinder the course of the negotiation or even destroy the whole negotiation.

There are many kinds of negotiation atmosphere and there are different standards. For example, some negotiations are positive, friendly and constructive, optimistic and enthusiastic; some are frank, natural, brief and straightforward; but some might be tense, contradictory, protracted or cold and perfunctory, even sedate and reserved. Some experts have summed up the following three kinds of negotiation atmosphere.

### 1. High-spirited atmosphere

High-spirited atmosphere refers to the situation in which the negotiation is animated as both parties are positive and enthusiastic, and are optimistic about the prospect of the negotiation, with pleasant elements as the leading tone of the negotiation. Usually, when one party gets the upper hand and hopes to reach an agreement with the other party, it should try to generate a high-spirited atmosphere.

### 2. Low-spirited atmosphere

Low-spirited atmosphere is one that is serious, depressing and downcast. It is the situation in which the negotiators are in low spirit and having an indifferent attitude, with unpleasant factors as the leading role. Usually when we still have the bargaining ability but cannot secure an absolute advantageous position and have to exert some pressure on the other party, we can attempt to create a low-spirited atmosphere.

### 3. Natural atmosphere

In a natural atmosphere, negotiation is neither animated nor oppressive. Both parties are in a natural and steady mood when they take part in the negotiation. Many negotiations are conducted in a natural atmosphere, and we don't need to work on it purposely. This kind of atmosphere will be of great help to convey accurate and trustworthy information. When we know little of our counterparts, we tend to adopt a natural atmosphere.

## Ⅱ. How to Create a Good Negotiation Atmosphere

The main purpose of international business negotiation is to make the biggest profit, so almost all businessmen hope to have a positive or good negotiation atmosphere. Then how is it possible to create such a negotiation atmosphere? At the first contact of both parties, facial expressions, eye contact and the force of the handshake, other behaviors and contents of the talk have already created an opening atmosphere as well as exerting an influence on the subsequent course of negotiation because the first expression is so important that it has basically set the tone and atmosphere for the negotiation.

Generally speaking, factors that influence the opening of the negotiation can be analyzed from the point of negotiators, negotiation surroundings and opening remarks.

### 1. Negotiators

Negotiators should have proper behavior, good temperament and be graceful. Usually negotiators should walk directly to the negotiating hall and meet the counterpart friendly and frankly in a good mental state. Negotiators should imagine the meeting beforehand and get ready for the meeting etiquette.

(1) A natural facial expression

Generally speaking, negotiators should have a relaxed, self-confident, frank and natural facial expression. The facial expression of the negotiators can reflect their state of mind. Whether a person is relaxed or nervous, self-confident or hesitant, in a high spirit or tired can all be reflected from their facial expressions, especially from the changes of their expressions in their eyes. For example, natural facial expression reflects sincerity and frankness; indifferent or cold facial expression reflects nervousness or cunning. You can tell at the first sight whether your counterparts are honest or cunning, active or sedate.

(2) A good appearance and manners

Before uttering any words, your appearance and clothes always make a strong initial impression on other people. A proper appearance, a neat and tasteful suit and considerate and polite manners will draw the others close to you. In general, your clothing should not be too serious or too informal. One point needs to be mentioned: The clothing must fit one's own character. Don't be too peculiar about your dressing or wear clothes of too large or too small size. Don't wear clothes of over-bright colors. Don't loosen the tie or unbutton the shirt or wind up the sleeves or do other things implying that you are tired or bored. Your clothing should be adjusted according to different weather, customs and culture.

(3) A proper speech and deportment

Logical discourse or utterance, a sense of humor, proper speed as well as graceful behaviors can quickly attract the other party's attention, leaving them a good first-impression.

(4) A good state of mind

Negotiators' confidence and vigor can enlighten and activate the negotiation atmosphere, which can stimulate the initiative of the other party; on the contrary, negative, indifferent and nervous manners will make the other party doubt your frankness or your competence.

**2. Negotiation environment**

An appropriate negotiation environment includes the choice of negotiation sites, arrangement of the meeting room (color and equipment), seats and media if necessary.

(1) Choice of sites and arrangements

If the negotiation is held at a meeting room or negotiating room, it indicates that the host party attaches great importance to the negotiation. If the negotiation takes place at a hotel, it's most likely that the host party hopes to create a warm and friendly atmosphere. If the site is chosen at the lobby or coffee bar of a hotel, it seems that the host party neglects the guests. If the negotiation is set in the scenic open air, it conveys a pleasant message that common agreement is easy to attain. If the negotiation is conducted in the mansion or the villa of the host, it may show that the host hopes to move the other party by establishing personal friendship in order to reach an agreement.

(2) Decoration of the site and arrangement of the seats

Usually negotiation atmosphere is very tense, so the site should be decorated with a mild color, for example, to put some flowers.

Formal international business negotiations pay much attention to the arrangement of seats. Polite seating order is to ask the guests to sit in front of the window with the back facing it and the hosting party sit with the back facing the door. The best approach is to choose chairs of the same size set opposite on each side of the meeting table, and the guests are seated with their back facing the window or anywhere comfortable, making them feel just like at home.

Hosts should know clearly what equipment will be used and get them prepared, such as microphone, equipment for interpretation, equipment for lightening, etc. In addition, hosts could prepare some coffee, tea or desserts, which will not only soothe the thirst or hunger but also help to adjust the atmosphere and reduce the tension. Meanwhile, negotiation should avoid being interrupted by telephones and visitors.

（3）Media and public opinions

Some important international business negotiations will get the attention of the media and public at home and abroad, and wise negotiators make good use of the media reports to create a good atmosphere for the opening.

### 3. Prologue

The prologue to a negotiation can be some light talk or some topics which both sides are interested in. Just like warm-up exercise for sports activities, this kind of prologue is quite necessary in international business negotiations. Before we enter into formal negotiations, some neutral topics can be chosen as opening remarks, such as the local weather, travel hearsay, films and theater performance, personal hobbies, jokes as well as the previous co-operations. These topics, on the one hand, are cheerful, light and easy to arouse the resonance; on the other hand, they are not related to business, and thus helpful to build a harmonious and friendly atmosphere.

At this stage negotiators preferably stand and they can be divided into groups. They can also make good use of such kind of introductory remarks to tell some jokes in order to exert psychological implications on the other party. In addition, we should make sure that the prologue do not take up too much time. It usually takes up about 5% of the whole talk. As long as they can activate the atmosphere and lessen the tension, that's OK and we should proceed to the next formal stage of giving opening statement and exchange ideas at once.

### Ⅲ. Opening Strategies

Opening strategies are methods or means of action that negotiators take to achieve a good beginning for the negotiation and to cultivate a favorable situation to one's own side. The purpose is to create the appropriate atmosphere.

At the opening stage, negotiators are getting to know each other and identifying the issues involved through various channels. There are no strict rules on opening or conducting a meeting, but several different approaches have been suggested. Some experienced negotiators advise to start off the meeting with a completely irrelevant topic. Others suggest that a humorous story can lighten the tension. Still others propose that the introductory remarks set forth some of the general principles of negotiation：

the goals of each party, your objective and attitude and how you will listen and evaluate all alternatives and suggestions. Also you can set forth the benefits to be gained for the other side by dealing with you. Remember, if a negotiator has the option to hear the other side's offer first, and then do so.

## 1. Types of opening strategies

（1）Resonant opening

Resonant opening aims to seek for common opinions or topics that both sides are interested in and which can bring about "resonance" so that both parties can go on to a further step. Psychological studies show that people tend to favor those who share the same opinions with them and are willing to adapt their opinions to those of the people who have "resonance" or identity with them. The commonly used ways of resonant openings are conferring approach, inquiring approach and complementing approach.

Conferring approach suggests that we ask for the opinions of the other party with a kind tone to boost discussion towards our goals (in fact, we have a clear picture in mind), then we approve of their proposals and are willing to follow their proposals (as it is the same with ours) to proceed with our work. But what we need to pay attention to is: When we agree with the other party, we should not make the other party feel flattered, instead, we let them feel we agree with them because we identify with them and we understand and share their ideas.

Inquiring approach is to design your answer in the form of a question to induce your counterpart to move toward the goal that you have set. For example, you may ask them questions like "How do you think about the idea that we put the price terms aside and come to them at the end of negotiation?"

Complementing approach encourages you to avail yourself of the opportunity to add your own opinions to that of the other party and talk them around to your way of thinking and let them speak in your voice.

☞ **Case study 4 - 2** **（A resonant opening by talking NBA）**

It was a negotiation between a Chinese automobile company and US Ford company, and the American side is in a stronger position. The Chinese side knew that the main negotiator was fond of basketball matches, so they managed to get the copies of all video materials of NBA matches undergoing that year and watched most videos at nights and weekends.

When the Chinese and American parties seated themselves and began the negotiation about the introduction of new models of cars, the Chinese vice president congratulated the American manager on the success of the team from his home state in the NBA match with the score of 78 to 63, much better performance than the year before! The American manager was immediately excited, "Do you like NBA matches? I've watched all the NBA matches in the US, about which my wife often complained." The Chinese vice president said, "My wife almost divorced me for my ignorance of the housework due to NBA matches!" The American representative smiled, "Our interests are quite alike—by the way, did Yao Ming play the game? How was his performance?" The Chinese vice president said, "He did not show up in the court for his injury on the foot." The American representative said, "What a pity! However, if Yao had played in the match, our team would have had a difficult time. Yao is something and Americans like him very much."

The Chinese vice president said, "Yao is China's pride. We also have got the Olympic hurdle champion Liu Xiang, as well as the Chinese world champions in women's tennis doubles..." then he changed the topic, "In recent years, China has achieved remarkable success in sports games. The common people especially the ones among the young professional managers and white collars are fond of going to the fitness clubs, picnics, hiking and excursion. They are keen on surfing the Internet, staying in the bars and traveling around the world, and enjoying the newly-emerging things. Just for this reason, we would like to introduce two models of sports cars (sedans and hatchbacks) from your company. We do hope your company will not follow the suit of German manufacturers who have refused to give China the latest models, which led to the fact that their large potential market shares in China have been taken away by Japanese and Korean sports car producers." The American representatives suddenly realized that their market share in the field of sports cars in China was still quite small, and as long as they can take quick actions, the profitable opportunities would belong to them. Hence, the representatives from Ford Company reached an agreement with the Chinese party on the introduction of new models very quickly.

(2) Frank Opening

With frank opening, negotiators convey their opinions to the other party frankly so as to begin the negotiation in a constructive way or to make a breakthrough in the negotiation. This strategy is usually used between regular clients because it can save lots of courtesies and time, and we can put forward our opinions and requirements directly, which may also make our partners trust us more.

Frank opinion also applies to the party with weak negotiation power. When we are quite clear about each other's strengths and weaknesses, frankly revealing our weaknesses to the other party can help us gain the understanding and leave a good impression on the counterpart if we demonstrate our sincerity in this way.

☞ **Case study 4 – 3**    (**Frank opening of a branch secretary**)

One day in September 2000, a branch secretary of the Communist Party in a village in Jiangsu Province had a negotiation with a foreign businessman. After exchanging their business cards, the Party branch secretary noticed that the foreign businessman was very alert about his status; therefore, the negotiation did not move on smoothly. Hence, the secretary frankly told the foreigner, "As a branch secretary, I am, in fact, the leader of the highest rank in our village. I have the right and power to make economic and managerial decisions in our village and I am not a layman of economic activities because so far I have set up many enterprises. Even though our economic development is not on a high level and our conditions are poorer than some coastal cities, we are farmers, diligent and simple, and our labor and land costs are much lower compared with those in the cities. We sincerely hope to cooperate with you. It does not matter whether our negotiation is successful or not, for at least you, a 'foreign' boss, can make friends with me, a Chinese 'country' folk." Hearing these frank words, the foreign businessman burst into laughter and was no longer overcautious and vigilant. As a result, they entered the next stage of the negotiation, talking about substantial issues at once.

(3) Evasive opening

Evasive opening, also known as reserved opening, means that at the beginning of the negotiation, instead of answering key questions raised by the other party definitely, directly or explicitly, we try to avoid revealing too much information and reserve some important information, so that the other party will have a feeling of mystery, then as they are wondering what we intend to do, they will follow our plan, driving the negotiation to the direction we desire and target.

There are some prerequisites for us to use evasive opening strategy: First, we are quite confident about our competitiveness; second, we should be good at deploying resources. Additionally, we should be trustworthy and should not convey false information. Otherwise, once revealed, not only will we be trapped in embarrassment, but also we will possibly lose our good reputation and business.

☞ **Case study 4 – 4**    **(Lure the "big fish" to "bite" and let it "eat")**

Jiangxi A & A Artistic Carving Factory has grown from a small factory which was close to go bankrupt into factory which got a high reputation with a production volume of more than USD5,000 in several years.

One day in 1999, there suddenly came three Japanese businessmen to the factory, who wanted to purchase the shrine items produced in the factory. One of them was from a big company and claimed to purchase all the shrine products of the factory. The over-excited factory leaders thought it over and wondered why the representatives from three companies came to the factory together as if they had made a prior appointment, since these companies originally handled the products from the Republic of Korea and Taiwan China. There had to be some reasons for their sudden visit.

Then, the factory leader arranged the visitors to settle down, but did not give them any replies. Meanwhile, the technology department quickly browsed the latest market information in Japan and found that the wood quality and the craftsmanship of their products were exquisite and superb, but the prices of the products were much lower than those from the Republic of Korea and Taiwan China, which was just the reason why the Japanese rushed here and vied with each other in placing orders.

After getting to know all of these reasons, the factory applied the evasive strategy—allowing the visitors more latitude first to keep tighter reins on them afterwards. At first, they did not pay much attention to the big company; instead, they took advantage of the psychology of the Japanese representatives from the other two companies who were eager to purchase the goods. The Chinese side arranged the guests to visit the exhibition room of their high quality products in the factory and asked them to compare the goods with those from other countries to get better knowledge about the merits of these goods. Furthermore, the factory demonstrated the items and determined their prices one by one according to their quality in the same way that a jeweler sells gold and jewelry, and as a result, the prices increased by two percents. In order to lure the "big fish" to "bite" and let it "eat" more as well, the factory first signed contracts with the two small companies at high prices (but in limited quantities). The large company was afraid to lose the order, and so frequently asked for a talk with the factory leaders and offered prices higher than that of the two small companies for its purchase of all the shrine products of the factory. The quantities of the items they ordered were much higher than those of the two small companies, which shocked the factory leaders, for their proposed orders were several times as much as the productivity of the factory.

The success of the Artistic Carving Factory is mainly due to their active and considerate marketing strategy. Firstly, the quality of their product is the first grade and superb. Secondly, the factory adopted a proper marketing strategy and negotiating order which makes the biggest dealer have a sense of crisis.

(4) Nitpicking opening

Nitpicking opening refers to the way in which at the very beginning of a negotiation, we blame the other party for their bad manners, diplomatic and cultural mistakes severely so as to make the other party feel guilty and nervous, to confuse them, to suppress their requests and to force the other party to make compromises and concessions.

However, nitpicking opening should be used cautiously, taking the actual situation into account. For instance, if we are in a weak position and need the other party's support during a negotiation, then we should handle problems with a little tolerance.

☞ **Case study 4 - 5**　(**American negotiators' nitpicking**)

A large state-owned company from Brazil came to America to purchase a set of large-scale equipment. The negotiation representatives went shopping in the morning and were late for the appointment. When they arrived at the American company, it was 14 : 50 in the afternoon, almost an hour later than the appointed time. The American representatives were very angry and they scolded them for not keeping the time or promise. Time was money and the delay had affected their negotiation with other clients. The Brazilian representatives were guilt of their unpunctuality and made an apology again and again. In the following negotiations, the fury of the American representatives made their partners very embarrassed and unable to bargain with them. Finally the contract was signed and when the Brazilian representatives came back to the hotel, they found that they had lost a great deal due to the price, but it was too late and there was no use to repent.

(5) Offensive opening

Offensive opening refers to the way in which we express our firm attitude through well prepared speech or behavior so as to gain the awe from the counterpart and force them to start the negotiation in accordance with our intention.

An offensive opening will get the negotiation trapped in a competitive, nervous and tense atmosphere from the beginning, and which might hurt the other party easily and affect the ongoing of the negotiation. Therefore, it should be used with great care.

☞ **Case study 4 - 6    (Toyota's attack)**

When first coming into the American market, Toyota Company from Japan wanted to find an American agency to promote the sales of its products because of its ignorance of the American market. When the Japanese representatives went to the negotiation place appointed by an American car dealer, they met with traffic jam and were delayed. The American representatives flew into fury and wanted to obtain more commission and other benefits. The Japanese representatives had no way to go and one stood up and said coldly (taking an offensive posture), "Sorry to have wasted your time because of our delay. However, we did not do it intentionally. We had thought the transportation in America would have been better than that in Japan, but it is really beyond our imagination (playing down the other party's posture), which caused the unpleasantness between us. And we do not want to waste your valuable time anymore. If you doubt our frankness for this, all we can do is to end this negotiation (launching an attack at the other party). As the terms and conditions we offer are very favorable, it will not be difficult for us to find other partners in the US (threatening the other party)."

The American representatives were shocked at what the Japanese representative said. In fact, they did not want to lose this opportunity, and they only intended to threaten the Japanese party, but they failed. Then they pulled in their horns, their anger dispersed, and they began to have the negotiation with the Japanese party at once, even-tempered and good-humored.

## 2. Factors to be considered in applying opening strategies

It should be noted that there are many factors to be considered in applying opening strategies.

What opening strategies should be applied mainly depends on the mutual relations between the two parties and the negotiating power of the two parties.

(1)Mutual relations between the two sides

a. Supposing that there was no cooperation or even no contact between the two sides previously, your first contact with your counterpart should be cautious and serious since you know nothing about the other side; you may leave a good impression of seriousness on your counterpart. Being the case of such a relationship, the main job in the opening stage is to break the strangeness and quell the mentality of guarding against each other. You may apply polite wording and introduce your team members and your enterprise, which can not only lessen the strange atmosphere effectively and leave a first impression of frankness and politeness but also give the two parties some time to know each other. At this moment, it is inappropriate to talk about the subject of the negotiation. You might adopt the strategy of resonant opening.

b. Though it's the first business contact between the two parties, they knew each other in the previous communication and the two sides are not familiar with each other. In this case, it is critical to enhance the relation between the two sides. You may take the initiative to establish a friendly negotiating atmosphere in order to promote the mutual relations. Negotiators can be enthusiastic in language and frank in attitude. You might adopt the strategy of frank opening.

c. If the two sides have had some previous cooperation and the scale and result have been satisfactory, you might adopt the strategy of frank opening since the two sides have known each other quite well. By using frank strategy, you can save time; you can recall earnestly the friendly cooperation and communication between the two parties and can state your points and your expectation frankly. This kind of opening strategy may speed up the negotiation. Surely you can use the strategy of resonant opening.

d. If the two sides are old business friends, but the process and result are not satisfactory, you should be cautious about using opening strategies. You may express your regret for the unsatisfactory mutual cooperation in the past and hope to improve the situation through the new cooperation. You may try to make clear about the attitude and expectations of the other side and get ready for the forthcoming negotiation. Negotiators can adopt different opening strategies like resonant opening, offensive opening or nitpicking opening.

(2) Negotiating power of the two sides

a. If the negotiating power of the two sides is evenly matched, a tense negotiation atmosphere easily occurs, and the two sides might both be on the alert. Under this circumstance, the strategy of resonant opening is a good choice and your tone of language and wording should be enthusiastic and calm.

b. If we are more powerful than our counterpart, we should be confident and aggressive on the one hand; on the other hand, we cannot outmatch the other side and frighten him away, then offensive opening, nitpicking opening or evasive opening might be used according to the actual situation.

c. If we are weaker than our counterpart, we should be proactive in terms of cooperation and be neither humble nor pushy, the strategy of frank opening might be the best choice.

Generally speaking, resonant opening strategy can be used in all kinds of situation, yet we should be prudent and careful enough in choosing offensive opening, nitpicking opening and evasive opening.

## Ⅳ. Statement in the Opening Stage

Statement of opening refers to the perspectives and principles concerning the relevant issues. Before the substantive negotiation, both parties will usually make a formal opening statement to clarify the basic principle regarding the matters on the interest (gains and losses) of both parties from the negotiation. The statement should be concise and brief.

The function of opening statement is to clarify the viewpoints, create advantageous atmosphere for your own party and explore the reactions from the other party. While making the opening statement, the speaker will usually cover the following aspects:

a. Reasons or the goals of the negotiation;

b. Negotiation plan or agenda;

c. Prospect and significance of the cooperation between the two sides;

d. The interest your party hopes to obtain（including the problems of principles that your party will not compromise or yield）；

e. Benefits your party brought to the other party in the previous cooperation if there was any（implying that the other party ought to have the gratitude and make compromises and concessions in turn）；

f. Issues your party wishes to discuss（releasing signals for the potential concession）；

g. The benefits your party has already brought to the other side；

h. Possible opportunities and obstacles for future negotiation.

It should be noted that statement of opening or some statement contents might be omitted or neglected for those informal negotiations.

☞ **Case study 4 – 7** **（Emotional resonance brought by a photo）**

The sales promotion of French Airbus was very difficult in those years because it was just the time of world economic recession. Belna Radijun from the sales department was sent to Air India for the negotiation of the market of airplane and his counterpart was Marshal Lahr, Chairman of Air India. When they met, Belna said, "It's you who makes me have the opportunity to return to my birthplace." Then he introduced his own life experience, and finally took out a photo on which Gandhi, who has the fame of mahatma in India, and a child could be found. He told Lahr, "I was the child. When my parents took me to Europe, we took the same vessel with Gandhi." Thus, the distance between the Air India representative and him was drawn closer by an old photo, and an emotional resonance was generated through Gandhi who was worshiped by all Indians, and the negotiation was very successful.

☞ **Questions for your consideration and discussion**

1. Do you think the opening stage of a negotiation is important?

2. How do you think can people create a good negotiation atmosphere?

3. What are the usual opening strategies? Which one would you like to apply?

4. What factors should be considered for choosing opening strategies?

5. What are the usual contents for a statement of opening?

# 第四章
# 国际商务谈判开局阶段

☞ **案例分析 4—1** （里根的开场白）

美国前总统里根曾经访问复旦大学,在复旦大学礼堂发表演讲。他的开场白紧紧地抓住了与复旦之间的"亲近"关系:"其实我和你们学校有着密切的关系,你们的谢希德校长同我的夫人是美国史密斯学院的校友,照此看来,我和各位同学自然也都是朋友了!"话音刚落,全场鼓掌。短短的两句话就使在场的中国大学生把这位碧眼高鼻的洋总统当作亲近的朋友,接下去的交谈十分热烈,气氛很融洽。

国际商务谈判是双方或多方合作的活动,为了使这种复杂的活动取得更加有效的结果,必须遵循一定的程序。这个程序通常包括四个阶段:开局阶段、报价阶段、磋商阶段和成交与缔约阶段。

谈判的开局阶段是指从双方见面开始到正式谈判开始之前的阶段。在这个阶段,谈判者互相问候,相互介绍,进行非正式话题交流,试探对方的意图或立场,目的是影响谈判的进程,争取使己方在谈判中获得一个有力的地位。

"良好的开端是成功的一半。"开局阶段是谈判的起点,也是双方认识、熟悉的第一步,在很大程度上影响着谈判的进程及谈判的结果。无论是交易或投资、购买或销售,开局的方式和氛围对谈判的进一步发展都具有十分重要的意义。一个有经验的谈判人员往往会试探对方的真诚及合作意愿。可以说,开局阶段会给整场谈判定下一个基调,甚至决定谈判的走向。

## 一、谈判开局阶段的气氛类型

国际商务谈判的开局气氛指的是一方或双方在谈判开始前创造的一种氛围。良好的谈判气氛能帮助谈判顺利进行;相反,不好的谈判气氛会影响谈判的进程,甚至破坏整场谈判。

谈判气氛的种类有很多,其标准也不同。例如,有的谈判气氛是热烈、积极、友好、乐观且富有建设性；有的是坦诚、自然、简洁直接；有的谈判则是在冷淡、对立、紧张、矛盾，或是庄重保留，甚至是拖延、敷衍的气氛中进行的。一些专家把谈判气氛总结为以下三种。

### 1. 高调气氛

高调气氛是指谈判中双方均积极、热情，对谈判的前景持乐观的态度；谈判中令人愉悦的成分占主旋律。通常当一方占了上风，希望能与另一方达成一致时，就要努力营造高调的氛围。

### 2. 低调气氛

低调气氛是指严肃、压抑和沮丧的氛围；是指谈判者情绪低落、态度消极，令人不快的元素居主导地位的气氛。通常当一方仍具有讨价还价的能力但不能获得绝对优势地位时，就必须对另一方施加一些压力，这种情况下可以尝试营造一种低调气氛。

### 3. 自然气氛

自然气氛是指在自然的气氛中，谈判既不活跃也不压抑。双方参加谈判时都保持自然和稳定的情绪。许多谈判是在一个自然的气氛中进行的，我们不需要刻意地营造。这种气氛有助于传达准确、值得信赖的信息。当对谈判对手不甚了解时，往往采用自然的气氛。

## 二、如何创造一个良好的开局气氛

国际商务谈判的主要目的就是要最大限度地赚取利润。因此所有的商人都希望在谈判的开局阶段能创造一个良好的开局气氛。那么怎样才能创造一个良好的开局气氛呢？其实，双方刚一接触，谈判人员的面部表情、眼神、握手的力度和其他行为以及谈话的内容就已经创造出了一种谈判气氛并且会对随后的谈判产生影响，因为对对方的第一印象非常关键，以至于会为整场谈判设立一个基调。总体来说，影响谈判开局局面的因素主要包括谈判人员自身的情况、谈判环境和开场白几个方面。

### 1. 谈判人员自身的情况

谈判人员要具有得体的言谈举止和良好的气质与风度。在谈判开始前，谈判人员要想象与谈判对手即将见面的场景，提前做好见面的准备，比如，在礼仪上是适宜握手还是点头，拥抱还是贴面礼。到达谈判地点后，径直步入会场，以友好坦诚的态度出现在对方面前，展现出大方、庄重、认真的良好精神状态。

#### （1）自然的姿态与表情

谈判人员的姿态与表情应当自然放松、坦诚自信。面部表情可以反映一个人的心态，比如一个人放松还是紧张、自信还是犹豫、情绪高涨还是处于疲劳状态都可以从其面部表情特别是眼神的变化反映出来。自然的面部表情反映一个人的真诚，冷漠的面部表情反映一个人的紧张或狡猾。通常人们第一眼就可以判断出其对手诚实还是狡猾,积极还是消极。

(2) 良好的气质与风度

一个人的气质与风度首先体现在其外表和举止上。开口讲话之前,人的外表和服饰总是会给对方一个强烈的第一印象,因此,得体的着装与化妆就显得非常重要。服装要得体,不能太严肃,也不能太随意,同时需要根据不同的天气、风俗、文化进行适当的调整。还要注意服饰的搭配,色调的协调,从整体上营造出适合谈判的良好气氛。有一点需要强调的是,服饰必须符合自己的特点,比如个头矮胖的人不宜穿白色圆领的衣服。谈判的场合,不宜穿过大、过小、过靓的服装;不宜将领带和领扣解开或挽起袖子;女士也不宜化浓妆。

(3) 得体的言谈举止

从谈判一开始,谈判人员条理分明且符合逻辑的言辞、适度的幽默、恰当的语速与优雅的举止都会马上吸引对方的注意力,会给对方留下一个深刻良好的印象,从而有助于良好开局气氛的形成。

(4) 良好的心态

谈判人员的自信与活力有助于甚至会激发良好的谈判气氛。相反,否定、消极、紧张的心态就会使谈判对方怀疑你的真诚与能力。

2. 谈判环境

谈判环境即谈判地点的选择、谈判会场的布置及座位的安排等。

(1) 谈判地点的选择

如果谈判地点选择在会议室或是谈判室,就说明主人非常重视该场谈判;如选在酒店宾馆,很可能是主人想创造一种热烈友好的谈判气氛;如选在酒店的大厅或是咖啡间,说明主人不太重视客人;如选在露天风景区,所传递的信息是这场谈判很容易达成协议;而如选在主人的家里或别墅,则说明主人希望与客人建立个人的友谊。

(2) 谈判地点的装饰及座位的安排

通常,谈判的气氛比较紧张,因此适宜用柔和的色彩进行会场的装饰,比如,可以摆放鲜花来调节单一的色彩。正式的谈判必需安排谈判人员座位。客人应坐在背靠窗户的位置,而主人应坐在背靠门户的位置。座椅应选择相同规格的,并摆放在谈判桌的两侧。也可安排客人坐在舒适的位置,使他们有宾至如归的感觉。

主人必须了解谈判都需准备什么设备。谈判设备的完备能够帮助谈判顺利进行,主要包括翻译设备、扩音设备和照明设备。如果有多方参与谈判,涉及多种语言的翻译问题时,还需要有完善的同声传译设备。扩音设备中音响的质量和音色也非常重要。同时,照明问题也要格外注意,应保证灯光明亮,但不会使人产生刺眼或疲劳等不良感觉。另外主人可以准备咖啡、茶水或是甜点等。比如咖啡、茶水,不仅仅是为了人们解渴,也有帮助调节气氛、减少紧张的作用。还有,谈判不应被电话或访客打扰。

（3）媒体和公众舆论

一些重要的国际商务谈判还会引起海内外媒体的关注。聪明的谈判者能利用舆论报道为谈判的开局阶段创造良好的谈判气氛。

3. 开场白

开场白可选择一些双方感兴趣的中性话题。在这个阶段，谈判人员不必过于拘谨，可选择一些轻松的话题，找到双方共同感兴趣的话题进行交流。就像体育比赛前的热身运动，开场白对于国际商务谈判是非常必要的。正式谈判开始之前，可选择一些中性的话题，如当地的天气、旅途见闻、某部电影电视剧、个人爱好、笑话或是先前的合作，等等。一方面，话题应当轻松愉悦，能够引起双方的共鸣；另一方面，它们与业务无关，因此有助于建立和谐友好的谈判气氛。

开场阶段双方刚刚见面，所以最好站着进行寒暄、介绍和开场；双方也可分成若干小组，互相交谈。这种中性话题的交流时间不应过长，大约占到整场谈判时间的 5%，只要能活跃气氛、消除紧张就可以了，接下来双方就可进行开场陈述和意见交流了。

## 三、开局策略

开局策略就是谈判人员为了使谈判能有一个良好的开端，使已方能在谈判中处于一个有利的地位而采取的行动或方法。目的是创造一个合适的谈判气氛。

在开局阶段，谈判双方互相了解，并通过各种渠道确定谈判中所要涉及的问题。如何开局以及如何进行下一步会谈并没有严格的规定，但有几种方法可以借鉴：一些有经验的谈判专家建议用与谈判主题完全无关的话题开局。另一些人认为，一个幽默的故事可以减轻和消除紧张。还有人提出，用一些介绍性的说明来阐述谈判的基本原则——各方需要取得的成果，你可能的目的和态度，以及你将如何倾听和评估所有方案和建议。另外，也可以在开局时指出谈判另一方可能从交易中获得的好处。

1. 开局策略的种类

（1）引起共鸣式的开局策略

引起共鸣式的开局策略就是寻找双方共同的观点或双方都感兴趣的话题，以便引起共鸣，使得谈判能顺利进行。心理学研究表明，人们往往喜欢那些与他们分享相同观点的人，并且愿意为那些能够产生"共鸣"或者意见一致的人改变自己的观点。经常采用的共鸣式开局包括协商法、询问法和补充法。

协商法是指我们用友好的语气征求对方的意见，为了朝目标迈进而展开讨论（事实上，我们已经有了清楚的认识），然后我们同意并愿意听从他们的建议（因为他们与我们意见一致）来继续我们的工作。但需要注意的是：当我们同意对方的观点时，我们不应该使对方觉得我方是刻意迎合；相反，我们要让对方觉得我们同意是因为我们认同他们的观点,了解和认可他们的想法。

询问法是指将你的回答设计成问题的形式,诱导对方走向你设定的目标。

补充法是指你寻找机会,将自己的观点加在对方的观点中,并说服他们同意你的想法,为你说话。

## ☞ 案例分析 4—2 　(NBA 引起的共鸣)

这是一家中国汽车公司和美国福特公司举行的一场谈判,美方处于优势地位。谈判前,中方了解到美方的主谈人员喜欢篮球比赛,因此,他们设法找到了当年进行的 NBA 比赛的所有录像,并且利用晚上和周末进行观看。

当中美双方落座,就引进新款汽车事宜开始谈判时,中方的副总裁首先祝贺美方经理所在那个州的球队在 NBA 比赛中取得了胜利,比分是 78 比 63,表现比前一年要好很多。美方经理马上激动了起来:"你喜欢 NBA 比赛吗? 在美国我看了几乎所有的 NBA 比赛,为此我老婆经常抱怨。"中方副总裁说:"因为我看 NBA 比赛,忽略了家务事,我妻子几乎要跟我闹离婚!"美方代表笑着说:"我们的兴趣非常相似——顺便问一下,姚明参加比赛了吗? 他的表现如何?"中方副总裁回答道:"他因为脚伤没有上场。"美方代表说:"非常遗憾! 然而,如果姚明参加了比赛,我们州的队伍会很难打。姚明,了不起! 美国人民非常喜欢他。"

中方副总裁接着说:"姚明是中国的骄傲。我们还有奥运会跨栏冠军刘翔,女子网球双打的世界冠军。"然后他改变了话题:"近年来,中国在体育比赛中取得了举世瞩目的成绩。老百姓,特别是年轻的职业经理和白领都喜欢去健身俱乐部;喜欢野餐、徒步旅行和短期旅游;喜欢网上冲浪,泡酒吧或是去世界旅游;喜欢新生事物。正是由于这个原因,我们想从你们公司引进两款型号的汽车(轿车和有仓门式后背的汽车)。德国的厂家拒绝给中国提供最新款式的汽车,结果他们在中国潜在的多数市场份额都被日本和韩国的跑车生产商占领了,我们非常希望贵公司不要步德国厂家的后尘。"美国谈判代表突然意识到他们的跑车在中国的市场份额还很小,只要他们能马上采取行动,盈利的机会就是他们的。因此,福特公司的代表与中方代表很快就引进新款车型达成了协议。

(2) 坦诚式的开局策略

坦诚式的开局策略是指人们直率地表达自己的意见,以便使谈判有实质性的进展或是取得突破。固定客户间通常采用这一策略,因为可以省去很多礼节,节省时间。人们可以直接提出自己的意见和要求,也可能得到对方更多的信任。

坦诚式的开局策略也适用于谈判力弱的一方。当谈判人员十分清楚彼此的长处和弱点时,坦率地向对方暴露自己的弱点来表明真诚,可以帮助己方获得对方的谅解并留下好印象。

☞ **案例分析 4—3**　（党委书记的坦言）

2000 年 9 月的一天，江苏的一位村支书同外商举行了一场谈判。双方交换名片以后，他发现外商对自己的身份持有强烈的戒备心理，妨碍了谈判的进行。于是，这位村支书当机立断，站起来对对方说道："我是党总支书记，是我们村里的最高领导。我也懂经济、搞经济，并且拥有决策权。到目前为止，我已经建起了很多企业。尽管我们摊子小，与沿海城市相比，我们的条件是差一些，但我们农民实在、质朴，而且劳动力成本和土地成本比城市要低很多。我们愿意与贵方合作。咱们谈得成也好，谈不成也好，至少你这个外来的'洋'先生可以交我这样一个'土'朋友。"寥寥几句肺腑之言，打消了对方的疑虑。外商爽朗地笑了起来，谈判顺利地向纵深发展。

（3）托词式的开局策略

托词式的开局策略也被称为保留式的开局策略，是指在谈判开始时，我们不具体、直接或明确地回答对方提出的关键问题，而是尽量避免太多太快地透露己方信息，有所保留，让对方有一种神秘的感觉。当对方想知道我们打算做什么的时候，他们就会按照我们的计划，推动谈判向我们希望的方向和目标发展。

使用托词式的开局策略有一些先决条件：第一，我们对我们的竞争力很有信心；第二，要善于部署资源。此外，我们应该是值得信赖的，不应该传达错误的信息。否则，一旦被揭露，不仅会使我们陷入尴尬，而且很可能失去良好的信誉和业务。

☞ **案例分析 4—4**　（待价而沽，引大鱼上钩）

江西 A&A 工艺雕刻厂原是一家濒临倒闭的小厂，经过几年的努力，发展为产值 5000 多万美元的规模，在业界享有良好声誉的大厂。其产品打入日本市场，战胜了其他国家在日本经营多年的厂家，被誉为"天下第一雕刻"。

1999 年的一天，日本三家株式会社的老板好像约好的一样在同一天接踵而至，到该厂订货。其中一家资本雄厚的大商社，要求原价包销该厂的佛坛产品。这应该说是好消息，但该厂想到，这几家原来都是经销韩国、中国台湾地区产品的商社，为什么争先恐后、不约而同到本厂来订货？其中必有原因！

于是他们安排三家客人都住了下来，同时技术部门马上查阅了相关的市场资料，得出的结论是本厂的木材质量上乘、技艺高超是吸引外商订货的主要原因，另外，他们的产品价格要比韩国和中国台湾的价格低很多。

因此该厂采用了"待价而沽""欲擒故纵"的托词式的开局谈判策略。先不理会那家大商社,而是积极抓住两家小商社求货心切的心理,把佛坛的梁、榴、柱分别与其他国家的产品做比较。在此基础上,该厂将产品当金条一样争价钱、论成色,使其价格达到理想的高度。首先与小商社拍板成交,造成那家大客商产生失落货源的危机感。那家大客商不但更急于订货,而且想垄断货源,于是大批订货,以致订货数量超过该厂现有生产能力的好几倍。

在该案例中,工艺雕刻厂谋略成功的关键在于其策略不是盲目的、消极的。首先,该厂产品确实好,而几家客商求货心切,在货比货后让客商折服;其次,是巧于审时布阵。先与小客商谈,并非疏远大客商,而是牵制大客商,促其产生失去货源的危机感,这样订货数量和价格才有大幅增加。

（4）挑剔式的开局策略

挑剔式的开局策略是指在谈判的初始阶段,一方严厉指责对方的不良行为或在外交和文化习俗方面的错误,以便对方产生内疚感,制造紧张气氛,迷惑对方,抑制对方的要求,从而迫使对方做出妥协和让步。

然而,考虑到实际情况,挑剔式开局应谨慎使用。例如,如果一方处在弱势地位并且在谈判中需要对方的支持,就应该更宽容地处理问题。

☞ **案例分析4—5**　（美国谈判代表的"挑剔"）

巴西一家国有公司到美国去采购大型成套设备。巴西谈判小组成员因为上午上街购物耽误了时间,当他们到达谈判地点时,比预定时间晚了45分钟。美方代表对此极为不满,花了很长时间来指责巴西代表不遵守时间,没有信用,并且说如果一直这样下去的话,以后很多工作很难合作,浪费时间就是浪费资源、浪费金钱。对此巴西代表感到理亏,只好不断地向美方代表道歉。谈判开始以后美方似乎还对巴西代表来迟一事耿耿于怀,一时间弄得巴西代表不知所措,说话处处被动,无心与美方代表讨价还价,对美方提出的许多要求也没有静下心来认真考虑,匆匆忙忙就签订了合同。等到合同签订完以后,巴西代表平静下来,才发现自己吃了大亏,上了美方的当,但已经晚了。

在该案例中,美国谈判代表成功地使用了挑剔式的开局策略,迫使巴西谈判代表自觉理亏,在来不及认真思考的情况下匆忙签订了对美方有利的合同。

（5）进攻式的开局策略

进攻式的开局策略是指一方通过精心准备的言语或行为来表达其坚定的态度,来获得对方的敬畏,强迫对方按照其意愿开始谈判。

进攻式的开局策略会使谈判从一开始就陷入竞争性的紧张气氛,容易伤害对方和影响谈判进程,所以应该小心采用。

☞ **案例分析 4—6** （丰田的进攻）

　　日本的丰田公司最初进入美国市场时,由于他们不了解美国市场,想寻找一个美国代理推销自己的产品。当日本代表前往一个美国汽车经销商指定的谈判地点时,他们遇到了交通堵塞而迟到了。美国代表因此而发难,想得到更多的佣金和其他的利益。日本代表无路可走。这时,一个日方代表站了起来,冷淡地说(采取了进攻的态势):"十分抱歉,由于我们的迟到而耽误了你们的时间。然而,我们不是故意的,我们本以为美国的交通要比日本的交通好,但却糟糕得超出了我们的想象(采用贬低对方的态势),因而造成了双方的不愉快。我们不想再浪费你们宝贵的时间,如果你们就此怀疑我们的真诚,我们所能做的就是终止这次谈判(发动向对方进攻)。因为我们报价的条款很优惠,我们会很容易在美国再找一个合作伙伴(威胁对方)。"

　　美国代表对日本代表的言辞感到震惊。事实上,他们不想失去这次赚钱的机会,只是想威胁一下日本方面,结果失败了。因此他们原形毕露,没有了恼怒,马上开始与日本方面平和、愉快地开始了谈判。

　　2. 使用哪种开局策略应当考虑的因素

　　使用哪种开局策略主要取决于双方的相互关系和谈判实力的对比。

　　(1) 相互关系

　　①双方第一次建立业务往来,以前从来没有接触过。如果过去双方从来没有过合作与接触,那么第一次的交往应该持一种谨慎和认真的态度。谨慎是由于对对方的不了解,认真可以给对方留下好的印象。在这种关系下,开局阶段的主要工作是打破这种陌生感,淡化双方的防备心理,尽可能使用一些礼节性的语言,还可介绍自己谈判团队的成员,介绍自己的企业情况等。这样不仅可以有效缓和陌生的气氛,不卑不亢地给对方留下诚恳、礼貌的第一印象,而且还能够给双方一定的时间相互熟悉。此时不宜谈论本次谈判的主题,以免给对方操之过急的印象,引起对方不必要的猜疑和不信任。因此,可以采用引起共鸣式的开局策略。

　　②双方第一次建立业务往来,但是以前曾有过接触。这种情况下,双方虽然是第一次建立业务往来,但在以往的交往中已经对对方有一定的了解,双方的陌生感不强,但是关系依然比较淡,关键点在于如何增进双方的关系。此时,可采用主动式的开局策略,尽快增进双方感情,争取一个友好的谈判气氛,把点头之交进一步升级。一般要求语言上做到热情洋溢,内容上可以涉及以往的接触过程,态度上随和自然,逐步过渡到熟悉、友好的气氛中来。可以重点采用坦诚式的开局策略。

　　③双方有过业务合作,合作规模比较大,合作结果双方都比较满意。这种情况下,双

方相互已经非常了解,再加上以往的合作结果比较圆满,开局可以采用坦诚式的开局策略。坦诚式的开局可以节约时间,不必再在相互熟悉上浪费时间,真诚、热情地畅谈双方过去的友好合作关系,坦率地陈述己方的观点以及对对方的期望;坦率地表明己方的立场。这样的开局策略可以加快谈判的进度。也可以采用引起共鸣式的开局策略。

④双方有过业务合作,合作规模比较大,但是合作过程和结果都不尽如人意。这种情况下应谨慎地选择开局策略。可以对过去谈判中双方的不妥之处表示遗憾,并希望通过本次合作能够改变这种状况。此时,不急于拉近关系,用礼貌性的提问来考察对方的态度、想法,了解对方对这次合作的态度,是期待还是带有偏见,通过开局进行观察,并为下一阶段的谈判做好准备。可以根据情况采用引起共鸣式、进攻式或挑剔式的开局策略。

（2）双方的谈判实力对比

谈判双方的实力对比表现为以下几种情况:

①实力相当。在双方实力相当的情况下,容易造成紧张的谈判气氛,双方都有较强的戒备心理。这种情况下,开局阶段应当注意语言和措辞,尽量做到热情和沉稳。可考虑使用引起共鸣式的开局策略。

②实力强于对方。在己方实力强于对方的情况下,开局阶段应该表现出自信和强势,但是又不能过于强势凌驾于对方之上,把对方吓跑,所以需要做到礼貌和威慑并重。可根据实际情况考虑使用托词式、挑剔式或是进攻式的开局策略。

③实力弱于对方。当己方实力弱于对方时,应该在开局表现出积极主动的合作态度,另外还要不卑不亢,避免对方在气势上占据上风。可重点考虑使用坦诚式的开局策略。

总体而言,引起共鸣式的开局策略几乎可以用于任何情况,后三种开局策略（托词式、挑剔式、进攻式的）要谨慎使用。

## 四、开场陈述

开场陈述就是在实质性谈判之前,双方通常还要做出正式的开局声明,澄清重大问题上的基本原则,强调双方的谈判利益（得失）,即双方阐明自己对有关问题的看法和原则。开场陈述的作用是明确观点,创造有利的氛围,试探另一方的反应,为随后开始的谈判奠定双方沟通的基础。开场陈述需要做到简明扼要、重视己方利益。

开场陈述应明确说明双方的意见。开场陈述应包括以下内容:

①谈判目标、双方谈判的原因和理由。

②谈判计划、议程安排。

③双方今后合作的意向及良好的合作前景。

④己方对于开局阶段所讨论问题的理解。

⑤己方希望与对方讨论的问题（释放可能做出让步的信号）。

⑥己方希望得到的利益与保证,包括不会做出妥协或者让步的原则性问题。首要利

益是什么,哪些方面至关重要。

⑦己方可做出让步和商谈的事项。在以前的合作中,己方已经给对方带来的好处(这意味着另一方应该心怀感激而做出妥协和让步)。

⑧接下来的谈判可能会存在的困难和障碍。

值得注意的是,对于一些非正式谈判,开场陈述甚至可以省掉其中一些内容。

☞ **案例分析 4—7**　（照片带来感情共鸣）

因为正值世界经济衰退,法国空中客车公司(Airbus)的推销相当艰难。公司派了销售部贝尔那·拉第峻去印度航空公司谈判飞机销售事宜。谈判对手是印度航空公司主席拉尔少将。贝尔那见到拉尔时说:"是你使我有机会回到我的出生地",然后介绍自己的身世,最后拿出一张相片,是印度有着"圣雄"之称的甘地和一个小孩。他告诉拉尔:"那个孩子是我,当年父母带我去欧洲时与甘地同乘一条船。"就这样,他用一张旧相片同印航谈判代表拉近了距离,再用印度人都很崇拜的甘地与对手产生了感情共鸣,结果谈判非常成功。

☞ **思考题与讨论题**

1. 你认为谈判的开局阶段重要与否?

2. 你认为如何才能创造一个良好的开局气氛?

3. 谈判的开局策略有哪几种? 你愿意使用哪一种?

4. 选择谈判的开局策略应当考虑哪些因素?

5. 开局陈述一般包括哪些内容?

# Chapter 5

# Offer & Counter Offer of International Business Negotiation

☞ **Case study 5 – 1**　(**Offer for Edison's invention**)

Edison, the famous American inventor, obtained a patent for one of his inventions when he worked as an electric technician in a company. The manager of the company intended to buy the patent and asked him about the transfer fee. Edison thought $5,000 would be a good price, but he didn't speak it out. Instead, he said to the manager, "You must have known the value of the patent to the company, so it's better that you offer a price." "How about $400,000?" the manager offered. Of course the negotiation ended smoothly. Edison got an unexpectedly remarkable sum of money, which provided funds for his later inventions.

As stated in chapter 4, offer and counter offer is another important stage in international business negotiations. Soon after the two sides greet and introduce each other, have a prologue and state one's positions, the negotiation will naturally proceed to the process of offer and counter offer.

## I. Who Should Offer First

### 1. Meaning of an offer

An offer, which can be also called a quotation, is the suggestion or the terms and conditions for acceptance in order to conclude a business. It is a notice of the price of certain goods at which the seller is willing to sell. In an offer, the seller not only quotes the price of the goods he wishes to sell but also indicates all necessary terms of sales for the buyer's consideration and acceptance. A formal quotation is equal to an offer. An offer is usually made or sent by the seller. If the buyer sends an offer, it is called a bid. Making a quotation or an offer is the most important and indispensable step in negotiating an export transaction.

So narrowly defined, a quotation is a way to indicate a particular price of a certain item or product, but broadly defined, it involves all that one party proposes for making a business, including commodity name, quality, quantity, price, packing, shipping, payment, even inspection and arbitration, etc. For large projects, it may include forms of cooperation, ratio of capital distribution, profit and loss distribution and the like. Of course, price or ratio of capital distribution and profit distribution are among the most important terms. A quotation or an offer has direct impact on the trend and result of a negotiation and thus it is of vital importance to the success of the negotiation.

Quotation may take two forms: oral or written. International business negotiation mainly takes the form of oral quotation. Oral quotation is characterized as convenient, prompt and flexible.

## 2. Who should offer first

Should I be the first to quote? Complex negotiations have lots of issues to be discussed, but there will inevitably come a time when you have to decide who makes the first concrete offer.

Making the first offer is significant for at least three reasons. First, it gives lots of information to the other side. The other party will learn whether you intend to be more aggressive or friendly and get a chance to size up your offer against his own target. He can immediately get a sense of whether the two of you are likely to come to an easy agreement. Second, once the other party knows your opening offer, he might adjust his own opening offer to be more or less extreme than planned. Adjustment of price in private is much easier than that in public. If you have already made a public opening offer and find it too extreme, you'll have to publicly back up and propose a more conservative opening, you risk confusing or angering the other party. If you have not made an opening offer, nobody will know if you changed it at the last minute. Finally, when the other party adjust his opening offer, he is also likely to be adjusting where the two parties are most likely to make the deal.

So it is often suggested that you should always refrain from quoting first, especially when you are not very familiar with the market. Because when you are not very well-informed about what you are quoting for, you may lose much money which you are supposed to have.

However, if you are well-informed about the pricing range, giving the first offer could be advantageous. First, by indicating the first figure, you have the chance to set the zone of realistic expectations for the deal. Second, social scientists have discovered a psychological quirk that they call the "anchor and adjustment" effect, which refers to a human tendency to be affected by the "first impression" numbers thrown to our field of vision. We tend to make adjustments from these arbitrary reference points.

Actually, quoting first have both advantages and disadvantages. On the one hand, it can make you take the initiative in the negotiation; on the other hand, it will reveal much information to the other side and he may make the relevant adjustment. Therefore, if you are confident that you are quite informed about the market, you can open the bargain yourself. Otherwise, you should let the other side give the first offer and guard against the anchor effect at the same time.

In factual businesses, usually it is the seller, the stronger party and the starter who make the first offer. If you are stronger than the other, usually you can offer first, so that you can put yourself in a favorable position; if you are evenly matched in terms of negotiating power, you might consider to offer first to take an initiative of the consequent negotiation; if you are obviously weaker, you'd better wait and let the other side to offer first. Besides, as per the usual practice, the seller or the organizer of the negotiation should be the first to offer.

## II. Principles of Making an Offer

### 1. How to make an offer（fix a price）

(1) Getting well-informed about the market and setting the range of quotation

It is highly recommended that the negotiators form a general idea about the range of prices before the negotiation and then adjust the quote in response to the actual situation. To set a reasonable range of prices for quotation, the negotiators should assess the situation (i.e. demand and supply) in the national and international markets, learn the price level and offers of their competitors as references, and make sure the prices will cover the cost of the transaction and earn a reasonable profit. By doing so, the negotiators can make an offer which is likely to be accepted.

(2) Setting the bottom line and determining the rock-bottom price

It is very important for a negotiator to make clear about his lowest price target, and he should bear the bottom line in his mind especially in the worst situation. First, it may help to prevent one side from accepting overly-harsh terms and conditions proposed by the other side. Second, it may help one side avoid losing potential benefits. Third, it can make negotiators to be cautious enough so as not to make a careless decision in haste out of a moment's excitement.

（3）Seeking optimum pricing level and determining your offer

After you have acquainted yourself with the market and set the range of quotation and determine the rock-bottom price, it is the time for you to make your decision for the pricing issue in negotiation. You should take all the relevant factors into consideration and select the most suitable price for your offer. Remember that only when your price is accepted by the other party, can it generate the expected effect.

（4）Making favorable comments

Making favorable comments is also very important. When you make your offer, never forget to make favorable comments on your product. For example, what advantages or strong points does your product or item have? And do make some comments on marketing information if it sells good.

Here, it is necessary to mention the so-called passive price and active price. In our daily life, sometimes it is very difficult to define or judge whether a price is high or low. A professor might feel it expensive to spend RMB100 for a blouse but he will not hesitate to spend RMB500 for a set of books. A young man might feel it expensive to spend RMB50 to buy a book but probably he will not mind spending RMB500 for a jacket. Some people might feel it expensive to spend RMB30 to take a taxi but he will not mind spending several hundred for a meal with his friends. In these three cases, the former prices are passive ones, and the latter are active ones. To conduct business negotiation with active price is an effective negotiation skill. If a buyer needs the goods badly, the price will take a back seat to other factors like the time of delivery, quantity and quality. So although price is the core in business negotiation, we should not keep a close watch only on the matter of price. It is very important to demonstrate the merits of a commodity and convert a passive price into an active one so as to achieve the success of a negotiation, which is also worthwhile for all negotiators to think seriously about.

### 2. Principles of making an offer

（1）Reasonableness

Reasonableness is the basic and first principle for making an offer in international business negotiation, that is "to sell dear" (at high price) or "to buy cheap" (at a low price). In other words, the seller should try to present his quotation at the highest price acceptable to the buyer; and the buyer should bid the lowest price the seller can bear. If it is possible, each seller and each buyer attempts to maximize his own potential profit. If a price is offered by a seller, it cannot be raised any more and it would be the top limit.

a. The higher the selling price is or the lower the buying price is, the more leeway you can preserve for your company so that you can take the initiative in the subsequent negotiation.

b. Doing so may exert great psychological pressure on the other side, diminishing their expectations since the quoting price from a seller will be the highest, and it can be only lower and lower.

c. There's a saying "What price, what goods." The price you quote may have an impact on how the other side assesses your strength, your product or your services.

d. The quoting price will have direct and significant impact on the concluding price. Generally, if the quoting price is higher, the concluding price will be higher.

（2）Appropriateness

Appropriateness is another principle for making an offer. To offer a high price certainly means the price should be high at a reasonable and realistic level and comes in line with the prevailing market. In other words, the offer should be based on reasonable profit, not on wild speculations. So negotiators should consider not only the profit they can get if they close the deal at the desired or quoted price, but also the demand and supply of the related commodity in the market and the price level. Therefore, they need to make careful comparisons and tradeoffs time and time again so that they might arrive at a price which best combines the probability that the quotation would be accepted and the desired price.

Yet it should be noted that in factual business, selling high does not mean going beyond a reasonable price; buying low does not mean making an unacceptable offer. That is to say, as long as the price is reasonable and acceptable, the sellers should be bold enough to risk asking a high price and the buyers audacious enough to offer as low as possible.

（3）Artistry

Artistry is the third principle for making an offer. Making an offer is also an art. You should be self-confident, firm, explicit and decisive when making an offer so that you can leave a sincere and earnest impression on the other side. And unnecessary explanation or statement might remind the other side that this is the issue you care most and thus might put you in a passive position.

A. Specific

When you make an offer, you should be explicit and straightforward. It is inadvisable to use ambiguous words like "about," "approximately" and "probably." A specific quotation allows the other party to know your expectations more precisely.

B. Decisive

You ought to be decisive and resolute when you present your quotation. Hemming and hawing should be avoided in an oral quotation; you should speak up clearly. In the case of a written quotation, a prompt reply is always the best policy. Only in this way can you appear capable and experienced. What is more, a prompt reply also indicates that you are confident.

C. No explanation

Once you have made your quotation in a straightforward and specific way without any misunderstanding, you do not need to follow it up immediately with explanations or illustrations, because there is no need for extra talking to explain something logical and reasonable, and it would not be too late for you to add your explanation of how you formulated your price, your calculation basis and methods if the other side should raise these questions.

(4) Principles for price explanation if necessary

After you have quoted your price, the other side will often ask you to explain. The following are the principles you should follow:

a. Do not answer if not asked.

b. Answer actively and clearly if you are asked to explain.

c. Put your emphasis on explaining those essential issues and your answer should be concise and comprehensive.

d. Try to explain orally, not in a written form.

### Ⅲ. Types of Making an Offer

#### 1. Offer dear

That is to offer a high price and leave a large room for bargaining, then to lower the price through granting all kinds of favors such as discount in quantity, discount in terms of payment so as to conclude the business.

#### 2. Offer a rock-bottom

It means a seller offers his lowest price and in the meantime he states the most favorable terms to his own party such as terms of payment and time of delivery. If the buyer asks to change those terms, then the seller will raise the quoted price. The main purpose is to use the lowest price to arouse the buyer's interest and exclude competitors.

### 3. Differentiation

Differentiated quotations are often employed as useful tools for creating more possible business. This strategy allows a company to buy or sell the same product at different prices based on their grades, quantity, delivery destination, shipment, methods of payment and other factors. Furthermore, for repeat business with long-term relationships or big accounts dealing in large quantities, sellers should consider granting a certain percent of price discount. The differentiated quotation is a common quoting strategy in international business negotiations.

### 4. Psychological pricing

(1) Conversion of units of measurement

The actual price is not changed, but is quoted differently through the conversion of the original units of measurement into smaller ones. For example, for sugar at a price of USD5.5 per kilo, the price can be changed to USD2.5 per pound; and for pearl powder at USD32.15 per kilo, the quotation can be USD0.9 per ounce. Though the actual price remains the same, a quotation at a correspondingly smaller unit seems to easily make the buyer feel the price is relatively low, and thus quite acceptable.

(2) Breaking up the whole into parts

The actual price is not changed, but the strategy of breaking up the whole into parts can be used. For example, cigars at USD5 per pack (of 10 pieces) can be quoted as at USD0.5 for each piece. This method easily makes people feel it is quite a bit cheaper.

(3) Decimal fraction

The decimal fraction is used to indicate price in a quotation. It is commonly believed that people have a psychological tendency to see USD99.99 as significantly cheaper than USD100 because many of them see the former as a price in the USD90 range while the later well above USD100. For example, a certain commodity may be priced at USD499 rather than USD500; or a price may be quoted at Euro999.99 instead of Euro1,000.00. In addition, the price is usually shown accurate to two decimal places. These prices ending in an odd number or decimal fractions not only imply to people that there is a discount or it is a bargain, but also convey the notion of high accuracy.

### 5. Midway price changes

Midway price change is also known as provisional shift of price. This is a tactic used when making a quotation with changing the price while negotiation is in process. With a provisional shift of price, the trend of quoted prices suddenly changes and moves in the opposite direction. The purpose of the shift is to win a negotiation. Specifically speaking, this means that when the seller has been reducing the price gradually, he may suddenly and unexpectedly raise the price; or the buyer has been increasing his quotation and then suddenly offers a lower price. This is an abrupt change in the direction the prices are moving. As a result, they may lower the aspirations of the other side by conveying to their counterparts the notion of a change in the market, or perhaps of new competition cropping up. In this way, they may finally persuade the other side to accept their quotation. Surely midway price changes should be used with enough care.

Besides, there are quotations through addition and comparison. The former is to decompose the quotation into several parts or levels respectively and then add these parts or levels together so as to avoid the situation of frightening away the customers with a high quotation. The latter is to present the counterpart with different price lists from different suppliers and make a comparison in terms of property, quality, services and other terms and conditions so that the counterpart might accept the quotation easily.

## Ⅳ. Counter Offer

If an offeree disagrees with the offer from the offeror and makes some changes, the changed offer is called a counter offer. So a counter offer may be defined as a new offer made in response to a previous offer by the other party during negotiations for a final contract. It means that the offeree doesn't completely agree to the terms in the offer. Making a counter offer automatically rejects the prior offer. A counter offer is not legally binding on both parties and the counter-offer process can go on for more than once until the business is finalized or called off.

### 1. Asking for a better price

After one party receives a quotation and thinks it is not in accordance with its targeted aspirations or expectations, it may request the offeror to adjust the price. This practice is referred to as asking a price, which can be either substantive or strategic, or be both substantive and strategic. The party will ask for a new quotation or offer substantively because its counterpart's quotation is too high, with a big gap to its own targeted price, and thus request that the counterpart make a fresh quotation.

(1) Approaches for asking a better price

Different approaches are adopted in different phases of negotiation.

a. In the initial phase, due to inadequate knowledge of the formation and background of the offeror's price, the offeree should choose to ask for an itemized price—refuse the offeror's quotation as a whole and request that the other side make another quotation, that is, renew his offer.

b. In the substantive phase, the offeree should ask for a price with a specific intention. He should identify those obviously unreasonable demands in the offeror's quotation one by one, and then ask the offeror to improve the quotation by reducing an indefensibly-high price to a proper level.

c. In the final phase, upon receiving the offeror's reply to the questions and demands one raised, the offeree should analyze the response and determine whether the quotation has actually been substantively adjusted or not.

(2) Times of asking for a better price and closing indication

As for asking for a price, there is no guideline on the ideal number of times to do so.

a. In an international business negotiation, the quoter usually does not adjust the quotation the first time it is asked by his counterpart. Changing the price immediately upon demand would imply that his initial quotation is padded, or that he is too eager to close the deal. Generally speaking, at the outset, the quoter invariably sticks to his price, indicating reluctance to adjust the price. Or although the quoter may promise to optimize his quotation, he will not make any substantive revision in consideration of strategic demand. As a result, in most cases, the offeree has to request price modification several times before he can break through the defense line of the quoter.

b. On average, a quoter typically makes two concessions before sending out signals indicating that there will be no more concessions. For example, the quoter might firmly claim, "This is the final price!" or may protest, "No, I'll lose too much money if I lower the price any more," or may look pathetic as if he has no way out and is letting you know, "I have tried my best! Then, what price do you think is acceptable to you?"

At this moment, the offeree should not be moved by such words. As long as the quotation is not modified substantively, it still has a large profit margin. The offeree must not rush to close the deal; instead, he should give his own analysis of the factors contributing to the quoted price, and try to find any overestimates or errors in the calculation of the price quoted by the offeror. At the same time, he should judge the limits of his counterpart's authority, the degree of the determination to close the deal, the cooperative relationship between the two parties, and so forth. With full knowledge of all these factors as a solid basis, he can continue to ask his counterpart to offer a more favorable quotation.

c. Occasionally, the offeree can prompt his counterpart with the following questions: Is it possible that the producer is mistaken about the price? Would you please consult the producer and see if they are in a position to lower the price? Could you please ask your superior for more detailed instructions?

(3) Attitude towards asking for a better price

In the process of bargaining, the party who asks a price should argue strongly on just grounds, but at the same time must show due respect to his counterpart. In particular, the following three points should be stressed:

a. Be amiable. As an old saying goes, "Do business with a smile and you will make a pile." Bear in mind that you should try your best to be considerate of your counterpart's feelings, and avoid falling into a deadlock at the very beginning of the negotiation.

b. Talk in a measured and consultative tone. If you exert pressure on your counterpart, you are quite likely to make the negotiation break down. You should choose proper ways to influence your counterpart with skill and patience so as to induce them to reduce their price.

c. Maintain an expectant atmosphere. As a bargainer, you should base your arguments on a well-founded analysis. Your suggestions should be timed so as to open the door to further price cuts before your counterpart can firmly close it. You should make your counterpart feel that you expect and are looking forward to their cooperation.

## 2. Making counter offer

After one party in a business negotiation has made an offer or gives a quotation, it is unusual for the other party to accept it unconditionally. Instead, the offeree, receiver of the offer, may follow it up with bargaining by considering it carefully, and asking the offeror to quote a more acceptable price or make a counter offer, which is the most active, dynamic and vital part of the whole business negotiation. Then, based on the revised quotation, the offeree gives an explicit response. This practice is called making a counter offer. By definition, a counter offer is an explicit quotation in response to the one made by the counterpart who has already revised his quoted price substantively.

(1) Why to make a counter offer

a. Making a counter offer helps to set the bargaining range or settlement range. The counter offer will enable the other party to estimate their counterpart's concession range and then propose a price which might be acceptable. For example, the seller makes an offer and the buyer makes a counter offer. The offer given by the seller sets the upper limits of the bargain and the counter offer by the buyer determine the lower limit. Thus the spread between the resistance points or the bargaining range is established, and the negotiators can start serious bargaining within this range.

b. Making a counter offer helps avoid offending the quoter. If one party repeatedly asks the other party (the quoter) to make concessions, the quoter may feel he is being ridiculed or teased. Especially, after the quoter has made a substantive improvement in his quotation and the other party still refuses to give an explicit response, the quoter will be annoyed.

c. Making a counter offer helps to prove one's sincerity in the transaction. Only by means of a definite counter offer can you indicate that bargaining can possibly be aimed for a deal. The counter offer shows that you would be willing to close the deal at the price that you counter offer.

d. Making a counter offer helps to determine the direction that a negotiation will take. A definite counter offer will enable the counterpart to figure out the tendency and scope of the price movement. As a result, they can decide their next move and know how to make the best response in the negotiation.

(2) How to make a counter offer

With regard to the price range, a counter offer can either be a proportional one or one based on cost analysis.

a. A proportional counter offer refers to a proposal in which one party asks the counterpart to adjust the quotation proportionally—to lower the total price by certain percent.

b. A cost-based counter offer is made on the basis of cost analysis of the items under negotiation, proposing an appropriate price for the counterpart's quotation.

c. Bargain item by item. In a counter offer, equipment of different types can be bargained for separately one by one, or different sets of equipment can be bargained for set by set. Alternatively, each factor in the negotiation such as design fees, material expenses and training fees and such components can be bargained for one by one.

d. Bargain by classifications. The items under negotiation may be classified by models or price range. For example, they can be divided into three classes based on their prices: high-priced, medium-priced and low-priced groups. Then, they can be bargained for one by one, with bargaining emphasis on the high-priced group.

e. Bargain as a whole. A counter offer might be made to bargain over the negotiating subject as a single entity, indicating a total price at which the two parties might close the deal.

（3）Starting point of bargaining

The starting point of bargaining refers to the counter offer, or initial offer with which the buyer responds to the asking price, and terms and conditions one side would like to accept for closing the deal—the first number he will quote to his counterpart. How high should the initial price be? This is directly linked to one's interests and also reflects the negotiation ability and skills of negotiators who make the counter offer.

The principle of setting the starting point of bargain is that it should be low but not too low. On the one hand, a good starting point must be low enough to maximize one's own interests and create enough room for concessions. On the other hand, the starting point cannot be too low or too far below the target point. It must be reasonably close to the acceptable price for the seller. In this way, it can maintain the seller's willingness to negotiate, rather than annoying the seller and placing the buyer in a weaker position.

There are three factors involved in setting the starting point for bargaining:

a. Has your counterpart made any substantial improvement in their quotation after you have asked for a better price?

b. What is the difference between the improved quotation and your desired closing price?

c. Have you planned to make further concessions after your initial counter offer?

(4) Times of countering the asking price and how to determine the bargaining range

There is no fixed optimal number of times for countering the asking price. It mainly depends on how much room is left for making concessions after you make the initial counter offer. On average, the bigger the gap between the counter offer and the asking price is, the more room you have for making concessions and thus the more times you can make concessions. Of course, if there is not a large gap between the asking price and the counter, you can make fewer concessions. In factual business, many people make concessions for about three times.

(5) Tactics of bargaining

a. Throw a stone to clear the road. That is to adopt all kinds of assumptions. Supposing we increase the quantity; supposing we sign a one-year contract; if we are in charge of the transportation; if we buy all of your stock; if we make the payment in advance; under one of the above conditions, what will be your most favorable price?

b. Use alternative solutions of the same value for the change of the counterpart's stand. In other words, get the different permutation and combination with the present terms and conditions.

There is a fable in ancient China named "Three in the morning and four at night" meaning changing one's mind often. It originated from the story of a master raising his monkey. The master gave his monkey three acorns in the morning and four at night, with which the monkey is not satisfied. Later on the master make a different arrangement, four acorns in the morning and three at night, and the monkey is happy. Sometimes, people in the negotiation are the same as the monkey in the story.

☞ **Case study 5 – 2**   (**A farmer selling corn**)

A farmer was selling corn in a market. His corn were so big that they attracted a lot of buyers. While selecting corn, one of the buyers noticed that there were worms on them. Then he made a fuss over the matter, "Hey, man! The corn are big, but there are too many worms. Are you selling corn or worms? I don't think anyone likes worms. You might as well take the corn back home and we would go to others for corn."

While talking, the buyer was making exaggerating and amusing acts which made the other people laugh. On seeing this, the farmer grabbed the corn from the buyer. "Man, you haven't had any corn before, are you? You cannot even tell what the best corn are. The worms on the corn show that the corn are insecticide-free in plantation and that they are healthy food." Then he turned around and said to the other people, "You folks are knowledgeable. Do you believe that the smaller corn, the corn without worms and the more expensive corn are of better quality than mine? If you take a close look at these corn, you'll find that except for the little hole bit by the worms, they are still big and good corn."

Then the farmer turned to the man who deliberately embarrassed him and whispered by the ear, "The corn are so big and tasty that I don't want to sell them at such a low price!"

In his remarks, the farmer cleverly covered all such characteristics of the corn as big, tasty, healthy and cheap, which convinced all of the people present. Therefore, his corn were sold out in a while.

## ☞ Case study 5 – 3　（Midway price changes）

John, an American businessman, went on a trip to São Tomé and Principe. In the window of a leather shop at the roadside, he spotted a leather suitcase with a folded handle identical to his own, which he had left in the hotel. Out of curiosity, John stopped to gaze at it. Seeing John standing outside the window, the shop keeper came out to greet him, and made a wild boast about the suitcase. He tried very hard to persuade John to buy it, but John would not be moved by him. John thought to himself: In any case, I won't buy it. But I'd like to find out how on earth he'll promote the sale. The shop keeper found that John was not interested in it, so he lowered the price again and again, from $30 to $24, $20 to $17, and to $15, but only found John shaking his head with a smile. Seeing this, he abruptly quoted a higher price, " $16 again," changing the trend of the downward price. John opened his eyes wide at once, "But just now, did you say $15? You are pulling my leg, aren't you?" The shop keeper was annoyed, " $15 is my purchase price, and I won't make any money!" "That's impossible!" John said, "Since you've said it was $15, you have to sell it to me at this price!" Although the shop keeper appeared to be reluctant to do so, he was quite happy in his heart that he sold the leather suitcase to John at $15.

## ☞ **Case study 5 - 4**    (**Retreating in order to advance**)

In an art gallery in Belgium, three paintings owned by an Indian were offered at a total price of USD25,000. They took the fancy of an American art dealer. He asked the gallery keeper and the Indian if they could sell him the paintings at a lower price. As he bargained and bargained, the Indian flew into a rage and burnt one of the paintings. The American was shocked and saddened, and asked the Indian how much the remaining two pictures were. The Indian said that they were still USD25,000. The American refused this more expensive demand. The Indian hardened his heart and burnt another painting. The American became anxious and immediately asked him not to burn the last one. When the American asked the price of the remaining painting, the Indian surprised him by quoting a price of USD30,000. Can you guess the result? The deal was done on the spot. The Indian burned the two paintings in a retreat in order to advance and gain more advantage or a greater concession. In this case, this tactic proved to be very effective.

## ☞ **Questions for your consideration and discussion**

1. What are the advantages and disadvantages of quoting first?
2. What are the principles for making an offer?
3. What points should we pay attention to when we fix a price?
4. What are the types of making an offer?
5. What factors should we take into consideration when we make a counteroffer?

# 第五章

# 国际商务谈判的报盘与还盘

☞ **案例分析 5—1** （爱迪生的专利报价）

美国著名发明家爱迪生在某公司当电气技师时，他的一项发明获得了专利。公司经理向他表示愿意购买这项专利权，并问他要多少钱。当时，爱迪生想只要能卖到5000美元就很不错了，但他没有说出来，只是督促经理说："您一定知道我的这项发明专利对公司的价值，所以价钱还是您自己说吧！"经理报价道："40万美元，怎么样？"还能怎么样呢？谈判当然是没费周折就顺利结束了。爱迪生因此而获得了意想不到的巨款，为日后的发明创造提供了资金。

报盘与还盘是国际商务谈判的一个重要阶段。正如第四章所述，通常，在开局阶段双方经过相互问候、介绍、交流并阐述己方立场观点以后，谈判很自然就转入报盘与还盘阶段。

## 一、谁先报价

### 1. 报盘（报价）的含义

报盘，通常也可以称为发盘或报价，是为了成交而提出的建议或条款。报价是卖方准备出售某种商品的一个价格通知，而报盘指的是卖方不仅报出了他愿意出售商品的价格，还标明了其他所有出售商品的条款。一个正式的报价基本等同于报盘。报盘一般由卖方做出，如果报盘由买方做出，则称之为递盘。报价或报盘是出口贸易商务谈判中一个最重要的不可缺少的步骤。

商务谈判中的报价，狭义的概念是指报出某种商品的价格，而广义的概念是指谈判一方向另一方提出自己要求的总称和过程，通常包括商品的名称、质量、数量、价格、包装、装运、支付等交易条件。对于大型工程，报价包括合作的形式、资金分配和盈亏分配的比率等。通常，报价并非单指价格，还包括与谈判有关的各种交易条件。报价直接影响谈判的走势和结果，事关谈判者最终获利的多少，是关系到商务谈判能否成功的关键所在。

报价包括口头报价和书面报价。国际商务谈判主要采用口头报价的形式,因为口头报价方便、迅速、灵活。

2.谁先报价

商务谈判的议题很多,有时候就面临谁先报价的问题。我应该率先报价吗? 率先报价,影响深远,其原因有三:首先,它为对方提供了大量的信息。另一方能获悉你是打算采用进攻的态度还是友好妥协的态度,并且有机会抓住你的报价来实现自己的目标。对方也会马上意识到你们双方是否有可能轻易地达成协议。其次,一旦对方知道你的开价,他就能够调整自己的开价,私下调整价格要比公开调整容易得多。最后,当对方调整了自己的开价后,他就可能调整了双方最终可能达成的价格。

因此,人们常常认为,永远不要率先报价,特别是当你对市场不是非常熟悉的时候。当你不了解标的物时,率先报价可能会使你遭到损失。

然而,如果你非常了解议价的范围,率先报价也可能是有利的。首先,通过提出第一个数字,你就会设定交易的现实期望区。其次,社会科学家已经发现了一种心理怪癖,他们称之为"锚定和调整"效应,是指人们往往容易被第一个进入我们视野的数字所影响。我们往往从这些主观的参考数值出发,进行调整。因此,如果你自认为对市场非常了解,你可以率先报价。否则,你应该让对方给出第一个报价。

报价的先后是一个微妙的问题,率先报价有一定的优势,也容易暴露出一些问题。优势在于:率先报价者容易掌握谈判的主动权,为报价划定一个基准框架,对谈判的影响大。若价格出乎对方预料,可以打乱对方的谈判战略部署,动摇对方的信心,从而掌握谈判节奏并取得谈判的胜利。弊端在于:泄漏己方的底线和价格范围,对方在了解我方起点的基础上,可适当做出价格调整,从而获得本来得不到的一些利益。既然率先报价有利亦有弊,那么我们该如何处理呢? 具体来讲要注意以下的问题:

①谈判实力。如果谈判实力强于对方,居有利地位,可率先报价。如果双方谈判实力相当,可率先报价,占据主动。如果谈判实力弱于对方,缺乏经验,就让对方率先报价,以便观察调整,以静制动。

②惯例法。按照惯例来讲,卖方率先报价,也可以由谈判的发起人率先报价。

## 二、报价应当遵循的原则

1.如何确立报价

(1)掌握行情是基础

谈判人员应事先对所报商品的价格有充分的了解,才能更好地报出价格。要对标的商品的国内行情和国际行情,特别是供求关系进行充分了解,也包括了解竞争对手的价位,从而使你的报价比较合理,而且有可能被接受。

（2）确定最低的可接纳的水平

谈判人员应首先明确底价，避免接受对方过于苛刻的条件，失去潜在的利益，还可避免心血来潮做出匆忙的决定。

（3）寻找最佳价位并确立报价

掌握了行情，确立了底价，就可以确定你报价的价位了。谈判人员应考虑到各种因素以确定最合适的价位。记住：你的报价只有被对方接受才具有实际的意义。

（4）要对你的产品做出有利的评价

报价的同时对你的产品进行有利的评价是至关重要的。一定要详细描述你所报商品的优点和功能；如果所报商品比较畅销，还可对市场行情进行一番评论。

这里有必要对消极价格与积极价格进行说明。在日常生活中可以发现，价格的高低有时很难界定，常带有浓厚的主观色彩。一个教授可能觉得花 100 元买一件衬衫很贵，但花 500 元买书却毫不犹豫；一位年轻人不肯花 50 元买本书，但花 500 元买一件衣服也不会心疼；有人舍不得花 30 元打出租，但却愿意花几百元请人吃饭。在这三种情况下，前面的价格说明当事人对价格的反应及行为消极，属于消极价格；而后面的价格，表明当事人对价格的反应及行为积极，便是积极价格。运用积极价格进行商务谈判，是一种十分有效的谈判技巧。谈判中常常会有这种情形，如果对方迫切需要某种货物，他就会把价格因素放在次要地位，而着重考虑交货期、数量、品质等。因此，商务谈判中尽管价格是核心，但绝不能只盯住价格，就价格谈价格。要善于针对对方的利益需求，开展消极价格向积极价格的有效转化，充分展示商品的优点，从而赢得谈判的成功。这是值得所有谈判人员认真思考的问题。

### 2. 报价应当遵循的原则

（1）合理性原则

对卖方来讲，开盘价必须"是最高的"，而对买方来讲，开盘价必须是"最低的"，这是报价的首要原则。首先，若我们为卖方，开盘价为我方的要价确定了一个最高限度。一般来讲，除特殊情况外，开盘价一经报出，就不能再提高了。最终双方成交的价格肯定在此开盘价格以下。若我们为买方，开盘价为我方的要价确定了一个最低限度。同样，没有特殊情况，开盘价也不能再降低，最终双方成交的价格肯定在此开盘价格以上。其次，从人们的观念上来看，"一分钱一分货"是多数人信奉的观点。因此，开盘价的高低，会影响对方对己方提供的商品或劳务的印象和评价。再次，开盘价较高，能够为卖方以后的讨价还价留下充分的回旋余地，使卖方在谈判中更有主动性，便于掌握成交时机。第四，开盘价的高低往往会对最终成交水平产生实质性的影响，即开盘价高，最终的成交价相对较高；开盘价低，最终的成交价也相对较低。

（2）综合性/适度性原则

作为卖方，开盘价要报得高一些，但绝不是漫天要价，而是高的同时还应合乎情理。如果报价过高，超出常理，又没有足够的理由，会让对方认为缺少诚意，或者被逼无奈而中止谈判,或者相对地"漫天要价",或者提出质疑,而又无法解释,其结果只能是被迫无条件地让步。在这种情况下,即使卖方已将交易条件降低到较公平合理的水平上,对方仍会认为尚有"水分"可挤,因而还会穷追不舍。因此,报价时,不仅要考虑按照自己的报价所能获得的利益,还需要综合考虑该报价能否被对方所接受。只有被对方所接受的价格才具有实际的意义。

(3) 艺术性原则

报价是一门艺术,报价人应该充满自信,报价时应该坚定、明确、果断,这样可以给对方留下认真诚实的好印象。任何欲言又止、吞吞吐吐的行为都会给对方带来不良感受,甚至会使对方产生不信任感。因此,开盘报价要明确、清晰而完整,以便对方能够准确地了解己方的期望。此外,报价时不要对己方所报价格作过多的解释、说明或辩解,因为对方不管己方报价的水分多少都会提出质疑。如果是在对方还没有提出问题之前,便主动加以说明,会提醒对方意识到己方最关心的问题,而这些问题很可能是对方尚未考虑到的。因此,有时过多地解释和说明反而会成为对方从中找出破绽或猛烈反击的突破口,甚至会使己方十分难堪,无法收场。

①具体。报价时应做到清楚直接,最好不用模糊的字词,如"也许""大概""可能"等。一个具体的报价可以让对方更精确地了解你的期望值。

②果断。报价时应做到坚决果断,不能犹豫,不能支支吾吾。迅速清楚地报价会使你在对方面前呈现出有能力、有经验、有自信的形象。

③无须解释。一旦你直接、具体、毫无疑义地报出了价格,根本就不需要进行解释。因为对合理、富有逻辑性的东西没有必要解释。如果对方就你如何拟定价格及你计算的基础和方法向你提问时,你再解释也不迟。

(4) 进行价格解释时需遵循的原则

在谈判双方中的一方完成报价后,另一方会要求进行价格解释。在进行价格解释时需要遵循以下的原则:

①不问不答。是指对对方不主动问的问题,报价方不要主动进行价格解释。

②有问必答。当对方提出疑问时,要给予积极的解答,不能含糊其辞,也不能故意隐瞒,吞吞吐吐。

③避虚就实。进行价格解释时应该注重实质问题的解答。回答应该言简意赅,不要在水分大的地方浪费时间。

④能言不书。能用口头解释和说明的,就不要用文字来书写。

## 三、报价的种类

### 1. 报高价

报高价也称欧式报价方式,是指卖方提出一个高于本方实际要求的谈判起点来与对手讨价还价，最后再做出让步从而达成协议的谈判策略。其模式是卖方报价虚头较大，根据买卖双方的实力对比和该笔交易的外部竞争状况，通过给予各种优惠来逐步软化和接近买方的市场条件，最终达成交易。

## 2. 报低价

报低价也称日本式报价方式。卖方报出最低价格，并列出对卖方最有利的结算条件。如果买方要求改变有关条件，则卖方就会相应提高价格。这种报价方式的主要目的在于用最低价引起买方的兴趣，排斥竞争对手。

## 3. 差异化报价

差异化报价是指在商务谈判中针对客户性质、商品的不同等级、不同的购买数量、交易时间、支付方式，以及不同的目的港口等因素，报出不同的价格。另外，针对重复订单和长期友好的业务关系，卖方还可考虑给予价格折让。差异化报价是国际商务谈判中经常使用的报价方式和策略。

## 4. 按人们心理的定价方式

### (1) 转换计量单位报价策略

实际价格不变，但通过转换成更小的计量单位报价。例如，白糖每千克 5.5 美元，可以转换成每磅 2.5 美元；珍珠粉每千克 32.15 美元，可以转换成每盎司 0.9 美元。尽管白糖和珍珠粉的两个价格实际上是一样的，但转变成更小的单位后很容易让买方感觉价格相对便宜了，更容易被买方接受。

### (2) 除法报价策略

实际价格不变，但使用化整为零的方法，即以商品价格为除数，以商品的数量或使用时间等为被除数，得出一种数字很小的价格，使买主对本来不低的价格产生一种便宜、低廉的错觉。例如，一盒(10 根)香烟 5 美元，可以报价每根 0.5 美元。这种方法也容易使人感到便宜。

### (3) 十进制的小数报价策略

使用十进制的小数标明报价中的价格，即利用人们的心理报价。例如人们普遍觉得99.99 美元比 100 美元便宜，因为很多人会觉得前一个数是 90 多美元，而后一个数则上了100 美元。同样，人们可能会报价 499 美元，而不是 500 美元；或报价 999 欧元，而不是1000 欧元。另外，前者的数字显得更为精确并给人一种经过认真计算过的感觉。

## 5. 中途改变报价

中途改变报价也称为临时变动价格，是谈判过程中的一种报价方式。即突然改变报价趋势，向相反方向发展的一种报价，目的是为了能够成交。具体来说，就是当卖方的报价越来越低时，突然出人意料地提高价格，或当买方的递盘价格越来越高时，突然报出了一个更低的价格。这种价格上的突然变化，会降低对方的期望值，使之更接近市场或竞争对手的价格,从而达到说服对方接受报价的目的。当然使用这种报价方式要谨慎。

此外,还有加法报价和对比报价。加法报价是指在商务谈判中,有时怕报高价会吓跑客户,就把价格分解成若干层次渐进提出,使若干次的报价最后加起来仍等于当初想一次性报出的高价。对比报价是指向对方抛出有利于己方的多个商家同类商品交易的报价单,设立一个价格参照系,然后将所交易的商品与这些商家的同类商品在性能、质量、服务与其他交易条件等方面做出有利于己方的比较,并以此作为己方要价的依据。

## 四、还盘(还价)

当受盘人不同意所收到的报盘的内容并且做出了一些修改变动,修改后的报盘就被称为还盘。还盘就是在谈判中不完全同意发盘的内容,为回复对方的发盘而做出的一项新的发盘。一项发盘一经还盘就失去了效力,还盘没有法律的约束力,可以进行多次,直至双方成交或谈判失败。

### 1. 要求报更好的价格

当一方收到另一方的报价并认为报价不符合预期,通常会要求报价人调整价格,即报出一个更好的价格。这种要求或许是真实的,或许是策略性的,也或许二者兼而有之。一方常会因为对方的报价太高,与己方的要求差距过大,因此要求报一个新的更好的价格。

(1) 要求报更好的价格的路径

在谈判的不同阶段要求报更好的价格的路径是不一样的。

①在初始阶段,由于对卖方价格背景信息的缺乏,买方会选择询问某个具体的价位。并从总体上拒绝卖方的报价,要求卖方重新报价。

②在实质性阶段,受盘人要求对方降价一定会有具体的意向。将对方明显不合理的需求一个个指出来,并要求对方将价格降到合理适中的价位。

③在最后阶段,当收到对方对所提问题的回复后,应对其进行分析并明确价格是否已经进行了实际性的调整。

(2) 要求调整价格的次数,表明成交的意愿

要求对方报更好的价格的次数,在理论上没有规定。

①在国际商务谈判中,报价人第一次被要求调整价格时通常不会调整。如果调整了就意味着最初的报价水分太大或是过于急于成交。一般而言,报价人开始总是坚持自己的报价,不愿调整价格。或报价人尽管承诺会优化报价,但出于策略的需要也不会做出实质性的调整。因此,在大多数情况下,需要多次要求报价人调整价格才行。

②平均来说,报价人会做出两次让步并且告知再也没有余地了。例如,报价人会坚称"这是我们最终的价格"或"不能再降了。如果再降价就亏太多钱了",或者会显露出为难之情,"我已经尽力了,那你能接受什么价?"

此时,讨价方不能被这些言辞所动,而急于成交。只要报价还没有进行实际性的修

改，就意味着报价仍有很大的利润空间。此时一方应分析各种影响报价的因素，找出价格估算的高估或失误之处，同时，应判断对方的权限，达成协议的意愿程度以及双方的关系，等等。在充分考虑这些因素的基础上，继续要求对方报出更优惠的价格。

③有时，讨价方可以问对方这样一些问题，比如：生产厂家是否把价格搞错了？能否再跟厂家联系一下，看能不能把价格降低一些？能不能请示一下你们的领导？

（3）讨价的态度

在讨价的过程中，讨价方应当理由充分，立场坚决，同时对对方应表示出应有的尊重。特别强调以下三点：

①与人为善。牢记应尽量体谅对方的感受，避免谈判一开始就陷入僵局。

②用慎重商量的语气交谈。如果你想给对方施加压力，谈判就有可能破裂。应当有耐心，选择合适的方式说服对方降低价格。

③保持一种期待（成交）的气氛。作为讨价方，理由要充分。你的建议要与谈判的进展同步，要让对方感觉到你期盼与他们合作。

2. 还盘（还价）

商务谈判中，一方报价后，另外一方一般不会无条件接受。相反，受盘人一般会讨价还价，要么要求报价人报出更优惠的价格要么进行还价，这是整个商务谈判中最重要、最具活力的部分。还盘就是针对一方报价或已经修改了的报价的明确的回复（新的报价）。

（1）为什么要进行还盘

①还盘有助于设立讨价还价或成交的区域。还盘可以使谈判的对方预估谈判的让步幅度，并且建议可能被接受的价格。例如，卖方发盘买方还盘的情况下，卖方的发盘就设定了讨价还价的上限，而买方的还盘则设定了讨价还价的下限。谈判双方就可在这个价格区间进行讨价还价。

②还盘可以避免冒犯报价人。当一方反复要求对方（报价人）做出让步时，报价人可能会有被愚弄的感觉。特别是当报价人已经在原报价的基础上进行了实际性的改进，而对方还不做出明确的回应，报价人可能就会恼怒。

③还盘可以证明一个人在交易中的诚意。只有通过明确的还盘，随后才可能进行讨价还价，进而达成交易。还盘意味着你愿意在还盘的价位上与对方成交。

④还盘有助于确定一场谈判的走向。一项肯定的还盘能使对方知晓谈判的走向和价格的幅度。由此对方能决定下一步的动作，明确如何最好地回复对方。

（2）如何进行还盘

有关价格幅度，还盘可以是（在原价基础上的）百分比，也可以是基于成本的分析。

①按百分比还盘。即谈判的一方建议另外一方按照百分比调整降低报价。

②基于成本的还盘。就是谈判中就商品的成本进行分析，提出一个合适的价格。

③逐项（条）讨价。还盘中，不同种类的设备、商品可逐个（套）进行。谈判中的每个因素，比如设计费、材料费、培训费等都可逐条进行还价。

④按照规格讨价。谈判中的名目可以按照模型或价格幅度分类。例如，可按照其价位分为三个级别：高价位、中价位和低价位。然后按每种价位进行还价，并以高价位作为重点。

⑤通盘进行讨价。还盘还可以将整场谈判的内容作为一个整体进行讨价，从而达成交易。

（3）讨价的起点

讨价的起点指的是一方为回复原发盘或还盘而做出的愿意与对方达成交易的条款，即一方报出的第一个价位或条款。这个价位的高低将直接与其利益相关，也反映谈判人员在还盘时的能力与技巧。

设置讨价起点的原则应当是低价位，但不能过低。一方面，一个合适的讨价起点应当足够低，能够使己方的利益最大化，并留下足够的让步空间。另一方面，这个起点又不能过低，距己方的目标点太远。起点价必须足够合理，接近卖方可接受的价格。这样就可使卖方继续谈判，而不会使其恼怒，以致使买方处于一个劣势地位。

讨价应考虑的三个因素：

①对方在你要求报出更好的价格后是否已经做出了实质性的改进？

②对方改进后的报价与你设想的成交价的差距有多大？

③你还盘以后是否还打算做进一步的让步？

（4）讨价的次数及如何确定讨价的幅度

讨价没有固定的、最优的次数，它主要取决于你第一次还盘以后进行让步的空间。总体而言，报价与讨价之间的差距越大，让步的空间越大，让步的次数就越多。当然，如果两者之间的差距不大，让步的次数就会减少。现实业务中，让步三次左右的情况居多。

（5）讨价还价的策略

①投石问路。你可以提出各种假设，例如，如果我们增加数量；如果我们签订为期一年的合同；如果我们负责运输；如果我们买下你们全部的库存；如果我们预付货款。在以上任何一种假设的情况下，你们最优惠的价格是多少？

②以同等价值的替代方案换取对方立场的松动。也就是用现有的条件进行不同的排列组合。

中国古时有一则寓言"朝三暮四"。说的是主人给猴子定量进食的故事：主人早晨给猴子吃三只橡子，晚上吃四只，猴子不满意；于是主人重新做了安排：早四只晚三只，猴子很满意。人在谈判中有时也是如此。

☞ **案例分析 5—2** （农夫卖玉米）

　　一个农夫在集市上卖玉米。因为他的玉米棒子特别大，所以吸引了一大批买主。其中一个买主在挑选的过程中发现很多玉米棒子上都有虫子，于是他故意大惊小怪地说："伙计，你的玉米棒子倒是不小，只是虫子太多了，你想卖玉米虫呀？可谁爱吃虫子呢？你还是把玉米挑回家吧，我们到别的地方去买。"

　　买主一边说着，一边做着夸张而滑稽的动作，把众人都逗乐了。农夫见状，一把从他手中夺过玉米，面带微笑却又一本正经地说："朋友，我说你是从来没有吃过玉米吧？我看你连玉米质量的好坏都分不清。玉米上有虫，这说明我在种植中没有使用农药，这玉米是天然食品，连虫子都爱吃，可见你这人不识货！"接着，他又转过脸对其他人说："各位都是有见识的人，你们评评理，连虫子都不愿意吃的玉米棒子就好吗？比这小的棒子就好吗？价钱比这高的玉米棒子就好吗？你们再仔细瞧瞧，我这些虫子都很懂道理，只是在棒子上打了一个洞而已，棒子可还是好棒子呀！"

　　他说完了这一番话，把嘴凑在那位故意习难的买主耳边，故作神秘状，说道："这么大、这么好吃的棒子，我还真舍不得这么便宜地就卖了呢！"

　　农夫的一席话，把自己卖的玉米棒子个大、好吃、天然、售价低这些特点都表达出来了，众人被他说得心服口服，纷纷掏钱购买，不一会儿工夫，农夫的玉米销售一空。

☞ **案例分析 5—3** （中途提价）

　　美国商人约翰到圣多美和普林西比去旅行。在街边一个皮革商店的橱窗里，他看到了一个折叠手柄皮箱，和自己放在酒店里的一模一样。出于好奇，他停下了脚步，端量着箱子。看到约翰站在窗外，店主便出来打招呼，并且对箱子夸奖了一番。店主使尽浑身解数想说服约翰买箱子，但约翰都不为之所动。约翰心里想，无论如何，我都不会买这个箱子，但我想看看，他到底会怎么进行推销。店主看到约翰对箱子不感兴趣，就一再降价，从30美元，降到了24美元，20美元，17美元，最后降到了15美元，但只见约翰微笑着摇着头。有鉴于此，他突然报出了一个高价"还是16美元"，改变了价格一直向下的趋势。约翰马上睁大了眼睛说："刚才你不是说15美元吗？你不是开玩笑吗？"店主恼怒了："15美元是这箱子的成本价，我根本就不挣钱！""那不可能！"约翰说，"既然你说价格是15美元，就必须将箱子以15美元马上卖给我！"尽管店主表面上显得不情愿，但他以15美元把皮革箱卖给了约翰，内心却很高兴。

☞ **案例分析 5—4　（以退为进）**

　　在比利时的一家美术馆,一个印度人带来的三幅画总共报价 25000 美元。一个美国艺术商非常喜欢这三幅画,就问艺术馆的人员及这个印度人能否便宜一点。随着美国人一次次的讨价还价,印度人勃然大怒,烧掉了其中的一幅画。美国人非常震惊和悲伤,问印度人剩下的这两幅画多少钱。印度人说还是 25000 美元,美国人自然拒绝了这个更加无礼(更贵)的要求。印度人狠了狠心,又烧掉了另一幅画。这时美国人非常焦急,马上请求印度人千万不要烧最后一幅画了。美国人问剩下这幅画的价格时,印度人令人吃惊地报出了 30000 美元的价格。你能猜出结果吗? 当场成交! 印度人烧掉了两幅画以退为进,获取了更大的利益。这个案例中,这个策略非常有效。

☞ **思考题与讨论题**

　　1. 先报价的优缺点各是什么?

　　2. 报价有哪些原则?

　　3. 如何确定报价?

　　4. 报价的种类有哪些?

　　5. 还盘应考虑哪些因素?

# Chapter 6

# Bargaining of International Business Negotiation

☞ **Case study 6 – 1**    (**Buying apples**)

It was the season of picking apples. A purchaser from a fruit company came to an orchard and asked the orchard owner, "What is the price per kilo?" "10 Yuan." "Is it OK for 8 Yuan?" "No, it is the rock-bottom price." The purchaser shook his head and left. Then there came another purchaser. "What is the price per kilo?" "10 Yuan." "What is the price for the whole basket?" "We don't sell by basket; it is 10 Yuan per kilo." The purchaser was in no hurry to make a bargain, but open the basket cover unhurriedly. He took up an apple, weighing in his hand and scrutinizing it. He said without haste, "The size of the apples is OK, but the color is not red enough, and this kind of apple cannot be sold at a good price!" Then he stretched out his hand into the basket, fumbling for a while, and drew out a smaller apple, "Sir, the apples on the surface of the basket are bigger ones, but there are many smaller ones in the bottom. How do you price the smaller ones?" While he was talking, he picked up an apple from the basket. "Look, some apples have been bitten by insects. Your apples are not red enough, big enough and cannot be classified as first-class apple." This time the seller could not keep silent and speak politely. "If you really want to buy, please make a counter offer." At last, the two sides concluded the business at a price of 9 Yuan per kilo.

In the above case, the first purchaser's counteroffer was refused, and the second purchaser could conclude the deal at a lower price. The most important reason is that the second purchaser adopted a nitpicking tactics of making a counteroffer and put forward the defects of color, size and quality and just to the point.

Bargaining stage, also called consultation stage or stage of making concessions, is the most complicated and pivotal stage for business negotiation. Usually it is the period the relevant parties invest most of their time and vigor since it is a process of consulting all material items, a contest of mutual strength, intelligence, technology and a process of understanding and cooperating with each other. In many cases, it is a tough and seesaw battle and is the most difficult and most important period in the negotiation. Whether the participants in a business negotiation can make any profit and how much profit they can make depends on the skills and strengths they employ in the bargaining phase.

## Ⅰ. Strategic Approaches and Considerations in Negotiating Consultation

### 1. Five strategic approaches in negotiation

The so-called strategic approaches are the attitudes negotiators adopt in negotiating consultation. Because of the different cultural background and education, everyone has his own unique negotiation style when it comes to dealing with conflicts. For example, some people are aggressive, dominating; some are inflexible, competitive; and some are dishonest; there are also people who are constructive, compliant and co-operative. According to Thomas and Kilmann (1974) (qtd. in: 罗立彬, 2013), these different approaches can be grouped into five distinct categories: collaborating, compromising, accommodating, controlling and avoiding.

### 2. Strategic considerations

Usually there are five considerations which will influence the strategy one might use in the process of business bargaining: repeatability, strength of both parties, importance of the deal, time scale and negotiation resources.

(1) Repeatability of a negotiation

Repeatability has an important influence on the styles and tactics of a negotiation. If it is a series of deals with one organization, there needs to be goodwill and lasting relationships with that organization, and a personal relationship is essential. If, on the other hand, the negotiation is for one time dealing with an organization not likely to be met again, then the situation is strategically different. It is not necessary to have the same concern to establish goodwill. Thus the first strategic consideration is the repeatability of the deal. If it is likely to be a repeat business, the first strategy (cooperating) mentioned beforehand can be a good option in the negotiation.

(2) Strength of negotiating parties

The second influence is each party's strength. If a party is the only dealer with whom a deal could be made，this party is in a strong position. If there are many potential competitors，this party is in a relatively weak position. Both the styles in which a party operates and the personalities of those who negotiate on their behalf will influence the choice of strategy by the opposing team. The second party's strength is the converse of the first. The second party is strong if they can dominate a market either as buyers or sellers，and weak if they are just one of many.

(3) Importance of a deal

The importance of a deal is a critical factor. If a negotiation is about a deal worth millions of dollars，the strategy needs to be different from that with thousands of dollars. Or negotiating a deal for a well-established product in a well-established market requires less strategic concern than launching a new product into a new market.

(4) Time scale

In an international business negotiation，the time scale for a deal may also influence the strategy. If it is imperative that the deal be concluded quickly，the negotiation strategy would surely be different from what it would be if there is little urgency. In the former case，the powerful side might choose "controlling" strategy while the weak side might give up (if the agreement to be reached leads to loss on its side or the conditions are unacceptable) or use "avoiding" or "accommodating" strategy.

(5) Negotiation resources

Negotiation resources may also influence strategies one might use. If there are few qualified negotiators but many projects to be negotiated，the negotiators cannot be spared for long periods on any one deal.

These are not the only strategic considerations. It's not possible to generalize about the special situations. However，these general considerations will basically influence the choice of strategy.

## Ⅱ. Bargaining Tactics

### 1. Striking weakness

You point out the unreasonable or impractical parts of the quotation raised by the other party，or any part which is not well-founded. You focus on these issues until your counterpart makes a new substantial concession.

## 2. Observing

During the bargaining process, you should keep a close eye on your counterpart's mood and guess his thoughts. What might be his next action? How far the other side might go and how much concession can he make?

## 3. Being flexible and well-prepared

Negotiators should be fully aware of the difficulties and criticality and get fully prepared. Just like the cards you have in your hand, you should know clearly about the items you might negotiate with the other side. You need to work out a few bargaining plans to choose from, identifying which should be held firm, which could be flexible, and how much flexibility you should allow. When both you and your counterpart refuse to budge over key issues, you can turn to the more flexible aspects and draw your counterpart's attention to them.

## 4. When to begin your bargaining

When both of the two sides have the intention to bargain, or the two sides have reached the agreement for future cooperation, it is the time to enter into the stage of consultation. This agreement is very important since obviously one single party cannot conduct bargaining. For example, "We have adjusted our price many times, and it is your turn to have some move." "We have also improved the price more than once, even to a greater extent than you do. Why do you only ask us to improve?" "Let's make efforts together to solve the problems." All these mean the bargaining stage will soon begin.

## 5. Allocation of your negotiating items

Pay attention to the following two points when allocating your negotiating items: Take everything into consideration, and consolidate step by step for your goal. Keeping the negotiating items confidentially is of vital importance. Negotiators should control their facial expressions so as not to reveal any secret. If happiness easily appears on your face when you succeed or scratch your ears and cheeks when feeling embarrassed, the other side can detect your thoughts easily.

## Ⅲ. Principles of Making Concessions

Making concessions is absolutely very important and indispensable to international business negotiations. In a sense, negotiations consist of only two parts: demanding and giving, which can be explained as asking the other side to make concessions and making concessions to the other side. Making concessions is no doubt necessary, but before making the concession, negotiators should think it over. Is it the right time to make concessions now? How should we make the concessions? What benefits can the concessions bring about? The general principle for making concession is to exchange a bigger interest with a smaller one.

### 1. Do not propose to make concessions easily

Experienced and intelligent negotiators will not propose to make concessions easily. Because though you might have taken up a favorable position in a negotiation, the concession you've made may boost up the confidence of the other side, and you will probably lose the initiative of the negotiation.

(1) Do not make concessions blindly

Before you have a clear picture of your counterpart's ultimate intentions, do not make concessions easily. The success of a business negotiation relies on many psychological factors. When a bargaining is in a stalemate, the two sides are contesting psychologically rather than contesting their benefits. So in negotiations, we should keep calm and do not propose to make concessions.

(2) Do not make any senseless concessions

As a last resort, or for long-term interests, or in exchange of your counterpart's concession, you may be forced to make concessions. Otherwise, you should never make a meaningless "sacrifice." If you need to make concession in a business negotiation, you should not make concession first, whereas you can make a proper concession at the time of being needed most or when the negotiation cannot go further. Furthermore, you should make the concession step by step, and be careful to compromise at the same range as your counterpart.

(3) Propose to make conditional concessions

When you have to make some concessions, you can append some conditions for your concessions instead of expressing agreement immediately. For the benefit maximization, negotiators should seek some benefits in return for each of your concession whenever it is possible.

(4) Choose the right time

Concessions should be made at a right time. If you make concessions too early, the other party may become greedy, asking you to make more concessions; but if you make concessions too late, you may fail to direct the desired outcome.

### 2. Make concessions effectively

Make concessions effectively so as to force the other side to make some concessions and prevent your counterpart from "reaching out for a yard after taking an inch."

(1) Set a definite goal of benefits

Never make any concessions without exchange, which is the principle a negotiator should abide by. You will be considered incompetent if you make meaningless concessions.

(2) Make clear which is important and which is less important

Try to analyze all negotiation items, and make concessions for those which are urgent to be made. Generally speaking, you should not make concessions first on matter of principle, on items of great significance or things the other side does not ask you to make concessions.

(3) Do not make it too easy for the other party to gain what he wants

Even though you are ready to make a concession, you should not be too "frank and straightforward," or you may cause your counterpart to think you are too easy to deal with. Do remember: Your counterpart is not likely to value the concessions that they get too easily. You should let the other party feel that it is very difficult for you to make any concessions. As per the viewpoint from psychology, people usually do not value the things that they have reaped but not sown by themselves.

(4) Firmly control the times, speed and margin of your concession

You should not make concessions too many times; otherwise, it will not only nibble away your interests but also reduce the effectiveness of your negotiation. Concessions should not be made too quickly or it will encourage the will and morale of the other side. You should not make a concession of a large margin, or the other side will get the hint that there is a lot of room left, and it may encourage the other party to see you as weak and vulnerable.

### 3. Have the overall situation in mind and take all factors into consideration

(1) Seize the big "fish" and release the small one

It is better to persuade the other party to make concessions on issues which are important to your side. Meanwhile, in various situations, you can make considerable concessions on less important issues.

(2) Do not automatically accept a bid to match concessions by an equal margin

This is usually a trap set by your counterpart. For example，the other party quotes $100 and you counter it for $60，then he says，"Let's meet each other half way and have the average $80." You should refuse to automatically accept it.

(3) Withdraw to get the second best

Sometimes if you realize it is impossible to reach your best goal，you should not continue to persist on the best possible result. Instead，it is wise to withdraw a little and work towards the second best target，and you may take the opportunity to secure the successful outcome of the negotiation in hand for the second priority，rather than the first.

(4) There is no need for returning a favor with a favor

You should feel at ease and justified to accept your counterpart's concession. It is not necessary to feel a sense of pressure，obligation or responsibility to match your counterpart's concession. Do not begin to consider at once what concessions to make in return for their concessions or the concessions you have gained will become meaningless or less valuable.

Besides，you should always keep the bottom line as a secret，and you'd better not let your counterpart know what your target is. The disclosure of one's deadline may bring about losses or trouble with subsequent negotiations.

## Ⅳ. Models or Styles of Making Concessions

Making concessions should be conducted in correct ways and be controlled in terms of the times，procedures and degree. But in factual negotiations，there's no fixed standard and rules to abide by. The specific tactics of making concessions depend on many factors such as the characteristics of negotiating objects，supply and demand，negotiating strategies，managing plans and objective environment. Negotiators should choose and use effective tactics of making concessions flexibly. The following are eight different kinds of concessions with characteristics respectively which are usually called eight models or styles.

Supposing there is a margin of USD100 to make concessions on the basis of the original price between the buyer and the seller，and you can make concessions by four times，there are usually 8 different models of making concessions as shown in Table 6-1.

Table 6-1 Eight commonly used patterns of making concessions          (Unit: USD)

| Concession tactics | Planned reduction | First step | Second step | Third step | Fourth step |
|---|---|---|---|---|---|
| 1 | 100 | 0 | 0 | 0 | 100 |
| 2 | 100 | 25 | 25 | 25 | 25 |
| 3 | 100 | 10 | 20 | 30 | 40 |
| 4 | 100 | 40 | 30 | 20 | 10 |
| 5 | 100 | 60 | 25 | 10 | 5 |
| 6 | 100 | 55 | 40 | −5 | 5 |
| 7 | 100 | 60 | 5 | 30 | 5 |
| 8 | 100 | 100 | 0 | 0 | 0 |

### 1. Keeping up until last concession 【0 – 0 – 0 – 100】

The characteristic of this pattern is that no concession is ever made before the negotiation, leaving no room for the other party to bargain. If the buyer is weak-willed, he will give up early; if the seller can not stick to it any longer, the buyer will gain a lot in the end. However, both the buyer and the seller risk falling into a deadlock with this pattern.

### 2. Concessions by equal margin 【25 – 25 – 25 – 25】

This pattern is characterized by making concessions of the same margin several times. This method encourages the other party to continue their efforts to strive patiently for more concessions of the same margin. Experienced negotiators do not use this approach in making concessions.

### 3. Progressive increase in concessions 【10 – 20 – 30 – 40】

This is even worse than the second pattern, and may result in greater loss to the seller because the buyer will believe that he can narrow the price difference continuously by an increasingly wider margin.

### 4. Progressive decrease of concessions with a minor range 【40 – 30 – 20 – 10】

This pattern has an obvious feature of a tendency of compromise and artistry. On the one hand, it indicates a strong wish of cooperation of the seller and implies to the buyer he has made almost his utmost to make the concessions. On the other hand, it means that the margin of each possible concession will be progressively smaller and the seller cannot go any further and that it is the time to conclude the deal. Generally speaking, this pattern is most widely used.

## 5. Progressive decrease of concessions with a large range【60 – 25 – 10 – 5】

The party making the concession has a strong desire to compromise, but unfortunately, the concession is limited. At the early stage of a negotiation, the party makes the concession in such a way that it can arouse the counterpart's expectation greatly, but as the concessions made become smaller and smaller, the other party might feel depressed and unwilling to accept what is proposed. This strategy is often used by the relative weak party.

## 6. Decreasing progressively and increasing in the end【55 – 40 – – 5 – 5】

This pattern is characterized by a sudden reverse in the progress of making concessions, to which the other party is sure to object strongly. However, the final concession will make them overjoyed at the unexpected gain. It is appropriate for a formal occasion since it seems that the party making concessions goes back on their words.

## 7. Unstable concession【60 – 5 – 30 – 5】

This method features a great concession made first which indicates a strong tendency to continue making great concessions, and followed by a dramatically-reduced concession margin which may make the counterpart feel dissatisfied. The third concession margin becomes relatively large again, and then is followed by another small concession. This process is very risky as it is very difficult for the other party to adjust to it. Experienced negotiators might try this method occasionally, depending on their counterpart's situation, to achieve an unexpected result.

## 8. Showing one's hand at the beginning【100 – 0 – 0 – 0】

This method is characterized by making only concession once and for all at the very beginning of the negotiation. The party who makes such a concession will lose any chance or room for maneuvering. Meanwhile, the counterpart will be overjoyed at first and then become extremely discouraged. This approach may cause the negotiation to fall into an impasse.

## Ⅴ. Tactics Used to Force the Other Party to Make Concessions

### 1. Excessively demanding

At the beginning of the consultation stage, one party will put forward very harsh terms and conditions for a transaction to lower the other party's aspirations, and then give preferential treatment or make concessions gradually later in the process. After the other party is aware of the benefits offered, they will be more ready to make corresponding concessions. In addition, the party using it may imply to the counter party that they are dealing with a tough opponent who will not be taken in easily by any tricks. This tactics can usually make the other side make concessions and leave a large room for bargaining.

### 2. Emotional outburst

In the negotiation process, sometimes negotiators cannot refrain from emotional outbursts, but at other times negotiators purposely burst into feigned anger as a deliberate tactic. When neither side is ready to yield, or if the counterpart's attitude and behavior are not appropriate, or when the counterpart raises an excessive demand, you may consider taking this opportunity to show your anger by raising your voice, and blame your counterpart and create an impasse. This is done to frighten him and make him reprove himself so that he will adjust his negotiation targets and make concessions.

If your counterpart uses emotional outburst, you should try to keep calm as if nothing has happened, or you may adjourn the negotiation, and can point out the impolite and inappropriate behavior of the other side, then you may call for a complete start of the negotiation.

### 3. Tag-team tactic

In a negotiation, this is a tactic of having several persons take turns in fighting one opponent to tire him out. When the negotiation is stalemated, you may excuse yourself from the meeting by saying that you have some other business to do and have another person replace you to continue the talk. Through constantly changing negotiation representatives, your side may try to postpone the negotiation or delay a decision until a time your side thinks favorable or when the other side makes concessions.

### 4. Divide and conquer tactic

If the members of your counter team have different ideas or disagree among themselves, you may take advantage of this disagreement by affirming and supporting positively those whose ideas favor your side and thus you form an invisible alliance with them. As a result, they lose negotiation power. In the end, they may have to retreat or concede.

### 5. Involving competition

To create and utilize competition is always an effective tool to urge your counterpart to make concessions. To create competition, you may invite many companies to take part in a bid and choose the highest bidder; or invite many potential buyers to take part in a collective negotiation at the same time and negotiate with one of them at minimum terms and conditions, forcing the counterpart to yield under the pressure of competition.

### 6. Red face and white face routine

This tactic is also known as the hardball and softball tactic, the stick and carrot tactic, the eagle and pigeon routine, or the good guy and bad guy routine. At the beginning of the negotiation, the tough negotiator, "white face" or "bad guy," fires the first shot or speaks first, giving offense to or threatening his counterpart or putting forward harsh and very high terms and conditions which are difficult to be accepted by the other side. As a deadlock approaches, the "red face" or "good guy" appears on the stage. He adopts a reasonable attitude and takes notice of his counterpart's emotions and makes concessions to certain extent. As a result, the counterpart may make even greater concessions in response.

When using this tactic, the "white face" or "bad guy" must be tough enough to be convincing, and the "red face" or "good guy" must appear on the stage or speak at exactly the right moment. In factual business, one single negotiator can also use this strategy by acting as a "white face" first, and if the other side cannot accept the proposed terms or the negotiation is approaching a deadlock, then he can change to be a "red face."

### 7. Making feint to the east but attack in the west

"Making feint to the east and attack in the west" is originally a military term. In a negotiation, one side may intentionally change topics and address issues that are not very important to the other side to distract their attention from their major issues. On answering or explaining matters concerning less-important issues, they might release information on the major issues.

### 8. The ultimatum

The ultimatum is also called "take it or leave it" strategy. If the other party refuses to accept your party's terms and conditions, your side can issue an ultimatum. When neither side is willing to make more concessions and the negotiation is deadlocked, you may set a deadline for the other side to accept your terms. That means when the other side fails to say "yes" to your proposal, you may declare that negotiations are finished.

Usually, you can use this tactic successfully if your side is more powerful. What is more, it should be used with decisive and firm wording at the last critical moment.

## VI. Strategies Used to Prevent the Counterpart's Attack

### 1. Limited authority

In negotiation, a negotiator with a limited authority tends to be in a more advantageous position than one who arrogates all authority to himself. The former may be able to ask the other side to make concessions one after another, but when he is asked to make concessions he can say he has only limited authority and thus may excuse himself from making any commitments. When you pay a visit to a customer abroad, and you are in a weak position, you may say, "Because of the limited information or materials, let's continue our talk tomorrow, OK?" and you might stop the attack from the other side in this way.

### 2. No precedents

"No precedents" means there is not any usual practice for a certain issue. When the other side raises an excessive demand, you may respond that there are "no precedents" which is a tactful excuse or reason to refuse other party's demand. This tactic doesn't focuses on people but on problems. So it is rather effective and convincing. For example, if your counterpart asks you to accept D/A, you may say that there are "no precedents," which means this kind of payment term has not been used so far.

### 3. Fatiguing tactics

When you meet a counterpart who is very aggressive and exerts pressure on you, you can adopt the tactics of a seesaw battle by stretching the negotiation to more rounds. In this way, you may prolong the negotiations, making the other party weary both in body and mind. You can then be able to turn defense into offense.

### 4. Adjournment

When the negotiation encounters some obstacles, either or both sides hope to adjourn the talk to have a break so that everyone has a chance to relax and recover their strength and energy. Meanwhile, they can adjust their strategies and ease tensions in an attempt to carry through the negotiation. Most of the time, this tactic enables you to have more private discussions and change an unfavorable atmosphere.

### 5. Seeking commiseration

Known also as a compassion tactic, seeking commiseration involves one party feigning weakness and embarrassment in order to gain the other party's sympathy or compassion. It will be effective when the user is really weaker than or equal to the counterpart, and sometimes it will influence inexperienced counterparts. For example, "If I accept your price, I might be fired!" or you might get the commiseration by shedding your tears.

### 6. Finding other's fault (nitpicking)

It means trying to force the other side to make concessions by finding the defects of the quality, property, cost, transportation, etc.

☞ **Case study 6 - 2 　(Buy a refrigerator skillfully)**

Robert, an Australian negotiator, once went to a store to buy a refrigerator. The shop assistant pointed to the refrigerator Robert was interested in and told him that the price was USD700. Then there appeared a wonderful bargaining.

Robert (hereinafter referred to as R): How many colors does this kind of refrigerator have?

Assistant (hereinafter referred to as A): We have 22 colors.

R: Can I have a look at the samples?

A: Certainly! (immediately fetch the sample book)

R: (Asking while watching) How many colors do you have for the goods in the store?

A: Now we have 12 colors, and which color would you prefer?

R: (Pointing at the color which is not available in store) This color matches the color of my kitchen!

A: I am so sorry. We do not have this color right now.

R: Other colors don't match the color of my kitchen. The color is not satisfying, and the price is so high. Can it be cheaper? Or I'll go to other stores. I think I can find the color I want in other stores.

A: OK, it can be cheaper.

R: There's also something wrong with this refrigerator. Have a look at here...

A: Nothing can be seen.

R: What? Though the defect is very little, there should be some discount for a refrigerator which has something wrong with its appearance.

A: ...

R: (Opening the door of the refrigerator and watching for a while) Does this refrigerator have an ice-maker?

A: Yes! This ice-maker makes ice cube for you 24 hours a day, and the electric charge is only USD0.03 per hour. (She thinks Robert is interested in this ice-maker)

R: That's terrible! My child has a slight asthma, and doctors forbid him to have any ice cube. Can you help me to dismantle it off the refrigerator?

A: This ice-maker cannot be dismantled since it is connected with the whole refrigerating system.

R: This ice-maker is of no use to me! But I have to pay for it and its electric charge in the future. It is unreasonable... Certainly, if the price can be lower...

The result is that Robert bought his desirable refrigerator at USD550, a rather lower price.

☞ **Case study 6 – 3**    **(Business of a mouse)**

One day in July last year, I went to the Computer City to buy a mouse. On the second floor of the Computer City, we took a fancy to a mouse. So there was a bargain over the price with the boss.

"What is the price for this mouse?"

"The lowest price is 40 Yuan!"

"What? It's too expensive!"

"It is not expensive! It is sold at 50 Yuan in other stores!"

"It is so expensive. I'll go to other stores to have a look."

"Wait, well! Considering you are students, I would like to sell you at 35 Yuan, the special price for students!"

"Are you kidding? The price for students is even 35 Yuan. It is that expensive?"

"It is not expensive! This mouse is completely new!"

"But the mouse is not any famous brand, so it should not be that expensive!"

"Well, what do you think the price should be?"

"10 Yuan. I think the mouse is worth this price at most!"

"It is far away from normal price! Nobody sell at this price in the Computer City! It's impossible to make business at this price!" The boss went back to the counter while talking with us. It seemed that there is no way to make this business.

"This mouse is essentially not bad," My friend said while holding and scrutinizing the mouse, "yet it is only too expensive!" Then he put down the mouse and was ready to leave.

"Well, how about 25 Yuan! What do you think?" The boss came out from behind the counter. It seemed that there's the possibility for the business again!

"It is still very expensive! Let's make it 15 Yuan! OK?"

"I only earn several Yuan. I'll lose money at 15."

"We are only consumers, and 15 is the furthest we can go!"

"Well, 20! You may take it!"

"18 Yuan is the limit. I'll go no further!"

"What? You even bargain with me for 2 Yuan!"

"Exactly! Only 2 Yuan! Don't haggle over with us students! 18 Yuan! We'll come to you again in the future, and we'll bring our classmates here! Since there is more business, you will make more money!"

"Alright, you have me there! OK, 18 Yuan! Bring your friends here."

So I bought the mouse at the price of 18 Yuan.

In the whole process of bargaining, we asked the price from 40 Yuan to 10 Yuan, then made proper concessions, and raised the price to 18 Yuan. The business was concluded at a price both sides are satisfied, and a win-win result was reached.

☞ **Case study 6 – 4**  (**Tom's tactics of bargaining**)

James is a doctor. His house was once hit by a hurricane and there were some damages. The house had been effected insurance in an insurance company, so he could lodge a claim. He would like the insurance company to compensate more but knows that the insurance company was very difficult to deal with. James was fully aware it was beyond his ability, so he went to Tom for help. Tom asked James how much compensation he expected to get so that he might have a minimum standard. The doctor answered he would like the insurance company to compensate him USD1,000. Tom asked a second time, "How much have you lost through this hurricane?" The doctor answered, "About over USD1,000, however I know that it's impossible for the insurance company to compensate that much!" Soon after, the claimsman from the insurance company came to Tom, "Mr. Tom, I know you, as a barrister, are specially negotiating for a large sum. However, I am afraid that we cannot compensate you too much. What do you think if I only compensate you USD300?" Years of experience told Tom that the other side said "only compensate" suggesting he himself also felt USD300 was very little and felt embarrassed to offer, there must be a second and third time to offer after the first one. So Tom kept silent deliberately for a long time, and then had a rhetorical question, "What do you think?" The other side was stupefied for a while and said, "Well, we are sorry. Please forget about the offer just now. How about USD600?" Tom got the information from the tone of the answer that the other side was not confident. So Tom asked, "Can it be more?" "Alright. What do you think if I increase to USD1,000?" Finally, the two sides reached the agreement at USD3,000, which was three times the figure the doctor expected.

☞ **Case study 6 – 5**　　(Sino-US electronics negotiation)

An American electronic corporation was going to sell equipment producing semiconductor to a Chinese import and export corporation. The American side sent representatives to Beijing for negotiation. The equipment was good in functions and suited the Chinese side. The two parties reached the agreement for the performance index very quickly and turned to pricing negotiation. The Chinese side thought: The equipment's functions are OK but the price doesn't work, so the price is expected to be lowered. The American side thought: Since the equipment is good, the price is naturally high and cannot be lowered.

Chinese side (hereinafter referred to as C): We can't accept if the price is not lowered.

American side (hereinafter referred to as A): The Eastern people like bargaining, and we Americans are loyal to friends. The price can be lowered by only 0.5%.

C: Thanks for your loyalty to friends, but the price is not reasonable.

A: How is it unreasonable?

C: The price of the equipment is much higher compared to its functions.

A: You are satisfied with our equipment, aren't you?

C: Yes, the functions can meet our requirement, but it does not mean the functions are the best. We can buy much better equipment at your offer.

A: We need to think it over.

The two sides resumed the negotiation after they had rested for a while. The American side made a further concession by granting another 3%, but the Chinese side was not satisfied, and asked the American make further reduction. The American didn't agree, asking the Chinese to make a counteroffer. The Chinese side asked to be granted by 15%.

On hearing this, the American kept silent for a while and then took out his air ticket and said, "It's difficult for us to accept you harsh conditions. In order to show our sincerity, we lower the price by another 2%. If you agree, we sign the contract; if you don't agree, I'll leave at 2: 00 p.m. tomorrow on time." Then he got up and was going to leave, saying, "I live in the Friendship Hotel. Please give me a reply before 12: 00 a.m. if you make the decision."

The Chinese side knew through their research that they could not accept the favor by 5.5%; the other side should at least lower the price by 7%. But how to negotiate further? The Chinese side made an investigation and found that there was no flight to the US at 2: 00 p.m. tomorrow at all. On 10: 00 a.m. the following day, the Chinese called the Americans at the hotel to express the sincerity to negotiate by making concessions and said they would only ask to be given a favor by 10%. The American was convinced of the sincerity on the Chinese side and agreed to meet again for the negotiation. Finally both of the two sides make further concessions by lowering the price by 7.5%.

☞ **Questions for your consideration and discussion**

1. What are the five strategic approaches and considerations in negotiation?

2. What are the principles of making concessions?

3. What are the usual models of making concessions? Which do you prefer? Why?

4. What are the tactics which can be used to force the other party to make concessions? Which ones are commonly used?

5. What are the strategies which can be used to prevent the counterpart's attack?

6. In case study 6 – 5, how did the two sides conclude the business? What strategies of making concessions were used?

# 第六章
# 国际商务谈判的磋商及让步

☞ **案例分析 6—1**　（买苹果）

　　苹果熟了,果园里一片繁忙。一家果品公司的采购员来到果园,询问园主:"多少钱一公斤?""10元。""8元行吗?""少一分也不卖。"采购员摇摇头走了。又一家的采购员走上前来。"多少钱一公斤?""10元。""整筐卖多少钱?""不论筐卖,10元一公斤。"采购员不急于还价,而是不慌不忙地打开筐盖,拿起一个苹果掂量着、端详着,不紧不慢地说:"个头还可以,但颜色不够红,这样上市卖不上价呀!"接着伸手往筐里掏,摸了一会儿摸出一个个头小的苹果:"老板,您这一筐苹果,表面是大的,可筐底不少小的,这怎么算呢?"边说边继续在筐里摸着,一会儿,又摸出一个带伤的苹果:"看,这里面还有虫咬,也许是苞伤。您这苹果既不够红,又不够大,算不上一级果,勉强算二级就不错了。"这时,卖主沉不住气了,说话也和气了:"您真想要,就还个价吧。"双方终于以每公斤9元的价格成交了。

　　该案例中,第一位采购员还价遭到拒绝,而第二个采购员却能以较低的价格成交,其关键在于后者在谈判中采取了挑剔还价的战术,恰到好处地提出色泽、大小、质量等方面的缺点,成功地压价。

　　磋商阶段也被称为讨价还价阶段。它是谈判中最复杂、最关键的阶段。因此这一阶段是一场硬仗和拉锯战,是最困难的阶段。此阶段是全部谈判活动中最为重要的阶段,故其投入的精力最多、涉及的问题最多、占用的时间最长。此阶段双方的焦点是讨价还价,而讨价还价的过程也就是彼此妥协让步的过程。

　　谈判的磋商阶段是指随着谈判开局阶段任务的完成和议题的深入而进入的中心阶段,即在谈判开始之后到谈判终局之前,谈判各方就实质性事项进行磋商的全过程。谈判的磋商阶段是谈判的实践阶段,这不仅是谈判主体间的实力、智力和技术的具体较量阶段,是谈判主体间求同存异、合作、谅解、让步的阶段,也是双方为了达成交易而显示各自真实意图与目的的阶段。谈判人员能否实现利润或实现多少利润主要取决于各自在这个阶段的实力和技巧。

## 一、谈判磋商阶段的战略路径与考虑

### 1. 谈判中的五种战略路径

所谓的战略路径就是谈判人员在谈判的磋商阶段采取的五种态度。由于每个人的文化背景和所受的教育程度不同，谈判人员在谈判中遇到冲突时会有不同的处理问题的战略路径。例如，有的人进取好斗，有的专横顽固，有的善耍花招，而有的则是合作顺从，富有建设性，等等。根据托马斯·基尔曼（1974）（转引自：罗立彬，2013）的观点，谈判中所有的战略路径可以归纳为以下五种：合作、妥协、顺从、控制和规避。

### 2. 采用战略路径的考虑

采用哪种战略路径，通常取决于以下五种基本的考虑：重复谈判还是一次性的谈判，双方的实力对比，交易的重要程度，时间限度和谈判资源。

（1）谈判的重复性

重复性（的谈判）对谈判的风格和策略有着重要的影响。如果与一个企业有一系列交易，就应与之建立友好持久的关系，特别重要的是要建立起个人之间的关系。另一方面，如果与一个企业的谈判是一次性的交易，将来不再见面，那形势就会截然不同，就不用那么着重建立友好的关系。因此，第一个战略考虑就是交易的重复性。如果可能是重复性的交易，正如前面所述，第一种策略（合作）会是谈判的一个不错的选择。

（2）谈判当事人的实力

第二个影响因素是每一方的实力。如果一笔交易只能跟某个当事人达成，那这个当事人就处于一个强势的地位。如果一个当事人拥有许多潜在的竞争对手，那该当事人就会处于一个弱势地位。一方谈判的谈判风格和谈判人员的性格都会影响到双方的战略选择。一方的实力的强弱刚好是另一方实力的相反方面。不管是买方还是卖方，如果他们能控制市场，他们就强势，反之就会弱势。

（3）一笔交易的重要程度

接下来的考虑就是一笔交易的重要程度。一场标的数百万美元的谈判显然与几千美元谈判的战略考虑是不一样的。同样，谈判一个成熟市场上完美产品的交易和推出一个新产品到一个新市场的战略考虑也是不一样的。

（4）时间限度

在国际商务谈判中，一场交易是否有时间限制也会影响战略的选择。如果交易必须快速达成，其谈判的战略与交易不急于达成的谈判是不一样的。在前一种情况下，强势的一方可能会选择"控制"的战略，而弱势的一方可能会选择放弃（如果达成协议就意味着赔钱或是条件不可接受）或者采用"规避""顺从"的战略。

（5）谈判资源

谈判资源同样会影响战略的选择。如果没有几个合格的谈判人员，而需要谈判的项目又很多，就不能安排谈判人员在某一笔谈判中花太长的时间。

除此以外，可能还会有其他的考虑，尤其可能会有一些特殊的情况。然而上述这些考虑基本会决定战略的选择。

## 二、讨价还价的策略

### 1. 攻其弱点

对方的报价中如存在不合理、不切实际或是令人难以置信的地方，就应给对方指出来并抓住不放，直到对方做出新的实质性的让步。

### 2. 认真观察，理解对方

揣摩对方的所思所想。在讨价还价的过程中，应密切留意对方的心境，揣摩对方的心思，下一步对方的行动会是什么？对方还有多大余地？

### 3. 准备充分，具灵活性

作为谈判人员，应该充分了解讨价还价阶段的难度和关键性。所以在进入该阶段时应该有充分的准备，特别是出手条件的整理。出手条件就像谈判桌上掌握的"牌"，有多少张牌、每张牌的分量有多大，都必须了解好、准备好。通常需要几套讨价还价的方案，并从中选择，确定哪个应当坚持，哪个可以灵活一些，灵活度有多大。当双方在关键问题上都拒绝让步时，就可以使用灵活的谈判方案。

### 4. 讨价还价阶段的开始时机

当双方都有讨价还价的意思表示，即谈判双方达成共识：该进入磋商阶段了。这个共识很重要，因为单有一方是不能进行讨价还价的。一般来说，意思表示是一种明示的协议。常见的表述有"我方已将还价做了多次调整，该贵方考虑新的态度了。""我方也有改进，且次数比贵方多，力度比贵方大，为什么还让我单方改善条件？""那让我们双方共同努力解决难题。"买方和卖方的说法均使彼此意识到新的阶段开始了。

### 5. 出手条件的配置

配置出手条件，即谈判砝码，主要把握两点：一是要统观全局、牢记总账；二是要谨记目标、步步为营。

讨价还价时的保密问题。出手条件是绝密的，一般只有主谈人与负责人知道。虽然在群体谈判时，可以集体参与谈判方案的设计，但底线的确定权仍是掌握在高层（领导与业主）和主谈人、负责人手中的，由主谈人配置出手的次数和条件。

此外，还应注意参谈人员的面部表情，若喜形于色，则易泄密。遇到僵持的局面，即着急,抓耳挠腮;得手,即喜上眉梢,均属泄密行为。主谈人不得如此,参谈人员也不得如此。情不自禁、缺乏控制力的人容易泄密。

### 三、妥协的一般原则

妥协让步对于国际商务谈判至关重要而且必不可少。从某种意义上讲,谈判就是由两个部分组成:要求和给予。换句话说,向对方提出要求和向对方做出让步。

妥协让步固然是必要的,但在让步之前,谈判手应该反复考虑:现在是否应该让步?该如何让步?让步能带来什么利益?让步的一般原则就是用己方较小的利益换取对方较大的利益。

#### 1. 不要轻易提出让步

高明的谈判手不会轻易提出让步,因为即便已经占据了有利的谈判地位,也有可能因为先做出让步而坚定对方的信心,也使对方强化了其立场,从而丧失了自己的谈判主动权。

（1）不要盲目地让步

在你完全了解对方的终极目的之前,不要随意做出让步。商务谈判的成功往往取决于许多心理因素。当讨价还价处于僵持阶段,双方谈判者的心理活动异常激烈,此时与其说双方是在计较利益,不如说是在做心理较量。所以谈判中首先要沉住气,不要主动提出妥协方案。

（2）不做无意义的让步

在万不得已的情况下,或是为了长期的利益,或是为了换取对方的让步,你可能不得不做出让步,不然,不要做无意义的牺牲。在商务谈判中,即使需要让步,也不应该轻易地先做出让步,只有在最需要的时候,或谈判无法进行下去的情况下,再做出适当的妥协;还要掌握让步的尺度,要循序渐进,不要轻易做出与谈判对手同等幅度的让步。

（3）提出有条件的让步

在面临不得不做出让步的情况下,要对让步附加某些条件,而不应是"随即同意"。从追求自身经济利益最大化的角度出发,只要有可能,就应该对每一步妥协寻求一定的回报,即换取对方的让步。可以先向对方提出让步条件,在对方认同己方提出的条件的前提下,再谈让步。

（4）选择正确的（让步）时间

如果过早让步,对方可能会变得贪婪,要求你做更多的让步;如果让步太晚,就可能会影响预期的最终谈判结果。

#### 2. 做到有效的让步

做到有效的让步,使己方的让步不至于使得对方得寸进尺,同时也迫使对方不得不让步。

（1）让步应有明确的利益目标

让步可以从对方手中获得利益补偿。无谓的让步会被对手视为无能。"没有交换,决不让步",这是一个谈判者首先应该遵循的。

（2）让步要分轻重缓急

对谈判的条目进行分析,急需让步的问题才能进行让步。一般不先在原则问题、重大问题,或者对方尚未迫切需求的事项上让步。

（3）不要让对手轻而易举地得到己方的让步

尽管你准备好让步,但不应太过"坦诚直接",要使对方感到获得我方的让步是十分艰难的。千万别让对手轻而易举地得到己方的让步。因为按照心理学的观点,人们对不劳而获、轻易得到的东西通常都不加重视和珍惜。

（4）严格控制让步的次数、频率和幅度

让步过程中应严格控制让步的次数、频率和幅度。让步次数不宜过多,一般3～4次。过多不仅意味着损失大,而且影响谈判信誉、诚意和效率;让步频率不可过快,过快容易鼓舞对方的斗志和士气;让步幅度也不可太大,幅度过大反映了己方条件"虚头大",会使对方进攻欲望更强,程度更猛烈。

3. 放眼全局,综合考虑

（1）抓大放小

就是最好能说服对方在对己方重要的问题上进行让步,同时在次要的问题上可向对方做出让步。

（2）不要不经思索地接受对方同等幅度的让步

这通常是对方给你设置的一个陷阱。例如,对方报价100美元,你还价60美元,对方接着说,"咱们各让一半,80美元吧。"你应不假思索地予以拒绝。

（3）退而求其次

有时你认识到不可能实现最好的目标时,就应放弃最好的目标。相反,这时应当争取次佳目标,而且你可以利用这个机会确保次佳目标的成功实现。

（4）没有必要投桃报李

对谈判伙伴的让步你应当感到正常和心安理得,没有必要有压力感,或是有义务或责任必须向对方做出让步。对于对方的让步不用马上考虑向他们做出回报,不然的话你所得到的让步将变得没有意义或是降低了它的价值。

另外,自己的底线应保密。最好不要让你的对手知道你的目标是什么,泄露你的底线可能会给接下来的谈判带来损失和麻烦。

## 四、让步方式(模型)

谈判的让步,强调要正确地控制让步的次数、步骤与程度,即采用正确的让步方式,不可使让步过多、过快、过大。但在实际谈判中，其"量"的概念是无法具体规定的，让步方式也不可能有成规可循，因为让步方式是受到交易物特性、市场需求状况、谈判策略、经营计划、客观环境等一系列因素制约和影响的。作为谈判人员，应根据具体情况，灵活选择和应用各具特点的有效的让步方式。下面介绍八种具有不同特点的让步方式，供谈判人员参考。

假设买卖双方在原有讨价还价的基础上，预计让步幅度还有 100 美元，且需要经过四次反复让步才能达成协议，这对让步方来说，有八种不同方式可供选择，见表 6-1。

表 6-1　八种常见的让步方式　　　　　　　　　　　　　　　　（单位：美元）

| 让步方式 | 让步尺度 | 第一次让步 | 第二次让步 | 第三次让步 | 第四次让步 |
|---|---|---|---|---|---|
| 1 | 100 | 0 | 0 | 0 | 100 |
| 2 | 100 | 25 | 25 | 25 | 25 |
| 3 | 100 | 10 | 20 | 30 | 40 |
| 4 | 100 | 40 | 30 | 20 | 10 |
| 5 | 100 | 60 | 25 | 10 | 5 |
| 6 | 100 | 55 | 40 | − 5 | 5 |
| 7 | 100 | 60 | 5 | 30 | 5 |
| 8 | 100 | 100 | 0 | 0 | 0 |

1. 强硬型的让步方式【0 − 0 − 0 − 100】

开始给人以立场坚定、态度强硬、缺乏合作与成交的诚意之感，但最后让步一次到位，"先苦后甜"，又必然会使对方兴高采烈。这种方式的采用者可能自恃实力雄厚，交易地位优越。但是，采用这种方式，又必须解决好两个可能存在的问题：一是对方在再三要求让步而均遭拒绝的情况下，可能等不到最后，就会离开谈判桌；二是最后让步虽然很晚，但幅度过大，往往会鼓励对方进一步纠缠，而且进攻可能会更加猛烈，有可能导致僵局。

2. 等值型的让步方式【25 − 25 − 25 − 25】

这种等值型的让步，是为了使让步"细水长流"，均匀地满足对方的要求与需要，并获取对方的好感。但是采用这种方式，必须让对方意识到最后的让步已使价格降至谷底，否则它将鼓励对方争取进一步的让步。因为在无任何暗示和让步余地较大的情况下，不再让步，较难说服对方，从而有可能使谈判陷入僵局。有经验的谈判人员不会使用这种让步方式。

3. 递增式（刺激型）的让步方式【10 − 20 − 30 − 40】

这种方式的让步幅度呈增值型，可能开始是为了使让步的口子开得小一点，以后充分显示成交的诚意。但是，这也存在一个明显的问题，就是会刺激对方要求进一步让步的胃口,而且其胃口可能越来越大,最终会使谈判难以收场,导致僵局,起码会使对方感到不满意。

4.递减式(稳妥型)的让步方式【40-30-20-10】

这种方式表现出强烈的妥协性和艺术性。它一方面告诉对方,我们已尽了最大努力,表示出了极强的合作愿望。另一方面,又暗示对方,让步的幅度越来越小,并且最后让步已基本到了尽头,不可能再进行让步了,最后成交的时机已经到来。一般来说,这是一种符合常理的常见的让步方式。

5.希望型(大幅度递减)的让步方式【60-25-10-5】

这种方式,让步人第一次让步幅度很大,对方会感到成交的希望很大,但此后让步大幅度下降,而且幅度越来越小,显示出让步方的立场愈来愈强硬,防卫森严,让步行为也较符合常理。一般适合势力较弱的一方。

6.虚伪型的让步方式【55-40--5-5】

这种方式在前两次就使让步达到了极限,表现出极大的热情与诚意,一定会使对方暗喜。但在第三次该让步的情况下,却诡称成本或其他数字计算有误,提高报价,可谓给对方当头一棒,对方显然不会接受,甚至会引起对方的误解和气愤,使谈判气氛紧张。第四次又纠正"错误",给对方一个小小的让步,可能会使对方得到一点安抚。

7.不稳定的让步方式【60-5-30-5】

这种方式的特点是第一次做出巨大的让步,显示出强烈的妥协愿望。但紧接着让步幅度骤减,第三步的幅度又较大,最后又是一个很小的让步幅度。这种方式风险较大,对方也较难适应。有经验的谈判人员根据情况可以一试,同样适合实力较弱的一方。

8.一步到位式的让步方式【100-0-0-0】

这种方式一开始便把所有的让步幅度给了对方,其用意显然是为了谋求尽快地达成协议,提高谈判效率,争取时间。但是,在谈判中坦诚是会带来风险的,它会使对方怀疑你是否真的坦诚,会使对方更猛烈地向你发起进攻,逼迫你再做让步。否则,就很容易引起僵局和谈判的破裂。当然,如果这种方式已成为交易中的惯例,或者谈判对象是老客户,彼此非常熟悉,也未必不可。

## 五、促使对方让步的策略

1.先苦后甜/过分要求/吹毛求疵

这是一种在谈判的开始阶段,谈判的一方先用苛刻的虚假条件使对方产生疑虑、压抑、无望等心态,以大幅度降低对手的期望值,然后在实际谈判中逐步给予优惠或让步。这种策略通常能使对方做出让步,并且留有讨价还价的余地。使用这种策略的人会使对方感到遇到了强硬的对手。这是较为常用的一种策略。

**2. 感情迸发**

在谈判的过程中，谈判人员有时难以控制自己的感情。但也有的时候是故意假装生气，感情激动、提高嗓门甚至离开会场。当谈判的双方都不让步时，如果对方的意见或是行为不合适，或者当对方提出了过分的要求，你就可以利用这个机会通过提高音量等方式显示你的恼怒，责怪对方创造了僵局。记住，这么做的目的是为了吓唬对方，以便使他调整谈判目标，进而做出让步。

如果对方使用这个策略，你应保持冷静，权当什么也没发生，或者你可以推迟谈判，指出对方无礼的不当的行为，然后你可以建议开始一场全新的谈判。

**3. 车轮战术**

车轮战术是指谈判桌上由几个人轮换着跟对方一个人进行谈判。当一方遇到关键问题或与对方有无法解决的分歧时，借口自己不能决定或其他理由，转由他人再进行谈判。通过更换谈判主体，侦察对手的虚实，耗费对手的精力，削弱对手的议价能力，为自己留出回旋余地，进退有序，从而掌握谈判主动权，直至对方让步。

**4. 分而治之，利用他人失误**

如果对方谈判成员发生了意见分歧，你可以利用这个机会去支持意见有利于你方的成员，从而使对方分化，对方的谈判力自然就会削弱而不得不进行让步。利用他人失误是指在谈判中对方出现了失误，你可以借机利用，让对方不得不进行让步。

**5. 利用竞争**

促使对方让步最有效的武器是利用竞争。你在跟对方谈判，可明示或暗示对方，让他们知道你正在或打算进行比价工作，让对方知道有竞争对手的存在。有时甚至可以邀请多个公司参加投标，从而选择对己方最有利的报价，或者可以邀请几个潜在的买主一同参加一场集体谈判，具体条款可以与每个买主单独进行，从而逼迫他们在竞争的压力下妥协让步。

**6. 软硬兼施**

软硬兼施又叫红白脸策略、胡萝卜大棒策略或是鹰鸽策略。在谈判初始阶段，先由唱白脸的人出场发言，他傲慢无理，提出苛刻的条件，而且态度强硬、立场坚定、毫不妥协，让对手产生极大的反感。当谈判进入僵持状态时，红脸人出场，他表现出体谅对方的难处，以通情达理的态度，照顾对方的某些要求，放弃自己一方的某些苛刻条件和要求，做出一定合理的让步。

软硬兼施策略的使用非常广。使用这个策略时，应当注意，白脸人要足够强硬，要强硬得逼真；红脸人一定要在合适的时机出现。在现实的谈判实践中，一个人也是可以使用这个策略的：如，开始你可以以"白脸"的面目出现，而当对方不接受你的条款或是谈判出现了僵局，你可以变为"红脸"，实施另一套方案。

### 7. 声东击西

"声东击西"是个军事术语和策略。在谈判中，一方可以有意通过转换话题，谈论对对方不是很重要的条款或是话题，以转移他们的注意力。他们在回答或解释非重要的话题、条款时，可能就会释放出一些有关主要议题的信息。

### 8. 最后通牒

最后通牒又被称为"要么接受要么放弃"策略。当对方拒绝接受你方的条款时，就可考虑使用这一策略。当双方都不肯再做让步时，谈判出现了僵局，就可以提出一个让对方接受你方条件的截止期限。这就意味着如果对方不同意你方的建议，就可以宣布谈判结束了。通常实力较强的一方使用这一策略成功的概率较大；使用这一策略时，措辞应当肯定坚决而且要把握好时机。

## 六、阻止对方进攻的策略

### 1. 限制策略

谈判中，拥有有限权力的谈判人员往往比拥有决定权的谈判人员更容易处于一个有利的地位。前者可要求对方做出妥协和让步，但是当他被要求让步时，他可以以他权力有限为借口而不用做出什么承诺。当你在国外拜访客户被要求做出让步时，你就可以说"由于材料和信息所限，咱们明天再谈，好不好？"从而阻止了对方的进攻。

### 2. 没有先例

没有先例指的是在某一个问题上到目前为止还没有尝试过。当对方向你提出了一个过分的要求，你可以回应"没有先例"，这是拒绝对方要求的一个机智的借口或是理由。这种策略强调的是问题，而不是人的因素。因此非常有效和具有说服力。例如，对方要求你接受承兑交单的付款方式，你就可以说"没有先例"，意味着，这种付款方式到目前为止从来没有使用过。

### 3. 疲劳战术

当对方非常强势好斗，一直给你施加压力，你可以采用拉锯战的战术，将谈判延长到多个回合。这样，就可以使对方身心疲惫，你就可能由防守转为进攻。

### 4. 休会

当谈判遇到一些障碍，谈判的一方甚至双方可能都希望延迟谈判，以便休息一下，恢复一下体力和精神。同时还可利用这个机会调整一下谈判策略，缓和一下局势，以便继续谈判。多数情况下，人们会利用这个策略进行一些私下单独的交流以改变不利的气氛或局面。

5. 示弱以求怜悯

寻求怜悯和同情包括谈判的一方假装弱势或是窘迫以便得到另一方的"可怜、同情"。在谈判中，如果一方的谈判力确实比另一方弱或实力相等，使用这一策略会比较有效。另外谈判桌上的新手较多地使用这一策略。例如，"如果接受你的价格，我会被炒鱿鱼的"，有时还可以通过"流眼泪"博得对方的同情。

6. 挑剔还价法

挑剔还价法是指在谈判中，谈判方通过再三对商品质量、性能、成本价格、运输等方面寻找"疵点"进行讨价还价，压低报价方的报价。

☞ **案例分析 6—2** （巧买冰箱）

澳大利亚谈判学家罗伯特有一次去买冰箱，营业员指着罗伯特要买的那种冰箱说："700 美元一台。"接着罗伯特导演了一台精彩的"讨价还价"。

罗伯特（以下简称罗）：这种型号的冰箱有多少种颜色？

营业员（以下简称营）：共有 22 种颜色。

罗：能看看样品吗？

营：当然可以！（接着立即拿来了样本）

罗：（边看边问）你们店里的现货有多少种颜色？

营：现有 12 种。请问您要哪一种？

罗：（指着样品上有但店里没有的颜色）这种颜色同我厨房的墙壁颜色相配！

营：很抱歉，这种颜色现在没有。

罗：其他颜色与我厨房的颜色都不协调。颜色不好，价钱还这么高，要不便宜一点？否则我就要去其他的商店了，我想别的商店会有我要的颜色。

营：好吧，便宜一点。

罗：可这台冰箱有些小毛病！你看这里……

营：我看不出什么。

罗：什么？这一点毛病尽管小，可是冰箱外表有毛病通常不都要打点折扣吗？

营：……

罗：（又打开冰箱门，看了一会儿）这冰箱带制冰器吗？

营：有！这个制冰器每天 24 小时为您制冰块，1 小时才 3 美分电费。（她认为罗伯特对制冰器感兴趣）

罗：这可太糟糕了！我的孩子有轻微哮喘病，医生说绝对不可以吃冰块。你能帮我把它拆下来吗？

营：制冰器没办法拆下来，它是和整个制冷系统连在一起的。

罗：可是这个制冰器对我根本没用！我现在花钱把它买下来，将来还要为它付电费，这太不合理了！……当然，假如价格可以再降低一点的话……

结果，罗伯特以相当低的价格——不到 550 美元买到了他十分中意的冰箱。

## ☞ 案例分析 6—3 　（一只鼠标的买卖）

去年 7 月的一天，我与朋友到电脑城买鼠标。在电脑城的二楼，我们看中了一只 SUNREEC 的鼠标，于是跟老板展开了价格的谈判。

"老板，这只鼠标多少钱？"

"最低 40 元！"

"不是吧？这么贵？"

"不贵了！其他的店铺卖 50 元呢！"

"这么贵，我还是先去别的店铺看看吧。"

"等一下，好吧！看你们是学生，给你学生价好了！35 元！"

"不是吧？学生价还要 35 元那么贵？"

"不贵了！你看看这鼠标是全新的！"

"但是你的鼠标又不是什么名牌货，用不着那么贵！"

"那么好了，你说多少钱？"

"10 元，我看你的鼠标最多值这个价！"

"太离谱了！这个价是不可能的！在电脑城里没有可能卖这个价的！这个价没法交易！"老板说着就站回柜台里去，眼看这笔交易是做不成了。

"这鼠标还不错，"我朋友拿着鼠标边端详边说，"就是太贵了！"说着就放下了鼠标，然后和我准备离开了。

"真拿你俩没办法！这样好了！25 元！怎么样？"老板又从柜台里走了出来，看来交易又有希望了！

"还是太贵了！15 元吧！"

"我也只是赚那么几块钱，15 元就亏本了。"

"我们也只是消费者，15 元已经是我们最大的让步了！"

"也罢，20 元！要就拿走！"

"这样吧，你也要赚钱，18 元！最后的让步了！"

"不是吧？那 2 元钱也要跟我算……"

"就是嘛！那 2 元钱就别跟我们学生计较了！18 元！以后我们还会来光顾的，而且还会带些同学来！带旺生意，你就赚得更多！"

"好了好了，真说不过你们！18元吧！多带些朋友来。"

于是我就以 18 元买下了这只鼠标。

整个过程中，我们把价格从 40 元压到了 10 元，然后再做出适当的让步把价格提升到 18 元。老板以赚钱的价格卖出了鼠标，我们也以较低的价格买到了满意的鼠标，达到了双赢的结果。

☞ **案例分析 6—4**　（汤姆的讨价策略）

詹姆斯是一位医生。有一次，詹姆斯的房屋遭受飓风的袭击，有些损坏。这房屋是在保险公司投了保的，可以向保险公司索赔。他想要保险公司多赔一些钱，但又知道保险公司很难对付，自己没有这种能力做到这一点，于是去请汤姆帮忙。汤姆问医生希望得到多少赔偿，以便有个最低的标准。医生回答说，他想要保险公司赔偿 1000 美元，汤姆又问："这场飓风究竟使你损失了多少钱？"医生回答："大约在 1000 美元以上，不过，我知道保险公司是不可能给那么多的！"不久，保险公司的理赔调查员来找汤姆，对他说："汤姆先生，我知道像你这样的大律师是专门谈判大数目的，不过，恐怕我们不能赔太大的数目。请问你，如果我只赔你 300 美元，你觉得怎么样？"多年的经验告诉汤姆，对方的口气是说他"只能"赔多少，显然他自己也觉得这个数目太少，不好意思开口；而且，第一次出价后必然还有第二次、第三次。所以他故意沉默了半晌，然后反问对方："你觉得怎么样？"对方愣了一会儿，又说："好吧！真对不起，请你别将刚才的价钱放在心上，多一点儿，比方说 600 美元怎么样？"汤姆又从对方回答的口气里获得了情报，判断出对方的信心不足，于是又反问道："能多一点儿吗？""好吧，1000 美元如何？"最后，以 3000 美元了结，竟是医生希望的三倍。

☞ **案例分析 6—5**　（中美电子谈判）

美国某电子公司欲向中国某进出口公司出售生产半导体使用的设备，派人来北京与中方洽谈。其设备性能良好，适合中方。双方很快就设备性能指标达成协议，随即进入价格谈判。中方认为设备性能可以，但是价格不行，希望降价。美国方面认为货好，价格自然就高，不能降价。

中方：不降价我们接受不了。

美方：东方人爱讲价，我们美国人讲究义气，只能降 0.5%。

中方：谢谢您的义气之举，但是价格是不合理的。

美方：怎么不合理了？

中方：设备是中等性能，但是价格远远高于其性能，不匹配。

美方：贵方不是很满意我们的设备吗？

中方：是的，性能方面符合我们的需求，但并不意味着就是最佳、最高水平的。如果用您的报价，我们可以买到更好的设备。

美方：我们需要考虑一下。

休息片刻后，双方再谈。美方改为价格再优惠 3％，但是中方仍然不能满意，认为价格没有达到中方的成交线，要求美方再降。美方坚决不同意，要求中方还价，中方给出价格优惠 15％ 的条件。

美方听后沉默了一会，从包里拿出机票说："贵方条件太苛刻，我方难以接受。为表示诚意，我再降 2％。如果同意，我们签订合同；如果不同意，我的机票是明天下午 2 点的，准时离开。"说完起身离开，临走前说："我住在友谊宾馆，如果有了决定请在中午 12 点前给我答复。"

中方研究之后，不能接受 5.5％ 的优惠，至少应该降到 7％。如何再谈呢？中方调查了第二天下午 2 点是否有飞往美国的航班，得到了否定的答案。第二天早上 10 点，中方给宾馆打电话，说明了诚意，表示中方也愿意让步，只要求优惠 10％。美方看到了诚意，也看到还有谈判的希望，表示愿意见面，继续谈判。最后双方再次都做出了让步，以优惠 7.5％ 的价格成交。

☞ **思考题与讨论题**

1. 谈判磋商阶段的战略路径与考虑有哪些？

2. 让步有哪些原则？

3. 让步的模式有哪些？你喜欢哪一种？为什么？

4. 迫使对方让步的策略有哪些？哪几种更常用？

5. 阻止对方进攻的策略有哪些？

6. 试分析案例分析 6—5，该谈判中双方是如何促成交易的？是否形成了僵局？使用了什么样的让步策略？

第三篇

知 识 篇

# Chapter 7

# Language Skills for International Business Negotiation

☞ **Case study 7 – 1**    (**Premier Zhou's resourceful reply**)

Premier Zhou Enlai is known worldwide for his eloquence. The art of language is best presented through his resourcefulness, courage and trenchancy.

There was a widely-spread story about Premier Zhou. At a press conference held in Beijing, a reporter from the West asked the Premier a question after he introduced the economic achievements in China. "May I ask how much money People's Bank of China possesses?" The question was obviously ridicule. But Premier Zhou answered diplomatically, "The People's Bank of China has 18.88 Yuan." All the people at present were astounded by the answer. It was curiously silent and you would hear a pin drop. Then Premier Zhou continued, "To be specific, we issue 10 Yuan, 5 Yuan, 2 Yuan, 1 Yuan, 5 Jiao, 2 Jiao, 1 Jiao, 5 Fen, 2 Fen and 1 Fen, totaling 18.88 Yuan." There appeared a big applause.

Language is the media to convey information. The whole process of international business negotiation is a process in which negotiators from different countries or regions communicate, discuss and persuade each other with mutually understandable language so as to achieve the negotiation goal. The information transfer is fulfilled between negotiators through listening, stating, asking, answering, debating, convincing, etc. Only if negotiators have good command of the rules of language and skills for business negotiations, can they turn the full power of language into an effective tool to achieve negotiation goals.

## Ⅰ. Techniques for Asking Questions

Asking questions is an important means for one party to acquire information from its counterpart. Negotiators always use ingenious questions to understand the counterpart's needs, get to know their thoughts, convey their emotions and provoke the counterpart's thinking. Attaching importance to and utilizing the skills of asking flexibly may give rise to mutual discussion, obtain information and even control the direction of the negotiation. Hence, we should have a clear picture about why to ask questions, what questions to ask, when to ask questions and how to ask questions.

### 1. Types of questions

(1) Closed questions

Closed questions are the questions that can evoke given answers under given conditions, to which the only answer is "Yes" or "No." Typical examples are "Will you ship the goods in September?" "When did you find the package broken the first time?" This sort of questions can help the questioners to get certain and specific information. Meanwhile, answering these questions does not take too much effort.

A. Selective or suggestive questions

Selective questions offer several situations among which the counterpart is asked to make a choice. For example, "Please note that we can get 2% to 5% commission from other suppliers." "Only today is OK, in the morning or afternoon?" That is, we give two or more choices among which the counterpart may choose. When selective questions are used, questioners should be careful to use a mild tone and an appropriate expression, so as to avoid giving a forceful or imposing impression. So please be prudent to use this kind of asking. Generally, people use it when taking the complete initiative of the negotiation or it might lead to an impasse. In addition, don't narrow down the choices within which the counterparts can choose, or they may find all the choices unacceptable.

B. Clarifying questions

Clarifying questions refer to the questions through which we urge our counterpart to re-state or complement their previous answers, such as "Just now you said the products will be delivered in October. Can you guarantee it?" "Just now you mentioned our bilateral trade plans to adopt the payment by L/C this year. Have you decided about that?" "What would be the situation if we adopt the second project?" This kind of question is aimed at making your counterpart clarify their attitude again after they have expressed certain ideas, ensuring that both parties can get accurate feedback and enhancing mutual understanding.

C. Reference questions

Reference questions refer to the questions asked on the basis of the opinions given by a third party. For example, "Dr. John said that the product had achieved the top-level of precision internationally. Do you agree?" "Mr. Zhang agreed to that point. What do you think of it?" This kind of question requires both parties to confirm the comments made by their well-known and mutually respected third party. It will always make a significant impact on the counterpart; but if one refers to an unfamiliar figure or institution, the outcome will just be the opposite.

(2) Open-ended questions

Open-ended questions don't limit the answer, and they can't be answered with a simple "Yes" or "No." For instance, "What do you think of the market prospects for the product?" "What is your impression on our corporation?" "What do you think of the present sales performance?" Questioners can always elicit more information, for there is no fixed range of answers to this kind of questions and they encourage the counterpart to talk freely.

A. Probing questions

When you don't know too much about the other side, you may ask questions in a tactful mood and tone on appropriate occasions. Probing questions are further questions based on the information the counterpart has already given, such as "The function of the product is good enough. Can you make some comments?" "You do not think there is any space for the price to be lowered. Are there other reasons apart from the two you have already cited?" Putting probing questions to the counterpart is like sending out scouts to see if anybody is about. They can be used to dig out more information, which is then used to make comparisons and analysis in order to find a better solution. Besides, if the other side agrees, he will answer you the question; if he refuses, you will not feel intolerable or embarrassed.

B. Conferring questions

Conferring questions are questions raised to the other side for his opinions, and the purpose is to make him agree with you. For example, "In March next year, the East China Export Commodity Trade Fair will be held in Shanghai. Do you think you will be able to be there then?" "Is it OK to deliver the goods in three batches?" "Let's make the commission 3%. Do you think it appropriate?" This kind of question is usually related to the counterpart's benefits, and may be viewed as a constructive way to ask questions in order to solicit the counterpart's opinions. Furthermore, this sort of question is generally easily accepted, and if refused, the atmosphere can still be harmonious, and the two sides still have opportunities to cooperate.

Besides, there are proof-seeking questions, multi-level questions, etc.

### 2. Questions that should not be asked

a. Hostile questions;

b. Questions about private life, job, income, family status, woman's age, religion and party beliefs;

c. Questions that indicate suspicions of the quality of the other party;

d. Other excessive questions irrelevant to the negotiation contents.

### 3. Techniques for asking questions

a. Prepare some questions beforehand that will be difficult for the counterpart to answer immediately. Preferably ask some questions that the other side cannot figure out a proper answer so that you may get unexpected effect.

b. Ask questions at a right moment. Asking a question too early will reveal the intention of the questioner, and asking your question too late will hinder the negotiation process. Usually questions should be asked when the other side has finished his statement or at the interval of his statement. Surely you can ask at the specified time according to the agenda or before or after you make the statement yourself.

c. Avoid raising doubts, or asking harsh questions like a judge in a trial, and do not speak with an overbearing air or ask a succession of questions at one time.

d. Ask different questions according to the age, position, personality, education level, and negotiation experience of the counterpart.

e. Test the honesty of your counterpart and see how the other side will deal with the matter, you may ask a question of which you already know the answer.

f. Keep silent after asking a question to wait patiently for the counterpart to answer it, and do not give additional remarks over and over again, which will make it impossible for the other party to answer the question.

g. Ask questions sincerely and in simple and short sentence patterns to stimulate the interest of your counterpart in answering the questions, or the counterpart will get impatient or feel fooled.

## II. Techniques for Answering Questions

Answering questions is no simple and easy job. There might be different possible answers to the same question, and different answers will have different effects. In international business negotiations, the motivations of the questioners are so complicated that simple words "Yes" or "No" cannot suffice. Every sentence from the answering is considered as a promise which is a psychological burden and pressure. An improper answer will endanger the success of the negotiation. Sometimes accurate answer may not be necessarily the best and proper answer. The key to answering a question is to know what should be said and what should not be said.

### 1. Think first, and then answer

Leave some time for contemplation before you answer the questions posed by the counterpart. Whether your answer is good or not does not depend on the speed of your answering. Your answer can be accurate and forceful as long as you have a clear picture about the motivation and intention behind your counterpart's questions. You may extend your thinking time through some accepted procedures, such as drinking water, adjusting your seat, browsing some materials, etc. Negotiators must abstain from racing to be the first to answer a question without careful thinking.

### 2. Answer selected questions

When the counterpart poses a string of questions with the hope of "sending out a scout to see if anybody is about," it's unnecessary to answer all the questions. Some of them might not be worthwhile to answer or you might partly answer the questions—especially questions that are unfavorable to your party. You should keep your bottom line as a secret. You can narrow down the questions or steer away from the main topic or talk ambiguously. For example, "Could we please take this question in separate parts?" "I can hardly agree with some parts of your questions..." "We usually deal with such problems in this way..." and so on.

### 3. Delay answering questions

Some of the questions posed by the counterpart are not impossible to answer, but it is better to adopt a delaying approach to deal with them until conditions are mature and the opportunity you want arrives. The first method is "delay first, then answer." This includes such responses as "Could you please repeat your question?" "I don't fully understand what you mean." "Before I answer your question, may I hear your suggestions?" The second method is to "delay instead of answering the question," which means that you do not answer at all. For example, "I don't have the first hand information to answer your question. I think you must hope I give you a detailed and satisfactory reply, which needs time. Do you think so?"

### 4. Ask a question in reply

Rhetorical questions can be adopted when the counterpart poses some probing, leading or proof-seeking questions, and you neither want to reveal details nor want to refuse the counterpart directly, lest you negatively influence the negotiation atmosphere. You may wish to limit the questions of your counterpart or to probe into details from your counterpart. For instance, the seller asks, "Why do you insist that international express be used?" (They are afraid that it will be too expensive.) The buyer answers, "Do we have any quicker and safer means of delivery besides international express services?" (The buyer is trying to relate it to the deal, and to block the counterpart from seeking other cheaper but slower means.) At a news conference, a reporter asked the then US president Regan, "Some people say that the Soviet people think that you will be reappointed US President, which means they want to meet with you. Do you think so?" "You should go and ask them why they want to meet with me!" replied Regan.

### 5. Give irrelevant answers

The method of giving irrelevant answers can be adopted when we are confronted with some harsh, sharp or complicated questions that are very difficult to answer in a positive manner. Apparently, we are answering the question, but in fact, we are answering another question related to the original one. This enables us to avoid a sharp question as well as escape the embarrassment of having no answers. For example, we can change the definition, transfer to a related topic, avoid the counterpart's strength and focus on his weakness, as we are offering a meaninglessly ineffective answer.

### 6. Use ambiguous and general answers

Answer sharp or sensitive questions posed by your counterpart in ambiguous, general and flexible ways. This may relax the negotiation atmosphere as well as keeping the secret of your own party. Take this sentence as an example, "We will solve the problem as soon as possible." "As soon as possible" here is flexible and general because it does not state any specific time, and at the same time leaves large space for your party. You might say like："For this question，I once heard that..." "I used to notice a piece of news from a newspaper，as far as my memory can reach，it is probably like this..." "...it all depends on..."

### 7. Refuse in a polite way

If you do not want to say "No" directly for fear of destroying the negotiation atmosphere when you disagree with your counterpart，you can confirm their opinions first，and then use a buffer to give them some comfort，and finally clarify your unchangeable attitude with polite negative words. For instance，"I completely agree with you，but..." "I understand your meaning and have the same thoughts as you on my mind，but..." "I know that it will cost less if you send the samples through common parcels，but..."

### 8. Silence

Sometimes silence can be adopted as a special "answering" strategy when there are some sensitive questions difficult or inconvenient to answer. Appropriate silence can work wonders. Your unexpected silence will make your counterpart feel uncomfortable："Did I ask the wrong questions or did they feel my question was not worth answering?" This kind of self-doubt and reflection will create intangible pressure. In order to escape embarrassment，your counterpart may abandon the previous requirement，transfer their topic or put forward new proposals. Japanese businessmen like adopting this kind of strategy to achieve their goals. Remember silence can be used only occasionally，or the whole negotiation will be too low-toned and low-spirited.

### 9. Interruptions

Some experienced negotiators often arrange a certain person to cut in or interrupt at the critical moment in the negotiation when facing some difficult questions so that they can get some time to think about the questions. For example，"There's an urgent document which needs your signature." or "There's a telephone call outside for you."

## Ⅲ. Skills of Watching/Observing Body Languages

Body language，gestures，or nonverbal language can convey information. Watching refers to observing the behaviors of the other side. Observing body language can be an important means for analyzing，obtaining information and understanding your counterpart. Through observing the behaviors and conversation, you might try to explore the psychological factors and judge the ideological changes of the other side, and determine your countermeasures. Body language used in negotiations mainly consists of facial expressions, limb language and some incidental behaviors.

### 1. Speaking eyes

"Eyes are the window of the soul." Changes of emotions, moods and attitudes can be reflected in our eyes. In general, people can hide their real intentions through controlling their tones and behaviors when they are speaking, but it is very difficult for them to hide their expression in their eyes. Eyes can usually convey the following five kinds of information:

a. If your counterpart often looks at you in the face or has eye contact with you, say, over 60%, it means that he is very interested in what you are talking about and is eager to learn about your attitude and determine your sincerity, so you are quite likely to make a deal with him. If the percentage is below 30%, it means that he has no interest in the talk.

b. If your counterpart blinks his eyes far more than natural frequency (normally, people blink their eyes about 8 times per minute, i.e. we blink once every 8 seconds and every blink should not last for more than one second), it is possible that your counterpart is bored with you or your talk, or maybe he has a sense of superiority and is indifferent to you.

c. If your counterpart does not look into your face while talking, or occasionally glances at your face then quickly shifts away, it may indicate dishonesty: he may play tricks on you, want to take advantage of you or lack interest in this deal.

d. If the pupils of your counterpart's eyes are enlarged and shining, it suggests that your counterpart is very excited about the talk and you stand a good chance of succeeding; the shrinking of the pupils as well as dull eyes can show that your counterpart is very negative or angry, so the possibility of a successful negotiation will be lowered.

e. If your counterpart's eyes keep shifting and often fail to contact yours, you can conclude that he is not interested in what you are talking about, or they are not honest.

### 2. Movement of upper limbs

By virtue of gestures or shaking hands with other people, it may help you to judge their psychological state and activities, and to convey some information to them. Gestures can strengthen the mood and might make the other side in a high spirit.

(1) Handshake

Standard handshake postures usually go like this: You should hold the palm of your counterpart with a firm but gentle force, and your counterpart should also return a firm handshake, which usually lasts for 1 to 3 seconds. Besides, you should keep an eye contact when shaking your hands with your counterpart. A handshake can convey the following messages besides courtesy and greetings:

a. Firm handshakes show enthusiasm, activeness and self-confidence. Most Americans prefer shaking hands in this way because of their open-minded character.

b. Loose handshakes show shyness, a timid nature, lack of self-confidence, a conservative nature or putting on airs.

c. Sweating palms show excitement or nervousness.

d. Shaking hands after staring arrogantly at the counterpart for a while indicates that one is observing his counterpart. In fact, this act implies that one wants to lower the status of the counterpart.

e. Palm-upward handshakes is a signal of frankness or in a passive or inferior position. Downward handshake is the sign to show that one wants to dominate the other side.

f. Holding one hand of the counterpart with both of one's hands and shaking upward and downward show sincere thanks, a request or the accomplishment of a deal.

(2) Arms

Arms crossed on the chest show a conservative nature, defensiveness or protection, and, at the same time, if both fists are clenched, it shows hostility.

(3) Fists

Clenching one's fists shows nervousness or challenge against the counterpart. Making noises by fingers-joint while clenching one's fists is usually a signal of wordless threat or preparing to attack the other side. During the negotiations, clenching one's fists might also be the signal of determination or dissatisfaction. Pressing and pinching one's finger joints to make cracking sounds with both hands one after another shows determination or may indicate relief from nervousness.

(4) Hands and fingers

a. Tapping or drumming one's fingers or pens shows that one is not interested in, disagrees with or impatient with what the counterpart is saying at the moment.

b. Resting one's elbows on the table and keeping one's fingers together show self-confidence, willfulness, authoritativeness or arrogance. It also has the function of overawing to the others.

c. Interlacing all the fingers before one's chest can show concentration, frankness, modesty and introversion.

d. With both of one's hands inserting into his waist means that he has a well-thought-out plan, and that he has had an adequate preparation mentally and physically for the matter he is confronted with. It might also be the sign of feeling superiority and domination.

e. To make a circle with one's thumb and index finger means OK in America, while it means MONEY for Japanese, and extreme provocative action for Tunisians.

### 3. Body posture and movement of the lower limbs

(1) Body posture

The static state of negotiators' body conveys some information. Usually, there are three styles of posture: horizontal posture, sitting posture and vertical posture. In business negotiation, most people usually adopt sitting style. Sitting style can undisguisedly reflect the psychological state of the negotiator: deeply sitting in a chair with one's back straight and upright demonstrates a kind of psychological superiority; arms crossing on the chest is a psychological expression of taking precaution measures; wryneck and sloping shoulder usually mean a poor automaticity of a person; trembling with fear or being in a haste means that the person is lack of confidence; holding one's head high usually conveys the meaning that he is confident and can be reliable.

(2) Movement of the lower limbs

Legs and feet are often the parts of a person to reveal one's subconsciousness. They can mainly convey the following information:

a. Putting one's knees together, with the upper body straight and upright. If your counterpart is speaking with legs putting together, upper body straight and maintaining this posture for a long time, it shows his respect and modesty, and may indicate that your counterpart hopes to accomplish this deal. Your counterpart's putting knees together with the upper body leaning backward shows cautiousness and thorough consideration, but lack of charisma and self-confidence.

b. Legs apart. If your counterpart is sitting with knees apart and upper body leaning back, it indicates that he has enough self-confidence and is not apt to make any concessions, ready to accept challenges from you. If he sits with one leg on another, it usually indicates that he will refuse you and protect his sphere of influence. If he often changes the posture of putting his legs, it usually means he is impatient, quite bothered and emotionally instable. Shaking one's feet or legs or patting floor with the tiptoe also show that one is impatient, bothered, or has no alternative, or wants to get rid of tension.

c. Sitting cross-legged. If a person is sitting cross-legged with upper body erect, it suggests that he is formal, square and not flexible, but is eager to close the deal. If he is cross-legged sitting across from his counterpart with his upper body leaning or bending forward toward his counterpart, it means that he wishes for cooperation. If he is sitting cross-legged with his upper body leaning backward, it may indicate his arrogance or refusal.

d. Sitting with ankle on knee. Putting one foot on the other knee with the upper body reclining against the sofa may be an indication of arrogance, precaution, suspicion or unwillingness to cooperate; talking eloquently with the upper body bending forward shows one is enthusiastic, not bothering about the trifles, punctilious, and willing to cooperate. Frequent changes of leg postures show discomfort, restlessness or impatience.

### 4. Abdominal language

Protrude one's abdomen reveals his psychological superiority, confidence and satisfaction. Some people say abdomen is the signal of will and courage. Uncovering the buttons of one's jacket means opening one's sphere of influence. Holding abdomen and curling up is a signal of defending psychology because of depressing and uneasiness. Tapping one's belly slightly is to demonstrate his graceful bearing, generosity and pride of oneself.

### 5. Messages conveyed through coughs

a. Preparing to make speeches.

b. Calming down.

c. Showing surprise or suspicion.

d. Covering lies.

e. Reminding your business partner to be careful of their words and behavior.

f. Reminding your counterpart of the time.

### 6. Playing with something that one has brought with him

a. Cleaning one's glasses or kneading one's eyes is a symbol of tiredness; looking at the clock on the wall or looking at your watch or mobile phone reveals that he is not interested in the topic. Suddenly pushing the glasses upward is an indication of anger or readiness to take counteraction.

b. Opening one's notebook slowly means he pays a close attention to the speech. Opening one's notebook quickly means he has found an important question.

c. Scribbling on a blank piece of paper is a symbol of impatience. Turning a pen around with one's fingers is a symbol of absent-mindedness.

d. Frequently looking at one's watch is a signal that say "That's enough for now." Closing a notebook and a laptop computer，resting both hands on the table，looking here and there and leaning the body backward means "It's time to bring this to an end!"

## Ⅳ. Other Tips

### 1. Brief tips for listening

Listening is an important factor to achieve success in socializing or contacting with others. A qualified and educated negotiator must have the habit of listening to his counterpart patiently. Listening is the simplest way to know the other side's need and understand the real situation. During the negotiation，listening with great concentration is more important than endless talking.

Listening aims at clarifying the facts and figuring out your counterpart's thoughts so as to adjust your moves. Active listening can help you know more about the other side's stands，views and attitudes and learn about their ways of communication，inner relationship and even the divergence of opinions in their team. Listening is one of the most efficient ways to improve relationship between both parties since listening carefully shows that the listener pays close attention to what the speaker is talking about. By listening，negotiators can obtain attitude-changing effect of the other side which is obviously beneficial to the success of a negotiation.

（1）To concentrate your attention by taking notes actively while listening

Concentration is the basic and significant part in the art of listening，accompanied with thinking and analyzing what you have heard. Taking notes is helpful for concentration. It can not only help you to recall and memorize what the speaker is saying，but also help you to make further inquiries or explanations. In business negotiation，you can obtain a large amount of information through listening，so it is one of the most basic requirements for a qualified negotiator.

(2) To listen with great presence of your mind

In negotiation, it is very important to try every means to know the idea of the other side, find out their need and prepare to react promptly. Listening initiatively is to listen selectively with attention to get to the point. We should avoid preconceptions and interrupting the speaker; do not hasten to judge, refute or give up listening. It is more important to listen with patience and take necessary notes for further speech.

(3) Try to distinguish what you have heard

If one side takes up most of the time for their own speech, there is little time for both parties to communicate and negotiate. Sometimes there might be the case that what you have heard is not logical, reasonable, or even repetition. So through listening, you can in the meantime take the opportunity to think how and what you should reply to your counterpart.

(4) Don't avoid those problems which you feel difficult to deal with

It is impossible to memorize all the contents of the conversation by brain in negotiation because everyone is in high tension. Therefore it is necessary to make notes or even make a recording. Sometimes the topics might have some concern with politics, economics, technology and interpersonal relationship. Though you probably don't agree, you should try to figure out the other's thinking. And in this way, it helps you to remember and recall the contents of the negotiation so as to make an inquiry over some questions; for another, it can make the other side feel appreciated and respected.

### 2. Brief tips for making statements

a. Opening statement is of vital importance. Express your point of view in a sincere and relaxed way so that a harmonious, friendly and positive negotiation atmosphere can be established.

b. Be clear and concise. Differentiate primary issues from secondary ones, and achieve unity and coherence.

c. Try to be accurate and consistent, objective and genuine and give a vivid and visual account.

d. Pay attention to your intonation, pronunciation, speed and necessary pause and repetition. Have a sense of propriety in speech or action.

### 3. Brief tips for persuasion

In negotiation, the basic principle for persuasion is to be reasonable, powerful and proper. That is to convince people by good reasoning, evidence and materials, and stop where it should stop.

a. Create conditions to persuade the other side: Establish good interpersonal relationships and win the trust of your counterpart and then try to persuade him.

b. Grasp the good timing for persuasion.

c. Seek the common ground and emphasize the consistency of the two sides.

d. Explain in details the effect of your opinions, especially the benefits which the other side can obtain on receiving your opinion.

e. Be patient and go from the easy to the difficult, and you cannot force the other side.

Note: The following are the efficient approaches to persuade bigots.

Firstly, give him an out. Some people have a strong sense of self-respect and don't like to admit his fault. You can give him an out by making some positive comments on his behavior, or mentioning the objective excuse for his mistakes which in fact provides him a chance to correct his mistakes. In this way he will easily accept your persuasion.

Secondly, wait patiently. For some bigots, you can wait for a period of time. Although your counterpart may not change his attitude, he will surely recall and think about what you have said.

Thirdly, adopt a roundabout route. You may take a roundabout route for some bigots. That means to keep away from the topic and say something that he is interested in and try to find out his weaknesses. He will find that you are the person who can be relied on and what you said is helpful for him.

Lastly, To keep silent. To those snarled problems and people who are unreasonable, you may keep silent and pay no attention. Probably they will reflect on their behavior and not insist on their point of view and might be convinced.

### 4. Brief tips for refusal

The principle to make a refusal in negotiation is to express the idea of NO on the one hand, and on the other hand, to let the other side understand and accept your response so as to keep some leeway for future cooperation. In business negotiation, you should have the ability to say both "YES" and "NO."

(1) To raise some questions and ask your counterpart to answer

Sometimes you may raise a string of questions against the excessive demanding. When your counterpart answers your questions, he will have to admit his demand is too excessive, and you can easily refuse him.

（2）To find excuses for refusal

Sometimes you can try to find some excuses for refusing your counterpart. For example, you may try to hang up the negotiation. In the end, the affair should be over since the situation has changed and you can easily refuse the other side.

（3）To make some compensation

Make some compensation at the time of your refusal. The compensation here usually does not refer to money, goods or interests, but some future commitment, concession or some information or services.

（4）To affirm first and then make the refusal

Try to find the common grounds first, affirm some of the points so as to tackle the confronting situation, and then state your point of view for refusal.

（5）To put forward some conditions

Sometimes refusing the other side will probably worsen the mutual relationship. You can put forward some conditions. If your counterpart can meet with your requirements, you can accept his point of view; if not, then you can achieve the goal of refusing him.

☞ **Case study 7 – 2**　（**A college student's interview**）

Ma Ming, a college graduate majoring in marketing applied for the position of salesman. On the day of job interview, he got up early and went to the interview full of confidence, carrying his application letter and various kinds of certificates which gave proof to his fruitful college life. It took him some time to locate the interview room in a building. However, when he knocked at the door and went into the room he saw three men leaning on sofa, smoking and chatting, with their legs crossed.

"Excuse me. Is this the interview room of ＊ ＊ company?" asked Ma Ming politely.

"No, it isn't. You've got the wrong place." one of the men responded.

Ma Ming was a little confused and turned back to check the number of the room, and then he came up and said, "I'm sorry, but this is exactly the place mentioned on the job advertisement."

"Well, it's too early for the interview." another man replied.

"Can I wait here and join you to have a chat?" asked Ma Ming.

"There's no need for you to stay here, for the positions have been filled." said one of the men.

"But according to the advertisement, tomorrow is the deadline for the position. Please give me a chance to let me introduce myself and I'm sure I won't disappoint you." Ma Ming insisted and gave a brief introduction of himself and his plans for the job.

"Good!" The three men smiled at each other.

Ma Ming finally got the job. But there were tens of applicants who came before him and were refused by the remarks of the three men. It turned out that the purpose of the three men's remark was to test such qualities of a salesman as the judgment, confidence, persistence and the ability to get along with others.

## ☞ Case study 7 – 3　(Mobutu's rhetorical question)

The former president of Zaire, Mobutu, was once interviewed by a Western reporter, "You're quite rich. It is said that your possessions amount to $3 billion. Is it true?" Obviously, this question was meant to disclose whether he benefited himself from abusing the power he had. Mobutu burst into laughter, delaying the time when he must answer, as well as giving himself time to think before he responded to this sharp and sensitive question. Then he asked this question in reply, "A Belgium congressman said that I owned $6 billion. Have you ever heard of that?" (Thus he gave an irrelevant answer as he raised a rhetorical question.) In this reply, he raised the rhetorical question by altering the reporter's question a little. This answer revealed nothing that the reporter could hold against him but left enough leeway for himself. The reporter got no detailed answers from that rhetorical and ineffective answer.

## ☞ Case study 7 – 4　(Statements in the opening stage)

Company A was a powerful real estate development company. On the option of its investment, it took a fancy to a piece of land which belonged to company B and had the potentials of appreciation, whereas Company B also had the intention of cooperation. So the two sides chose go-getters for a negotiation for the transfer of possession of the land.

Representative of Company A: "Probably you also know something about our company. Our company was established by the joint venture between Company C from the US and Company D which is famous in China. We are economically powerful and has made outstanding achievement in real estate development in recent years. Last year we also developed XINHAI garden in your city, and we learn that Mr. Wang, your general manager, is also our purchaser. Several companies from your cities are seeking for cooperation with us, hoping to transfer their land in hand to us for which we have not declared our stand readily. This piece of land of your company has great appeal to us. We are going to remove the original residents and develop a residential quarter. The relevant personnel of our company have conducted an extensive investigation among the residents and enterprises in this region. Basically, there is no resistance. Time is money, we hope we can reach the agreement concerning this problem at the fastest speed. What do you think?"

"We are pleased to have an opportunity to cooperate with you. Though we did not have any contact with you before, we have gained some understanding about you. We have offices spread over the country, many of which are in the houses built by your company. This may be a destiny that ties you and us. We really have the will to sell this piece of land, but we are not anxious to slip out of our hand because besides your company, several companies like XINGHUA and XINGYUN also have a keen interest in this piece of land, they are actively consulting with us. Of course, we are willing to cooperate with you first if your conditions are relatively reasonable and your price is more favorable. We might also help you to simplify the concerned formalities so as to make your project to start work as soon as possible."

## ☞ Questions for your consideration and discussion

1. What are the techniques for answering questions?

2. What are the techniques for asking questions?

3. What are the skills of observing body languages?

4. What are the techniques for listening, making a statement, making a refusal and persuasion?

5. In case study 7 – 1, what were the advantages of Premier Zhou's reply? What would be the effect if Premier Zhou refused to reply? How would it be if Premier Zhou answered directly?

6. What do you think of the opening statements of the two sides in case study 7 – 4?

# 第七章

# 国际商务谈判技巧

☞ **案例分析 7—1** （周总理的巧妙回答）

周恩来总理的口才蜚声海内外。他应变机敏、气魄非凡、言辞犀利、柔中有刚,是谈判中能够出色运用语言艺术的典范。

有一则周总理的故事流传很广。在北京举行的一次记者招待会上,周总理在介绍我国经济建设的成就及对外方针后,一名西方记者问道:"请问,中国人民银行有多少资金?"这明显是一种讥笑。对此,周总理婉转地说道:"中国人民银行的资金嘛,有 18.88 元。"这一回答,全场愕然。顿时场内鸦雀无声,静听他细做解释。"中国人民银行发行面额为 10元、5 元、2 元、1 元、5 角、2 角、1 角、5 分、2 分、1 分共 10 种主辅人民币,合计为 18.88 元。中国人民银行是由全中国人民当家做主的金融机构,有全国人民作后盾,信誉卓著,实力雄厚。它所发行的货币,是世界上最有信誉的一种货币,在国际上享有盛誉。"一番话,语惊四座。接着,全场爆发出热烈的掌声。

语言是传递信息的媒介,是人与人之间进行交际的工具。商务谈判则是人们运用语言传达意见、交流信息的过程。而谈判中的信息传递与接受则需要通过谈判者之间的问、答、听、看、叙、辩以及劝和拒绝等方式来完成。在很大程度上,语言的应用效用往往决定了谈判的成败。因此,谈判人员必须综合运用这些方面的技巧,以便准确地把握对方的行为与想法,传递自己的意见与观点,进而达到谈判预期的目的。

## 一、谈判中"问"的技巧

如何"问"是商务谈判中非常重要的语言技巧。通过巧妙而恰当的提问可以摸清对方的需要,掌握对方的心理,传达信息,表达自己的感情,引起对方的思考,从而达到探求情报、获取信息、引导话题、继续谈判的目的。如何"问"是很有讲究的。重视和灵活地运用提问的技巧,不仅可以引起双方的讨论,获取信息,而且还可以控制谈判的方向。哪些问题应该问、可以问、怎样问,哪些问题不可以问,以及什么时候、什么场景适合提问等,都有一些基本的常识和技巧需要了解和掌握。

1. 提问的类型

(1) 封闭式的提问

封闭式的提问指在特定的领域中给出特定的答复（"是"或"否"）的问句。例如："您是否能在 9 月份装货？""贵方第一次发现包装破损是在什么时候？"这样的提问可以使提问者获得特定的资料，而答复这种问题并不需要太多的思索。

①选择建议式的提问。这种问题旨在将本方的意见抛给对方，让对方在一个规定的范围内进行选择回答。例如："请对方注意，我们从其他供应商那里可以得到 2%～5% 的佣金。""只有今天可以，上午还是下午？"按理说，在提出这种问题之前，提问者应先得到对方将付佣金的承诺，但是这种提问却将这一前提去掉，直接强迫对手在给出的狭小范围内进行选择，可谓咄咄逼人。但使用这种提问方式要特别慎重，一般应在我方掌握充分的主动权的情况下使用，否则很容易出现僵局甚至导致谈判的破裂。即使选用这种提问方式，也要尽量做到语调柔和，措辞得体，以免给人留下专横跋扈、强加于人的不良印象。

②澄清式或探索式的提问。通常，这是针对对方的答复，重新提出问题以便对方进一步澄清或补充原先答复的一种问句。例如："您刚才说这笔交易可以在 10 月份交货，贵方能保证吗？""刚才你们说今年的贸易将使用信用证付款，贵方已经决定了吗？""如果我们采用第二套方案，结果会怎样？"这种方式的提问不但可以进一步探求更为充分的信息，而且还可以显示提问者对对方答复的重视，可以确保谈判双方进一步沟通，还是针对对方的话语进行信息回馈的有效方法，是双方密切配合的理想方式。

③借助式的提问。这是借助第三者的意见来影响或改变对方观点的提问方式。例如："约翰博士说该产品的精密度已达到国际领先水平，您同意吗？""张先生已经同意，您对这个问题是怎么看的呢？"采用这种提问方式，应当注意所提到的第三者必须是对方所熟悉而且最好是他们十分尊重的人，这样就会对他们产生很大的影响力。但如果提起一个对方不熟悉的人或谈不上尊重的人，则可能会引起对方的反感。

(2) 开放式的提问

开放式的提问指在广泛的领域引出广泛的答复，不能简单使用"是"或"不是"来回答的问题。例如："您认为产品的市场前景如何？""您对我公司的印象如何？""您对当前的销售状况有什么看法？"由于开放式的提问不限定答复的范围，答复者可以畅所欲言，提问者也可以得到广泛的信息。

①婉转探讨可能性式的提问。即在没有摸清对方虚实的情况下，采用婉转的语气或方法，在适宜的场合和时机向对方提出问题。例如："这种产品的功能还不错吧？ 您能评价一下吗？""您认为产品不能降价，除了您说的原因，还有其他原因吗？"这种问题是试探性的，一般会得到更多的信息。如果对方有意，他定会接受提问，如果不满意，他的拒绝也不会使我方难堪。

②协商式的提问。即为使对方同意己方的观点,采用商量的口吻向对方提问。例如:"明年三月华东交易会将在上海举行,您会参加吗?""您看是否可以分三批交货?""您看佣金定为 3% 是否合适?"这种提问,语气平和,对方容易接受。而且,即使对方没有接受你的条件,谈判的气氛仍能保持融洽,双方仍有继续合作的可能。

此外,还有证明式的提问(要求对方做出证明或解释)、多层次式的提问(一个问句包括多种内容)等。

**2.通常不应该提问的问题**

①带有敌意的问题。

②有关对方个人生活、工作方面的问题。对于大多数国家和地区的人来说,回避个人生活和工作方面的问题已经成为一种习惯。比如,对方的收入、家庭情况、女士的年龄、对方国家的政党以及宗教等问题都是应当回避的。

③直接指责对方品质和信誉方面的问题。因为这样做不仅会使对方感到不快,而且还会影响彼此之间的真诚合作,甚至还会引起对方的不满和怨恨。

④其他与谈判内容无关的问题。

**3.提问的技巧**

①要预先准备好问题。谈判之前应当对预计要提出的问题进行充分的准备,最好能准备一些对方不能够迅速想出适当答案的问题,以期收到意想不到的效果。一些有经验的谈判人员,往往是先提出一些看上去很一般并且比较容易回答的问题,而这个问题恰恰是随后所要提出的比较重要的问题的前奏。

②要注意提问的时机。提问问题过早,会暴露己方的意图,过晚则会影响谈判的进程。提问一般在对方发言停顿、间歇或完毕之后;在议程规定的辩论时间内;或在己方发言的前后。

③避免使用威胁性、讽刺性的语言,特别要注意不能像法官那样进行盘问、审讯,不要强行追问。

④根据对方的特点进行提问,比如根据对方的职务、年龄、性格等。

⑤可以在适当的时候将一个已经发生的并且答案也是己方所知道的问题提出来,验证一下对方的诚实程度及其处理问题的态度。

⑥提出问题后应闭口不言,等待对方回答。如果这时对方也是沉默不语,则无形中给对方施加了一种压力。由于己方提出了问题,对方就必须以回答问题的方式来打破沉默,或者说打破沉默的责任应当由对方来承担。

⑦态度要诚恳,言辞应简短。用诚恳的态度来问对方,以此来激发对方回答问题的兴趣。另外,所提出的问题句式越简短越好,而由问题引出的回答则越长越好。因此,我们应尽量用简短的句式来向对方提问。

## 二、谈判中"回答问题"的技巧

谈判中回答问题不是一件容易的事情。因为谈判者对回答的每一句话都负有责任，每一句回答都将被对方理所当然地认为是一种承诺，这就给回答问题的人带来一定的精神负担和压力。同一个问题，可以有不同的答案。因此，一个谈判者水平的高低，在很大程度上取决于其回答问题的水平。在谈判中针对问题所做出的准确、正面的回答未必就是最好的回答，有时回答得越准确就越是愚笨。回答的真正艺术在于知道该说什么和不该说什么。

### 1. 让自己获得充分的思考时间

回答问题的好坏，并不是看你回答速度的快慢。作为答复者应保持清醒的头脑，沉着稳健，不慕所谓"对答如流"的虚荣，而应当让自己获得充分的思考时间，判断出对方提问的动机。你可以通过喝一口水、调整一下自己的坐姿和椅子、整理一下桌子上的资料或翻一翻笔记本等动作来考虑一下对方的问题，之后再作答。这样做既显得自然、得体，又能做到三思而后答。当然，间隔的时间也不能太长。

### 2. 不要全盘托出

通常，面对对方的提问，特别是当对方提出一连串问题来投石问路时，不要"全盘托出"，不能毫无保留地回答，你的"底牌"不能轻易地亮出。在谈判中，有的问题不值得回答，有些问题只需做出局部回答，如果你老老实实地"全盘托出"，就会暴露自己的底线。同时，当你"全盘托出"之后，对方不需继续提问就获得了对他们有用的信息，这样就失去了对方向你继续反馈信息和与你进行进一步交流的可能。

### 3. 拖延答复的时间

在谈判中，有时可采用拖延答复的方法，如："我没听明白您的问题，您再重复一遍好吗？""在我回答您的问题之前，我想先听听您的建议。"当对方提出问题而你尚未考虑出满意答案并且对方又追问不舍的时候，你可利用资料不全或需要请示等借口来拖延答复。例如："对于您所提问的问题，我没有第一手资料来做答复。您肯定希望我们为您做详尽而圆满的答复，但这需要时间。您说对吗？"不过延迟答复并不是拒绝答复，因此，谈判者还需进一步思考如何来回答问题。

### 4. 以问代答或无效回答

以问代答是用来应付那些一时难以回答或不想回答的问题可采用的方法，即把对方踢过来的球再踢回去。例如，谈判进展不是很顺利的情况下，一方问道："您对合作的前景怎么看？"对方可采用以问代答的方式："那么，您对合作的前景又是怎么看的呢？""至于……那就取决于您的看法如何了。"又比如，卖方问："贵方为什么坚持使用国际快递？"（担心太贵），买方回答"除了国际快递，还有更快的寄送方法吗？"（与生意联系在一起，阻止买方采用更便宜但更慢的方法）。这时双方自然会认真加以思考，这对于打破窘境会起到良好的作用。

在一次记者招待会上，记者问里根是否相信这样的说法：由于苏联人认为他会再次连任美国总统，所以想和他会晤。记者表面上以苏联人想会晤里根的原因来提问，实际上涉及他是否想连任美国总统的敏感问题。对此，里根回答说："究竟是什么原因使他们想和我会晤，你得问他们。"这就把同一问题转手扔回给对方，做出的是个无效回答。显然，无效回答是说了等于没说，但是它在各种类型的谈判中，为了回避棘手的难题起着独特的作用，同时展现出人们语言表达的风采与智慧。

5. 避正答偏、顾左右而言他

有时，对于对方提出的问题可能很难直接从正面回答，但又不能以拒绝的方式来逃避问题。这时，谈判高手往往用"答偏"的办法来回答，即在回答这类问题时，故意避开问题的实质，而将话题引向歧路，借以破解对方的进攻。比如，可以跟对方讲一些与所提问题既有关系而又没有实际关系的问题。说了一大堆话，看上去回答了问题，其实并没有回答。经验丰富的谈判人员往往在谈判中运用这一方法。此法似乎显得谈判员头脑糊涂，其实这种人高明得很，对方也拿他们没有办法。

6. 可采取推卸责任的方法或不确切地回答

有时候面对毫无准备的问题，人们往往不知所措，或者即使能够回答，但由于某种原因而不愿回答。在这种情况下，可以这样回答："对这个问题，我虽没有调查过，但曾经听说过……"或"贵方的问题提得很好。我曾经在某份资料上看过有关这一问题的记载，就记忆所及，大概是……"这样对那些为了满足虚荣心及自己也不明确提问目的的提问者常能收到较好的效果。另外对于某些问题，可以模棱两可地、富有弹性地进行回答，不把话说死。例如："对类似的问题，我们过去是这样处理的……""对于这个问题，那要看……而定。"

7. 委婉地进行回答

在谈判中，当你不同意对方的观点时，不要直接使用"不"这个具有强烈对抗色彩的字，而应适当运用"转折"技巧，巧用"但是"，先予以肯定、宽慰，再委婉地表示否定继而阐述自己不可动摇的立场，这样就会赢得对方的同情和理解。例如："我完全理解您的意思，也赞成您的意见，但是……""我理解您的处境，但是……""我也明白价格再低一点会更好，但是……"

8. 礼貌地拒绝不值得回答的问题或干脆保持沉默

对于某些不值得回答的问题，可以礼貌地加以拒绝。例如在谈判中，对方可能会提一些与谈判主题无关或基本无关的问题，回答这种问题不仅浪费时间，而且会扰乱你的思路，甚至有时是对方故意提的一些容易激怒你的问题，其用意在于使你失去自制力。回答这样的问题，只会损害自己的利益，可以一笑了之。对于那些不便回答的问题，还可以采取沉默的方式,有时同样可以获得奇妙的效果。因为你的沉默,往往会给对方一种无形的压力,使对方感到不安。为了打破沉默,对方只好中止自己的要求,或提出新的方案,或自己转移话题。日本商人很喜欢采用该策略以达到他们的目的。当然,使用沉默这种方式一定要十分慎重,因为,有时这样做就会显得不太礼貌,或者让人觉得软弱可欺,甚至可能意味着放弃发言权。

9."重申"和"打岔"

对于一些棘手的问题,有经验的谈判者常先安排某人在谈判的节骨眼上打岔,以赢得己方思考一时难以回答而又必须回答的问题的时间,比如"有紧急文件需要某先生出来签字"或"外面有某某先生的电话"。有时回答问题的人自己可以借口去洗手间方便等。

### 三、谈判中"看/观察"的技巧

谈判中的"看"就是指"观其行"。通过仔细观察对方的举止言谈、每一个细微动作,我们可以捕捉对方内心活动的蛛丝马迹,也可以通过揣摩对方的姿态神情,探索引发这类行为的心理因素,进而判断对方的思想变化,决定己方的对策,使谈判朝着有利于己方的方向发展。人的姿态和动作语言所传递的信息是真实可信的。

1.眼睛的"语言"

眼睛被人们誉为"心灵的窗户"。它具有反映人们深层次心理的功能,其动作、神情、状态是最明确的情感表现。通常,人们在讲话的时候可以通过控制声调和行为来掩饰其真实的意图,但是眼睛的动作却很难隐藏。眼睛的动作及所传达的信息主要有:

(1)目光凝视讲话者时间的长短

通常,在与人交谈时,正常情况下视线接触对方脸部的时间应占全部谈话时间的30%～60%。超过这一平均值,可认为对谈话者本人比对谈话内容更感兴趣;低于这一平均值,则表示对谈话者和谈话内容都不怎么感兴趣。

(2)眨眼的频率

一般人每分钟眨眼8次左右,每次眨眼不超过1秒钟。如果每分钟眨眼次数明显超过8次,一般表示对话题不感兴趣。如果眨眼时间超过1秒钟的时间,一方面表示厌烦,不感兴趣;另一方面也表示自己比对方优越。在谈判中,切忌凝视或长时间地连续眨眼,以免引起对方反感。

(3)眼神中是否逃避

倾听对方谈话时,几乎不看对方,表示听话人在试图掩饰什么。一位有经验的海关检查人员在检查过关人员已填好的报关表时,还要再问一句:"还有什么东西呈报没有?"这时,他的眼睛通常不是看着报关表,而是看着过关人员的眼睛,如果一个人不敢正视对方的眼睛,那么就表明该人在某些方面可能有试图掩饰的情况。

（4）瞳孔的变化

眼睛瞳孔放大,炯炯有神,表示此人处于欢喜与兴奋状态;瞳孔缩小,神情呆滞,目光无神,则表示此人处于消极、戒备或愤怒的状态。一般而言,瞳孔放大传递出正面的信息,缩小则传递出负面的信息。实验证明,瞳孔所传达的信息是无法用人的意志来控制的。

（5）眼睛是否闪烁不定

眼睛闪烁不定是一种反常的举动,常被认为是掩饰的一种手段或是性格上不诚实的表现。做事虚伪或者当场撒谎的人,其眼睛常常闪烁不定,以此来掩饰其内心的秘密,这是他们的一个共同特征。

2. 上肢的"语言"

手势或手与手的接触,可以帮助我们判断对方的心理活动或心理状态,同时也可以帮助我们将某种信息传递给对方。手势是谈判中辅助语言的手段,它能使语言表达得更贴切、更恰当,它能加强谈判者的语气,也能使对方的精神振奋起来。

（1）握手

标准的握手姿势应该是:用手指稍稍用力握住对方的手掌,对方也用同样的姿势用手指稍稍用力回握,时间大约为1～3秒钟,另外握手的同时应保持与对方目光的接触。如果双方握手出现与标准姿势不符的情况,便可能有除了问候、一般礼貌以外的附加含义。

①如果对方用力握手,则表明此人具有好动、热情的性格,这种人做事往往喜欢主动。大多数美国人因为性格外向喜欢采用这种握手方式。

②如果对方的握手不用力,甚至轻轻触碰到你的手掌,一般说明这个人缺乏自信,也可能是傲慢矜持、爱摆架子的表现。

③如果对方手掌出汗,表示对方处于兴奋、紧张或情绪不稳定的心理状态。

④握手前先凝视对方片刻,再伸手相握,一般是表明该人想在心理上先战胜对方,将对手置于心理的弱势地位。先注视对方片刻,意味着对对方进行审视,看看对方是否值得自己同其握手。

⑤掌心向上伸出与对方握手,往往表示其坦诚的态度或是其处于被动、劣势或受人支配的状态。在某种程度上,手掌心向上伸出握手,有一种愿与对方合作的含义。如果是掌心向下与对方握手,则表示想取得主动或支配的地位。另外,手掌心向下,也有居高临下的意思。

⑥用双手紧握对方一只手,并上下摆动,往往表示热烈欢迎对方的到来,或表示真诚感谢,也可能表示有求于人或肯定契约关系等含义。

（2）两臂

两臂交叉于胸前,表示保守或防卫;两臂交叉于胸前并握拳,往往是怀有敌意的标志。

（3）拳头

拳头紧握,表示向对方挑战或是自我紧张情绪的表现。握拳的同时如伴有手指关节响声,或用拳击掌,则表示向对方发出无言的威吓或发出攻击的信号。握拳会使人肌肉紧张,能量比较集中,一般只有在遇到外部的威胁或挑战时,人们才会紧握拳头,以准备进行抗击。在谈判中,握拳也表示下决心或不满。将指关节弄出响声往往是下定决心或是紧张状态的一种释放。

（4）手与手指

①用手指或手中的笔敲打桌面,或在纸上乱画,往往表示对对方的话题不感兴趣、不同意或不耐烦的意思。

②两手手指并拢并置于胸的前上方呈塔尖状,表示此人充满信心。它通常可表现出此人高傲与独断的心理状态,对他人起到一种威慑的作用。

③手与手连接放在胸腹部的位置,是谦逊、矜持或略带不安的心情的反映。不停地搓手通常是"为难"的表现。

④手叉腰间,这表示胸有成竹,对自己面临的事情已做好了精神上或行动上的准备,同时也表现出某种优越感或支配欲。有人将这看作领导者或权威人士的风度。

⑤拇指与食指合成一个圈,对美国人来说意味着"OK";对日本人来说则表示"钱";而对突尼斯人来说则意味着极端的挑衅行为。

3. 体态及下肢等的"语言"

（1）体态的"语言"

体态的"语言"是指谈判者身体的静态姿势所传递的信息。通常,人的体态主要有三种:躺卧式、坐式和直立式。商务谈判中通常采取坐式。坐姿一般能毫不掩饰地反映谈判个体的心理状态:深深坐入椅内,腰板挺直,是谈判者想表示出一种心理上的优势;交叠双臂多是一种防范性心理的表示。此外,谈判者的某些姿势（体态）也可以传达某种信息:歪头斜肩、伸脚舞腿,通常说明这是个自律性差、不爱整洁的人;战战兢兢、慌张不定、两脚打颤,说明这个人缺乏自信;昂首挺胸、步履稳健、风度十足,说明这个人富有信心,值得信赖。

（2）下肢的"语言"

人们的腿和脚往往是最先表露潜意识情感的部位。它们主要的动作和所传达的信息有:

①双膝并拢,上身挺直,并且能保持较长时间,通常表明其比较诚实而且尊重对方,愿意与对方达成交易。

②双腿分开,上身后仰,表明其自信,不愿做出让步,并愿意接受对方的挑战。如果一条腿架到另一条腿上,一般是拒绝对方并保护自己的势力范围的信号。如果频繁变换架腿姿势,则表示情绪不稳定、焦躁不安或不耐烦。摇动脚部、用脚尖拍打地板或抖动腿部,表示焦躁不安、无可奈何、不耐烦或欲摆脱某种紧张感。

③盘腿而坐。如果一个人盘腿而坐,上身挺直,表明他正直、拘谨、不灵活但急于成交。如果盘腿而坐,身体前倾,表示他愿意与其对方成交,如果盘腿而坐,身体后仰,则表

示一种傲慢或拒绝。

④双脚交叉而坐，往往表示从心理上压制自己的表面情绪。比如对某人某事持保留态度，表示警惕、防范，或表示尽量压制自己的紧张或恐惧。跷着二郎腿身体斜靠沙发，表示怀疑、警觉、傲慢，不愿合作。身体前倾，侃侃而谈，表示不拘小节，热情，愿意合作。对女性来讲，如果再将两个膝盖并拢起来，则表示拒绝对方或一种防御的心理状态。这往往是比较含蓄而委婉的举动。

**4.腹部的"语言"**

凸出腹部，表现出自己的心理优势、自信与满足感。有人说腹部是意志和胆量的象征。揭开上衣纽扣而露出腹部，表示开放自己的势力范围；抱腹蜷缩，表示出不安、消沉、沮丧等情绪支配下的防卫心理；轻拍自己的腹部，表示自己有风度、雅量，同时也包含着经过一番较量之后的得意心情。

**5.咳嗽传递的信息**

①准备发言。

②镇定不安的情绪。

③表示惊奇或怀疑。

④掩盖谎言。

⑤提醒对方注意自己的言行。

⑥提醒对方注意时间。

**6.其他动作的"语言"**

①猛推一下眼镜，说明因某事而气愤；摘下眼镜，轻轻揉眼或擦擦镜片，可能反映其精神疲劳，或对争论不休的问题感到厌倦，或是喘口气准备再战。

②慢慢打开笔记本，表示关注对方的讲话；快速打开笔记本说明发现了重要问题。

③手中玩笔，表示漫不经心，对所谈的问题没有兴趣，或显示其不在乎的态度；拿着笔在空白纸上画圈或写数字等，双眼不抬，若无其事的样子，说明已经厌烦了；放下手中的物品，双手撑着桌子，头向两边看、向后看，双手抱臂往椅子上一靠，暗示对方"没有多少爱听的啦！随你讲吧。"

④扫一眼室内的挂钟或手腕上的表，或是把桌上的笔收起，把记事簿合上，或是轻轻拿起桌上的帽子，都是准备结束的架势。若再抬眼看着对方的眼睛，似乎在问，"可以结束了吧？"

## 四、谈判中"听""说""劝""拒绝"的技巧

### 1.谈判中"听"的技巧

与人交往取得成功的重要秘诀就是多听。一个合格的谈判人员一定具有认真倾听对

方的习惯。倾听是了解对方需要、发现事实真相的最简捷的途径。没有什么方式能比倾听更直接、更简便地了解对方的信息了。倾听可以给对方留下良好的印象,可以使你更直接地了解对方的立场、观点、态度。因此,谈判人员必须十分注意捕捉对方思维过程的蛛丝马迹,及时跟踪对方动机,认真倾听对方的发言,从而掌握谈判的主动权。

（1）通过记笔记来集中精力

绝大多数人即席记忆并保持的能力是有限的,为了弥补这一不足,应当养成在倾听别人讲话时做笔记的习惯。一方面,笔记可以帮助自己回忆和记忆,而且也有助于在对方讲完话以后就这些问题向对方提出质询,同时,还可以帮助自己做充分的分析,理解对方讲话的确切含义与精神实质;另一方面,通过记笔记可以给讲话人留下一个重视其讲话内容的印象,当听话人停笔抬头看看讲话者时,又会对其产生一种鼓励的作用。对于商务谈判来说,一般情况下,信息量都很大,所以一定要动笔做记录,不能因相信自己的记忆力而很少记笔记。

（2）要专心致志、集中精力地听

谈判人员在倾听对方讲话时应做到聚精会神,同时还要以积极的态度去倾听。精力集中地听,是倾听最基本、最重要的原则。因此,我们应当时刻集中精力并用积极的态度去倾听,可以主动与讲话者进行目光接触,并做出相应的表情以鼓励讲话者,比如,可以扬一下眼眉,或是赞同地点点头。这些动作的配合可以帮助我们集中精力,起到良好的收听效果。作为一名商务谈判人员,应该养成有耐心地倾听对方讲话的习惯,这是商务谈判人员良好个人修养的一个标志。

（3）要有鉴别地倾听对方的发言

通常,人们说话时是边说边想,来不及整理,有时表达一个意思要绕着弯子讲许多内容,也根本谈不上什么重点突出。因此,听话者就需要在用心倾听的基础上,鉴别传递过来的信息的真伪,去粗取精,去伪存真,这样才能抓住重点,收到良好的效果。

（4）不要回避难以应付的话题

有时谈判的话题往往会涉及一些诸如政治、经济、技术以及人际关系等方面的问题,可能会令谈判人员一时回答不上来。在这个时候,切记不可持充耳不闻的态度,只有用心去领会对方提出的每个问题的真实用意,才能找到难题的真实答案。另外,为了培养自己急中生智、举一反三的能力,应多加训练和思考,以便自己在遇到问题时不慌不乱。对方所讲的,即使不认可,不能回答,也应先记录下来。

2. 谈判中"说"的技巧

①开场陈述至关重要。要开宗明义,明确本次谈判所要解决的主要议题,并表明己方的基本立场。应以诚挚和轻松的方式来表达自己的观点,创造一种和谐、友好、积极向上的洽谈气氛。"好的开始是成功的一半"就是这个道理。

②简洁通俗,主次分明,生动具体。

③措辞得当,富有弹性,客观真实。

④注意语调、语速及必要的停顿和重复。

3. 谈判中"劝"的技巧

在谈判中,说服对方的基本原则是:要做到有理、有力、有节。有理,是指要以理服人,而不是以力压人;有力,是指说服的证据、材料等有较强的力量;有节,是指在说服对方时要适可而止,不能得理不让人。

①创造说服对方的条件:建立良好的人际关系,取得对方的信任,抓住对方的心理进行诱导劝说。

②把握说服的时机。

③寻找双方的共同点,强调利益的一致性。

④说明你的意见可能导致的影响,特别是对方接受意见后的益处。

⑤说服要有耐心。由浅入深,不可胁迫。

注:以下是说服"顽固者"的方法。

第一,"下台阶"法。当对方自尊心很强,不愿意承认自己的错误时,你不妨先给对方一个"台阶"下,再肯定他正确的地方,或者说一说他错误存在的客观依据,也就是给对方提供一个改正错误的条件和机会。这样,他就会感到没有失掉面子,因而也就容易接受你善意的说服。

第二,等待法。有些人可能一时难以说服,不妨等一段时间,对方虽没有当面表示改变看法,但对你的态度和你所讲的话,他会加以回忆和思考的。

第三,迂回法。当有的人正面的道理已经很难听进去时,不要强行地进行说服,而应采取迂回前进的方法。即暂时避开主题,谈论一些他感兴趣的事情,从中找到他的弱点,然后针对他的弱点,发表己方的看法,让他感到你的话对他是有用的,感到你是令人信服的。这时,他会更加冷静地考虑你的意见,更容易接受你的说服。

第四,沉默法。对于一些纠缠不清的问题,如果又遇上了不讲道理的人,可以当作没有听见,不予理睬,对方就会觉得他所提出的问题可能没什么道理,于是自己也就感到没趣了,可能就会不再坚持自己的意见,从而达到说服对方的目的。

4. 谈判中"拒绝"的技巧

谈判中拒绝的原则是:既要明确地表达出"不",又能让对方理解和接受,从而为以后的合作留有一定的余地。在商务谈判中,会说"是"的谈判者,不是最优秀的谈判者,只有善于说"不"的谈判者才是成熟老练的谈判者。既会说"是",又会说"不"的人才可能被称为谈判家。

(1) 提出问题让对方回答

有时候,面对对方的过分要求,你可以有针对性地提出一连串的问题。通常,如果对方回答你这一连串的问题，那么他将意识到他所提的要求太过分了，从而达到拒绝的目的。

（2）找借口达到拒绝的目的

有时候可以寻找一些借口来拒绝对方。比方说，谈判者可以用拖延时间的手段达到拖延谈判的目的，最后因"事过境迁"，各种宏观条件发生了如谈判者预料或声称的那种变化，最后达到拒绝的目的。

（3）对对方进行补偿

这种方法就是在拒绝对方的同时，给予某种补偿。这种补偿一般不是可以兑现的金钱、货物或某种利益等，而是某种将来情况下的允诺、某种未来有条件的让步、某种未来的前景，甚至是将来会提供的某种信息、服务，等等。

（4）先肯定再转折

就是先不亮出自己的观点，而是从对方的观点、意见中找出双方的共同点，再加以肯定赞赏，或者站在第三者的角度对对方的观点表示理解，从而减少对方的对抗心理，减弱其心理防线，然后再用婉转的语言陈述自己的观点，来拒绝对方，甚至说服对方。

（5）提出一定的条件

有时候直截了当地拒绝对方势必会恶化双方的关系，甚至导致对方对你的攻击。如果在拒绝对方之前，先要求对方满足你的某个条件，若对方能满足你，你就可以满足对方的要求；如果对方不能满足你，那你也无法满足对方的要求，从而达到拒绝对方的目的。

☞ **案例分析 7—2** 　（一个大学生的应聘）

某校市场营销专业的毕业生马明前去应聘推销员。一早他就准备好求职信以及能证明他大学期间辉煌历史的各种证书，满怀信心地去面试了。他左转右转寻至某大厦某层某号房，敲门，推门进去后看见三个男子正跷着二郎腿，斜躺在沙发上吞云吐雾地闲聊。

"请问这是某公司的招聘办公室吗？"马明很有礼貌地问。

"你搞错了，这不是某公司的招聘办公室。"一男子侧着身答道。

马明一愣，回身看看房号，又走了进来："对不起，招聘启事上写的地址应该是这里。"

"哦，现在还没到面试的时间呢。"另一男子答道。

"那我可以坐在这跟你们一起聊聊天吗？"马明问道。

"别等了，应聘的人已经满额了。"又一男子说。

"可是招聘启事上的截止时间是明天。请务必听听我的自我介绍，给我一个机会，我会给你们一个惊喜。"马明坚持用简短的语言把自己的情况及工作设想说完。

"行！"那三个男子相视一笑。

马明就这样通过三句半话被录用了。而在他之前,有数十名应聘者被这三句话打发走了。原来他们的三句话考的是推销员应该具备的判断力、自信心、融洽性和锲而不舍的推销素质。

### ☞ 案例分析 7—3　（蒙博托的反问）

扎伊尔前总统蒙博托有一次接受一位西方记者的采访。"你很富有,据说你的资产有30 亿美元,这是真的吗?"很显然,这个问题的深层含义就是他是否有滥用职权、以权谋私的问题。蒙博托哈哈大笑起来,以便在回答这个尖刻敏感的问题之前能够使自己思考一下如何回答。然后他以问代答,"一个比利时记者说我有 60 亿美元的资产,你听说了吗?"（通过反问给出了不相关的回答。）在这个回答中,总统改变了记者的问题,提出了反问。西方记者无法通过这个无效的反问回答得到他想知道的信息,而总统却给自己留下了充分的余地。

### ☞ 案例分析 7—4　（开场陈述）

A 公司是一家实力雄厚的房地产开发公司,在投资的选项上,相中了 B 公司的一块极具升值潜力的地皮。而 B 公司也有合作的意向。于是双方精选了得利的干将,对土地的转让问题进行谈判。

A 公司代表:"我公司的情况你们可能也有所了解,我公司是美国 C 公司与 D 公司（全国著名的）合资创办的,经济实力雄厚,近年来在房地产开发领域业绩显著。去年在你们市还开发了鑫海花园,听说你们的王总也是我们的买主啊。你们市的几家公司正在谋求与我们的合作,想把他们手里的地皮转让给我们,但我们没有轻易表态。你们这块地皮对我们很有吸引力。我们准备把原有的住户拆迁,开发成一片居民小区。我们公司的有关人员已经对该地区的住户、企业进行了广泛的调查,基本上没有什么阻力。时间就是金钱啊,我们希望能以最快的速度就这个问题达成协议,不知你们的想法如何?"

"很高兴能与你们有合作的机会。你我双方以前虽然没有打过交道,但我们对你们的情况还是有所了解的。我们遍布全国的办事处也有多家在你们建的大厦里,这可能是一种缘分吧。我们确实有出卖这块地皮的意愿,但我们并不急于脱手,因为除了贵公司外,兴华、兴运等一些公司也对这块地皮表示出了浓厚的兴趣,正在积极地与我们接洽。当然了,如果你们的条件比较合理,价钱比较优惠,我们还是愿意优先与你们合作的,还可以帮助你们简化有关手续,使你们的工程能早日开工。"

☞ **思考题与讨论题**

1. 谈判中"问"的技巧有哪些?

2. 谈判中"回答问题"的技巧有哪些?

3. 谈判中"看"的技巧有哪些?

4. 谈判中"听""陈述""拒绝""劝说"的技巧有哪些?

5. 案例分析 7—1 中,周总理这样答复记者提问有何好处? 如果周总理当时直接拒绝答复,效果会如何? 如果据实答复又会怎么样?

6. 你认为案例分析 7—4 中双方的开场陈述如何?

# Chapter 8

# Etiquette for International Business Negotiation

☞ Case study 8 – 1 　(Casual dressing leading to the failure of business negotiation)

A Chinese enterprise was negotiating the export business of field mower with a German company. As per the etiquette, the Chinese members arrived at the meeting room five minutes earlier. On seeing the guests, all Chinese members stood up and applauded. Unexpectedly, there was no expecting smile on the faces of the Germans, but twinge of annoyance. What is more, the negotiation schedule for the whole morning as planned was ended hastily within half an hour and then the Germans left in a hurry. The Chinese negotiators learned afterwards that the reason for the Germans' departure was the inappropriate dressing of the Chinese negotiators. In the case of German negotiators, men and women were in suits and leather shoes. Whereas as for the Chinese negotiators, except the manager and interpreter who were in suits, some wore jackets, some wore cowboy suits and one of the engineers even wore work clothes.

As everybody knows that Germany is a country which attaches great importance to etiquette and the German people are famous for their earnest in handling affairs in the world. They think business negotiations are formal and important activities, and people should be dressed formally. In the eyes of the Germans, the informal and casual clothes of the Chinese negotiators can be explained in two aspects: they don't respect the other party; they don't attach importance to the negotiation. So it is not necessary to hold the negotiation any more.

Etiquette refers to the universal demand for a negotiator's appearance, speech and behavior with which one should be strict with himself and show respect to the others. Etiquette is a very important part in international business negotiations. It is a passport to the success for both sides of the negotiation and the rule that every participant in the negotiation should obey. Indecent etiquette or a small mistake in etiquette will present impoliteness in front of the opposite side and lead to embarrassment, which would not only undermine the feelings of both parties, but also affect other aspects of yourself and evaluation, and lead to misunderstandings and failure of a business negotiation.

So etiquette is considered to be an indispensable part of negotiations. As a negotiator in the international business, it is necessary and even essential to have some knowledge of etiquette for international business negotiations and to take corresponding measures.

## Ⅰ. Basic Principles for Etiquette of International Business Negotiations

### 1. Equality, mutual benefit and mutual respect

Equality and mutual benefit are the basic principles in international business negotiations. Equality means everyone is equal regardless of his sex, color of skin, nationality and job title. Mutual benefit means that participants in the negotiation both "give and take," that is, both sides can benefit from the negotiation. Only when both sides in the negotiation abide by this rule can they set up a stable and harmonious cooperative relationship and can the negotiation go smoothly.

Respect is the emotional basis for etiquette. In the interpersonal communication nowadays, all people are equal, no matter whether they are higher or lower in their rank, or whether they are old or young, strong or weak, big or small in their nationality. To respect leaders, customers, elders, guests and friends is not humble, but a manifestation of etiquette. Only by respecting others can we win others' respect. Only by respecting each other can we establish and maintain harmonious and pleasant interpersonal relations and lay a solid foundation for the cooperation. That is why people say "harmony brings wealth." Besides, respecting others is also a manifestation of self-respect. We should respect others at anytime, anywhere.

### 2. To show sincerity for others and to seek similarities by reserving difference

To establish a good image of an individual or an organization is the main reason for business people to have etiquette. Therefore, etiquette is not just meaningful for its normality but also a way to the success of business. Nowadays, people place more and more emphasis on etiquette in business activities. Only when we obey the principle of sincerity can we obtain the final interests. That is to say the businessmen and the enterprises need to cherish their image and reputation.

In international business communications, the disparities among different countries should not be neglected and denied. The disparities, especially those in our counterpart's country deserve special attention. What is important is that we need to know and learn those disparities instead of judging whether they are good or bad, and then decide what we have to do to achieve our goal.

### 3. To keep your words and to maintain your image and dignity

The most important and fundamental principle in international business negotiations is keeping your words. It means that you should seriously and strictly abide by all the promises that you have made in any formal international communications. You must fulfill your promises. Once you have a date with someone, you must keep your appointment. Especially, you need to abide by any formal appointment related to time.

In international business negotiations, people pay much attention to the image of their counterparts. They also place much emphasis on their own image through normal and decent behavior, especially their first impression on formal occasions on the business partners who do business with them for the first time.

### 4. To present appropriate enthusiasm and to be neither haughty nor humble

Communications and understandings are very important for building good personal relations. But without appropriate distance, the result will be totally opposite to the expectation. While communicating with foreigners, not only should we be enthusiastic and friendly, but we also should present our appropriate enthusiasm and friendliness.

Being neither haughty nor humble is a basic principle for foreign-related etiquette. Its main requirement is that everyone should realize that he stands for his own country, his own nationality and his own enterprise in the eyes of the foreigners when engaging in international communications. Hence, his behavior should be decent and polite. He should neither present excessive haughtiness or servility before foreigners nor be too arrogant or aggressive.

### 5. To do as the Romans do and to respect others' privacy

International Business negotiation is a business activity concerning different cultures of different countries. People in different countries have formed different business habits since they have different political and cultural backgrounds and have different local customs, practices and manners.

Respecting others' privacy is a main principle in the foreign-related etiquette. It is also an important rule that we need to strictly obey in international business negotiations. Different from Chinese tradition, in international communications, the westerners generally do not like Chinese-style greetings; they pay more attention to privacy. Hence, in the process of communication, we must voluntarily try to avoid asking such questions as income, expenditure, age, marriage status, health condition, family address, personal experience, religious belief and politics. Take "age" for example, we all know that AGE is a taboo for girls, but actually it is also a taboo for old people, because OLD means NO USE in Western society and has the meaning of OBSOLETE, which is completely different from the situation in China where elder people win much respect of the society and the families.

### 6. To pay attention to details and "Ladies first"

As the saying goes "Details determine success or failure." In business negotiation, people should pay attention to their words and deeds. Sometimes an unhealthy living habit might lead to the failure of a negotiation only because your counterpart does not like it.

"Ladies first" is a very important etiquette principle acknowledged by international community. It mainly applies to social activities among people of different sex. It means that on any social occasions every male adult has the obligation to positively and voluntarily respect women, attend women, understand women, take care of women and protect women with practical actions. Men should also try every means to solve women's difficulties or problems. If men's incaution leads to women's embarrassment and predicament, that is indicative of men's dereliction of duty.

### 7. Not to be too modest and the usage of appropriate language

Modesty is one of the Chinese virtues. However, excessive modesty and compromise without principles, severe lack of confidence are even obstacles to social communications. Especially, when we do business with Westerners, lack of confidence will make our counterparts suspect our abilities. In international communications, when referring to self-evaluation, although we should not boast or play up, it is also not necessary to belittle or play down ourselves.

When conversing with others, do not use too many gestures. Instead, we should keep an appropriate speed and voice, and speak in a gentle and calm manner. Your wording should be popular and easy to understand. Try to explain profound theories in simple language instead of using vulgar words. And your speech should be logical and reasonable.

## Ⅱ. Reception Etiquette

### 1. Welcoming guests

Welcoming the guests and seeing them off is the most basic and a vital part in international business negotiations, through which the hosts express their friendship and hospitality. Host negotiators should prepare well for every aspect of the meeting, such as welcoming the guests, choosing the meeting site or arranging the meeting agenda. Welcoming guests can especially leave the first impression on your counterparts, so it is of extremely importance.

（1）To attach importance to the reception and to make relevant preparations

The host should set up a reception group, collect information about the guests and the negotiation, make a reception plan and try to make everything perfect so as to make guests feel comfortable and thus both parties will find it easier to build a good relationship with mutual understanding and trust.

（2）To have a proper reception standard and to arrive earlier when welcoming guests and seeing them off

To welcome guests, a proper person of corresponding rank or position with the guest should be sent. If the person cannot go and meet the guests, a polite explanation is needed.

When the two sides meet for the first time, they usually have an initial impression of each other. Whether this first impression is good or not will influence the negotiation. A good impression will help both sides to build a good relationship while a poor impression might be an obstacle to reaching an agreement. So the host should confirm the time and flight of the guests and arrive at the airport or railway station earlier to show respect for the guests. Never make your guests wait for you. When your guests are leaving, pick them up in their hotels and take them to the airport or railway station. Or you might go directly to the airport or railway station to say goodbye to them. Remember: You should arrive earlier!

（3）To treat guests politely and to provide satisfactory service

The host should prepare transportation vehicles beforehand. After meeting the guests, greet them actively like "How are you" "Welcome to our corporation." Then you can give them your name-cards and make a self-introduction. Usually, hosts should book the hotel in advance for the guests and bring them to the hotel. Besides, the host should advise the guests the negotiation plan and agenda, and stay for a while if necessary. Before saying goodbye, make sure to tell guests when, where and how you will contact them the following day.

### 2. Making introduction

When two sides meet, it is necessary to make introduction. Introduction usually includes name, title or position in the company. Introduction, especially your name, should be made clearly and distinctly, making sure the other party can hear it accurately. Also, make sure you get the other party's name right. If you are not sure, repeat it or ask them to repeat it.

(1) Introducing team members

Usually the main negotiator of both sides is responsible for introducing his team members respectively. The introduction is usually made from the superiors and ladies. "Mr." is used for men, "Miss, Mrs. or Ms." are used for women. "Comrade" should not be used in business negotiation since it has the meaning "homosexual" in some western countries.

(2) Introducing superiors or leaders

When you introduce your superiors or leaders, special attention should be paid to the coincidence that your leader has a surname which might have a quite different meaning and which may cause misunderstanding or embarrassing situation. For example, Chinese surnames like "FU," "DAI," "JIA" might share the same pronunciation with another Chinese word which has a different meaning. Besides, when making introduction, we should be careful in using the first word of those surnames together with the first word of their positions, which might cause misunderstanding. Proper introduction should go like this: "This is our general manager, Mr. DAI Bing"; "This is our deputy general manager, Madam DIAO."

(3) Salutation

Be cautious for the salutation when you are new to a corporation. Do not use "senior fellow apprentice" or "LAO DA (elder brother)" casually, or other people might think that you don't respect your superiors or you want to seek relations. Proper salutation for your superiors is Manager Zhang or Director Wang. Furthermore, if several leaders are together, you should salute them from the higher rank to the lower. If you really don't know what to do, you might ask politely, "I am a new comer. How should I salute you?"

### 3. Exchanging business cards

One of the first impressions you will make on your foreign counterpart is through your business card. Here are some specific suggestions regarding business cards:

a. Have your card translated into two languages. One side is printed in your native language and the other side is in the language of the country which you are doing business with.

b. Always hand your cards to your counter negotiators with the printed face up. If it is a bilingual card, be sure that the side in the local language is facing the person who will receive the card.

c. Never fling a card across the table or onto a desk.

d. Use both of your hands to receive the other's card and be sure to take time to read it. Give it a deliberate study instead of merely giving a glance. This shows your respect. Never put it into your pocket without reading it.

e. Give your card to the highest-ranking individual or leader of the negotiation group first. This is a sign of respect and avoids embarrassing the low-ranking members of the negotiation group who may even refuse your card if their leader has not yet received one.

### 4. Shaking hands

Shaking hands is a common and most widely used etiquette when people are introduced to each other. Though shaking hands is a very ordinary way to show respect and courtesy, it reflects your image and the image of your corporation. Therefore there are some factors negotiators have to be aware of.

(1) Proper way of shaking hands

When people meet and greet or when they are introduced to others, they hold out their right hands, keep a distance of about one single-step, and their palm and ground should be vertical. Remember always to greet people with a firm handshake of three to five seconds. Keep eye contact and smiling to show your earnest and respect while shaking hands with others.

(2) The strength of a handshake

Never shake hands too loosely or too firmly. A loose hand-shake gives an impression of lack of confidence. On the other hand, an over-firm handshake might actually hurt others. Usually people should use 3 – 5 kilograms for a handshake.

(3) The right order of shaking hands

When shaking hands with others, be cautious about the right order. Wait for the host, the elder, the higher-ranking ones and ladies to extend their hands first. And if you are younger, or of lower rank, sometimes you should bow a little and use both of your hands to shake in order to show respect. When a man is introduced to a female counterpart, always wait for the woman to offer her hand first.

(4) Taboos for shaking hands

a. In many countries, left hand cannot be used for shaking hands and giving name-cards.

b. Generally, it is not proper to shake hands in gloves.

c. When other people extend their hands first, you should not refuse.

**5. Taking cars**

In the reception concerning foreign affairs, it is necessary to learn the etiquette of taking cars and make clear about the superiors and inferiors of the seats. Generally speaking, the superiors and inferiors of the seats are mainly decided according to the comfort and convenience. The most important guest should be seated at the right side of the host when taking cars.

(1) Sedan cars

a. If there is a full time driver, the seat on the right in the back row and beside the car window is the honored one. Guests should be invited to get into the car from the right side while host enters from the left. If the guest takes the seat of the host, just let it be. The seat on the left in the back row is considered the second honored seat. The right seat in the front row is the last.

b. If the host drives the car by himself, co-driver seat is considered as the No.1 seat, and the seat on the right in the back row is the second choice.

c. If a host couple drive a car, the host couple usually sit in the front, and the guest couple sit in the back.

(2) Cross-country vehicle

Generally speaking, co-driver seat is considered the best seat in terms of comfort and convenience, the seat on the right in the back row is considered as the second.

(3) Business travelling bus

No strict rules have to be followed. But usually the first row at the back of driver's seat is considered as the most important, and usually the seat which is close to the bus door is the No. 1 honorable seat.

It should be noted that the rules are just the opposite in countries like Great Britain where drivers sit on the right side and drive along the left side.

## 6. Choosing the negotiation room and arranging the seats

（1）Choosing the proper negotiation room

The company's meeting room can be used as the negotiation room. If possible, prepare two or three rooms. One room will be used for negotiation, the other two for both sides' private discussions. An additional room could be set aside for people to take coffee or refreshment.

（2）Arranging the seats in appropriate order

A. Rectangular or oval table

Rectangular or oval tables are always used in bilateral negotiations. On most occasions, the negotiation parties will sit face to face. If the table is positioned horizontally facing the door, the seats facing the door are the ones for the honored guests while the opposite seats are for the hosts. Interpreters will be seated at the right side of the speakers. It is advisable to prepare name cards to avoid mistakes.

B. Round table

Participants will sit around the table for the meeting. This arrangement minimizes the status differences among people and helps to build a friendly atmosphere.

C. U-shaped table

Small discussions can be held with people sitting on sofas, without a table. Hosts would be seated on the right and guests on the left. In this case, interpreters will sit behind the speakers.

It should be noted that in formal international communications, according to international practice, the right, the center and the front row gains more respect, this is also the fundamental rule for international business negotiations.

## 7. Exchanging gifts

Most people value exchanging gifts since it is an accepted way to build and cement strong personal relationships. Before you prepare to give others some gifts, consider the following points:

a. A golden rule to keep in mind for any gift you select is quality. Choose quality items that are not ostentatious. Gift with your company logo is a better choice.

b. Good choices are quality writing instruments, branded whiskey or cognac, picture books about your city or region or country, and products your home country is famous for. Universally, chocolate is a good choice.

c. Electronic items, desk and office accessories make good gifts. Business gifts useful for a business person, or an executive or a staff member are electronic items such as laser pointers, calculators and address books. Desk and office accessories that make good gifts include fine quality pens, pen and pencil sets, business card holders, good leather briefcases. If the person smokes cigarettes, a nice cigarette lighter could be given.

d. A gift, regardless of its expense, should always be wrapped; failing to wrap a gift signifies an uncaring attitude and undermines the importance of the gift.

e. When preparing gifts, you should be aware of some culture-specific taboos. Avoid sharp objects such as knives because in some cultures they symbolize the ending of a relationship. In China, avoid clocks and watches, which are considered bad luck because the word for clock sounds like another Chinese word that refers to death. Pork/wine for Muslim, comb for Japanese should be avoided.

f. People usually exchange gifts after the agreement is signed, sometimes after the meeting. Many companies and some governments have strict policies regarding their employees accepting gifts. To avoid troubles, it is imperative that you learn the policies affecting the companies you do business with.

### Ⅲ. Dinner Etiquette

Negotiations often feature dinner parties, which contribute to a more relaxed and less tense atmosphere where both sides can behave less aggressive. In such an atmosphere, people will be more willing to make concessions or offer more attractive conditions. Table manners usually play an important role in making a good impression on the counterpart. They are visible signs of manners and therefore are essential to negotiation success.

#### 1. Steps hosts should follow

Sometimes good organization of a dinner party facilitates the ability to reach an agreement quickly or motivates the other side to make some concessions. Spend some time and you will be rewarded sooner or later. Generally, there are two main kinds of dinner parties: formal and informal ones.

(1) What

Make sure that you know the objectives for holding this party and then decide whether it should be a formal or informal one.

(2) Who

Decide whom you are going to invite and all together how many people should be included. Take into consideration the status, nationalities, national habits and customs of the guest party members.

(3) When

Choose the right time. It would be better if you could ask for the guests' suggestions. Never make the mistakes of inviting people to attend a dinner party during their country's legal holidays.

(4) Where

To choose the appropriate venue for a dinner is really a delicate matter. Of course, never host your guests in the hotel where they are staying. Then your choices will depend on how much your budget is, what goals you want to reach and how many people you are going to invite. Always remember you should not ask your guests where they would like to eat when scheduling the meal.

(5) Where to sit

The closer to the host, the higher the status is. Usually the person on the right side of the host is the most important one at the dinner party and the person to the left is less important. In no case should your guest be facing a mirror or the bathroom or kitchen doors.

## 2. Negotiators as guests

Being guest negotiators, remember the old saying "when in Rome, do as the Romans do." This is the golden and basic rule and a very important etiquette principle you should always follow in international communications. Accept the arrangements made by the host, and observe what others do and how they do. Doing this can help you avoid making silly mistakes that might jeopardize the success of the negotiation.

When you are abroad to be guests, you need to respect the custom and etiquette of the host. Because of the disparities of social systems and cultures among different countries, different regions, there will be much difference in ways of thinking and views on some issues. Therefore, when you set your foot on another country or meet some foreigners, you need to learn the customs and etiquettes of that nation firstly. Even with close friends, attention should be paid to basic etiquette and special custom of your partners in the negotiation. By doing so, it is easier to promote the understanding and communication between the two sides. It is also helpful for expressing your friendliness better and more appropriately.

### 3. Seating orders for dinner

（1）Basic principles for seating orders

Seats will be considered as more important and honorable in the situations like facing the door, further to the door, in the middle, on the right or against the wall, and having an open and wide view.

（2）Order or sequence of different dinner tables

If it is a large dinner or a banquet party, the middle table is usually the honorable table, and then the right table is considered as the second important, and the left table the third. Tables nearer to the main table are more important than that further to the main table.

（3）Specific seating order

The central seat facing the door is usually considered as the principle seat. The most honorable guest will sit on the right and No.2 guest will sit on the left of the host.

（4）Seating etiquette for western-style dinner

The most important etiquette for western-style dinner is LADIES FIRST. For example, female host usually takes the No.1 host seat and male host takes the No.2 host seat. As for other seating etiquette, it is more or less the same with that of Chinese dinner.

### 4. Other specific etiquette for dinner party

（1）Attending the dinner party

Reply promptly when you receive the invitation of the party so that your host can be sure about the number of people coming to the dinner and thus begin to arrange the dinner party. Come to the dinner party on time or a few minutes early, and never be late. As a host, don't order drinks before all guests arrive.

（2）Taking a seat and leaving the dinner party

You should not take a seat before leaders, seniors, or ladies have taken their seats. Sit straight, and do not lean on the table or put your elbows on the table, and try to keep your elbows off the table. Do not leave the party before the most important person leaves. If you have to leave because of urgency, excuse yourself to the host and try to leave without being noticed by others at the party.

（3）Dining in the dinner party

a. Never start eating without the signal from the host. Don't speak with your mouth full of food, which is not only unpleasant to eyes, but could also lead to choking! Don't wave utensils in the air, especially knives or the utensils with food. If you want to smoke, you should ask for the permission. Put napkin on your knees. Your dining speed should synchronize with the host.

b. Don't forget to make polite conversations with guests around you, especially lady guests. Dinner parties are not just about the food, but more a social occasion. It is not appropriate to talk about sad or terrifying matters or you will destroy the pleasant atmosphere.

c. Keep your voice low and pleasant; follow the tone set by the host as to the discussion of business. Loud eating noises such as slurping and burping are very impolite, the number one sin of dinner table etiquette in Western countries! It is perfectly acceptable to slurp your noodles in some cultures, such as Chinese culture. In Chinese culture, doing so will exhibit your enjoyment of your food. But it is considered bad manners in Western cultures. Anyway, you should keep quiet when you drink soup, and never slurp soup at the table. Chew quietly, keep bites small. Eat at a leisurely pace.

d. Use public chopsticks to fetch dishes instead of your own table ware. Picking teeth or licking fingers are very unattractive! The only exception is when eating meat or poultry on the bone, in which case a finger bowl should be provided. Excuse yourself when leaving the table. After the dinner party, do say "thank you" to the host and sing high praise for the dishes. Do not make negative comments about the dinner party. Shake hands to show your courtesy before you leave.

e. Drinking too much wine can be very embarrassing! It is quite acceptable not to finish each glass. In any case, drinking should not affect your normal jobs.

### 5. Conversation taboos

a. Always maintain eye contact with the person you are talking to. If you want to join other's conversation, say "hello" first. Apologize to others if you have to leave in the middle of a discussion.

b. If there are more than three persons in the conversation, remember to cover other topics now and then. Do not make others feel absented. If there is something you do not want to share with others, choose another chance or just leave the room and find somewhere else. Whispering in front of others is very impolite.

c. Politics, religion, death are always the pitfalls you should avoid. Do not ask people about their personal information such as income and property. The common topics could be about weather or news.

d. Be cautious with wording and phrasing when you talk with others. Always be polite, using "please," "thanks," "sorry," "excuse me," "see you soon," etc. to show your respect.

## Ⅳ. Etiquette of Answering and Making Telephone-calls

### 1. Answering telephone-calls

(1) Answering calls

Answer calls as soon as you hear the ring. You'd better answer a call within 3 seconds, or you will leave a bad impression on the other side.

(2) Greeting

In order to show respect for the other party, usually you should greet to the other side first, like "Hello," and then tell the other side who you are.

(3) Politeness

Treat your partner politely and speak with a smile on your face so that the other side can feel your attitude and manner from your intonation. By doing so, you can leave a good impression on him.

(4) Attitude and enunciation

Speak distinctly and remember that you cannot smoke or eat something or even drinking tea while you're answering a call, otherwise the other side will think that you are not concentrating on the phone.

(5) Answering questions and taking notes

Answer questions politely and take notes earnestly. Your answer should be concise to the greatest extent and you should take notes of the important messages in the phone if necessary.

(6) Hanging up the phone

Try to hang up the phone after the other side do or put it down gently. Before you hang up, you may repeat those important particulars.

### 2. Making telephone-calls

(1) Preparation

Confirm receiver's name, telephone number, contents of the call and order and the purpose of the call.

(2) Greetings and informing your name

For example, "Hello, I am Zhang from ABC Corporation."

（3）Confirming your object and greeting again

For example，"Is Mr. Li there?" "May I speak to Mr. Li?"

（4）Content of your call

Make sure to convey the content of your call. The time，place and figure should be accurate.

（5）Conclusion

The ending of the call should be sincere in mood and amicable in manner.

Note：In case a telephone dropped off，it is the telephone-maker who should dial again.

## V. Dressing Etiquette

Dressing etiquette is very important in international business negotiation. Proper dressing not only embodies beauty of personal appearance but also shows your respect for others，and it has a direct impact on the success or failure of the negotiation. Generally，dressing for international business negotiation should be traditional，formal and elegant.

### 1. General principle for dressing

In the communication with others，people usually pay their first attention to the dressing of others. Successful dressing has a close connection with one's appearance. Business people should abide by the following principles：

a. Do not pursue the fashion blindly. Some people might ignore their occupation and identity because of fashion. There are so many fashionable dresses each year like beautiful evening or dancing dress，but they might not be suitable for you. Besides，each person has his own height，appearance and temperament，so he should have his own dressing style.

b. Dressing should be fit for one's own conditions. In choosing dress，you should take many factors into consideration such as age，identity，body form，facial appearance and character. For example，a short and fat person，or one with thick neck and round face，should choose clothing in deep color or in V shape，whereas a tall and slim person，or one with a long neck，can make a choice for light color and high collar clothing.

c. Dressing should coordinate with your occupation，occasion，communication objective and your partner which is a very important principle and cannot be ignored. For example，if it is a formal social occasion，your clothing should be serious and in good taste. If you are to attend an evening party, then you can choose beautiful, light and bright-colored clothes; if it is festival or a holiday, your clothing can be light and informal.

## 2. Dressing for ladies

As everybody knows, skirt suits are considered as the most appropriate occupation clothing for ladies. Generally, ladies should pay attention to the following points for dressing.

a. In international business negotiation, ladies should avoid wearing too showy and exaggerating clothing. Do not pursue too fashionable especially unearthly clothing.

b. Avoid ultraconservative clothing. Ladies can add a piece of scarf or some trinket to their suit so as to restrain from the feeling of stiffness.

c. Avoid too sexy and exposed clothing, or you will leave a feeling and impression of frivolity and vase on other people.

d. Pay attention to the beauty of entirety. Professional females should put emphasis on the beauty of entirety for the dressing-up from their heads to their feet. For example, their hair-style, trinkets, footgear and haversack should fit for the color of their clothing. Generally speaking, there are three main kinds: One is suit with the same color for the up and down to be embellished by some trinket; the second is similar color for the up and down which usually has rather coordinated effect, and the third is contrasting colors for the up and down which usually has a feeling that everything is fresh and new.

## 3. Dressing for men

In international business negotiation, Western-style clothes is the most ideal business wear for men which is beautifully designed, prudent, natural and unrestrained. Shell fabric for Western-style clothes had better choose pure woollens or materials which contain a high percentage of woollens which is dignified, comfortable and elastic. The recognized color for business circles is navy blue, light grey for young men and dark grey for elder people.

(1) Dressing of Western-style clothes

Western-style clothes are popular all over the world. Thus there is a conventional standard and requirement for the dressing. People should pay attention to the following points.

A. Buttons of Western-style clothes

All buttons should be buckled up for double breasted Western-style clothes; only the upper button should be buckled up for single breasted Western-style clothes if there are two buttons; only the middle button should be buckled up for single breasted Western-style clothes if there are three buttons; and no button should be buckled up for leisure Western-style clothes.

B. Pockets for Western-style clothes

The upper pockets of Western-style clothes are for decorated handkerchief, and the lower pockets and pockets in the trousers are for the purpose of decoration and beautification and nothing should be put in.

(2) Shirts

Shirts should match the Western-style clothes in formal occasions, and the best color is white. Lower hem of the shirts should be fortressed into trousers. Button on the neckline should be buckled up properly if wearing a tie.

(3) Ties

On formal occasions, a tie should be worn. Ties should be chosen according to its material, style, color and design. Besides, the length should be appropriate, and the color should match with the Western-style clothes.

(4) Socks and shoes

Color of socks usually should be in dark color, or the same color with trousers or shoes. You'd better not choose white socks. In terms of wearing Western-style clothes, the only choice for shoes is leather shoes, and preferably black shoes. Casual shoes cannot be fit for Western-style clothes, and there should be no design and ornaments on the leather shoes.

(5) Others

A proper briefcase is of vital importance and indispensable to men. Briefcases should be made of leather in black or dark color, preferably with the same color of your shoes. Hand-held rectangle briefcase is a standard one. Furthermore, sleeves should not be rolled up when wearing Western-style clothes and try not to wear a woollen sweater.

☞ Case study 8 – 2    (Failure of negotiation due to improper handshaking)

The director of a factory went to the Canton Fair and it happened that his sales manager was negotiating the contract with the client from Indonesia. On seeing the director, the manager immediately introduced his boss to the client. As there was a briefcase in his right hand, the director extended his left hand and shook hands with the client who extended his right hand. But the smile on the client's face suddenly vanished and the enthusiasm he had just now in negotiating no longer existed. And after a while, he excused himself and left the booth.

In some countries, left hand cannot be used in doing such things as signing, shaking hands, taking foods, etc., otherwise it will be regarded as rude and impolite behavior because left hand is usually used for some dirty things. The failure of the negotiation lies in the director's ignorance of the cultural differences. He shook hands with the client with his left hand, which is an accepted practice in Chinese culture.

☞ Case study 8 – 3    (One cooperative project failed because of a spit)

A Chinese medical apparatus factory had reached a preliminary agreement for introducing the assembly line of infusion tube with an American merchant and they were expected to sign the contract the following day. But while the factory director was accompanying the foreign merchants to visit workshops he spat at a wall corner and then wiped it with his shoe sole. The American merchant was disgusted with what he had seen, and found an excuse to cancel the said agreement the following day.

☞ Case study 8 – 4    (Should private questions be asked?)

Yang Lu speaks fluent English. One day she accompanied her manager to meet a group of English customers. While entertaining the guests at the banquet, she chatted with a guest Sophie enthusiastically in order to create a good atmosphere. When they got acquainted with each other, Yang Lu asked Sophie, "How old are you?" Sophie gave an irrelevant answer, "Just guess!" Yang Lu felt snubbed and asked further, "You must have got married at this age?" To her surprise, Sophie turned her head aside and took no notice of Yang anymore. Until their separation, they did not say a word.

☞ **Case study 8 – 5** （Has Zhang Qiang made any mistakes?）

Zhang Qiang found a job in the foreign trade department in a large corporation. One day, the telephone rang, and Zhang picked up the phone. It was an American customer who wanted to talk with the manager. Since the manager was not in the office, Zhang began to talk with this customer. The customer talked a lot and Zhang didn't take any notes. Until the following morning, he remembered the phone call and told the manager, but he could not recall the specific contents of the phone. Afterwards, the manager made a telephone to inquire this customer for which the customer felt quite strange. Several days later, Zhang Qiang was transferred from his post.

☞ **Questions for your consideration and discussion**

1. What are the basic principles for etiquette of international business negotiations?
2. What is the etiquette for making introduction in business activities?
3. What is the etiquette for handshake in business activities?
4. What is the etiquette for taking a car in business activities?
5. What is the etiquette of answering and making telephone-calls?
6. What is the etiquette for a business dinner party?
7. What are the general principles for dressing in business activities?

# 第八章
# 国际商务谈判礼仪

☞ **案例分析 8—1** （着装随便导致商务谈判失败）

    中国某企业与德国一公司洽谈割草机出口事宜。按礼节，中方提前五分钟到达了公司会议室。客人到后，中方人员全体起立，鼓掌欢迎。不料，德方人员脸上不但没有出现期待的笑容，反而均显示出一丝不快的表情。更令人不解的是，按计划一上午的谈判日程，德方半小时便草草结束，匆匆离去。事后中方了解到：德方之所以提前离开，是因为中方谈判人员穿着不当。德方谈判人员中男士个个西装革履，女士个个都穿职业套装，而中方人员除经理和翻译穿西装外，其他人有穿夹克衫的，有穿牛仔服的，有一位工程师甚至穿着工作服。众所周知，德国是个重礼仪的国家，德国人素以办事认真而闻名于世。在德国人眼里，商务谈判是一件极其正式和重大的活动，中国人穿着太随便说明了两个问题：一是不尊重他人；二是不重视此活动。既然你既不尊重人，又不重视事，那就没有必要谈了。

    礼仪是指在人际交往中，自始至终以一定的、约定俗成的程序和方式来表现的律己、敬人的完整行为。商务礼仪是商务活动中对人的仪容仪表和言谈举止的普遍要求。在国际商务谈判中，如果不了解相关的礼仪，就可能产生尴尬、误解，轻则引起笑话，重则可能因此而失去许多谈判成功的契机。因此，礼仪在商务谈判中占有十分重要的地位，是商务谈判不可缺少的组成部分，甚至可以说关系到商务谈判的成功与否。因此，作为一个谈判人员了解并遵循有关商务谈判中的礼仪是非常重要的。

## 一、国际商务谈判礼仪的基本原则

### 1. 平等互利，相互尊敬

    平等互利是国际商务谈判的基本原则。平等意味着在谈判中不管性别、肤色、国籍或职务，双方都是平等的。互利意味着谈判的参与者应平等交换，即都能从谈判中获益。谈判中只有双方都遵循这个原则，才能建立起稳定、和谐、合作的谈判关系，谈判才能得以顺利进行。

尊敬是礼仪的情感基础。在当今人际交往中，人与人是相互平等的，无论职务高低、年龄长幼、民族大小、种族强弱，人格上没有贵贱之分。尊敬领导，尊敬客户，尊敬长辈，尊敬宾朋不但不卑下，而且是一种讲究礼仪的表现。只有尊敬对方，才能获得对方的尊敬。只有相互尊敬，才能建立和保持和谐愉快的人际关系，才会给事业上的合作提供良好的基础。所谓和气生财，就是这个道理。此外，尊敬他人还是一种自重的表现，我们任何时候都应该尊敬他人，以礼待人。

2. 真诚待人，求同存异

商人讲究礼仪的主要原因是为了树立个人和企业的形象。因此，礼仪也是实现商业目的的方法。做生意不是短期行为，当今社会，人们经商越来越重视礼仪。只有遵循真诚待人的原则，着眼于未来，才可能获得最终的利益。

在国际商务交往中，不应忽略不同国家之间的差异，特别是对谈判中与自己贸易伙伴的差异更应关注。重要的是我们需要了解这些差异，而不是判断这些差异的善恶，进而决定我们在谈判中要实现的目标。

3. 遵守诺言，保持形象

遵守诺言是国际商务谈判中最重要的基本原则，意思是人们应当严格遵守在正式国际交往中所做出的诺言。比如，如果与某人约会，一定要按时赴约。在国际商务谈判中，人们通常非常关注合作伙伴的形象，同时也很重视自己日常得体的形象。人们尤其重视在正式场合他们留给首次与其做生意的商业伙伴的第一印象。

4. 热情有度，不卑不亢

交往和理解对建立良好的人际关系至关重要，但如果不保持适当的距离，结果将适得其反。与外国人进行交往，我们不能单靠热情友善，而应热情有度，亲密有度。不卑不亢是涉外礼仪的一条基本原则。基本要求是，每个人都应清楚在国际交往中，我们代表的是自己的国家，自己的民族，自己的企业。因此，我们的行为应当得体、优雅。我们不必卑躬屈膝，也不必傲慢逼人。

5. 入乡随俗，尊重隐私

国际商务谈判是涉及不同国家、不同文化的商业活动。谈判者来自不同的国家，有着不同的政治背景和宗教信仰，不同的文化背景，不同的风土人情和风俗习惯，这些会导致不同的商业习惯。因此，我们要真正做到尊重交往对象，就必须了解和尊重对方所独有的风俗习惯。

在涉外交往中，尊重隐私既是国际礼仪的一项基本原则，也是国际商务谈判人员必须遵循的规矩。在国际交往中，各国的文化和习俗差异很大，对于隐私的理解也大不一样。一般来说，在对外交往中不要涉及与收入、年龄、健康、婚姻、信仰和政见等相关的话题，这些都属于隐私的范畴。比如说年龄问题,大家都知道是女孩子特别忌讳的话题。其实,不仅仅女孩子如此,西方国家的老年人也特别忌讳,因为"老"在西方是"没用"的意思,有被淘汰的意思,这与我们中国人尊老敬老,老年人喜欢说自己"老"的习惯完全相反。

### 6. 注意细节,女士优先

俗话说"细节决定成败"。在国际商务谈判中,一定要时刻注意自己的言行,有时候可能由于自己平时的不良生活习惯引起客户的反感,从而导致谈判的失败。女士优先是国际社会认可的重要礼仪,适用于不同性别之间的社会活动。这一礼仪就是指在任何社交场合,每个成年男性都有义务主动积极地用实际行动照料、保护、理解和尊重女性。男性应尽力解决女性的问题和困难。如果由于男性的不小心而导致女性的尴尬和困窘,就是男性的失职。

### 7. 谦虚适度,语言得体

谦虚是中华民族的美德。然而过分的谦虚、无原则的妥协以及缺乏自信都是社交的障碍。在国际商务谈判中,过谦和缺乏自信会使对方认为你能力不足,要做到不卑不亢,反对一味地抬高自己,但也绝对没有必要妄自菲薄。谦虚适度原则就是要把握好各种情况下的社交距离及彼此间的感情尺度,也就是说待人既要彬彬有礼,又不低三下四;既要殷勤接待,又不失庄重;既要热情大方,又不轻浮谄谀。

交谈中,手势不要过多,语速不要太快,声音大小要适当,语调应平和沉稳。一般来说,声音大小要让全场参与者听得见,声音有强弱变化;讲话速度要快慢适中,重要地方应放慢;音调变化要根据内容改变,有高昂、有低沉,并配合面部表情;有时使用短暂的顿挫可促使听者期待或思考;措辞要通俗易懂,深入浅出,避免粗俗或咬文嚼字;逻辑顺序要合理,不要颠三倒四。

## 二、接待礼仪

### 1. 迎接礼仪

迎来送往是商务接待活动中最基本的形式和重要环节,是表达主人情谊、体现礼貌素养的重要方面。尤其是迎接,是给客人良好第一印象的最重要工作。迎接客人要有周密的部署,应注意以下事项。

（1）高度重视,做好谈判的准备工作

谈判的主场人员应成立迎接小组,收集客人的相关信息,制订迎接计划。尽量让客人感到舒适,以便能够为谈判创造良好的条件和环境。

（2）接待规格要恰当,接站和送行应提前到达

对前来访问、洽谈业务、参加会议的外国或外地客人,应安排与客人身份、职务相当的人员前去迎接,迎接人员与客人原则上要对口对等。若因某种原因,相应身份的主人不能

前往，前去代为迎接的人应向客人做出礼貌的解释。迎接客人，首先应了解确认对方到达的车次、航班，提前到达机场或车站，恭候客人的到来，决不能让客人等候；送行客人，同样应了解好相关信息，提前到达客人所在的酒店。

（3）礼貌待人，服务周到

迎接客人应提前为客人准备好交通工具，不要等客人到了才匆忙准备。接到客人后，应首先问候"一路辛苦了""欢迎您到我们公司"，等等，然后向对方做自我介绍。如果有名片，可递给对方。通常，主人还应提前为客人准备好住宿，帮客人办理好一切手续并将客人领进房间，同时向客人介绍住处的服务、设施，将活动的计划、日程安排交给客人，把准备好的地图或旅游图、名胜古迹介绍材料等送给客人。将客人送到住地后，主人一般不要立即离去，应陪客人稍作停留，热情交谈，谈话内容要让客人感到满意，比如客人参与活动的背景材料、当地风土人情、有特点的自然景观等。考虑客人一路旅途劳累，主人不宜久留，让客人早些休息。分手时将下次联系的时间、地点、方式等告诉客人。

2. 介绍礼仪

双方见面，相互的介绍必不可少。介绍应清楚，包括姓名、头衔及在公司的职务，保证对方能听清楚，还要确保听清对方的信息，如不肯定，可重复一下或让对方重新介绍。

（1）介绍小组成员

一般是双方主谈各自介绍自己小组的成员。顺序是女士优先，职位高的优先。称呼通常为"女士""小姐""先生"。对一般男子用"先生"，对未婚女子用"小姐"，对已婚女子用"女士"，对有头衔的则应冠以头衔，也可用职称或职务替代。中国人的称呼"同志"，翻译成英语是"comrade"，在西方某些国家的意思是"同性恋"，为避免误会，在商务谈判中不宜用此词。

（2）介绍上司

介绍上司时应注意上司姓氏与职务的语音搭配。中文当中有些姓氏一字多意，介绍时与职务相连可能会出现另外一层含义，应特别注意以避免引起误解或尴尬。例如：傅处长、戴总经理、贾董事长等。这里"傅"与"副"同音，"戴"与"代"同音，"贾"与"假"同音，但含义却不一样。

还应注意以下几种情况。

对正职，以姓＋职务第一个字：范局、戴校、季院等。

对副职，以姓＋职务第一个字：祖副、薄副、舒副、纪副、岳副、辜副等。

对女性副职：席副、晏副、幺副、邵副、刁副等。

对上述特别的姓氏，介绍时合适的称呼应当为：这是我们总经理戴兵先生；这位是我们公司的副总经理席旭燕女士。

（3）称呼

初入职场称呼要谨慎。"师兄""老大"别随便叫，否则有不尊重上司、攀亲之嫌。保险的称呼为：直接呼上司职位"张经理""王主任"；称呼多位时，应从职位高的开始，如李总经理、张经理；如对对方称呼不清楚时，可礼貌地问对方"先生，我是新来的，不知该怎么称呼您?"

3. 交换名片

你给谈判对手的第一印象就是通过你的商业名片完成的。以下是几个有关名片的建议：

①将名片译成两种文字：名片的一面用你本国的语言，另一面用英语或贸易合作伙伴国家的文字。

②递名片应正面朝上。如果是双语名片，应确保朝着接受名片人的一面是其本国语言。

③千万不要将名片隔着桌子抛掷给对方。

④为表示尊重对方，用你的双手接受对方递来的名片，并且一定花点儿时间读一下，不是扫一眼，而是认真地看看或是出声读出来，千万不要一眼不看就装进口袋。

⑤给名片也要双手递交，一定要首先将你的名片给级别最高的人，这也是尊重对方的一种表示，并且可以避免谈判小组中级别较低人员感到尴尬。谈判中，如果领导还没接名片，级别低的成员可能会拒绝你分发的名片。

4. 握手礼仪

握手是国际上最常用、最通用的一种礼仪。握手貌似简单，但这个小小的动作却关系着个人及公司的形象，影响到谈判的成功。

（1）正确的握手方式

通常，人们在见面问候或被介绍的时候行握手礼。握手时，双方各自伸出右手，彼此之间保持一步左右的距离，手略向前方伸直，手掌与地面呈 90 度，同时注意上身稍向前倾，头略低，面带微笑地注视对方的眼睛，以示认真和恭敬。握手时不可东张西望或面无表情。握手的时间以 3～5 秒为宜。

（2）握手的力度

握手的力度要适中。如果是一般关系或初次见面，只需稍用力握一下即可；如果关系密切，双方握手时则可略用力，并上下轻摇几下。注意握手不宜用力过大或过小（约 3～5 千克）。

（3）伸手的先后顺序

伸手的顺序通常依据以下几个原则：职位高者优先；长辈优先；女士优先；主人优先。

（4）握手的禁忌

①不能用左手。在很多国家，用左手握手或递给别人名片被认为是不礼貌的行为。

②一般不戴手套握手。

③当对方伸出手时，切忌迟迟不伸手。

5. 乘车礼仪

在涉外接待中,如遇乘车,必须明白座位的尊卑,否则,不仅会表现得不礼貌,还会贻笑大方。一般来说,座位的尊卑以座位的舒适和上下车的方便为标准。

(1) 小轿车

①如果有专职司机驾驶,以后排右侧为首位,左侧次之,中间座位再次之,前排右侧为末席。

②如果由主人亲自驾驶,以副驾驶位为尊,后排右侧次之,左侧再次之,后排中间座为末席。

③主人夫妇驾车时,则主人夫妇坐前座,客人夫妇坐后座,男士要服务于自己的夫人,宜开车门让夫人先上车,然后自己再上。

(2) 越野吉普车

越野吉普车功率大,底盘高,安全性也较高,但通常后排比较颠簸,而前排副驾驶的视野和舒适性最佳。因此越野吉普车无论是主人驾驶还是司机驾驶,都应以前排右座为尊,后排右侧次之,后排左侧为末席。

(3) 商务旅行车

我们在接待团体客人时,多采用商务旅行车接送客人。此类汽车座位的确定,一般考虑乘客的乘坐舒适性和上下车的便利性。因此,商务旅行车以司机座后第一排靠近车门的位置即前排为尊,后排依次为小。其座位的尊卑,依每排右侧往左侧递减。

应当注意的是,上述规则在英国等国家则刚好相反,因为他们的司机坐在车的右侧并且沿路的左侧行驶。

6. 选择谈判地点及安排座位

(1) 选择谈判地点

公司的会议室可以作为谈判室。如果可能,可准备两三个房间:一个用于谈判,另外两个作为双方各自讨论的地方,另外还可准备一个茶歇的地方,供谈判人员喝咖啡、吃点心。

(2) 恰当地安排座位

①双边谈判常用长方桌或椭圆形桌子。大多数情况下,双方采用面对面的座位。若谈判桌横放,面门是客方的位置,背门是主方的位置。翻译人员就座于主谈人员右边的位置。最好再放置名帖以避免混淆。

②圆桌。圆桌淡化了人们职位的差别,可随便就座,帮助人们建立友好的谈判气氛。

③U型座位。如果是小型谈判,人们可以坐在沙发上:主人居右,客人居左,译员坐在谈判人员的后面。

应当注意的是,在正式的国际交往中,根据国际惯例,座次排序的基本原则是:以右为上,居中为上,前排为上。

7. 交换礼物

在国际商务交往中,大多数人都很重视礼物的交换,以加强双方的关系。准备礼物应注意以下几点:

①注意礼物的品质,不应过于昂贵,礼物上如有己方公司的徽标是不错的选择。

②文具、品牌酒、能代表本国本市的画册或产品都很好,巧克力很常用。

③电子物品、办公桌上的饰物都是很好的礼品,如激光笔、计算器、通讯簿,或者笔、笔架、名片夹、公文包等。如对方吸烟,香烟、打火机均可。

④无论价值如何,礼物都应好好包装,以示重视。

⑤准备礼品时,应注意一些文化差异。应避免送刀一类的利器,在一些文化中利器代表关系的终结。在中国不应送钟表,"钟"与"终"同音,有不吉利的含义。还有伞、鞋等也不适合做礼物。在国际上,穆斯林忌猪肉和酒,日本人忌送梳子,等等。

⑥通常,交换礼物的时机在双方签署协议后,也可在双方会议结束后。有些国家或者很多公司对雇员接受礼品有严格的规定。为避免出现问题,有必要对这方面予以了解。

## 三、宴请礼仪

许多商务谈判都会涉及商务宴请的问题。商务宴请可以给双方提供放松的气氛和环境,在宴请的环境下,人们更愿意做出让步或提出更有利于成交的条件。在宴请上花一些时间和精力准备,从长远来看是值得的。因此在商务用餐的时候,我们应该注意一些宴请的礼仪问题。商务用餐的形式分成两大类,一类是比较松散的自助餐或自助酒会,另一类是正式的宴会,即商务宴会。商务宴会还有中式宴会和西式宴会两种形式。

1. 主人宴会前应考虑的问题

(1) 目的

一定要弄清楚你召集这次宴会的目的是什么,并确定宴会是正式的还是非正式的。

(2) 邀请人员

确定你要邀请哪些人参加宴会,总人数是多少。要考虑到参加人员的职务、国籍、习惯等因素。

(3) 时间

要选择合适的时间,最好能征求客人的建议,不要在客人法定的假期进行。

(4) 地点

选择合适的宴会地点也颇有学问。主要取决于宴请预算、你想达到的目的、你要宴请的人等。不要在客人下榻的酒店宴请客人,也不用问客人想吃什么。

（5）座次

越靠近主人，地位越高。以右为尊，不要将客人安排在面朝镜子、浴室或是厨房门的座位。

2. 做客的礼仪

作为客人，身在国外，基本礼仪就是"入乡随俗"。接受主人的安排，看看主人怎么做。这样你就能避免一些影响谈判成功的低级错误。

当我们走出国门，我们应当尊重主人的习俗和礼仪。不同国家和地区，不同民族的社会制度和文化存在着差异，他们考虑问题的方式和主观想法也会有着明显的不同。因此当我们踏上他国的土地，我们首先应当了解这个国家的习俗和礼仪。在谈判中，即使是亲密的朋友，也应关注对方的习俗和基本礼仪，只有这样，才有助于促进双方的了解和沟通，更好地表达双方的友谊。

3. 宴会的座位礼仪

（1）排序基本原则

①面门为上，以远为上。即以正对门、远离门为上座。

②居中为上，居右为上。即中间最尊，右边次之，左边再次之。

③靠墙为上，开阔为上。即以背靠后墙和视野开阔为尊。

（2）桌次排序

如果宴会规模较大，有两桌及两桌以上时，则必须定其尊卑。其原则是：如有三桌，则以中间为尊，右旁次之，左旁为卑。如有三桌以上，以主桌位置作为基准，同等距离，右高左低，同一方向，近高远低。

（3）座次排序

面门居中位置为主位，由主人中地位最高者即主陪入座。越接近首席，一般位次越高。其他宾客按照同等距离，右高左低的顺序入座。

（4）西餐宴会的座位礼仪

西餐宴会强调女士优先，女主人坐第一主位，男主人坐第二主位。其他与中餐座次类似：以右为尊，男主宾坐于女主人右侧，女主宾坐于男主人右侧。距主位越近，地位越高。

4. 餐桌上的礼仪及禁忌

在商务宴请中，餐桌上有许多应注意的礼仪，必须谨记。

（1）宴会前

作为客人，收到邀请后，应尽快给主人回复，以便主人进行相应的安排。还应准时赴宴或提前几分钟到达。客人到齐之前，主人先不要点酒水。

（2）就座和离席

就座时应等领导、长者及女士坐定后，方可入座。坐姿应端正，与餐桌保持适当的距离,不要将手肘放在桌面上或靠在桌上,脚踏在自己座位下,不可任意伸直,不得将手放在邻座椅背上。用餐后,须等主人、领导、长者及女士离席后,其他宾客方可离席。如果必须提前离开,一定要和主人说明后再安静地离开。

（3）用餐

①用餐时要温文尔雅,从容安静。餐巾打开后,放在双膝和大腿上,不要系入腰间或挂在衣领下。主人还没发话或是暗示,客人不要开吃,口内有食物时应避免说话。不宜抽烟。应当坐直,不可用筷子敲打盘子。进餐的速度宜与男女主人同步,不宜太快或太慢。

②在餐桌上不能只顾自己,也要关心别人,尤其要招呼两侧的女宾。商务宴请不仅仅是吃饭的活动,更是社交活动。餐桌上不要谈悲伤、恐惧的事情,否则会破坏欢愉的气氛。

③说话的声音应和悦,注意主人定的基调。在西餐中,喝汤出声被认为是一种最不文明的现象。中餐式宴会,特别是有外宾在场,吃饭不要发出明显的响声,如啜食或饱嗝,都很不礼貌,这在西方国家被视为最重要的餐桌礼仪。

④自用餐具不可伸入公用餐盘夹取菜肴,取菜舀汤应使用公筷公匙。剔牙齿或舔手指会很不雅观。如需用手吃肉或家禽,则应准备洗指碗。用餐后,餐具摆放整齐,不要凌乱放置。客人应对主人表示感谢并主动握手道别。

⑤酗酒醉酒是一件很尴尬的事情,不要每次都干杯。饮酒量不应超过自己酒量的五成,以不影响工作为宜。

5.谈话的技巧

①与他人交流谈话,一定要保持与对方目光的接触。如果想要加入别人的谈话,应先打招呼,如在谈话过程中不得不离开,需向对方道歉。

②谈话中如有三个或更多的人,应注意时常进行话题的切换,不要不顾他人的存在。如有什么事情不想与第三人分享,应另寻机会或单独找个机会。在别人面前窃窃私语是非常不礼貌的。

③应当避免交谈政治、宗教、死亡等话题。不要询问对方的个人信息,比如收入和财产等。天气和新闻通常是较好的话题。

④与人谈话还要注意措辞,应随时注意礼貌,为表示对他人的尊敬,多使用一些礼貌的字词"请""谢谢""对不起""打扰一下""再见"等。

## 四、打电话礼仪

1.接听电话的礼仪

（1）听到铃响,迅速接听

听到电话铃声后应迅速拿起听筒,最好在三声之内接听。若很长时间才接听,会给对方留下不好的印象,在接听后最好先道歉。

（2）先要问好，再报家门

一般接听后的第一句话是"您好"，然后再报出自己的名字，让对方知道接听的对象是谁，这也体现了对对方的尊重。

（3）礼貌待人，微笑说话

当我们打电话给客户时，若一接通就听到对方亲切、优美的招呼声，心里一定会很愉快，使双方对话能顺利展开，对该客户也有了较好的印象。因此，接电话时要有礼貌，这样一开始就会给客户留下良好的印象。此外，打电话时要保持良好的心情，即使对方看不见你，也可以从欢快的语调中体会到你的态度。

（4）姿态端正，声音清晰

打电话过程中绝对不能吸烟、喝茶、吃零食。懒散的姿态对方也能够"听"出来，因此打电话时，即使对方看不见，也要当作对方就在眼前，尽可能注意自己的姿态。同时，在说话时语调要稍高一些，吐字要清楚，便于对方听清。

（5）礼貌应答，认真记录

回答对方要有礼貌，讲话应尽量简练，只要把意思说清楚即可。如遇到需要记录的内容，应一边拿话筒一边记录。认真听取并记录对方的谈话内容也体现对客户的一种尊重。

（6）礼貌告别，后挂轻放

挂电话前为了避免错误，应重复一下电话中的重要事项，再次明确对方的目的之后，向对方说一声谢谢。另外，要尽量等对方挂下电话后，再轻轻放下听筒。

2. 拨打电话的礼仪

（1）准备

确认对方的姓名、电话号码，准备好要讲的内容、说话的顺序，明确通话所要达的目的。

（2）问候、告知自己的姓名

"您好！我是××公司×××。"一定要报出自己的姓名。

（3）确认对象

"请问××部的×××先生在吗？"必须确认通电话的对象。与要找的人通话后，应重新问候。

（4）电话内容

"今天打电话是想……"应先将想要说的内容告诉对方，时间、地点、数字等要传达准确。

（5）结束语

"谢谢""麻烦您了""那就拜托您了"等，做到语气诚恳、态度和蔼。

注意：打电话时，如果发生掉线、中断等情况，一般应由打电话方重新拨打。

### 五、着装礼仪

着装礼仪在国际商务谈判中非常重要。得体的着装，不仅体现个人的仪表美，而且还是对他人的尊重，直接影响着谈判的成败。在国际商务谈判中，一般要求穿着传统、庄重和高雅。

#### 1. 着装的一般原则

俗话说，人靠衣裳马靠鞍。与人交往，我们首先注重的是人的着装。人们常常发现，一件漂亮的衣服，穿在不同的人身上，其效果和感觉并不相同。成功的着装与仪表有着紧密联系。商务人士在着装时应遵循以下几个原则：

①不盲目追求潮流或模仿。现代人容易受潮流的影响，经常为了追求时尚而忽视了自己的职业与身份。时装设计师们为了刺激大众的购买欲望，每年都会推出各式新款时装，这些时装或许是很出色的晚装、舞台装，却未必是合适的职业装。再者，每一个人的身材、五官、气质不同，着装风格也不会相同，穿在别人身上漂亮得体的服装，穿自己身上则不一定合适。

②着装应与自身条件相适应。选择服装应该与自己的年龄、身份、体形、五官、性格和谐统一。就形体条件而言，一般来说，身材矮胖、颈粗脸圆的人，宜穿深色低"V"字形或大"U"字形领套装，浅色高领服装则不适合；而身材瘦长、颈细长、脸长的人宜穿浅色、高领或圆领服装；方脸者则宜穿小圆领或双翻领服装；身材匀称、形体条件好的人，着装范围则较广。

③着装应与职业、场合、交往目的和对象相协调。着装要与职业、场合相宜，这是不可忽视的原则。正式社交场合，着装宜庄重大方，不宜过于浮华；参加晚会或喜庆场合，服饰则可明亮、艳丽些；节假日休闲时间着装应随意、轻便些。

#### 2. 女士着装

众所周知，目前女装款式中，裙式套装被公认为职业女性最适当的职业装，这几乎成了一项不成文的规定。裙式套装既不失其女性本色，又能切合庄重与大方的原则。一般来说，在国际商务谈判中，女士着装要注意以下要点：

①避免过分前卫的服饰。在国际商务谈判中，女士要显得稳重大方，不宜穿花哨、夸张的服装，也不要选择过于追求流行的服饰，尤其是怪异的装扮。

②避免极端保守的服饰。太过保守的着装会使人显得呆板，因此可以在套装上增添配饰、点缀丝巾或小饰物，使其免于呆板之感；也可以将几组套装作巧妙的搭配，这样既不显得呆板，又符合经济节约的原则。

③忌穿过分性感或暴露的服装。过分性感或暴露的服装会给人以轻浮、不稳重的感觉，更会给人留下"花瓶"的印象。

④注意"整体美"。职业女性还必须注意,除了注意穿着考究以外,从头至脚的整体装扮也应强调"整体美",比如发型、佩饰、鞋袜、挎包等要与服装相协调,颜色要搭配。一般来说,着装配色和谐的保险做法有三种:一是上下装同色,即套装,并以饰物点缀;二是同色系配色,利用同色系中深浅、明暗度不同的颜色搭配,整体效果会比较协调;三是利用对比色搭配,即运用明亮度对比或相互排斥的颜色搭配,会产生相映生辉、令人耳目一新的效果。

3.男士着装

在国际商务谈判中,西装是男士最理想的职业装,它美观大方,穿起来稳重、潇洒,因此,男士在国际商务谈判中一般应穿西装。西装面料的要求比较高,高档西装应选择纯毛料或含毛量较高的面料,这些面料厚重、舒软、有弹性;面料图案一般宜选择无图案面料,有时也可选择带隐形细竖条的面料。公认的商界人士西装的颜色是藏青色,另外,也可以选择浅灰(适合年轻人穿)和深灰色(适合年长者穿)。

(1)西装的穿着

西装是一种国际性服装,在穿着上有一套约定俗成的规范和要求,若穿着不当,不仅影响自己的形象,对别人也是一种失礼行为。男士穿西装时必须注意以下问题:

①西装的扣子。双排扣西装,应将扣子全部扣上;单排扣西装,两粒扣西装扣上边的一粒,三粒扣西装扣中间的一粒,休闲西装一般不扣扣子。

②西装的口袋。西装上衣胸部的口袋是放折叠好的装饰手帕的,其他东西不宜装入。两侧的衣袋也只作装饰用,不宜装物品。裤子两边的口袋也不宜装东西,以求裤型美观。

(2)巧配衬衣

正式场合穿西装,内应穿单色衬衣,最好是白色衬衣。衬衣的领子大小要合适,领头要挺括、洁净,衬衣的下摆要塞在裤子里。领口的扣子要扣好,若不系领带时应不扣。衬衣内一般不穿内衣,若要穿,也应注意要从衬衣外看不出穿了内衣。

(3)选配领带

在正式场合穿西装一定要打领带。佩戴领带时,除了要注意质地、款式、色彩、图案等几个要点外,还要掌握领带的系法。领带系好后,领带结大小要适中,造型要漂亮。领带的长短要得当,其最佳长度是,领带的大箭头应正好抵达腰带扣,过短、过长都不雅观。另外,领带的颜色不宜太绚丽,应尽量与衬衣和西服颜色协调。如是多色领带,尽量不要超过三种颜色。

(4)袜子和鞋

袜子的颜色应以深色为主,也可与裤子或鞋的颜色相同,不宜穿白袜子。鞋子要穿皮鞋,最好是牛皮鞋,而且光感、硬度要好,不宜变形。休闲鞋不适合与西装配套。皮鞋的颜色最好为黑色,棕色皮鞋往往不太适合。在正式场合穿的皮鞋,应当没有任何图案和装饰。

（5）其他注意事项

公文包是男士外出办公不可离身之物。对穿西装的男士而言，外出办事时如果不带公文包，会使其神采和风度大受损害。公文包材质多以牛皮、羊皮为佳，颜色以黑色或深色为主，最好与皮鞋的颜色一致。标准的公文包是手提式的长方形公文包。另外，穿西装时不要挽起袖子；尽可能不穿羊毛衫，即使穿，也不要穿带图案的羊毛衫，而且颜色要与西装协调。

☞ **案例分析 8—2**　（错误的握手导致谈判的失败）

某厂长去广交会考察，恰巧碰到销售部经理和印尼客户在热烈地洽谈合同。见厂长来了，销售部经理忙向客户介绍。厂长因右手拿着公文包，便伸出左手握住对方的右手。谁知刚才还笑容满面的客户忽然间笑容全无，并且就座后也失去了先前讨价还价的热情，不一会儿便声称有其他约会，匆匆离开了展位。

在一些国家，左手是不能用来从事如签字、握手、拿食物等工作的，否则会被看作粗鲁的表现，因为左手一般是用来做不洁之事的。这次商务谈判失败，就是因为厂长不了解这一文化差异，用了对中国人来说可以接受的左手与对方握手，最终错过了交易机会。

☞ **案例分析 8—3**　（一口痰吐掉一个合作项目）

我国国内一家医疗器械厂与美国客商初步达成了引进"输液管"生产线的协议，第二天就要签字了。可就在该厂的厂长陪同外商参观车间时，随口向墙角吐了一口痰，然后用鞋底擦了擦。这一幕让外商很反感，第二天该美国客商借故取消了该协议。

☞ **案例分析 8—4**　（私人问题该不该问？）

某公司的杨露小姐英语口语很好，某一天陪着经理会见英国来的客户。在宴会招待客人时，为了避免冷场，她热情地与客人索菲小姐寒暄起来，两人越聊越起劲，后来杨露问对方："你今年多大岁数呢？"索菲小姐所答非所问地说："你猜猜看。"杨露自觉没趣，又问道："你这个岁数，一定结婚了吧？"更令杨露吃惊的是，对方居然转过头去，再也不理她了。一直到客人离开宴会，两个人再也没说一句话。

☞ **案例分析 8—5**　（张强有什么失误？）

张强大学毕业后不久到某大公司外贸部门就职。一天，电话铃响了，张强拿起后一听是美国客户打来的，要找外贸部经理。因为经理不在，张强便与客户谈起来。客户说的内容比较多,他没有完全记下来。打完电话后直到第二天早上,他才想起这件事,随后告诉了经理,但具体内容却记不清了。之后经理又打电话问客户,客户觉得很奇怪。这件事后不久,张强被调离了外贸部门。

☞ **思考题与讨论题**

  1. 国际商务谈判礼仪的基本原则有哪些?

  2. 商务活动中,介绍他人时有哪些礼仪?

  3. 商务活动中,握手时应注意什么礼仪?

  4. 商务活动中,乘车时应注意什么礼仪?

  5. 接听和拨打电话有哪些礼仪?

  6. 商务宴请有哪些礼仪?

  7. 商务活动中,着装应注意什么问题?

# Chapter 9

# Customs, Taboos and Negotiation Styles of Negotiators from Different Countries

☞ **Case study 9 – 1**    (The story of green hats)

In 1992, a Chinese delegation consisting of 13 experts from different fields went to the US for the purchase of chemical equipment and technology of about USD 30 million. The American side tried every means to satisfy the Chinese delegates, one of which was to send every Chinese delegate a present after the first round of negotiation. The present was a beautifully wrapped red box, for "red" symbolizes luck. However, when the Chinese opened the boxes in the face of the Americans, their facial expressions were frozen; inside each box was a golf cap, particularly, it was green. The following day, the Chinese delegation gave an excuse and left.

The present from the American side, so to speak, is deliberately arranged. On the one hand, the present box is red, since in Chinese culture red symbolizes luck; on the other hand, the present itself is a fashionable golf cap, which suggests playing golf after signing a contract. In the 1990s, playing golf was an elegant but luxurious activity to Chinese. However, the American side made a big mistake, for "green hat" is a taboo in Chinese culture.

## I. Customs, Taboos and Negotiation Styles of Americans

In the 18th century, a large number of pioneers came to America from Europe seeking freedom and happiness. The pioneering spirit of their dogged perseverance and optimistic aggressiveness made them set up a new paradise—The United States of America which is now the most powerful country in the world. They are very practical and always judge a person by his success or failure. English and US Dollar sit on the important position in the business arena. Americans, being proud of their nation's achievements and importance, have strong self-esteem.

### 1. Customs and taboos of Americans

People usually shake hands in American business community, and it is enough to shake their hands twice: One is at the beginning of the visit and the other is at the end. Both gentlemen and ladies should extend their hands actively. Although Americans appear informal and casual, they are formally dressed when they go to work or attend a dinner. For example, people usually wear black or plain color clothes for attending funeral or wedding ceremonies. Ladies should wear skirts instead of cowboy pants when they are at their office. When going upstairs and downstairs, they follow the established practice of ladies first and seniors first so as to ensure their safety.

Tip, about 15%, is usually not included in a bill when people have their meals at restaurants. When communicating with Americans you should avoid being too modest and paying too much attention to ceremonies. Being too modest or a polite formula is considered as incapability or having an evil design. The proper distance in social communication is about 50 centimeters. Private matters such as age, personal income, political tendency and even the price of buying a certain commodity should not be asked.

During business contacts, people usually don't present gifts to others if they are not familiar with each other. Asking for a dinner and presenting a gift often take place after they have had a harmonious relations or a negotiation has come to a success. To be a guest in an American family, you should bring some gifts like candies, chocolate, brandy or flowers, but remember: The number of flowers should not be 13. Perfume, clothing, and cosmetics should not be given to women as gifts which indicate over intimacy between the two sides.

### 2. Negotiation style of Americans

(1) Being direct, frank and confident

During the process of negotiations, Americans state their position and principles directly, even of the unacceptable condition. It is widely accepted that Americans are endowed with prevailing confidence. They believe transaction is based on the foundation of interests. The negotiation style of Americans is to take the initiative in every round and raise their plans without hesitation. Americans are confident and firmly believe their judgment.

(2) Valuing efficiency

Americans are used to settling problems by legal system. The transaction progresses under the guidance of law. Americans especially lay emphasis on the compensation in contract. Once unexpected situation arises, the predetermined agreement will come into effect.

American companies usually have a clear division of work. They have high efficiency both in information collection and decision-making. Time is another issue that plays an important role in the American negotiation style. Don't be late for the appointment and do have a schedule for every arrangement.

(3) Being realistic and pragmatic

Americans pay close attention to interests, so they are realistic and pragmatic in negotiations. Interests are the utmost target for Americans, but they will not ask for the unreasonably high price. Americans highly respect law regulations and their agreement fulfillment rate is very high. In their eyes, business is business, and should not be mixed with friendship.

(4) Being good at bargaining

Americans are well-trained bargainers and will fully prepare for each condition in the contract. They consider concrete benefits first rather than private relationships. In addition to the quality, specifications, packing, quantity, price, time of shipment and payment terms, they will also talk about the design and development, manufacturing technique, selling, and after-sale services. To negotiate with Americans, make sure that right is right, and wrong is wrong.

(5) Valuing quality, appearance design and packing of commodities

Quality is the most basic requirement of commodities, and appearance design and packing is, in their opinion, an important factor to embody the state of consumption in a country and to stimulate mass consumption. They spare no efforts to improve the interior quality, appearance design and packing of their own products and they are also very strict with that of their imported goods.

(6) Being humorous

Americans are famous for their humor in their character. Suppose there is a fly in a glass of beer, British would instruct a waiter gently to change a glass of beer; French would pour out the beer; Japanese would ask the manager to come and rebuke him; yet Americans might say to the waiter, "Please place beer and flies respectively in the future, then guests who like flies may put flies into the beer. What do you think?" In negotiations，American businessmen prefer to transfer information in light and humorous language or make joke to liven things up.

## Ⅱ. Customs，Taboos and Negotiation Styles of Japanese

Japan's economy began to develop rapidly from 1955 soon after the Second World War. It had become the second economic power by 1980s. Chinese Confucianism has been deeply rooted in Japanese culture，meanwhile，Western culture，especially American culture，has a great influence on Japan.

### 1. Customs and taboos of Japanese

Japan is a state of ceremonies. What Japanese people do is bound by strict ceremonies. Take bowing for example，which is a unique way of greeting when people meet，though handshake is very popular on some social occasions，traditional bowing is still a kind of orthodox and standard ceremony which is applicable to all kinds of occasions such as greeting，inquiry，appreciation，meeting and seeing off guests. When Japanese people meet，they often bow. For general bowing ceremony，people bend down by 30 to 45 degrees. Different degree of people's bending down has different meanings.

Name cards play an important role in Japanese business activities. They think name card manifests a person's social status so people always bring their cards with them. In terms of the exchange of name cards，it is the younger or inferior who should give their cards to the other side first，which has been considered as a kind of ceremony. When presenting a gift，they pay much attention to their social hierarchy or grades. Generally a gift should not be of a great value，or they might think your identity and status are higher than theirs.

Japanese people dislike the color purple，which they think is sorrowful. The color green is what they want to shun and avoid and is considered as misfortune. The numbers 9 and 4 are also what they want to shun. Japanese people also avoid taking a picture with one person on the left and another on the right which they think is the prelude of misfortune. They are disgusted with things having images of fox which is a symbol of greedy. Besides，comb should not be sent as a gift because the pronunciation of comb is similar to that of death. The color red，a token of luck in China，is not welcomed in Japan. People use both of their hands to accept a gift. It is a usual practice not to open the gift in the face of the giver，and when you meet the giver again in the future，you should mention the gift and extend your thanks.

## 2. Negotiation style of Japanese

（1）Valuing ceremonies

When meeting for the first time, "I'm sorry" is a pet phrase for Japanese. They are very meticulous about ceremonies which might be indifferent or even ridiculous for westerners. So it is necessary to know and abide by the relevant ceremonies before negotiating with Japanese. Giving presents is a custom in Japan. Japanese are generous in giving gifts.

（2）Valuing interpersonal relationship, especially long-term cooperative partnership

In business negotiation with Japanese, a good personal relationship is half of the success. Interpersonal relationship is even more important than contract clauses. It is the usual practice for Americans and Europeans to make contract clauses as much specific and detailed as possible, especially the aspect of bilateral responsibilities and claim for compensation. But Japanese people don't think contract is the most important. They think as long as the two sides have established good and trusted cooperative relationship, they may consult the relevant clauses through renegotiation though one side cannot do according to the contract. It will be of great benefit to negotiation to make your contact with a Japanese merchant through an intermediary who has better reputation. Furthermore, Japanese people pay close attention to harmonization of interpersonal relationship. Never come straight to the point and talk about the main subject in your first consultation with a Japanese. You'd better talk about things they are interested in such as culture, philosophy or history in an indirect way. In Japan, patience is closely related to friendship. Personal relationship is highly emphasized in business. Japanese are willing to know their business partners and maintain a long-term relationship.

（3）Having strong team spirit

Group decision-making and collective responsibility are the two aspects found in negotiation with Japanese. This has made the Japanese insist on their own proposition and attempt to persuade their counterpart to make concessions. It is difficult for a Japanese to change his decision. To negotiate with Japanese, you should manage to communicate with people from all levels. This is why it takes long time for Japanese to make the decisions. But as long as a Japanese merchant has made the decision, he will go into actions promptly. Japanese are well-known for their strictness with contracts and promises. The careful discussion about contract details will lay the foundation for future work.

（4）Having strong sense of hierarchy

Social status and ranks is a sensitive issue in Japan, to which they pay much attention and often restricts their decision-making in business and social contact. All Japanese enterprises have a tendency of respecting elders. Those who have the qualification of being the representatives of the companies usually have a working experience of 15 to 20 years. To negotiate with Japanese, it is better to send the negotiators who have higher status and ranks than the Japanese counterparts so as to ensure the success of the negotiation. Besides, the social status of women in Japan is quite low, and women are generally not allowed to participate in the operation and management in large companies. Japanese will not bring a female companion to attend important occasions.

（5）Preference for euphemistic and indirect negotiation style

During negotiation, they usually inquire and answer questions in an indirect manner. They avoid direct criticism, direct refusal and embarrassing questions. Japanese dislike direct conflicts with their counterparts. Patience is an important factor for success. Negotiation with Japanese needs patience and sincerity. If you ask your Japanese counterpart to declare his stands concerning contract contents in haste, the negotiation will not go smoothly. So you should be prudent both in your actions and your wording when negotiating with Japanese. Be careful to deliver an ultimatum. Don't disturb Japanese when they are thinking in silence. You may make use of the time to think, observe and figure out your countermeasures.

Besides, in a consultation, Japanese have the habit to echo with others, or nodding heads with the meaning of "yes," but it should be noted that this does not mean he agrees with you. Instead, it simply means he has understood what you have said or he is listening.

## Ⅲ. Customs, Taboos and Negotiation Styles of Germans

### 1. Customs and taboos of Germans

Germany, with highly developed industry, is one of the strongest economies in the world. Germans lay emphasis on regulations and discipline. They surely abide by those expressly stated, and avoid those explicitly banned. The superior quality of German products is based on sophisticated technology. Germans are persistent, prudent and creative.

Germans value cleanness and tidiness not only of his own life but also of the environment of the society. They pay a lot of attention to their dressing, and will wear work clothes during their working hours. They are informal in their wear at home, but will wear formally as long as they go out or receive guests at home.

Germans are very punctual, and they will not change the agreed time unless there are any special circumstances. Germans prefer quiet life and dislike noise and excitement. In most cases, they are straightforward, and seldom give an ambiguous reply. They will immediately tell you "OK" if they can do what you ask them to do, and they will refuse you if they cannot do for you.

Germans also pay much attention to ceremony. When two persons meet, no matter whether they know each other or not, whether they meet in the street, elevator or at offices, they will greet each other. When having meals at restaurant, they will greet other customers by nodding their heads. When people meet or say goodbye to each other, they usually shake their hands. Good and intimate friends might embrace each other if they haven't seen each other for a long time.

In Germany, "ladies first" is the principle people abide by on many occasions such as getting on cars, going into rooms or elevators. Men should open doors and hang clothes for women, women can simply say "thank you," and they need not feel embarrassed. In conversations, Germans will respect others and not inquire into private matters of the other side such as income, marriage status, woman's age, etc. They will not make fun of other people.

Germans attach importance to presenting gifts. Generally, Germans will bring gifts with them if they are invited to be a guest, for example, a bunch of fresh flowers, or one or two bottles of grape wine or a meaningful book. Flowers might be a good choice for welcoming guests or visiting a sick person. For attending wedding or birthday ceremony, or for a festival, the gift should be practical and meaningful. Most people will open the gift in the face and extend thanks to the giver when they receive a gift.

### 2. Negotiation styles of Germans

Germans are obstinate and self-confident. They are prudent and dedicated to their jobs. They make plans for everything, and attach importance to efficiency and perfection.

(1) Being well-prepared

Germans will make full preparation for the negotiation. Their research not only includes the product itself, but also includes the company, the macro environment, the credit, finance, management, and production of the company. They will try to get as much detailed and first-hand information as possible so that they can negotiate with high proficiency and be able to achieve success one way or another.

(2) Being self-confident and stubborn, lacking flexibility and compromise

Germans are very confident with their products, strict with technological standard, and often take their domestic products as the standard in negotiation. The changes in price will cause confusion on German side, or even lose the opportunity. The same is true that once Germans give a price, the condition will be basically fixed. Thus it is not difficult to understand that Germans seldom bargain or only make a small bargain.

(3) Being responsible with contracts and keeping their promises

Germans attach importance to the performance of contracts and have a strong sense of rights and obligations. Before signing contracts, they would study and check every item in the contracts very carefully. Once contracts come into effect, Germans will observe them without any hesitation. It is natural that Germans will also be strict with their counterparts.

(4) Being efficient and practical

Germans have a strong sense of time and enjoy the reputation of being highly efficient. They believe in the principle of "at once." From the fact whether the documents on office desk can be dealt with quickly and effectively, German people can judge whether a negotiator is capable or not. Germans are serious and particular about efficiency in everything. So in making contacts with Germans, try not to be late, or they might be disgusted with you or even lose faith in you.

## Ⅳ. Customs, Taboos and Negotiation Styles of the British

UK, the earliest industrialized country and the former world financial and trade center, was called "the empire on which the sun never sets," which formulates their national characteristics of being conservative and prudent.

### 1. Customs and taboos of the British

UK is famous for "gentlemen." In contact with ladies, men can shake hands only after ladies extend hands first. An appointment should be made beforehand for a meeting, and negotiators should be punctual. Presenting gifts is common, and it is the best if your gifts bear the name of your company. When you are invited you should bring some gifts with you, such as flowers or chocolate.

There are three taboos in UK: Not jumping in the queue, not asking ladies' age and not bargaining. British people have the habit of queuing up; they might queue up for getting on a bus or train, or buying newspapers. It is improper to ask a lady of her age, because she thinks age is her own secret, and everyone wants to keep young forever. "You look like much younger" is a suitable compliment for a middle-aged woman. When shopping in UK, bargaining is a taboo. The British do not like bargaining and think bargaining is a matter of losing face.

The number "13" and "Friday" are the other taboos for the British, which are the signs of misfortune and boding. The Friday is called "black Friday" if that day happens to be the 13th day of that month, and no activities should be held. The number "3" is another unlucky number. And you should not light cigarettes for more than two persons with a lighter or a match each time. British people are disgusted with the color deep green, which makes people depressed. They dislike designs with goats and elephants, which are a sign of stupidity. Designs with peacocks, black cats and greenish lily flowers are also taboos for British people since they think peacock is a disastrous bird, black cat the sign of misfortune, and greenish lily flower a token of death.

### 2. Negotiation styles of the British

(1) Being prudent, earnest and particular about ceremonies

British businessmen are good at stating their positions and opinions briefly. But they are, in most cases, quiet and calm, self-confident and careful, not agitated, risk-taking and boasting. They would rather make business of small profit but with low risk than make business of large margin of profit but with higher risk. British people pay much attention to ceremonies; they are reserved and will not reveal too much emotion in negotiations. So, to negotiate business with British, you should be clean and tidy with your appearance, and your speech should be elegant and your behavior dignified.

(2) Being inflexible and disliking long-time bargaining

The British appear to be inflexible in negotiation and refuse to accept other possibilities besides the alternatives already provided by them. They don't like long-time bargaining and hope an agreement can be reached soon. Except for important negotiations, one hour is enough for most cases. Pay attention to the approaches and strategies for negotiations with the British. For those important business negotiations, you should hold talks with decision-making persons such as the president, managing director and general manager.

（3）Following strictly with the agreed time

To conduct business activities with the British, you should usually make an appointment beforehand and arrive ahead of time so as to win their trust and respect. After you receive treat from British businessmen, you should write to extend your thanks. British people enjoy a high reputation in terms of doing business and they are strict with themselves in almost everything.

（4）Valuing relationships

British people are prudent and careful in contacting with others. Once friendship is set up, the relationship is long-lasting and helpful for the business.

The Great Britain is an old capitalist nation. Concept of class is deeply rooted in this society. The "commoner" and the "noble" are different in many aspects. For instance, the upper class read *Times*, *Financial Times*; middle class read *Daily Telegraph* while the lower class people read *Sun and Mirror*. Comparatively, in foreign affairs, the British pay more attention to their counterpart's identity, experience and achievements.

## Ⅴ. Customs, Taboos and Negotiation Styles of the French

France has made great achievements in social sciences, literature, science and technology in recent decades. French people are very proud of their nationality; they are open and cheerful in character; they are enthusiastic, earnest, hard-working and are good at enjoying their lives.

### 1. Customs and taboos of the French

French people usually shake their hands when they meet with guests on social occasions. Women enjoy a quite higher status in social life. To shake hands with ladies, men should wait for them to extend their hands first. Ladies can have gloves on when shaking hand but men cannot. The principle of "ladies first" is carried out in almost all kinds of situations, say, proposing a toast on a dinner table, entering a room, having a seat, etc. It is also the case when people extend their thanks to the host / hostess when saying good-bye in a visit.

The social communication distance is quite closer in France than that in other Western countries, for they think it appears to be intimate. The French prefer cock and consider it a token of "sunshine" and it is the national bird of France because cock has both viewing value and economic value in addition to the function of heralding and announcing the arrival of dawn. French people also like flower-de-luce, the national flower of France, which is considered as pride of their nationality, symbol of power, and token of the country.

French people tend to express or emphasize their ideas with their gestures. Yet their gestures mean differently in comparison with ours. For example, when people separate our thumb and index finger, it means eight in China, but in France it means two. To express the meaning of "it's me," Chinese people point to their noses, but the French point to their chests. When they point downwards with their thumbs, it has the meaning of "bad" or "poor."

To French, the number "13" and "Friday" are unlucky. It is a taboo for a man to present perfume to a woman since it has the suspicion of over-intimacy and hatching a sinister plot. They don't like others to inquire about their political tendency, wage and other private affairs. It is improper to present gifts to the other side when people meet for the first time. Presenting gifts at the first meeting is considered being not good at social communication or even may be considered being vulgar.

### 2. Negotiation styles of the French

（1）Being easy to get along with

Personal friendship has effect on business relationship. To build up personal relationship is to build up firm business relationship. French people pursue individualism and value interpersonal relationship. They attach importance to individuals. In business negotiations, it has been the practice to adopt individual responsibility system which is quite efficient. French businessmen prefer to handle affairs through interpersonal relationship since it will be much easier and quicker than through normal channels. Before business consultation, French people hope to know about the representatives of their counterpart and to establish harmonious relations between the two sides.

（2）Preference for horizontal negotiations

French merchants prefer to sketch an outline for the negotiation beforehand, then reach a principled agreement and finally confirm the specific contents concerning the negotiation. Furthermore, French people tend to concentrate on the main clauses, and they will not pay so much attention to the details.

（3）Not having a strong sense of time

In public places, such as an official banquet, there is an informal custom that the higher the guest's status is, the later he will be. So you should be patient if you want to make business with them. But French people will not forgive those who are late, and they will receive them coldly.

In August，France is in vacation and any business negotiation will have to be sheltered for a while. The business in July will have to wait until September. Besides，French negotiators often insist on using French as the negotiating language，for in their eyes French is the most honorable language in the world.

## Ⅵ. Customs，Taboos and Negotiation Styles of Russians

USSR was the firs socialist country in the world and collapsed in 1991. Russia is now still one of the most important and powerful countries in the world.

### 1. Customs and taboos of Russians

In Russia，"right" means "superior," "noble" and "lucky;" "left" means "inferior,""humble" and "unlucky," and this concept is deeply rooted in Russian people's mind. People even connect right with male and left with female. When dressing，Russian people will have their right sleeve on first，and it will be unlucky to have the left sleeve on first. If there is a nevus on the right cheek，it will be considered as a lucky one; if a nevus is on the left cheek，then it is considered as an unlucky one.

Russian people like drinking，smoking and dancing. Dancing is a tradition in Russia. They lay much emphasis on their appearance and are fond of making up. In public places，they pay attention to their behavior，for example，they never put their hands into their pockets or sleeves. They don't take off their coats casually though it is hot.

In Russia，the number "13" is an unlucky number. When entertaining guests，they never invite 13 people. No.13 does not exist for residential house number. Same as in Western countries，it will be called "black Friday" if that Friday is just the 13th day of that month. The numbers "1" and "7" are considered as lucky numbers.

Salt is worshipped and treasured by Russian people，and it is also used as offerings for worshipping ancestors. They think salt has the power to drive out evil spirits and get rid of misfortune. Mirror is thought to be a holy article. Breaking a mirror means the ruin of spirit. According to the traditional Russian custom，knives and pins cannot be sent to others as gifts. Handkerchief cannot be presented as a gift either since it indicates separation. Two persons should not wipe perspiration with one piece of handkerchief. It is a taboo to whistle at home or in public places because whistle can attract ghost.

## 2. Negotiation styles of Russians

(1) Valuing private relationship

Private relationship plays an important role in Russian trade. They pay much attention to the language exchange and prefer to express their intentions directly. Russian merchants often neglect time. To consult with them, the expected time is often delayed and the ending time might also be postponed and the negotiation might be often interrupted. The negotiation with Russians might be more difficult since they are influenced greatly by their dilatory style of work.

(2) Being conservative and inflexible

Russians, used to the planned economy, are conservative in negotiations and too prudent to make any innovation and adaptation. They stick to tradition and lack flexibility. The USSR was a foreign trade controlled country with a highly planed foreign trade system. It was impossible for any enterprise or person to import or export any commodities. All importing and exporting plans were decided by the government and would be approved, checked, administrated and supervised by the relevant organizations. So people have been used to act according to rules. Even after the collapse of the USSR, some Russians still have the obvious features under the planned system. In negotiations concerning foreign affairs, they prefer to act according to rules and plans.

(3) Being interested in technical details and claiming clauses in negotiations

Russians businessmen might spend a lot of time on discussion of technical matters of a product. So in the negotiations with Russians, it's better to have a technical expert in the negotiation team so as to state the technical details accurately and punctually. Besides, you should be careful for the contract wordings and be prudent with the claiming clauses.

(4) Being good at bargaining

Russians businessmen have the wisdom and strong ability of bargaining and are specialized bargainers. They can always force their counterparts to reconcile even when Russians have disadvantages in financial resources, advanced technology and equipment. They are good at seeking cooperative and competitive partnership. For example, if they want to import a certain project, they will first of all invite for bids, and then make a choice without haste among those competitors. They might even make mischief among the competitors to have a fierce competition and they will reap profits from it. Russian can be called old-hands and experts in terms of bargaining. They will not believe and accept a quotation no matter how calculated and fair it is, and they will make every endeavor to ask the other side to make some concessions.

Besides, Russians are specialized in bartering. Because of the lack of foreign exchange, Russians prefer barter trade in international business. Russians make use of the barter trade skillfully. In order to maintain the attractiveness, they won't require paying with their own products to their counterpart who expects hard currency. A common practice is that Russians will beat the price quotation to the bottom and then require to pay partly or all with products.

## Ⅷ. Customs, Taboos and Negotiation Styles of Koreans①

### 1. Customs and taboos of Koreans

Koreans advocate Confucianism and respect elders. Young people should pick off their sunglasses when they talk to elders. When having meals, elder people are served first, and only after the elder begin to eat, can the others start eating. Traditional Korean etiquette for greeting is making a bow. When younger generation or juniors meet with elders, the former should bow, greet and stand aside, waiting for the latter to go first. In the Republic of Korea, if you go to other's home attending a dinner, you should bring a gift. When proposing a toast during a dinner, you should hold the wine bottle with your right hand, putting your left hand on the bottom of the bottle, then make a bow, deliver a felicitation and lastly pour a drink for three times. Toast proposer's wine glass should be lower than the guest. After finishing the toast, the proposer should make another bow and then leave the dinner table.

Liquor is the best gift for males in the Republic of Korea but it is not suitable for females except that you make it clear that the liquor is prepared for her husband. Generally speaking, Korean men prefer those famous brands of goods like textiles, ties, lighters and electric shavers. Korean women prefer cosmetics, handbags, gloves, scarves and seasonings used in the kitchen.

There are many taboos for Koreans. People cannot say unlucky words, quarrel or get angry when they meet on New Year's Day or other festivals. During the first three days of the first month of the lunar year, people should not put out the garbage or sweep the floor; they should by no means kill chickens or butcher pigs. It is a taboo to make a fire on Cold Food Festival. People should shun trimming their nails at others'

---

① It refers to people from the Republic of Korea in this book.

home or the two families will become enemies. People should shun wearing hats while having meals or they will live in poverty all their life.

### 2. Negotiation styles of Koreans

(1) Valuing etiquette and being able to create a good negotiation atmosphere

Koreans will choose the negotiation site deliberately and prefer to hold talks in famous hotels and pay much attention to negotiation atmosphere in the opening stage. They usually passionately greet their counterpart and introduce their names and positions to the other side. When they are asked what drinks they would like to have, they often choose the drinks the other side prefers in order to show their respect.

(2) Being fully prepared for negotiations

Korean businessmen have accumulated rich experiences in trade practice for a long time and can usually gain the upper hand in the trade negotiations which are unfavorable to them. So they are considered as negotiation nemesis by Western countries. Koreans manage to know about their counterparts and make full preparation before a negotiation. There are many things they would like to know and consult beforehand, such as the business items, scale, fund, management style and the market price of the commodities. Once they sit together with the counterparts for negotiation, they have been surely well prepared for it.

(3) Valuing negotiation skills

Korean businessmen often use tactics such as "feint to the east and attack in the west," "excessively demanding," "fatiguing tactics" and even "nibble strategy" at the last moment. Besides, when signing the contract, Korean merchants are often ready to sign contract in three languages—language of the two sides plus English. Three languages are equally authentic.

Furthermore, it should be noted that Korean people are affected by both Confucian culture and American culture. Korean's personality is on the one hand sensitive about one's reputation, and on the other hand very independent and straightforward. So when in contact with Koreans, we should know the blend of the two cultures.

## Ⅶ. Customs, Taboos and Negotiation Styles of Negotiators from Other Countries

### 1. Customs, taboos and negotiation styles of Arabians

(1) Customs and taboos of Arabians

There are many religious branches among Arabian people and they live by tribes for the sake of geography, religion and nationalities. They are obstinate and conservative; they have a strong sense of family, hierarchy and national cohesion.

Arabian people believe in Islam and have many taboos. For example, Arabians refuse to eat and drink before sunset during Ramadan. They cannot be cross-legged when they sit down. We should respect their belief or there might be conflicts. Gifts should not be presented for the first meeting or it will be considered as bribery. Gifts with animal designs should not be sent to them, because they think animals might bring them misfortune. Gifts should be exchanged with your right hand or both of your hands. Don't send a gift to the hostess or a married lady. The first etiquette for Arabians when they meet is to embrace and kiss on their cheeks: three times on the left, three times on the right and again three times on the left, and then the two people shake their hands.

(2) Negotiation styles of Arabians

a. Make friends first and then do business. Usually it takes Arabians a long time to make a decision, and they don't like negotiating business through telephone. If you want to promote sales of your products to them, you might succeed after many visits to them. In making contact with them, you simply have to leave a favorable impression on them and gain their trust so as to establish a friendly relationship. Arabians are very hospitable and receive any guests heartily. Therefore, a negotiation is often interrupted by unexpected visits and the host will leave for the new visitors. Arabians will give others a misconception that they have no concept of time, because they stop or delay a negotiation casually.

b. Arabians show special preference for bargaining. Bargaining is so important that people think that a negotiation without bargaining is not considered as a serious one. Prices either in big stores or small stores can all be bargained. The marked price is only sellers' quotation. It is especially true in business negotiations, and they even think that people who bargain again and again without buying anything can get more respect from the seller than those who buy something immediately without any bargaining.

c. Negotiations are conducted through agents. In Arabian world, agent is inevitably a critical part in business either with the private businesses or with governments. Almost all Arabian governments insist that business should be conducted through agents who can get commission from the business. A good agent can be of great help to developing business. He might help his employer contact the government organizations, urge the parties concerned to make decisions as soon as possible and arrange other matters such as recovering the payment of goods, use of labor services, cargo transportation and storage.

## 2. Customs, taboos and negotiation styles of Indians

(1) Customs, taboos of Indians

India is a country with an ancient civilization. There is a distinct gradation and a strict hierarchy system in Indian society. The usual way of greeting is to put one's palms together devoutly before their chest or raise one's hand to give a sign. People put their palms together for greeting when their hands are empty; if there is something in one of his hands, then he can raise his right hand to salute. Embracing is a usual etiquette. People usually embrace when they meet again after a long separation or someone will go on a long journey or when they expect some great event to occur. Touch one's foot is the most solemn and formal ceremonies. Presenting a garland and putting it on around the guest's neck is also a usual etiquette to welcome guests in India. The more honorable your guest is, the thicker the garland will be. To mark an auspicious nevus is also the etiquette to welcome guests. On joyous festivals, Indians prefer to make a red dot between two eyebrows on women's forehead by using cinnabar. Some candies or a bunch of flowers can be a usual gift for visiting a friend.

In southern India, people shake their heads to show their agreement. The color white, a curve moon design and greenish lily flowers are taboos for Indian people. "1," "3" and "7" are the unlucky numbers. When talking with Indians, matters concerning religion, national contradiction, India-Pakistan conflict, nuclear weapons and sexual relations are all sensitive topics.

(2) Negotiation styles of Indians

a. Indian people have a lower rhythm and prefer to talk and attack after the other side has stated opinions. Indian merchants are conservative and traditional in their mind. They don't like a quick speed when doing business. So many westerners are unable to understand what it is all about for Indians' restrained attitude and low speed. Actually, What Indians aim at is that they want their counterpart to be impatient and show their hands earlier so that they can begin attacks afterwards.

b. The rate of Indians to fulfill agreement is not high, and they might breach the contract easily. Indian merchants have a habit of comparing the prices of two customers in the presence of their customer, and often find excuses of avoiding fulfilling their responsibilities when they meet with obstacles of a business. If they have faults and are blamed, they will surely explain again and again. So when negotiating with Indians, the contract clauses and stipulations must be rigor and strict so as to avoid the subsequent conflicts.

### 3. Customs, taboos and negotiation styles of Southeast Asians

Southeast Asian countries mainly include Singapore, Malaysia, Thailand, Indonesia, the Philippines, Vietnam and Cambodia. These people mainly have the following features.

Firstly, Southeast Asians attach much importance to hierarchy. Due to the cultural background, they are very sensitive to social status hierarchy. The seniors, especially the male seniors, enjoy high social respect.

Secondly, Southeast Asians have no concept of time. Southeast Asians are not strict with time. Because of the unsatisfactory infrastructure and climate, people don't interpret procrastination as lack of sincerity. But Singapore is an exception; Singaporeans have a strong sense of time and are very punctual for negotiations.

Thirdly, Southeast Asians like bargaining. So when negotiating with them, you should leave enough room when you make an offer.

(1) Singaporeans

In Singapore, people are forbidden to smoke in public places or you will be fined 500 Singapore dollars. "4,""6,""7,""13" and "69" are considered as negative numbers. They consider the color black as misfortune. And the color purple is not welcomed. They prefer the color red, blue and green. Designs with pigs and tortoises are their taboos.

Singaporeans are also responsible with contracts and keep their promise. They attach importance to the performance of contracts. There are many family businesses. It is important to establish personal relationships when doing business with Singaporeans.

(2) Malaysians

In Malaysia, you cannot point at others with your index finger, which is a kind of defilement. Tortoise is their taboo which is considered as an unlucky animal. Pork and dog meat are forbidden. Malaysians lay much emphasis on interpersonal relations, ceremonies and hierarchy. Relationship is more important than contract clauses in solving conflicts, and they think the presence of a lawyer is a manifestation of lack of trust between the two sides.

## 4. Negotiation styles of Latin Americans

Latin America includes South America and Central America. Brazil and Mexico are two major countries. Brazilians are very good bargainers, and they often refuse your offer directly. What they mean is that they want to know your deadline. So when negotiating with Brazilians, you should leave enough room when you offer and enough time for the possible long negotiation.

Making business in Mexico, it will be a valuable treasure if you can speak fluent Spanish. It is advisable that you should make it clear that whether an interpreter is needed in the negotiation. It is a good idea to translate your booklet which introduces your company and your products into Spanish.

Generally speaking, Latin American businessmen have a poor record of credibility and are inclined to break contracts. Contracts in Latin America are not strictly observed. The revision of a signed contract often happens. The fulfillment of contracts is sometimes not guaranteed.

Close personal relationships are very important to the success of negotiations. Latin Americans highly value friendship. To guarantee the success of negotiation, you should try to set up close personal relationships with them, and keep patient and not probe into the social problems.

The economic development is in different stages in Latin America, and high inflation often appears, therefore, in international trade, you should choose stable hard currency. Besides, their life rhythm is slow and they look down upon women.

## 5. Negotiation styles of Scandinavians

Scandinavian countries consist of Finland, Norway, Sweden, Denmark and Iceland. Scandinavians are good-natured, modest, gentle and humorous. Business people are generally well-educated and heartily observe the etiquette in either formal or informal negotiations. If they are hosts, they will arrange the schedule to the most satisfaction of guests. The quality of products is the pride of Scandinavians.

Scandinavians are punctual, relatively calm in negotiations and make every effort to avoid rashness. They arrange the work carefully and implement the project in strict accordance with the schedule.

Scandinavians are honest, frank and perseverant. They often reveal their points frankly and are well-known for constructive proposals. In a negotiation, participants should consider more about cooperation, and be straightforward and rational, and always seek stableness and harmony.

Sandinavians dislike endless bargaining and prefer a relaxed negotiation rhythm. Another common interest in Scandinavian countries is Sauna, an indispensable part of life. The invitation of Sauna at the beginning of business negotiations indicates a promising start. In some circumstances, conversations can be taken during Sauna time, which will eliminate the inconveniences in formal negotiations.

## 6. Customs, taboos and negotiation styles of Italians

Ladies are respected in Italy; "ladies first" can be reflected on any social occasion. There are many festivals in Italy: religious festivals, folk festivals and national memorial days. About one third of the days are festivals throughout a whole year. "13" and "17" are considered as unlucky numbers in Italy. The color purple has negative meaning and is not welcomed. Design of chrysanthemum is a taboo, for chrysanthemum is considered as funeral flower.

Italian businessmen or travelers are smartly dressed. Their offices are well-equipped. The comfortableness of life, such as accommodations, is highly expected.

Italians, unlike other Europeans, usually do not keep strict timetable and are often late for appointments. Even the schedule for carefully organized activities is not guaranteed without any notice. Their jobs are slack and perfunctory with low efficiency. They are extrovert and sentimental and are subject to changing mood.

Italians like quarrelling. They often quarrel loudly for trifles and neither gives way to the other. If possible, they will quarrel all day long. Especially in terms of price they will not yield an inch, but they will not pay too much attention to the quality, property and time of shipment though they surely hope the product they have bought can be normally used.

## 7. Customs, taboos and negotiation styles of Canadians

The number "13," Friday, the color black and the design of greenish lily flowers are taboos for Canadians. Their preference is the color white and the design of maple leaves. Canada is famous for red maple leaves in the world.

Canadian people are mainly the descendants of British and French immigrants. In general, most British Canadians believe in Christianity and speak English; they are relatively conservative and introvert. French Canadians believe in Catholicism and speak French; they are relatively open and untrammelled.

Most British Canadian merchants live in Toronto and western Canadian districts and French Canadian merchants mainly live in Quebec. British Canadians are conservative, strict in negotiating language and attach importance to credibility. Once a contract is signed, the performance of the contract is immediately fulfilled. However, French Canadian merchants are quite different. They are amiable, easy-going and generous for entertainment of their guests, but when it comes to practical issues, they become dilatory and unpredictable. As a result, in order to avoid the possible disputes and troubles, you should be prudent and the contracts should be accurate in details as much as possible.

### 8. Customs, taboos and negotiation styles of Australians

Handshake is the usual way of greeting in Australia. Australians have a strong sense of time. For business consultations people should make an appointment in advance and be punctual. For private visits a gift should be prepared.

Australians have kept the traditional style of British gentlemen; "ladies first" is very popular. Yawning and stretching oneself casually in public places are ungraceful and impolite behaviors. They are disgusted with the number "13" and "Friday" with the influence of Christianity. Don't make an appointment with Christians on Sundays.

Australian merchants have high efficiency in their work. They usually start on their negotiation soon after a brief greeting with their guests for the first time. Generally, Australian negotiators have the right of decision-making. They don't like the way of making a high offer and spend a long time on bargaining. Instead, they often adopt invitation of bids and conclude business at the lowest price.

Australian merchants are easy-going but scrupulous in separating public from private interests. Their entertainment has nothing to do with business. They are very prudent and careful in signing a contract. Once an agreement is reached, the agreement performance rate is also rather high.

### 9. Negotiation styles of Jews

Jews have a small population but a great influence on the world. They have the fame of "world merchant," strong commercial awareness and unusual talents and ability of doing business. There are so many Jewish celebrities such as Mose, Jesus, Marx, Freud, Einstein, Picasso, Beethoven, Kissinger, Rockefeller, Soros, Morgan and Harmer. About 30% of the Nobel Prize has been won by Jews.

Jews respect contract. Their contract performance rate is very high. In Jewish culture, contract has absolute authority, and is not allowed to be disobeyed. It's worthwhile to note that in their eyes contract, complex or simple, has no difference in importance and all should be observed with same seriousness.

Jews will make sufficient preparation for any negotiation, which is well recognized in business world and diplomat arena. Jews always show clear attitude in negotiation. Jews only negotiate with persons who have the right to make the final decision. They will investigate their counterparts about their position and decision level.

Jews are knowledgeable and good at bargaining. They are well-known for their wide knowledge and have a strong ability of prediction. They are ready to take notes about everything that they think important. They can calculate the profit or the loss immediately they get the data. They specialize in negotiation and bargaining and are strict with the contract clauses.

### 10. Negotiation styles of overseas Chinese

Overseas Chinese are people who have settled down in all parts of the world in recent one or two centuries, cannot be neglected in business community. Most of them made their fortune firstly by virtue of managing a restaurant, a tailor's shop or a barber's shop. What they dealt with was business with a small capital. They were decisive, good at bargaining and began to work soon after they made up their mind.

☞ **Case study 9 – 2**　（**How to make them jump off the vessel**）

A few businessmen were having an international trade negotiation on a vessel when suddenly the vessel began to sink.

"Ask those men to take on the life vest and jump off the vessel immediately!" The captain ordered the chief mate.

A few minutes later, the chief mate came back. "Those men won't jump." He reported.

So the captain had to go in person. In a while, he came back and told the chief mate, "All of them have jumped down."

"But how did you make it?" The chief mate could not help asking.

"I told the British jumping was good for health, then he did. And I said to the French it was a fashion, to the German it was an order, to the Italian it was forbidden...."

"Then how did you persuade the American?"

"It's easy," said the captain, "I told him I have effected the insurance for him."

## ☞ Case study 9 – 3   (A story of thumbing up)

Let's look at the experience of an British businessman in Iran. The British had been in Iran for one month and everything went well. He developed a good relationship with his Iranian colleague. In the negotiation, he respected Islamic culture, avoided any political issues which were potentially explosive in the negotiations. And to his delight, he successfully signed a contract with his Iranian counterpart. After signing the contract, he thumbed up to his counterpart when there arose an intense atmosphere unexpectedly. An Iranian official rose to his feet and left the room. The British was completely confused by the situation, not knowing what had happened. Meanwhile, his Iranian colleague also felt embarrassed, at a loss what to say.

In Britain, thumbing up signifies praise, meaning "great" or "very good." However, in Iran, it has a negative meaning, indicating dissatisfaction or even disgust, which is a rather rude gesture.

## ☞ Case study 9 – 4   (Misunderstanding resulting from interpretation)

The president of a transnational corporation visited a well-known Chinese manufacturing enterprise, talking about the cooperation and development between the two sides. The Chinese general manager made an introduction proudly to the guest, "Our corporation is a state-owned grade-2 enterprise..." The interpreter translated the "grade-2 enterprise" into "second-class enterprise" without a second thought. On hearing this, the guest's attitude changed greatly, responding perfunctorily and left. On his journey back, he complained, "How can I cooperate with a second-class Chinese enterprise?"

## ☞ Case study 9 – 5   (Importance of social contacting distance)

A manager of an American petroleum company held a negotiation of petroleum import with an Arabic representative from OPEC. In the climax of the negotiation, the Arabic representative drew closer and closer until the distance between them was only 15 centimeters. The American manager felt a little bit uncomfortable, and thus he receded and kept a distance of about 60 centimeters between them. The Arabic representative frowned, hesitating a little, and drew closer again while talking.

The American manager was unaware of the Arabian culture and not familiar with the manners and customs, so he receded a second time. Meanwhile, his assistant was shaking his head fretfully, giving a hint of stopping him from receding. Though the American manager did not fully understand his assistant, he stopped receding. As a result, a satisfying agreement for both sides was reached between the Arabic representative who felt natural and the American manager who felt uncomfortable.

After the event, the American manager sighed with emotion after knowing the Arabic manners and customs, "An important petroleum business was almost ruined!"

☞ **Questions for your consideration and discussion**

    1. What are the negotiation styles of Americans?

    2. What are the negotiation styles of Japanese?

    3. What are the negotiation styles of western European countries?

    4. What are the negotiation styles of Russians?

    5. How much do you know about the negotiation styles of other countries or areas?

    6. What can you learn from case study 9 – 5?

# 第九章
# 主要国家商人的风俗、禁忌与谈判风格

☞ **案例分析 9—1** （绿帽子的故事）

1992 年,中国的 13 名不同专业的专家组成一个代表团,去美国采购约 3000 万美元的化工设备和技术。美方自然想方设法令中方满意,其中一个环节是在第一轮谈判后,送给中方人员每人一个小纪念品。纪念品的包装很讲究,是一个漂亮的代表吉祥的红色盒子。可当中方代表团高兴地按照美国人的习惯当面打开盒子时,每个人的表情却显得很不自然——盒子里面是一顶高尔夫球帽,但颜色却是绿色的。第二天,中方代表团找了个借口,离开了这家公司。

美国人这次送礼,可以说也是经过精心策划的,一是礼品盒的颜色是红色的,红色在中国代表吉祥;二是礼品本身是时尚的高尔夫球帽,意思是签订合同后去打高尔夫球,这在 20 世纪 90 年代对中国人来说是很奢侈的,也是很有品位的。但美国人的工作还是没有做细,而且犯了中国男人最大的忌讳——戴绿帽子。

## 一、美国人的风俗、禁忌与谈判风格

18 世纪,大批拓荒者冒着极大的风险从欧洲来到美洲,寻求自由和幸福。顽强的毅力和乐观向上、勇于进取的开拓精神,使他们在一片完全陌生的土地上建立了新的家园。他们重实际,重功利,时时处处以成败来评判每个人,在当今世界上取得了巨大的经济成就。从 20 世纪 30 年代开始,美国一直是世界上头号的政治、经济和军事强国,英语成为最广泛的商业语言,美元也是国际结算中最常使用的货币,这就形成了美国商人独特的风俗与谈判风格。

### 1. 美国人的风俗与禁忌

美国商界一般以握手为礼。握手不宜太频繁,在访问开始和结束时各握一次手就足够了。不论是男士还是女士,都应主动向对方伸出手。虽然美国人给人以随意、不正式的印象,但在上班、赴宴会的场合穿着都很正式。美国人穿衣的规矩极多,总体而言以适合时宜为主。例如参加丧事、参加婚礼,则应着黑色或素色的衣服;女士在办公室应着裙装,避免穿牛仔长裤。上下楼梯也有一定规矩，上楼时应让女士、长者先行，目的是保障女士、长者的安全。

在饭店吃饭，小费通常不包括在账单里，一般是 15％。与美国人交往时，忌过分客套和谦虚。他们看不惯谦虚、客套的表白。他们认为过分的谦虚是一种无能的表现，甚至可能被他们看成是心怀不轨。谈话的双方不能距离太近，一般 50 厘米左右的间距为好。忌讳询问他人的年龄、个人收入和政治倾向，也不能问他人买东西的价钱。他们认为这些都属于个人私事，不需要别人过问和干涉。

在业务交往中，彼此关系如果不熟不要送礼，宴请和送礼宜在双方关系融洽和谈判成功之后。到美国人家里做客，忌空手而去，宜送糖果、巧克力或白兰地，也可以送花。但花束的枝数或朵数不能是 13。忌向妇女赠送香水、衣物和化妆用品，因为在美国人眼中这些东西显得关系过于亲密。

2. 美国商人的谈判风格

(1) 谈判时直入主题

美国商人性格开朗、自信果断，办事干脆利落，语言干脆坦率。他们在谈判中习惯于迅速将谈判引向实质阶段，不兜圈子，不拐弯抹角，不讲客套，并将自己的观点全盘托出。他们欣赏谈判对手的直言快语。在发生纠纷时，他们态度认真、坦率、诚恳，有时甚至会因观点不同而争执得面红耳赤。

(2) 注重效率，珍惜时间

美国人的生活节奏极快，法律意识很强。他们注重效率，喜欢每一场谈判都能速战速决。美国商人特别守时，他们认为守时是尊重对方的表现，按事先安排的议程行事是高效率的体现。有时为了谈判的成功，他们会耐心地去适应对方的谈判节奏。美国人习惯于按照合同条款逐项进行讨论，解决一项，推进一项，尽量缩短谈判时间。

(3) 关注利益，积极务实

美国人重实际，讲功利，做生意以获取利润为唯一目的。只要条件、时间合适就可进行洽谈。美国商人非常重视合同的法律性，履约率很高，同时也很注重违约条款的洽商与执行。美国商人认为生意就是生意，不应与友情混在一起，经济利益绝对分明。

(4) 精于讨价还价

在谈判桌上美国人会全盘平衡，面面俱到。美国商人常常从总交易条件入手谈判，再谈具体条款。除讨论项目的品质、规格、包装、数量、价格、交货期以及付款方式外，还包括该项目的设计与开发、生产工艺、销售、售后服务以及双方更好的合作事项。他们有理有据，从国内市场到国际市场到最终用户，以智慧和谋略取胜。同美国人谈判，是与非必须分辨清楚，如有疑问要毫不客气地问清楚，以免日后造成纠纷。

(5) 最关心商品的质量及其外观设计和包装

商品的质量是商品最基本的要求。商品的外观设计和包装是体现一个国家消费状况、刺激大众消费的一个重要因素。美国商人不遗余力地追求和提高自己商品的内在品质、外观设计和包装水平,努力把好出口商品质量及包装这一关。同样,他们对进口商品的要求也很高。

（6）性格幽默

美国人性格幽默也素有盛名。假如在餐厅盛满啤酒的杯中发现了苍蝇,英国人会以绅士风度吩咐侍者换一杯啤酒来;法国人会将杯中啤酒倾倒一空;日本人会令侍者去把餐厅经理找来,训斥一番;而美国人则可能对侍者说:"以后请将啤酒和苍蝇分别放置,由喜欢苍蝇的客人自行将苍蝇放进啤酒,你觉得怎样?"在谈判过程中,美国商人也喜欢用轻松幽默的语言表达信息,或讲讲笑话活跃气氛。

## 二、日本人的风俗、禁忌与谈判风格

从第二次世界大战后的 1955 年开始,日本的经济飞速发展,到 20 世纪 80 年代已成为世界第二经济强国。中国的儒家思想在日本的文化中根深蒂固,同时日本又受西方特别是美国文化的影响很大。

### 1. 日本人的风俗与禁忌

日本是一个礼仪之邦,日本人所做的一切事情,都会受到严格的礼仪约束。比如说日本人在见面时行独特的鞠躬礼,虽然在日本社交场合中握手已相当普遍,但传统的鞠躬仍然是一种正统和正规的礼仪,它被用于问候、迎送客人、表示感谢、赞赏、询问等各种场合。日本人见面多以鞠躬为礼。一般来说,人们相互之间行 30 度到 45 度的鞠躬礼,鞠躬弯腰的深浅不同,表示的含义也不同,弯腰最低,也是最有礼貌的鞠躬称为"最敬礼"。

日本人在商务活动中很注意名片的作用,他们认为名片表明一个人的社会地位,因此总是随身携带。名片交换时,适宜地位低或者年轻的一方先给对方,这种做法被认为是一种礼节。递交名片时,要将名片正面对着对方。赠送礼品时,日本人非常注重阶层或等级,因此不要赠送太昂贵的礼品,以免他们误认为你的身份比他们高。

日本人不喜欢紫色,认为紫色是悲伤的色调;最忌讳绿色,认为绿色是不祥之色。他们忌讳数字 9 和 4;他们还忌讳三人一起合影,认为中间的人被左右两人夹着,是不幸的预兆。日本人对装饰有狐狸图案的东西甚为反感,因为狐狸是贪婪的象征。礼物忌送梳子,因为梳子的发音与死相近。在中国象征吉利的大红大绿,金光灿烂的图案,在日本不受欢迎。接送礼物要双手,不要当面打开礼物,当接受礼物后,再一次见到送礼的人一定要提及礼物的事并表示感谢。

### 2. 日本商人的谈判风格

（1）注重礼仪

在初次见面时,日本人的第一句问候语是"我是某某,初次见面,请多关照"。"对不起"也是日本人的口头禅，即使是很平常的要求与行动，也会在说话前加一句"对不起"。虽然说许多礼节在西方人看来是无关紧要的，甚至是可笑的，但日本人却做得一丝不苟，严肃认真。因此，在同日本人进行谈判时，应该事先了解和遵守必要的礼节，否则可能会失去他们的信任与好感，甚至导致谈判陷入僵局。

（2）注重人际关系

日本商人比较重视建立长期的合作伙伴关系。在商务谈判中，如果与日本人建立了良好的个人关系，赢得了他们的信任，那么谈判就成功了一半。合同条款比起人际关系是次要的，合同在日本一向被认为是人际协议的外在形式。比如，欧美人习惯把合同条款写得具体化、详细化，尤其是双方责任及索赔方面；而日本人认为合同并不是最主要的，只要建立了良好的信任合作关系，即使做不到合同所保证的，也可以通过再谈判来重新协商合同条款。初次与日商打交道时，找一个信誉较好的中间人，会对谈判成功大有益处。另外，日本人很注意人际关系的和谐。在与日商进行第一次洽谈时，切勿开门见山，直切主题。可以通过一番寒暄，或是用迂回的方式谈谈文化、哲学、历史等他们感兴趣的话题。

（3）团队意识很强

日本文化所塑造的是以集体为核心的价值观念和精神取向，形成了世界闻名的团队精神，体现在谈判中是集体决策，集体负责。这种团体感决定了日本人在谈判中往往会坚持自己的主张，努力说服对方做出让步，要让日本人改变决定是十分困难的。在同日本人谈判时，应该把重点放在所有有关的部门管理人员上，而不仅仅只是高层管理人员。日本人的决策时间长，究其原因，就是群体意识的影响。但日本商人一旦做出决定，行动起来却十分迅速。

（4）等级观念强烈

日本是个等级制度森严的社会，几个日本人聚集在一起，就会根据年龄、头衔、所属机构的规模及威望等排列次序，并以此来决定自己的言行举止。他们非常注重级别，这种观念常常制约着他们在商务和社交方面的决策。日本企业都有尊老的倾向，一般能担任公司代表的人都是有 15～20 年经历的人。所以同日本人进行谈判时，派出的人员最好身份、地位都比对方高一些，这样会更有利于谈判的成功。另外，日本妇女在社会中地位较低，一般都不允许参与大公司的经营管理活动，日本人在重要场合也是不带女伴的。

（5）喜欢采用委婉、间接的谈判风格

在谈判中，他们通常用间接的方式来询问和回答有关问题，对对方提出的要求不直截了当地说"不"，而是用非常含蓄的语句来避免直接否定的答复，这样既保住了对方的面子，又间接地表达了"不"的含义。日本人不喜欢与对方发生直接冲突，而是尽力避免冲突。忍耐是成功的重要因素，跟日本人谈判要有耐心和诚意，如果迫不及待地要求对方就合同的内容表示态度，谈判就不会顺利进行，甚至会导致关系恶化。因此，在同日本人的谈判过程中言行一定要谨慎，语气要尽量平和委婉，切忌轻易下最后通牒。谈判间的一段沉默并不表明对方无兴趣或处于困境,日本人把沉默视为思考问题的机会,当谈判出现沉默时,不要像通常那样找话题打破沉默,应该利用这一段时间静静地去观察、思考,同时推敲并组织你的对策。

另外,日本人谈话时习惯频繁地随声附和或点头称是,但是,值得注意的是,这并非全都意味着对你的观点表示同意,有时只不过是说明他听明白了或表明他确实在听对方的讲话而已。

### 三、德国人的风俗、禁忌与谈判风格

#### 1. 德国人的风俗与禁忌

德国是高度发达的资本主义国家,德国人非常注重规则和纪律,干什么事都十分认真。凡是有明文规定的,德国人都会自觉遵守;凡是明确禁止的,德国人绝不会去碰它。德国人很讲究清洁和整齐,不仅注意保持自己生活的小环境的清洁和整齐,而且也十分重视大环境的清洁和整齐。德国人也很重视服装穿戴。工作时就穿工作服,下班回到家里虽可以穿得随便些,但只要有客来访或外出活动,就一定会穿戴得整洁。

德国人非常守时,约定好的时间,无特殊情况,绝不轻易变动。德国人多喜欢清静的生活,除特殊场合外,不大喜欢喧闹。多数情况下,他们都比较干脆。凡是他们能办的,他们都会马上告诉你"可以办";凡是他们办不到的,他们也会明确告诉你"不行",很少给人模棱两可的答复。

德国人比较注意礼仪。两人相遇时,不管认识不认识,也不管是在路上、办公室、宾馆、电梯等地方,都相互打招呼,问声"您好"。餐馆吃饭时,也要向已就座的顾客点头问候。朋友见面以握手为礼,告别时亦如此。十分要好的、长时间未见的朋友相见或要长期分开时可以相互拥抱。在交往过程中,大多数人往往用"您"以及姓氏之前冠以"先生"或"女士"作为尊称。只有亲朋好友和年轻人之间互相用"你"以及名字称呼。

在德国,女士在许多场合都受到优先照顾,如进门、进电梯、上车等,都是女士优先。男士要帮女士开轿车门、挂衣服、让座位等。女士对此只需说声"谢谢",而不必感到不好意思,或者认为对方不怀好意。在与人交谈时,德国人很注意尊重对方,不询问他人的私事(如女性的年龄,对方的收入等),也不拿在场的人开玩笑。

送礼在德国也很受重视。应邀去别人家做客时,一般都带礼物。大部分人带束鲜花,也有一些男性客人带瓶葡萄酒,个别人带一本有意义的书(或者是自己写的书)或者画册之类。在欢迎客人(如车站、机场等场所)、探望病人时,也多送鲜花。在祝贺他人生日、节日或者婚嫁等时,可寄送贺卡;如送贺礼,则以实用和有意义为原则,而不是以价格高低论轻重。所送之礼物都要事先用礼品纸包好。许多人在收到礼物后会马上打开观看,并向送礼人表示感谢。

2. 德国商人的谈判风格

德国人的民族特点是倔强、自信。他们办事谨慎,富有计划性。他们有敬业精神,工作上重视效率、追求完美。

(1) 严谨认真,准备周密,在谈判前准备充分

他们会对所要谈判的标的物以及对方公司的经营、资信情况等均进行详尽认真的研究,掌握大量翔实的第一手资料,以便在谈判中得心应手,左右逢源。

(2) 自信固执,缺乏妥协性和灵活性

德国商人往往对自己的产品极有信心,在谈判中常常会以本国的产品为衡量标准。他们对企业的技术标准要求相当严格,如果要与德国人谈生意,务必要使他们相信你公司的产品可以满足德国人要求的标准。德国商人的自信与固执还表现在他们不善于在谈判中采用让步的方式。他们考虑问题比较系统、缺乏灵活性和妥协性。他们总是强调己方方案的可行性,千方百计迫使对方让步。

(3) 诚实守约

德国人重视合同的履行,素有“契约之民”的雅称。他们崇尚契约,严守信用,权利与义务意识很强。德国人在签订合同之前,往往要仔细研究合同的每一个细节,并认真推敲,感到满意后才会签订合同。合同一经签订,他们会严守合同条款,一丝不苟地去履行。他们不轻易毁约,同样,他们对对方履约的要求也极其严格。

(4) 时间观念强,效率高

德国人的座右铭是“马上解决”。他们判断一个谈判人员是否有能力,只需看其办公桌上的文件是否能得到快速有效地处理。不论是工作还是其他事情,他们都非常认真,讲究效率。因此与他们打交道,最好不要迟到。对于迟到的谈判人员,德国商人对之不信任的反感态度会无情地流露出来。

## 四、英国人的风俗、禁忌与谈判风格

英国是老牌的资本主义国家,是曾经的“海上霸王”、世界的贸易中心和金融中心,曾被称为“日不落帝国”。

1. 英国人的风俗与禁忌

英国以“绅士”而著称。男士与女士交往,只有等女士先伸出手时再握手。会谈要事先预约,赴约要准时。赠送礼品是普通的交往礼节,所送礼品最好标有公司名称,以免留下贿赂对方之嫌。如被邀请,则应捎带鲜花或巧克力等合适的小礼品。

在英国有三个禁忌:排队不能加塞、不能问女士年龄、不能砍价。英国人素来有排队的习惯,你可以看到他们一个挨一个地排队上公共汽车、上火车或买报纸,加塞是一种令人不齿的行为。如果你问一位女士的年龄,是很不合适的,因为她认为这是她自己的秘

密,而且每个人都想永葆青春,没有比对中年妇女说一声"你看上去好年轻"更好的恭维了。在英国购物最忌讳的是砍价。英国人不喜欢讨价还价,认为这是很丢面子的事情。

英国人很忌讳数字"13"和"星期五",视其为厄运和凶兆的数字和日期。如果"星期五"这天正好是"13"日,则被认为是"黑色星期五",人们在这一天都不会举行活动。他们还忌讳数字"3",尤其是在点烟的时候,无论用火柴还是用打火机,只能点到第 2 个人,然后要把火熄灭后,再给第 3 个人点。英国人对墨绿色很反感,视其为令人懊丧的颜色。英国人忌用山羊图案,视山羊为讨厌的动物;忌用大象图案,认为大象是蠢笨的象征;忌用孔雀图案,认为孔雀是祸鸟;忌用黑猫图案,认为黑猫是不祥之兆;忌用百合花图案,把百合花看作是死亡的象征。

2. 英国商人的谈判风格

(1) 谨慎认真,讲究礼节

英国商人善于简明扼要地阐述立场,陈述观点。在谈判中,表现更多的是沉默、冷静、自信、谨慎,而不是激动、冒险和夸夸其谈。他们宁愿做风险小、利润少的买卖。英国人在商谈中讲究礼节,保持矜持,不过分流露感情。同英国人谈生意,要仪表整洁,谈吐文雅,举止端庄。

(2) 不灵活,不喜欢长时间讨价还价

英国商人希望谈一两次便有结果。除了重要谈判,一般一小时就够了。同英国人谈生意,谈判的方法和策略是很重要的。重要的业务谈判,要与公司的决策人物,如董事长、执行董事兼总经理商谈,而且要提前约见。

(3) 严格遵守约定的时间

通常与英国商人进行商务活动一定要事先预约,并最好提早到达,以取得他们的信任和尊重。在商务活动中,接待客人的时间往往较长,当受到英国商人款待后,要给对方写信以表示感谢,否则会被视为不懂礼貌。英国人做生意颇讲信用,凡事规规矩矩。

(4) 重视人际关系

在对外交往中,英国人一旦与他人建立了友谊,就会十分珍惜,长期信任。

## 五、法国人的风俗、禁忌与谈判风格

近几个世纪以来,法兰西民族在社会科学、文学、科学技术等方面都取得了卓越的成就,法国人的民族自豪感很强。他们性格开朗、热情,对事物比较敏感,工作态度认真,十分勤劳,善于享受。

1. 法国人的风俗与禁忌

法国人在社交场合与客人见面时,一般以握手为礼。法国女子在社会生活中地位较高。同女士握手时,一定要等其先伸手,她们可戴着手套,而男士一定要摘下手套;无论在何处，男士都要让女士先行。法国人在餐桌上敬酒先敬女后敬男，哪怕女宾的地位比男宾低也是如此。走路、进屋、入座，都要让妇女先行。拜访告别时也是先向女主人致意和道谢；介绍两人相见时，一般职务相等时先介绍女士。

法国人在同客人谈话时，总喜欢相互站得近一点，他们认为这样显得更为亲近。他们偏爱公鸡，认为它既有观赏价值和经济价值，还有司晨报晓的功能，因而它可以用作"光明"的象征，并奉为国鸟。他们还非常喜爱鸢尾花，认为它是自己民族的骄傲，是权力的象征、国家的标志，并敬为国花。

法国人在交谈时习惯于用手势来表达或强调自己的意思，但他们的手势与我们的有所不同。如，我们用拇指和食指分开表示"8"，在法国人看来则表示数字"2"；表示"是我"这个概念时，我们指鼻子，他们指胸膛。他们还用拇指朝下表示"坏"和"差"的意思。

他们认为数字"13"以及"星期五"都是不吉利的，甚至能由此引发什么祸事。法国人还忌讳男人送给女人香水，因为这有过分亲热和图谋不轨之嫌。他们还不愿意别人打听他们的政治倾向、工资待遇以及个人的私事。如果初次见面就送礼，法国人会认为你不善交际，甚至认为你粗俗。

### 2. 法国商人的谈判风格

(1) 奉行个人主义，珍惜人际关系

法国的管理者也具有独裁主义的风格。他们重视个人力量，很少有集体决策的情况。在商务谈判中，多实行个人负责制，因此谈判效率较高。法国商人很重视交易过程中的人际关系，因此，通过内部关系来办事比通过正常渠道要容易和迅速很多。在谈论业务之前，法国人希望对对方谈判代表有一定的了解，并建立和谐的关系。

(2) 偏爱横向式谈判

法国商人喜欢先为谈判协议勾画出一个轮廓，然后达成原则协议，最后再确认谈判协议各方面的具体内容。另外，法国商人习惯于集中精力磋商主要条款，对细节问题不是很重视。

(3) 时间观念不是很强

在公共场合，如正式宴会，会有一种非正式的习俗，那就是主客身份越高，他就来得越迟。所以，要与他们做生意，就需要有耐心。但法国人对他人的迟到往往不予原谅，对于迟到者，他们会很冷淡地接待。

此外，在谈判中法国人往往会坚持使用法语。他们认为法语是世界上最高贵的语言。法国人也很珍惜假期，他们会毫不吝惜地把一年辛辛苦苦挣来的钱在假期中花光。每年8月份，大部分法国人都放下手中的工作去旅游度假，因此，与法国人做生意要避开其假期。

### 六、俄罗斯人的风俗、禁忌与谈判风格

苏联是世界上第一个社会主义国家。1991 年苏联解体。俄罗斯仍是世界上最有影响力的国家之一。

#### 1. 俄罗斯人的风俗与禁忌

在俄罗斯右为尊、为贵、为吉，左为卑、为贱、为凶，这一观念根深蒂固，并将男右、女左联系起来。心情不好可能是起床时左脚先着地的原因；穿衣时，俄罗斯人必定先穿右袖，先穿左袖是不吉利的；右颊长痣是吉痣，而左颊长痣是凶痣。

俄罗斯商人喜欢喝酒、抽烟，喜欢跳舞。跳舞是俄罗斯族的传统，一般每个周末都举行舞会。俄罗斯人注重仪表，爱好打扮。在公共场所比较注意举止，从不将手插在口袋里或袖筒里，天热时也不轻易脱下外衣。

在俄罗斯，数字"13"被人们视为凶险、不吉祥的象征。俄国人请客从不请 13 个人；住宅的门牌号没有 13 号。"13"被称为鬼数。如果一个月份中的 13 日碰巧又是星期五，那就更是不吉利的日子，称为"黑色星期五"。传说，夏娃给亚当吃禁果、耶稣被钉死在十字架上，都是在 13 日、星期五。而"1"和"7"则被认为是吉祥的数字。

俄罗斯人对盐十分崇拜，并视之为珍宝，也是祭祖用的供品，认为盐有驱邪消灾的力量。镜子被认为是神圣的物品，打破镜子意味着灵魂的毁灭。俄罗斯人视蜘蛛为吉祥动物。

俄罗斯传统习俗中不能送他人尖利的东西，如刀、别针等物，不能送别人手帕，因为送手帕预示着分离；两个人用同一手帕擦汗，预示终会分离。忌在家里和公共场所吹口哨，口哨声会招鬼魂。

#### 2. 俄罗斯商人的谈判风格

(1) 注重建立私人关系

关系在与俄罗斯人的贸易中具有关键的作用，想要办事必须有一些良好的私人关系。但同其他同样注重关系的国家有些不同，俄罗斯商人比较重视语言交流，他们习惯于使用较为直接的语言来表达自己的思想。俄罗斯商人缺乏时间观念。同俄罗斯商人会面，常常在预定时间之后开始，结束时间也比预定时间要晚，并常常会被打断。俄罗斯人受到官僚主义办事拖拉作风的影响，做事断断续续，大大增加了谈判的难度。

(2) 固守传统，缺乏灵活性

苏联是个外贸管制的国家，实行高度计划的外贸体制。任何企业或个人都不可能自行进口或出口任何产品，所有的进出口计划都是经过专门部门讨论决定，并经过一系列环节审批、检查、管理和监督。在这种高度计划体制中，人们已习惯于照章办事，上传下达，忽视了个人创造性的发挥。苏联解体后，在涉外谈判中，一些俄罗斯人还是带有明显的计

划体制的烙印,在进行正式洽商时,他们喜欢按计划办事。

（3）重视谈判项目中的技术内容和索赔条款

在与俄罗斯商人进行洽谈时,要有充分的准备,可能会就产品的技术问题进行反复大量的磋商。另外,为了能及时准确地对技术细节进行阐述,在谈判中要配置技术方面的专家。同时合同的语言要精确,不能随便承诺某些不能做到的条件。对合同中的索赔条款也要十分慎重。

（4）讨价还价能力强

俄罗斯商人非常善于寻找合作与竞争的伙伴,也非常善于讨价还价。如果他们想要引进某个项目,首先要对外招标,引来数家竞争者,从而不慌不忙地进行选择。并采取各种离间手段,让争取合同的对手之间竞相压价,相互残杀,最后从中渔利。俄罗斯人在讨价还价上堪称行家里手。不管报价是多么公平合理,经过怎样的精确计算,他们也不会相信,他们要千方百计地挤出其中的水分,达到他们认为理想的结果。

## 七、韩国人的风俗、禁忌与谈判风格

### 1. 韩国人的风俗与禁忌

韩国人崇尚儒教,尊重长者。和长者谈话时要摘去墨镜。吃饭时应先为老人或长辈盛饭上菜,老人动筷后,其他人才能吃。韩国人见面时的传统礼节是鞠躬;晚辈、下级走路时遇到长辈或上级,应鞠躬、问候,站在一旁,让其先行,以示敬意。

在韩国,如有人邀请你到家里吃饭或赴宴,你应带小礼品,最好挑选包装好的食品。席间敬酒时,要用右手拿酒瓶,左手托瓶底,然后鞠躬致祝词,最后再倒酒,且要一连三杯。敬酒人应把自己的酒杯举得低一些,用自己杯子的杯沿去碰对方的杯身;敬完酒后再次鞠躬方可离开。

酒是送韩国男人最好的礼品,但不能送酒给女士,除非你说清楚这酒是送给她丈夫的。在赠送韩国人礼品时应注意,韩国男性多喜欢名牌纺织品、领带、打火机、电动剃须刀等,女性则喜欢化妆品、提包、手套、围巾类物品和厨房里用的调料。

韩国人禁忌颇多。逢年过节相互见面时,不能说不吉利的话,更不能生气、吵架。农历正月头三天不能倒垃圾、扫地,更不能杀鸡宰猪。寒食节忌生火。忌在别人家里剪指甲,否则两家今后会结怨。吃饭时忌戴帽子,否则终身受穷。

### 2. 韩国商人的谈判风格

（1）注重礼仪,并能创造良好的谈判气氛

韩国人十分注意谈判地点的选择。他们一般喜欢选择有名气的酒店进行会晤,并且特别重视谈判开局阶段的气氛。见面时总是热情地与对方打招呼,向对方介绍自己的姓名、职务等。当被问及喜欢哪种饮料时,他们一般选择对方喜欢的饮料,以示对对方的尊重。

（2）准备充分

韩国商人在长期的贸易实践中积累了丰富的经验，常在不利于己方的贸易谈判中占上风，被西方国家称为"谈判高手"。韩国人非常重视谈判前的咨询准备工作。他们往往在谈判前会对对方进行咨询和了解，如经营项目、规模、资金、经营作风以及有关商品的行情，等等。一旦韩国人与你坐在一起谈判，那么可以肯定地说，他们已对这场谈判进行了周密的准备。

（3）注重谈判技巧

韩国商人时常使用"声东击西""先苦后甜""疲劳战术"等策略。有些韩国商人直到最后一刻仍会提出"价格再降一点"的要求。此外，韩国人在完成谈判签约时，喜欢用合作对象国家的语言、英语和韩语三种文字签订合同，且三种文字具有同等效力。

另外，值得注意的是，韩国商人既受儒家文化的影响，也同时受美国文化的影响。韩国人的个性中既有爱面子、受儒家思想影响很深的一面，又有独立性强、性格直率的一面。因此，同韩国人打交道时，应注意两种文化的融合。

## 八、其他国家和地区人们的风俗禁忌与谈判风格

1. 阿拉伯人的风俗、禁忌与谈判风格

（1）阿拉伯人的风俗与禁忌

由于地理、宗教和民族等问题的影响，阿拉伯人以宗教划派，以部落为群。他们性情固执，比较保守，家族观念和等级观念很强，不轻易相信别人，整个民族具有较强的凝聚力。

阿拉伯人信奉伊斯兰教，禁忌很多。如斋月期间白天不能吃喝，坐着不能架起二郎腿。与阿拉伯商人谈生意，务必尊重他们的信仰，免得造成麻烦。初次见面不宜送礼，否则有可能被误认为是行贿。送礼时不要送带有动物形象的东西，他们认为动物会给人带来厄运。交换礼物时，用右手或双手，忌用左手。不能单独给女主人送礼，也别送东西给已婚的女子。阿拉伯人见面的第一个礼节是拥抱亲脸，从左边开始亲三次，右边亲三次，回到左边再亲三次，然后两人握手。

（2）阿拉伯商人的谈判风格

①先交朋友，后谈生意。阿拉伯人通常要花很长时间才能做出谈判的决策。他们不希望通过电话来谈生意。当外商想向他们推销某种商品时，必须经过多次拜访，有时甚至第二次、第三次拜访都接触不到实质性的问题。与他们打交道，必须先争取他们的好感和信任，建立朋友关系。他们热情好客，会谈也经常会被其他客人的到访而打断。另外阿拉伯人时间观念较差，一场谈判有时可能无缘无故地被延迟或终止。

②阿拉伯人对讨价还价情有独钟。在他们看来，没有讨价还价就不是一场严肃的谈判。无论是大商店还是小商店均可讨价还价，标价只是卖主的报价。在商务谈判中更是

如此，他们甚至认为，不还价就买走东西的人，还不如讨价还价后什么也不买的人更受卖主的尊重。

③通过代理商进行商务谈判。几乎所有阿拉伯国家的政府都坚持让外国公司通过代理商来开展业务，代理商从中获取佣金。一个好的代理商对业务的开展大有裨益。他可以帮助雇主同政府有关部门取得联系，促使有关方面尽早做出决定；帮助安排货款的收回、劳务使用、物资运输、仓储等诸多事宜。

**2. 印度人的风俗、禁忌与谈判风格**

(1) 印度人的风俗与禁忌

印度是文明古国。印度社会层次分明、等级制度森严。常见的问候方式一般是双手合十于胸前，或举手示意。两手空着时，则合十问候；若一手持物，则举右手施礼，切不可举左手。拥抱也是常见之礼。若久别重逢，或将远行，或有大事发生等，则要拥抱。摸足则是行大礼。献花环在印度是欢迎客人常见的礼节，主人要献上一个花环，戴到客人的脖子上。客人越高贵，所串的花环也越粗。点吉祥痣也是印度人欢迎宾客的礼数。每逢喜庆节日，印度女人爱用朱砂在前额两眉中间涂上一个圆点。一份糖果或是一束鲜花是印度人访朋问友经常送的礼物。

在印度南部的一些地方，人们惯于以摇头表示同意。印度人忌讳白色，忌讳弯月图形，忌讳送人百合花。"1""3""7"三个数字，均被他们视为不吉利的数字。同印度人交谈时，千万不要主动涉及有关宗教与民族矛盾、印巴冲突、核武器、两性关系等问题。

(2) 印度商人的谈判风格

①节奏较慢，后发制人。印度商人观念传统、思想保守。印度商人在做生意时并不喜欢速战速决，而是慢慢来，以静制动。因此很多西方人感觉印度商人"矜持"，不紧不慢，让人摸不着头脑。实际上印度人是想让对方心里产生急躁，过早摊牌，从而暴露出其真实的意图，以达到他们后发制人的目的。

②履约率不高。印度客商有一个习惯，习惯拿东家的价格给西家看，再拿西家的价格给东家看。印度商人在商务谈判中遇到问题时也常常喜欢找借口逃避责任；如果出现失误、受到指责时，他们会不厌其烦地重复解释。所以，与他们进行商务谈判，合同条款的规定务必严密、细致，力求消除日后发生纠纷的隐患。在没有利害关系时，他们还是比较容易合作的，然而一旦发生利害冲突，他们就会判若两人。

**3. 东南亚人的风俗、禁忌与谈判风格**

东南亚国家主要包括新加坡、马来西亚、泰国、印度尼西亚、菲律宾、越南和柬埔寨等。这些国家的人们等级观念根深蒂固，人们对社会等级、社会地位非常敏感；长者，特别是男性长者，享有很高的社会地位。总体来说，东南亚国家的人们时间观念较差，由于基础设施和气候等原因,人们认为迟到或是拖延时间并不是缺乏诚信的表现。但新加坡是个例外。新加坡商人时间观念很强,有准时赴约的良好习惯,认为准时赴约是对客人的尊重和礼貌。东南亚国家的商人很喜欢讨价还价,因此跟他们做生意,报价时应留有足够的余地。

（1）新加坡人

在新加坡,法律规定公共场合严禁吸烟,违者罚款 500 新元。要吸烟最好征得对方同意。

新加坡人认为"4""6""7""13""37"和"69"是消极的数字,他们最讨厌"7"。新加坡人视黑色为倒霉、厄运之色,紫色也不受欢迎。他们偏爱红色,也喜欢蓝色和绿色。忌讳猪和乌龟的图案。

新加坡人一旦订立了契约,就绝对不会违约,很重信义,珍惜朋友之间的关系,对对方的背信行为十分痛恨。在新加坡家族企业较多。在与新加坡人做生意时,首先就有必要拉关系。

（2）马来西亚人

马来西亚人认为,用食指指人是对人的一种侮辱。马来西亚人忌讳乌龟,认为这是一种不吉祥的动物。他们禁吃猪肉和狗肉,忌讳使用猪制品。

马来西亚人注重人际关系、礼节和等级制度。在解决纠纷时,他们更注重关系而非合同条款。在许多马来西亚人看来,律师的存在是双方缺乏相互信任的表现。

4. 拉丁美洲人的谈判风格

拉丁美洲包括南美洲和中美洲,其中巴西和墨西哥是两个最主要的国家。巴西人是很有名的难对付的杀价高手,他们经常非常直接地拒绝你的开价。然而,这种直率并不是有意地想无礼或者发生冲突,他们是想让对方知道他们的观点。所以在与他们谈判时,要为漫长的谈判程序留出足够的时间,同时在最初出价时要留足余地,为让步留出空间。

在墨西哥做生意,一口流利的西班牙语是一笔宝贵的财富;在拜访客户之前考察一下是否需要翻译将是明智的做法。也可以到墨西哥之前将介绍公司和产品的小册子翻译成地道的西班牙文。

总体来说,拉美商人信誉较差,履约率比较低。签订合同以后再修改合同时有发生。他们生活节奏较慢,作风拖拉,效率不高。跟他们做生意需把握好货款的支付方式。

拉美人高度重视友谊。为了保证谈判的成功,一定要先与他们建立起私人之间的朋友关系。要有耐心,不要探讨他们的社会问题。

拉美国家之间的经济发展水平差异较大,经常出现通货膨胀,因此与拉美人做生意要注意选择硬货币。另外,他们常常看不起谈判成员中的女性成员。

5. 斯堪的纳维亚人的谈判风格

斯堪的纳维亚国家包括芬兰、挪威、瑞典、丹麦和冰岛。这些国家的人们和蔼文雅、谦虚幽默；商人们有教养、守规矩。作为主人，他们定会令客人满意，产品质量是他们的骄傲。

斯堪的纳维亚人认真守时，在谈判中相对镇定。他们讲究实际，会严格按照谈判之前制订的计划洽谈项目。

斯堪的纳维亚人谦虚、坦诚，坚持不懈。他们经常坦诚地表明自己的观点并且提出富有建设性的建议。在谈判中，参与者应着眼于合作，要坦率、理性，还要力求稳定与融洽。

他们不愿无休止地讨价还价，喜欢悠闲的谈判节奏。桑拿浴是他们生活中不可缺少的一个部分。如在谈判之初受邀去桑拿浴便是一个良好的开端。有时他们会一边桑拿，一边交谈，这会减少正式谈判中的一些不便。

6. 意大利人的风俗、禁忌与谈判风格

在意大利女士受到尊重，特别是在各种社交场合，女士处处优先。意大利节日很多，全年有大约三分之一的日子属于节日。有的是宗教节日，有的是民间传统节日，有的是国家纪念日。意大利人普遍忌讳数字"13"和"17"。紫色被意大利人视为消极的颜色而不受欢迎。他们忌讳菊花图案，视菊花为"丧花""妖花"。他们讲究穿戴，向往舒适的生活。

意大利商人时间观念差。意大利商人常常不遵守约会时间，甚至有的时候不赴约也不打招呼，或单方面推迟会期。他们工作松松垮垮，不讲效率。他们情绪多变，喜怒无常。

意大利人特别喜欢争论。他们常常为了很小的事情而大声争吵，互不相让。如果允许，他们会整天争论不休，特别是在价格方面，更是寸步不让。但是，他们对产品质量、性能以及交货日期等事宜都不太关注，虽然他们当然希望所买或销售的产品能正常使用。

7. 加拿大人的风俗、禁忌与谈判风格

加拿大人也忌讳数字"13"和"星期五"。他们忌讳黑色，偏爱白色，认为白色是纯洁的象征。他们也忌讳百合花图案，喜欢枫叶图案，加拿大是世界上驰名的"枫叶之国"。

加拿大国民的主体是由英法两国移民的后裔所构成的。一般而言，英裔加拿大人大多信奉基督教，讲英语，性格上相对保守内向一些。而法裔加拿大人则大多信奉天主教，讲法语，性格上显得较为开朗奔放。

英裔加拿大商人大多集中在多伦多和加拿大的西部地区，法裔加拿大商人主要集中在魁北克。英裔的商人保守，重视信用，商谈时语言严谨；一旦签订契约，违约的事情就很少出现。法裔商人则大不相同，开始接触时，非常和蔼可亲，平易近人，款待也很客气和大方。但是，谈到实际问题时，他们就判若两人，讲话慢吞吞的，难以捉摸。因此，同法裔商人谈判时应力求慎重，签约时应力求详细明了和准确，否则难免引起纠纷和麻烦。

8. 澳大利亚人的风俗、禁忌与谈判风格

握手是澳大利亚常见的招呼方式。澳大利亚人的时间观念很强,商务约会必须提前预约并准时赴约;私人拜访则需携带礼物。

澳大利亚男子秉承了英国传统绅士的作风,讲究"女士优先"。在社交场合打哈欠、伸懒腰等小动作,是非常不雅观、不礼貌的行为。在数字方面,受基督教的影响,澳大利亚人对"13"和"星期五"反感至极。周日是澳大利亚基督徒的"礼拜日",所以一定不要在周日与其约会,这是非常不尊重对方的举动。

澳大利亚商人重视办事效率。他们往往和第一次见面的客人进行简短的寒暄后,即着手进行谈判。所派出的谈判人员一般都具有决定权。他们不喜欢开始报高价,再慢慢讨价还价的方法,而一般会采用招标的方式,最低价成交。

澳大利亚商人待人随和,公私分明。他们的款待与生意无关,不要以为在一起喝过酒生意就好谈了,相反,他们在签约时非常谨慎。但是一旦签约,发生毁约的现象也相对较少。

9. 犹太人的谈判风格

犹太人尽管人口很少,但对世界的影响力很大。他们有"世界商人"的美称,具有很强的商业意识,经商才华出众。犹太人名人辈出,如:摩西、耶稣、马克思、弗洛伊德、爱因斯坦、毕加索、贝多芬、基辛格等;华尔街金融大鳄洛克菲勒、索罗斯、摩根、哈默等都是犹太人;全世界约百分之三十的诺贝尔奖由犹太人获得。

犹太人重合同守信誉,履约率高。在犹太文化中,合同有着绝对的权威,不允许违约。在犹太人看来,不论是复杂重要的合同,还是简单的合同,都同样严肃重要。

犹太人参加谈判时总是有备而来,并且有着清楚的谈判目标和建议。他们会在谈判之前阅读大量的有关资料,搜集相关情报。他们认为,在谈判中要想从容不迫、控制谈判气氛,就必须做好一切准备。犹太人很会讨价还价,交易条件也会比较苛刻;他们在谈判中也不会轻易接受对方的条件。对于协议条款他们总是认真斟酌。

犹太人知识渊博,善于讨价还价。他们的预测力很强。在谈判中,常能根据得到的数据立即计算出盈亏结果,能在谈判中抢先做出判断,使对方陷于被动。他们尤其擅长从事珠宝首饰,做与"吃"有关的生意。

10. 华侨的谈判风格

在商界,华侨也是不可忽视的群体,他们大多都是近一两百年定居于世界各地的中国人。大多数华侨都是凭三把刀(菜刀、剪刀与剃头刀,即要么开餐馆,要么开裁缝店或是理发馆)起家的。他们经营的都是小本生意,因此,作风果断,善于讨价还价。

☞ **案例分析 9—2** （如何让他们跳船）

　　几个商人在一条船上开国际贸易洽谈会,船突然开始下沉。"快去叫那些人穿上救生衣,跳下船去。"船长命令大副。几分钟后,大副回来了。"那些家伙不肯跳。"他报告说。于是,船长只得亲自出马。不一会儿,他回来告诉大副:"他们都跳下去了。""那么您用了什么方法呢?"大副忍不住问道。"我告诉英国人跳水是有益于健康的运动,他就跳了。我告诉法国人那样做很时髦,告诉德国人那是命令,告诉意大利人那样做是被禁止的……""您是怎么说服美国人的呢?""这也很容易,"船长说,"我就说已经给他们上了保险了。"

☞ **案例分析 9—3** （竖起大拇指的故事）

　　让我们看一下一个英国商人在伊朗的故事:英国商人同伊朗同事建立了联系,一个月来事事顺利;在谈判中尊重伊斯兰文化,避免了任何比较敏感的政治闲谈。最终,英国商人兴高采烈地签署了一项合同。他签完字后,对着他的伊朗同事竖起了大拇指。顿时现场出现了紧张气氛,一位伊朗官员离开了房间。这位英国商人摸不着头脑,不知发生了什么事情,他的伊朗同事也觉得很尴尬,不知如何解释。

　　在英国,竖起大拇指是赞成的标志,意思是"很好";然而在伊朗,它是否定的意思,表示不满,近似令人厌恶,是一种无礼的动作。

☞ **案例分析 9—4** （翻译引起的误解）

　　某跨国公司总裁访问中国一家中国著名的制造企业,商讨合作发展事宜。中方总经理很自豪地向客人介绍说:"我公司是国家二级企业……"此时,翻译人员很自然地用"second-class enterprise"来表述二级企业。不料该跨国公司总裁闻此,原本很高的兴致突然冷淡下来,敷衍了几句立即起身告辞。在归途中,他抱怨道:"我怎么能同一个中国的二流企业合作?"

☞ **案例分析 9—5** （社交距离的重要性）

　　美国有家石油公司的经理曾经与石油输出国组织的一位阿拉伯代表谈判石油进口协议。谈判中,阿拉伯代表谈兴渐浓时,身体也逐渐靠拢过来,直到与美方经理只有 15 厘米的距离才停下来。美方经理稍感不舒服,向后退了退,使二人之间保持约 60 厘米的距离。只见阿拉伯代表的眉头皱了一下,略为迟疑后又边谈边靠了过来。美方经理并没有意识到什么,因为他对中东地区的风俗习惯并不太熟悉,所以他随即又向后退了退。

这时,他发现他的助手正在焦急地向他摇头示意,用眼神阻止他这样做。美方经理虽然并不完全明白助手的意思,但他还是停止了后退。于是,在阿拉伯代表感到十分自然、美方经理感到十分别扭的状态下达成了使双方均满意的协议,交易成功了。

事后,经理在了解了阿拉伯人谈判习惯以后,感慨地说:"好险! 差一点断送了一笔重要的石油生意。"

☞ **思考题与讨论题**

1. 美国人有什么样的谈判风格?

2. 日本人的谈判风格有哪些特点?

3. 与西欧人进行谈判要注意哪些问题?

4. 俄罗斯人的谈判风格有哪些特点?

5. 其他国家和地区人们的谈判风格你了解多少?

6. 在案例分析9—5中,

(1) 阿拉伯代表为什么对美国代表的后退皱了眉头?

(2) 这项谈判最终成功的关键是什么?

(3) 在国际商务谈判文化差异方面,本案例给我们哪些启示?

# 参考文献

［1］白远. 国际商务谈判[M]. 北京：中国人民大学出版社,2004.

［2］白远. 国际商务谈判(英文版·第二版)[M]. 北京：中国人民大学出版社,2008.

［3］蔡玉秋. 商务谈判[M]. 北京：中国电力出版社,2011.

［4］陈福明,王红蕾. 商务谈判[M]. 北京：北京大学出版社,2006.

［5］陈双喜. 国际商务谈判[M]. 北京：中国商务出版社,2006.

［6］陈莞. 实用谈判技巧[M]. 北京：经济管理出版社,2003.

［7］陈文汉,徐梅. 商务谈判实务[M]. 北京：清华大学出版社,2014.

［8］丁建忠. 商务谈判(第二版)[M]. 北京：中国人民大学出版社,2006.

［9］窦然. 国际商务谈判(英文,第二版)[M]. 上海：复旦大学出版社,2015.

［10］杜岩. 商务礼仪[M]. 北京：北京航空航天大学出版社,2009.

［11］方其. 商务谈判：理论、技巧、案例(第二版)[M]. 北京：中国人民大学出版社,2008.

［12］冯华亚. 商务谈判[M]. 北京：清华大学出版社,2006.

［13］黄卫平等. 国际商务谈判[M]. 北京：中国人民大学出版社,2011.

［14］黄伟,钱莉. 国际商务谈判[M]. 北京：冶金工业出版社,2012.

［15］贾书章. 现代商务谈判理论与实务[M]. 武汉：武汉理工大学出版社,2007.

［16］蒋三庚,张弘. 商务谈判[M]. 北京：首都经济贸易大学出版社,2006.

［17］金正昆. 商务礼仪概论[M]. 北京：北京大学出版社,2006.

［18］景楠. 国际商务谈判[M]. 北京：对外经济贸易大学出版社,2014.

［19］李品媛. 现代商务谈判(第三版)[M]. 大连：东北财经大学出版,2005.

［20］林晓华,王俊超. 商务谈判理论与实务[M]. 北京：人民邮电出版社,2016.

［21］刘婷. 国际商务谈判(英文版)[M]. 北京：对外经济贸易大学出版社,2012.

［22］刘文广,张晓明. 商务谈判[M]. 北京：高等教育出版社,2005.

［23］刘向丽. 国际商务谈判[M]. 北京：机械工业出版社,2005.

［24］刘园. 国际商务谈判[M]. 北京：对外经济贸易大学出版社,2012.

［25］罗立彬. 商务谈判(双语版)[M]. 北京：电子工业出版社,2013.

［26］毛国涛.商务谈判[M].北京：北京理工大学出版社,2006.

［27］全英.国际商务谈判[M].北京：清华大学出版社,2003.

［28］宋贤卓.商务谈判[M].北京：科学出版社,2004.

［29］汤秀莲.国际商务谈判[M].天津：南开大学出版社,2005.

［30］田玉来.国际商务谈判[M].北京：中国铁道出版社,2011.

［31］王琪.现代礼仪大全[M].北京：地震出版社,2005.

［32］王茹.国际商业谈判[M].北京：知识产权出版社,2013.

［33］王杨眉,李爱君.商务谈判[M].郑州：郑州大学出版社,2016.

［34］吴仁波,刘昌华.国际商务信函[M].杭州：浙江大学出版社,2016.

［35］杨芳.商务谈判[M].上海：华东师范大学出版社,2011.

［36］杨震,解永秋.模拟商务谈判案例教程[M].北京：中国轻工业出版社,2014.

［37］易开刚.现代商务谈判[M].上海：上海财经大学出版社,2006.

［38］袁其刚.国际商务谈判[M].北京：高等教育出版社,2007.

［39］张国良.国际商务谈判[M].北京：机械工业出版社,2015.

［40］张吉国.国际商务谈判[M].济南：山东人民出版社,2010.

［41］张燕.国际商务谈判[M].北京：立信会计出版社,2012.

［42］郑方华.业务谈判技能案例训练手册[M].北京：机械工业出版社,2006.

［43］周忠兴.商务谈判原理与技巧[M].南京：东南大学出版社,2003.

# Appendix I

# Materials for Simulated Negotiation

## I. Children's Wear-selling

**Background:** One day, Edward Khalily, an American businessman, came to the booth of Chinese Company A and Mr. Fang, the general manager, received him. After looking carefully at the samples of children's wear exhibited, he was quite satisfied with the products. Then suddenly, he turned to Mr. Fang and said he wanted to order 5,000 pieces at the price of USD20 for each. Mr. Fang did not answer directly and gave his counteroffer of USD45 per piece.

At this Mr. Khalily shouted and said USD45 was HK's retail price. His boss would get crossed at him if he ordered at such high prices. Mr. Fang replied confidently that the price was indeed HK's retail price, however, there was no such kind of products with the same color and design on the market. Besides, the price was not high at all. Mr. Fang further emphasized that since it was the first time they did business with each other, he hoped to establish good relationship first, so he actually offered him a very favorable price.

Mr. Khalily could not keep calm any longer. He offered USD23, USD25, USD28, and finally USD32. Mr. Fang simply said "friendship exists despite of failure in business." Mr. Khalily left without a word.

Two days later, Mr. Khalily came back to the booth of Company A.

**Requirements for the simulation:**

1. You are asked to continue the negotiation between Mr. Fang and Mr. Khalily from where it stopped. You should get the negotiation plan and the relevant matters ready in advance.

You can make the simulation in groups of two or more than two persons.

2. Key points of negotiation: The seller Mr. Fang knows the market of children's wear and has offered at USD45 per piece for the product of superior quality. The buyer

Mr. Khalily is planning to order at USD32 for each.

3. Specific requirement

(1) Use the knowledge you have learned.

(2) Use your imaginations and reach an agreement.

(3) Don't talk the price only. It is the best for the buyer to make the deal at USD32, but the price should not exceed USD41; for the seller, it is the best to conclude the business at USD45, but the minimum price is USD38.

(4) Use as many negotiating strategies as possible like "excessively demanding," "red face and white face," "involving competition," "the ultimatum."

(5) Use a different trade term.

4. Note: For trade negotiation, the two sides should usually make clear for the following clauses.

(1) commodity name          (2) specification/quality

(3) packing                (4) quantity

(5) price                  (6) time of shipment

(7) payment terms (L/C; D/P; D/A; advance payment; pay after arrival of the goods)

## II. The Trade Negotiation of Thiourea Dioxide

**Background of the buyer:** The ITOCHU Corporation in Japan (ITOCHU in short) is a large comprehensive trade corporation which has great domestic popularity and also international popularity. The corporation has a wide business field such as heavy machinery, electronics, chemical industry, food, weaving, etc. The chemical industry is one of the fields in the comprehensive corporation while Thiourea Dioxide is just one business among its trading. This corporation has established representative offices in China and has a big scale. It has a close relationship with Chinese companies and knows a lot about Chinese business. What is more, it has a good knowledge about Chinese Thiourea Dioxide market. During the establishment of the Shandong Guangming Chemical Factory, the principal in Beijing's representative office and the people from the headquarter both visited the factory.

**Background of the seller:** With the import of technology, Shandong Guangming Chemical Factory (Guangming Factory in short) has reformed itself and built a Thiourea Dioxide product line with advanced technology, and owns the right of import and export. The quality of Thiourea Dioxide is good while the factory could guarantee its output. Being one of the products in the factory, the annual production of Thiourea Dioxide could reach 10 thousand metric tons.

**Brief introduction of the product:** Thiourea Dioxide is a kind of white chemical product in powder which is mainly used in dyeing, printing and paper-making industry. It is also called Formamidine sulfunic acid and is environmental friendly during the process of usage. It can replace sodium hydrosulfite with low cost. The trade this time is one thousand metric tons.

**The relationship between the buyer and the seller:** Guangming Factory and the purchaser ITOCHU have a close relationship. When Guangming Factory reformed its technology, it bought production facility via ITOCHU. After that, it has been a supplier to ITOCHU. The trade between the two sides is satisfying.

**Background of the market:** At present, in Chinese market the price of the product in 50 kilogram fiber drum is USD1,000 – 1,250 per metric ton FOB CMP. Last year, Guangming Factory and ITOCHU had a contract of 500 metric tons of Thiourea Dioxide, the contract price for the goods in 50 kilogram fiber drum being USD1,240 per metric ton. This year the manufacturer has a positive attitude toward reducing price with the decrease of the procurement price.

**The stage and target of the negotiation:** The two parties have reached an agreement in terms of technical exchange and the price explanation. Guangming Factory and ITOCHU entered the bargaining stage. This negotiation aims to increase the volume of the order and set the stage for a long-term order. According to the situation of Chinese market, it is best for the buyer to make the deal at USD1,000 per metric ton. If not, USD1,230 per metric ton is acceptable, given the quality and the stability of the production of Guangming Factory. For the seller, it is good enough to trade at USD 1,240 per metric ton as last year. If this price does not work, considering the cooperating relationship between the two parties and the change of market quotation and competition, they can reach the agreement with no less than USD1,130 per metric ton.

**Simulation requirements:** The negotiation organization (personnel arrangement and staffing), the preparation of the negotiating project, and the host and development of the negotiation.

### III. Negotiation on the Claim due to Whey Powder Quality Problem

**The seller's background:** Holland Filly Feedstuff Co., Ltd. (hereinafter abbreviated as Filly) is a professional feedstuff manufacturer that produces extractive and addictive feedstuff at large scale and takes up a remarkable market share both in the domestic market and in the European market. The Asian market is one of its target markets. Several years ago, it established office in Beijing, which actively contacts the agents and end users in China. For years, due to the continuous efforts of this office, it has taken up a certain market share with its extractive and addictive feedstuff. The whey powder business with Beijing Shijitong Import and Export Co., Ltd. was one of the most achievements in its market exploration in China, to which the office in Beijing and head office in Holland pay much attention.

**The buyer's background:** Beijing Shijitong Import and Export Co., Ltd. (hereinafter abbreviated as Shijitong) is a comprehensive import and export company whose parent company is a large multinational corporation that enjoys high reputation in the market at home and abroad. It mainly contacts the sectors of agriculture and animal husbandry and imports a great amount of extractive feedstuff. Especially, it imports much whey powder for breeding of porkets from Europe, on which the domestic users have a positive feedback. This business has become one of its long-term businesses.

**Product:** Whey powder is classified into food and feedstuff. The former is mainly used for the raw material for ice cream so the requirements are strict with its acidity, bacteria, ash content, etc.; the latter is mainly used as the feedstuff for the breeding of porkets. For processing purpose, it must keep in powder during packing and transportation.

**Customer relation:** Shijitong and Filly know the operation strength of each other from the third party and show respect for and trust in each other. With the office of Filly being set up in Beijing, the first business between them was done. Although it was the first business, the scale was large, and they signed within one month two feedstuff-grade whey powder contracts with total quantity up to 400 tons which amount to USD180,000. This indicated that both parties desired to have large business in Chinese market.

**Claim clause:** In June, the buyer and the seller signed two contracts with the total quantity up to 400 tons and the buyer opened two letters of credit that month. According to the terms and conditions of the letters of credit, the seller should deliver the first batch of goods, i.e. 200 tons whey powder before July 15 from Rotterdam Port, while the second batch of goods, i. e. another 200 tons whey powder before August 31. In fact, the first batch with amount up to USD90,000 reached Tianjin Port in the mid of August. The buyer obtained the bills after making the payment and accepted the goods. However, when opening the containers, the buyer found some of the goods had been agglomerated. The buyer immediately contacted the forwarder. After excluding the possibility of water penetration into the ship and the responsibility of the insurance company, the buyer deemed that this was the quality problem and contacted the seller for the issue.

**Negotiation target:** The buyer should lodge a claim to the contract violator for reasonable compensation in conformity with the usual international practice. The seller must argue on reasonable ground to reduce the compensation pressure, but the follow-on contract must be fulfilled well.

**Negotiation place and time:** March 2018, in Beijing

**Simulation requirements:** The negotiation organization (personnel arrangement and staffing), the preparation of the negotiation project, and the host and development of the negotiation.

## IV. Negotiation over Establishing Discarded Tire Processing and Production Base by Capital Pooling

**Capital introducer:** Shandong Xiangyu Environmental Protection Industrial Co., Ltd.

**Investor:** Browning Environmental Protection Technology Development Co., Ltd. (US)

**Company introduction:** Shandong Xiangyu Environmental Protection Industrial Co., Ltd. (hereinafter abbreviated as Shandong Xiangyu Company) is a key private enterprise engaging in R&D of environmental protection processing technology and devices for using recyclable resources. Introduced by the foreign investment introduction agency of the local government and after a thorough market research on the project of discarded tire processing and the methods to use recyclable resources, the company decided to adopt a new technology and pool the capital to set up a discarded tire processing and production base in Shandong Province.

Browning Environmental Protection Technology Development Co., Ltd. (US) (hereinafter abbreviated as Browning Company) is a specialized company engaging in R&D of petrol chemical environmental protection technology and the technology of using recyclable resources. Its self-developed thermal decomposition technology for processing discarded tire is in the leading position in the world. Introduced by Shandong provincial government delegation which visits the US for investment introduction, this company is greatly interested in cooperating with Shandong Xiangyu Company to establish a joint venture.

**Negotiation Background**: Like developed countries, the discarded tires in China have increased year after year and have become a "black pollution." With the rapid development of China's automobile industry and the increase of automobiles in society, the environmental problems caused by discarded tires have become even more serious. Presently, China has more than 500 enterprises producing reconverted rubber with an annual production capacity of 400,000 tons. However, only 60 enterprises produce rubber powder with discarded tires as the raw material and their total annual production is less than 50,000 tons. In all, only 26 million to 30 million discarded tires can be processed with these two technologies every year. In view of the 60 million discarded tires produced in China each year, there are still more than 30 million of them that cannot get prompt and effective treatment. These discarded tires are scattered in society that fire disasters and secondary public hazards can easily arise as well.

Solutions to recycle and utilize discarded tires and wasted rubber products will contribute greatly to the multi-purpose utilization of resources and recyclable resources, and they also work as important measures to make rational use of resources so as to complete environmental protection. Furthermore, these measures are taken to promote the transition of mode of national economic growth, which has attracted much attention from governmental agencies at central and local levels. In this regard, it is greatly significant to adopt new high-technology and develop large scale production and processing methods to solve the problem of utilizing discarded tires and recyclable resources.

Thermal decomposition technology is to heat discarded tires and rubber products in high temperature, making it revolve into oil, flammable gases, carbon powder and steel wire balls. Recently, British researchers have made improvements in the thermal decomposition technology and changed the previous aerobic condition into the present anaerobic condition and further increased the economic value of the resolved materials, giving the technology a broader application prospect. The government has also adopted effective policies to support the project.

**Negotiation Process**: Arranged by Shandong provincial government delegation which visited the US for investment introduction, Shandong Xiangyu Company held an initial business talk with Browning Company in Jinan in June 2017. Browning Company gave an introduction to the thermal decomposition technology for which it possesses a patent，the equipment manufacturing process and the technology application effect within the US. Shandong Xiangyu Company presented the planned discarded tire processing base，specifically its construction site，factory buildings，supporting facilities and the resources of discarded tire recovery in Shandong province. The two parties have achieved a common perception—to integrate the available resources owned by each side to set up the largest discarded tire processing base in Shandong province. So they confirmed the intention to set up a joint venture. They also reached a consensus on constructing three production lines with an investment of 60 million Yuan. Lastly，a conclusion is reached，which is to establish a normalized exclusive business channel to recover discarded tires in Shandong province.

**The divergences between the two sides：**

1. Disputes on the share-holding right of the joint venture. Shandong Xiangyu Company believes that the present assessed value of its available working site and factory buildings and the supporting facilities is 31 million Yuan，plus the invested 5 million Yuan，its total input reaches 36 million Yuan，accounting for 60% of the total investment. So it is reasonable for them to possess the majority of shares in the joint venture. But Browning Company believes that it has invested the right to use the thermal decomposition technology and the assessed value of the patented technology should be regarded as share value，plus the three thermal decomposition production lines manufactured in the US，the total value of its investment has exceeded that of Shandong Xiangyu Company. Therefore，it should enjoy the share-controlling right.

2. Whether Browning Company's right to use the technological or its technological patent can be calculated into total shares. According to Shandong Xiangyu Company，since the joint venture is jointly invested by the two sides，Browning Company should share the complete patent of thermal decomposition technology with Shandong Xiangyu Company so as to ensure the joint venture to enjoy the possession of the patent exclusively and prevent Browning Company from transferring the patent to a third party. This practice is beneficial for the joint venture to conduct R&D and possess the derived novel intellectual rights. But Browning Company insists that only the right to use the technology，rather than the patent，will be invested as shares and the ownership of the patent should be continuously possessed by itself so that it can transfer the patent and the exclusive technology to other companies. As a result，the lately developed derived technology will be maintained in its own company.

3. The issue of how to manufacture the main equipment, thermal decomposition furnace. In Shandong Xiangyu Company's opinion, the three production lines will be constructed by the joint venture. If the main equipment, thermal decomposition furnace, is manufactured and supplied by Browning, its cost will be greatly high and a lot of inconvenience of transporting the equipment will arise as well. Therefore, Browning Company should provide the designing blue prints and the manufacturing technology and all the equipment should be manufactured in China. Correspondingly, other supporting equipment will be purchased and manufactured in China as well. In this way, large amount of investment will be saved. But Browning Company believes that since it has invested a complete set of equipment, namely the production lines, in the joint venture together with the thermal decomposition technology process, and the manufacturing technology, especially the manufacturing of the main equipment—the thermal decomposition furnace—which involves the kernel secret of this technology, thus the whole set of equipment should be manufactured in the US, and the three production lines will be input into the joint venture as its own investment.

**Negotiation Task:** In view of the situation, the two sides agree to have another negotiation in March 2018, and try to sign a contract.

**Negotiation time and place:** March 2018, in Jinan.

**Suggestions to both sides:**

1. What is the basis for deciding on the share right and the right to acquire the majority of shares in the joint venture? How to fully understand and flexibly use the basis to help oneself take an advantageous position in the negotiation and have the share controlling right?

2. What is the essential difference between the right to use technological patent and the right to the technology? And what results will be brought to the joint venture when each makes its own investment in the joint venture? Which model of investment is more beneficial for each of them?

3. Since the two sides have confirmed the intention to make a joint investment, what sensible approaches need to be adopted by each side? What practice is more beneficial for the joint venture and how to make the negotiation successful?

**Simulation requirements:** The negotiation organization (personnel arrangement and staffing), the preparation of the negotiation project, and the host and development of the negotiation.

# 附录 I

# 模拟谈判资料

## 一、儿童服装买卖谈判

**背景资料**：在广州交易会上，美国商人爱德华来到中国 A 公司的展位，方总经理接待了爱德华先生。爱德华反复认真地查看了儿童服装的样品，并对样品很满意。他转过身对方总说"我想以每件 20 美元的价格订购 5000 件"。方总没有直接答复，而是还价每件 45 美元。

对此爱德华大叫了起来："什么，这个价格是香港的零售价格，如我按这个价格订货，老板肯定会炒我的鱿鱼！"方总自信地说："类似的服装香港的零售价格差不多如此，但香港没有这样的颜色和款式。考虑到成本和加工费等因素，这个价一点也不高。因为这次是双方首次做业务，首先应建立起友好的关系，我们其实给你报了最优惠的价格。"爱德华再也无法保持镇定了，把买价从 20，提高到 23、25、28，最后提高到 32 美元。方总只是说"买卖不成仁义在"。爱德华没再说什么便离开了 A 公司的展位。

两天后爱德华又来到中国 A 公司的展位。

**谈判要求：**

1. 请以两/多个人为一组模拟中美双方之间的第二次谈判。双方都应提前做好谈判方案。

2. 谈判要点：方总经理了解儿童服装市场，其商品独特且质量上乘，故报价每件 45 美元；爱德华想订购 5000 件，价格为每件 32 美元。

3. 具体要求

（1）用所学的知识进行模拟，发挥你的想象力。

（2）需达成交易，不要仅谈价格。

（3）根据市场的现状，买方能以最低价 32 美元成交最好，最高争取以不高于 41 美元的价格成交；卖方能以 45 美元成交最好，最低争取以不低于 38 美元的价格成交。

（4）尽可能多地使用谈判策略"过分要求""软硬兼施""利用竞争""最后通牒"。

（5）提出与对方要求不同的贸易术语。

4. 买卖谈判中,谈判双方通常主要应明确以下条款。

(1) 品名 　　　　　(2) 规格

(3) 包装 　　　　　(4) 数量

(5) 价格 　　　　　(6) 交货期

(7) 付款方式(信用证/DP/DA/汇付/预付货款,或货到付款)

## 二、甲脒亚磺酸的贸易谈判

**买方背景:** 日本伊藤忠商事株式会社(简称伊藤忠)是日本大型综合商社,在国际和国内均有相当高的知名度。经营的业务范围较广,在重机、电子、化工、食品、纺织等行业均有投资或贸易业务。其化工部是该综合商社中的一个部门,而甲脒亚磺酸仅为其贸易业务中的一项。该公司很早就在中国设立代表处且规模不小,也与中国企业交往很多,对中国的业务很熟悉,对中国的甲脒亚磺酸市场了解也比较全面。光明化工厂的建设过程中,伊藤忠的北京代表处及本部均派人去过现场。

**卖方背景:** 山东光明化工厂(简称光明厂)经过技术引进,改造了老厂,建成了具有先进技术的甲脒亚磺酸生产线,又有进出口权。甲脒亚磺酸生产质量好,产量也有保障,年产量可达 1 万吨。

**产品简况:** 甲脒亚磺酸为白色粉末状晶体,在印染、造纸等行业已得到广泛应用。在使用过程中对环境无污染。可替代保险粉,成本很低。本次交易 1000 吨。

**客户关系:** 光明厂与买家伊藤忠株式会社关系密切,过去技术改造时,还通过该公司买过生产设备,产品下线后,又给伊藤忠公司供货。双方合同履行愉快,交易从几十吨到几百吨呈逐渐上升趋势,人员往来较多,彼此关系密切。

**市场背景:** 目前甲脒亚磺酸中国市场 FOB 主要口岸 50 千克纸板桶带包装价在 1000~1250 美元/吨。去年买卖双方曾有过 500 吨甲脒亚磺酸的合同,合同价为 FOB 天津港 50 千克纸板桶包装,1240 美元/吨。

**谈判阶段与目标:** 技术交流已完成,双方达成一致,价格解释与评论已完成,进入讨价还价阶段。这次是为了增加订量并为长期订货创造条件的谈判。根据中国市场的现状,买方能以最低价 1000 美元/吨成交最好。若不能以此价格成交,考虑到光明厂的供货质量与供货量的稳定性,则争取以不高于 1230 美元/吨的价格成交;卖方能以去年的价格1240 美元/吨成交已经很好。若不能以此价格成交,考虑到双方的合作关系,结合行情和竞争的变化,则争取以不低于 1130 美元/吨的价格成交。

**模拟要求:** 谈判组织(人员调配及分工安排)、谈判方案的准备、谈判的主持与展开。

## 三、乳清粉质量索赔的谈判

**卖方背景:** 荷兰飞利饲料公司(以下简称飞利公司)是饲料的专业生产企业,尤其是精饲料及饲料添加剂产量较大,在荷兰本土及欧洲市场占有一席之地。亚洲市场是其市场开拓的目标之一。几年前也在北京开设了办事处,积极与中国的代理商及最终用户进行接触。几年来,由于其代表处的不懈努力,逐渐使其精饲料与饲料添加剂两类产品挤入中国市场。与北京世纪通进出口公司的乳清粉业务是当年市场开拓的重要成果之一。其驻京代表处和荷兰总部均予以高度重视。

**买方背景:** 北京世纪通进出口公司(以下简称世纪通公司)是一家综合性进出口公司,其母公司系大型的跨国企业集团,在国内外市场均有一定的信誉。该公司在农牧业领域的贸易较多,进口的精制饲料量较大。尤其是乳猪饲养的乳清粉,世纪通公司从欧洲采购较多,国内的用户对其采购的乳清粉质量反映很好。该项业务也成了该公司的一项重要的长线业务。

**产品情况:** 乳清粉分食品与饲料两类。食品级的乳清粉主要用作冰激凌的原料,其酸度、细菌、灰分等指标要求很严格。饲料级的乳清粉,主要作为饲养乳猪的精饲料。为了加工需要,从其包装运输要求上必须使其保持粉状。

**客户关系:** 买方世纪通公司与卖方荷兰飞利饲料公司是先从第三方处知道对方的经营实力,彼此互有敬重与信任。后经飞利公司北京代表处的努力,终于成交了第一批业务。虽然双方是第一次做生意,但决心均很大,在一个月内就签订了两份总计数量为400吨、18万美元的饲料级乳清粉合同,充分表明双方渴望在中国市场把该项业务做大。

**索赔事由:** 买卖双方已于六月签订了两份合同,共400吨乳清粉。买方于当月开出两份信用证。信用证条款要求卖方第一批200吨乳清粉最晚于7月15日前从荷兰鹿特丹港发运,第二批200吨货最晚于8月31日前发运。第一批货200吨(9万美元)于八月中旬到达中国天津港,买方向开证行承兑后取得了单据办理了接货手续,但当打开货柜时发现部分货物已结块。买方立即与船公司联系,排除了船舱进水的可能性及保险公司责任后,认为是货物质量问题,并就此问题向卖方交涉。

**谈判目标:** 买方要依照国际惯例,就合同违约向出口方索取合理赔偿。卖方要据理力争,减轻赔偿压力,但后续合同应当履行。

**谈判时间及地点:** 2018年3月,北京

**模拟要求:** 谈判组织(人员调配及分工安排)、谈判方案的准备、谈判的主持与展开。

## 四、合资建立废旧轮胎处理厂的谈判

**招资方:** 山东翔宇环保产业有限公司

**投资方:** 美国布朗宁环保科技开发有限公司

**公司介绍:** 山东翔宇环保产业有限公司(以下简称山东翔宇公司),是山东省内专门从事环保处理和再生资源利用装置生产研发的骨干民营企业。据政府招商介绍,山东翔宇对废旧轮胎处理与再生资源利用项目进行充分的市场调研后,决定采用先进技术并合

资建设山东废旧轮胎处理生产基地。

美国布朗宁环保科技开发有限公司(以下简称布朗宁公司),是从事石油化工环保及再生资源利用技术研发的专业公司,其研发的废旧轮胎热分解处理技术工艺处于世界领先水平。经山东省政府赴美国招商团接触洽谈并介绍,布朗宁公司对与山东翔宇公司合资合作十分感兴趣。

**谈判背景:** 与世界发达工业国家相同,废旧轮胎的逐年递增已成为一种"黑色污染"。随着中国汽车工业的高速发展和社会汽车拥有量的增加,废旧轮胎带来的环保问题也越来越严重,处理压力也越来越大。中国现有再生胶企业500多家,年生产再生胶近40万吨,利用废旧轮胎生产胶粉的企业近60家,年生产胶粉不足5万吨。这两项处理措施合计年可利用废旧轮胎2600万～3000万条。按我国每年产生废旧轮胎6000万条总量计算,仍有3000多万条废旧轮胎未得到及时有效处理。这些废旧轮胎零散积存于社会环境中,不仅极易引发火灾,而且易形成二次公害。

如何回收利用废旧轮胎和废旧的橡胶制品,是搞好资源与再生资源综合利用的重要课题,也是合理利用资源、保护环境、促进国民经济增长方式转变和可持续发展的重要措施,已引起国家与地方政府有关部门的高度重视。尤为重要的是采用高科技加工处理技术,形成大规模的生产加工手段,解决废旧轮胎回收处理与再生资源的利用方向。特别是热分解技术,用高温加热废旧轮胎和橡胶制品,促使其分解成油、可燃气体、碳粉和钢丝团。最近英国研究人员对已有的热分解技术进行了改革,由先前的有氧状态变成无氧状态,进一步提高了分解产物的经济价值,从而使该项技术具有了更广阔的应用前景,政府也将在政策上大力扶持。

**谈判进展:** 经山东省赴美国招商的领导协调安排,山东翔宇公司与布朗宁公司于2017年6月在济南进行了初次洽谈。布朗宁公司介绍了其拥有专利权的热分解技术工艺水平状况、设备制造过程及在美国国内的应用效果。山东翔宇公司也介绍了拟建设废旧轮胎处理加工基地的场地、厂房、配套设施和山东的废旧轮胎回收资源情况。双方一致认为,整合双方已有的资源要素,合资建设山东最大规模的废旧轮胎处理加工基地的主要条件已具备,确定了合资意向,并就建设三条生产线及总投资规模为6000万元等方面达成共识。

**双方的分歧点:**

1. 合资企业的控股权争议。山东翔宇公司认为,己方的厂房场地及配套设施等固定资产评估现值3100万元,再加上投入的500万元资金,投入总额达3600万元,占总投资6000万元的60%,理应由己方控股。布朗宁公司认为,己方投入的是高科技热分解专有技术使用权,应按专利技术评估价值入股,加上在美国制造作为投入的三条热分解生产线价值2100万元,己方实际投入总价已经超过中方投入,应拥有合资企业控股权。

2. 布朗宁公司应是专有技术使用权入股还是专利技术入股。山东翔宇公司认为,既然双方合资,要求布朗宁公司将其热分解技术专利入股,以确保合资企业自身拥有热分解专利技术,避免美国企业再行转让第三方,有利于继续研发并拥有衍生新技术知识产权。布朗宁公司则认为不能将此项技术以专利入股,只能以专有技术使用权入股,保留该项技术专利所有权和专有技术可再转让他人的权利,继续研发衍生技术仍归己有。

3. 主要设备热分解炉及生产线配套设备制造问题。山东翔宇公司认为合资企业准备上三条生产线,主要设备热分解炉如果由美方制造提供,成本高,运输也不方便,应由布朗宁公司提供技术设计图纸,全部由合资企业在中国安排制造,其他配套设备则完全应由中国制造或采购,可节省大量投资。布朗宁公司认为,热分解生产线全套设备是随同热分解技术工艺一并投入合资企业的,特别是主要设备热分解炉的生产制造涉及该项技术核心秘密,应该由布朗宁公司在美国全套生产后以三条生产线作为己方投资到合资企业内,不宜在中国制造。

**谈判任务：**鉴于此,双方约定于 2018 年 3 月再行谈判,争取签约。

**谈判时间及地点：**2018 年 3 月,济南

**给双方的提示：**

1. 确定股权和控股的依据是什么? 如何充分理解并灵活运用该依据,使己方处于主动,实现控股权?

2. 技术专利权与专有技术使用权在本质上有什么不同? 各自投入到合资企业后分别对合资企业产生怎样的后果? 哪种投入方式对己方的权益更加有利?

3. 既然双方合资意向确定,在三条生产线设备制造问题上,各方应采取怎样理性做法,对合资企业有利且促使合资谈判成功?

**模拟要求：**谈判组织(人员调配及分工安排)、谈判方案的准备、谈判的主持与展开。

# Appendix II

# Terms Related to Negotiation 与谈判相关的术语

## I. Modes of Trade, Products, Organizations and Titles
### 贸易方式、产品、机构组织与职务

1. Modes of trade 贸易方式

| | |
|---|---|
| agency | 代理 |
| distribution | 经销 |
| joint venture | 合资企业 |
| cooperative production | 合作生产 |
| auctions | 拍卖 |
| leasing trade | 租赁贸易 |
| counter trade | 对销贸易 |
| compensation trade | 补偿贸易 |
| bidding/tender, invitation to tender | 招标 |
| submission to tender | 投标 |
| consignment | 寄售 |
| assembling with the supplied materials or parts | 来料加工或装配 |
| bilateral trade | 双边贸易 |
| multilateral trade | 多边贸易 |
| barter trade | 易货贸易 |
| bidder | 投标者 |
| bidding | 递盘 |
| broker | 经纪人 |
| brokerage | 经纪费 |
| counter purchase | 互购 |
| distributor | 分销商 |
| exclusive sales | 包销 |

| | |
|---|---|
| sole/exclusive agent | 独家代理人 |
| sales/selling agent | 销售代理人 |
| purchasing/buying agent | 采购代理人 |
| commission agent | 佣金代理人 |
| general agent | 总代理人 |
| manufacturer's agent | 厂家代理人 |
| advertising agent | 广告代理人 |
| shipping/forwarding agent | 运输代理人 |
| insurance agent | 保险代理人 |
| agency agreement | 代理协议 |
| agency commission | 代理佣金 |
| sole agency agreement | 独家代理协议 |
| entrepot trade | 转口贸易 |
| futures | 期货 |
| futures exchange | 期货交易所 |
| futures trading/transaction | 期货交易 |
| forward contract | 期货合同 |
| hedging | 套期保值 |
| product buyback | 产品回购 |
| processing trade | 加工贸易 |
| processing of imported materials | 来料加工 |
| import/export quota | 进口(出口)配额 |
| sale by sample | 凭样品销售 |
| sealed/closed bid | 密封递盘 |

2. Products 产品

| | |
|---|---|
| chemicals | 化工品 |
| textiles | 纺织品 |
| cereals oil and food stuffs | 粮油食品 |
| native produce and animal by-products | 土产畜产 |
| instrument | 仪器 |
| light industrial products | 轻工产品 |
| nonferrous metal | 有色金属 |
| metals and minerals | 五金矿产 |
| arts and crafts | 工艺品 |

| | |
|---|---|
| machinery and equipment | 机械设备 |
| medicines and health products | 医药保健品 |
| electronic products | 电子产品 |
| complete plant | 成套产品 |
| tobacco | 烟草 |
| silk | 丝绸 |
| oil and gas | 石油天然气 |
| coal | 煤炭 |

3. Organizations 组织机构

| | |
|---|---|
| APEC | 亚太经合组织 |
| Asian Development Bank | 亚洲发展银行 |
| Asian Infrastructure Investment Bank（AIIB） | 亚洲基础设施投资银行 |
| Bank of Communications | 交通银行 |
| Bank of China | 中国银行 |
| Industrial and Commercial Bank of China | 中国工商银行 |
| China Merchants Bank | 招商银行 |
| China Construction Bank | 中国建设银行 |
| China Agricultural Bank | 中国农业银行 |
| China Customs | 中国海关 |
| China Entry-Exit Inspection and Quarantine Bureau（CIQ） | 中国出入境检验检疫局 |
| China Council for the Promotion of International Trade（CCPIT） | 中国国际贸易促进委员会 |
| European Union（EU） | 欧盟 |
| International Chamber of Commerce | 国际商会 |
| International Monetary Fund（IMF） | 国际货币基金组织 |
| International Standard Organization（ISO） | 国际标准化组织 |
| Organization of Economic Cooperation and Development（OECD） | 经济合作和发展组织 |
| Organization of Petroleum Exporting Countries（OPEC） | 石油输出国组织 |
| Unite Nations Conference on Trade and Development（UNCTAD） | 联合国贸易与发展会议 |
| World Bank | 世界银行 |

| World Trade Organization（WTO） | 世界贸易组织 |
| state-operated/owned corporation | 国有公司 |
| collective-owned enterprise | 集体企业 |
| private-owned enterprise | 私营企业 |
| township/rural enterprise | 乡镇企业 |
| small and medium-sized enterprise | 中小企业 |
| large-scale industry | 大型企业 |

4. Titles 头衔职务

| chairman/president | 董事长,总裁 |
| chief executive officer（CEO） | 首席执行官,执行总裁 |
| independent director | 独立董事 |
| managing director | 执行董事 |
| general manager | 总经理 |
| executive vice president | 执行副总裁 |
| director of client service | 客户主管 |
| sales manager | 销售经理 |
| （deputy）director/director general | （副）司/局长,董事长 |
| （deputy）division chief | （副）处长 |
| section chief | 科长 |

## Ⅱ. Trade Terms, Currencies, Price, Settlement, Payment and Insurance
## 贸易术语、货币、价格、结算与保险

1. Trade terms 贸易术语

| International Rules for the Interpretation of Trade Terms by（INCOTERMS International Chamber of Commerce） | 国际商会国际贸易术语解释通则 |
| Trade terms/price terms | 贸易术语,价格术语 |
| Cost and Freight（CFR） | 成本加运费（指定目的港） |
| Cost，Insurance and Freight（CIF） | 成本、保险费加运费（指定目的港） |
| Carriage Paid To（CAP） | 运费付至（指定目的地） |
| Carriage and Insurance Paid To（CIP） | 运费和保险费付至（指定目的地） |
| Ex Works（EXW） | 工厂交货（指定地点） |
| Free Alongside Ship（FAS） | 船边交货（指定装运港） |

| | |
|---|---|
| Free Carrier（FCA） | 货交承运人(指定地点) |
| Free on Board（FOB） | 船上交货(指定装运港) |
| Delivered at Terminal（DAT） | 运输终端交货 |
| Delivered at Place（DAP） | 目的地交货 |
| Delivered Duty Paid（DDP） | 完税后交货(指定目的地) |
| CIF Liner Terms | 成本加运费、保费价(班轮条件) |
| CIF Ex Ship's Hold | 成本加运保费舱底交货价 |
| CFR Landed | 成本加运费卸至码头价 |
| Delivered at Frontier（DAF） | 边境交货(指定地点) |
| Delivered Ex Ship（DES） | 目的港船上交货(指定目的港) |
| Delivered Ex Quay（DEQ） | 目的港码头交货(指定目的港) |
| Delivered Duty Unpaid（DDU） | 未完税交货(指定目的地) |
| FOB Liner Terms | 装运港船上交货价(班轮条件) |
| FOB Under Tackle | 装运港吊钩下交货 |
| FOB Stowed | 包括理舱费在内的装运港船上交货价 |
| FOB Trimmed | 包括平舱费在内的装运港船上交货价 |
| FOB Stowed and Trimmed（FOBST） | 包括理舱费、平舱费在内的装运港船上交货价 |

2. Currencies 货币

| | |
|---|---|
| Australian Dollar（AUD） | 澳大利亚元 |
| Chinese Yuan（CNY） | 人民币元 |
| Canadian Dollar（CAD） | 加拿大元 |
| Egyptian Pound（EGP） | 埃及磅 |
| Euro（EUR） | 欧元 |
| Great British Pound（GBP） | 英国英镑 |
| Greek Drachma（GRD） | 希腊德拉马克 |
| Hong Kong Dollars（HKD） | 港元 |
| Italian Lira（ITL） | 意大利里拉 |
| Indian Rupee（INR） | 印度卢比 |
| Japanese Yen（JPY） | 日元 |
| Korean Won（KRW） | 韩国元 |
| Mexican Peso（MXP） | 墨西哥比索 |
| Macao Pataca（MOP） | 澳门澳元 |
| New Zealand Dollar（NZD） | 新西兰元 |

| United States Dollar（USD） | 美元 |
| Vietnamese Dong（VND） | 越南盾 |
| Singapore Dollar（SGD） | 新加坡元 |
| Russian Ruble（RUB） | 俄罗斯卢布 |
| South African Rand（ZAR） | 南非兰特 |

3. Price 价格

| best price | 最好的价格 |
| better price | 更好的价格 |
| bottom price/rock-bottom price | 底价 |
| competitive price | 具有竞争力的价格 |
| contracted price | 合同价格 |
| cost price | 成本价 |
| dumping price | 倾销价 |
| estimated price | 预估价 |
| forward price | 期货价 |
| feasible price | 可行的价格 |
| favorable price | 优惠价 |
| lowest price | 最低价格 |
| monopoly price | 垄断价格 |
| spot price | 现货价 |
| net price | 净价 |
| nominal price | 名义价格 |
| price adjustment | 价格调整 |
| reference price | 参考价格 |
| reasonable price | 合理价格 |
| suitable price | 合适的价格 |
| unit price | 单价 |
| total value/total amount | 总价 |
| retail price | 零售价 |
| wholesale price | 批发价 |
| commission | 佣金 |
| discount | 折扣 |

## 4. Settlement and payment 结算与付款

| | |
|---|---|
| drawer | 出票人 |
| drawee | 受票人 |
| payer | 付款人 |
| payee | 收款人，受款人 |
| endorsement | 背书 |
| endorser | 背书人 |
| endorsee | 被背书人 |
| bill of exchange | 汇票 |
| promissory note | 本票 |
| cheque/check | 支票 |
| issue | 出票 |
| presentation | 提示 |
| acceptance | 承兑 |
| dishonor | 拒付 |
| payment | 付款 |
| recourse | 追索 |
| collection | 托收 |
| collection application | 托收申请 |
| collecting bank | 托收行 |
| negotiating bank | 议付行 |
| reimbursing bank | 偿付行 |
| confirming bank | 保兑行 |
| opening/issuing bank | 开证行 |
| presenting bank | 提示行 |
| paying bank | 付款行 |
| remitting bank | 汇付行 |
| advising/notifying bank | 通知行 |
| accept draft | 承兑汇票 |
| applicant | 开证申请人 |
| bona fide holder | 善意持票人 |
| beneficiary | 受益人 |
| banker's draft | 银行汇票 |
| bank guarantee for loan | 借款担保函 |

| cash against documents（CAD） | 凭单付现 |
| discount | 贴现 |
| cash with order | 订单付款 |
| commercial draft | 商业承兑汇票 |
| remittance by banker's demand draft（D/D） | 票汇 |
| documentary collection | 跟单托收 |
| clean collection | 光票托收 |
| documentary credit | 跟单信用证 |
| deferred payment | 延期汇票 |
| deposit | 押金 |
| documents against acceptance（D/A） | 承兑交单 |
| down payment | 预付定金 |
| documents against payment（D/P） | 付款交单 |
| D/P at sight | 即期付款交单 |
| D/P after sight | 远期付款交单 |
| Letter of Credit（L/C） | 信用证 |
| letter of guarantee | 担保函,保函 |
| money order | 汇款单 |
| mail transfer（M/T） | 信汇 |
| telegraphic transfer（T/T） | 电汇 |
| payment in advance | 预付 |
| payment by installments | 分期付款 |
| principal | 委托人 |
| reciprocal credit | 对开信用证 |
| remittance | 汇付 |
| documentary L/C | 跟单信用证 |
| sight L/C（ L/C at sight，L/C by sight draft) | 即期信用证 |
| time/usance L/C | 远期信用证 |
| revocable L/C | 可撤销信用证 |
| irrevocable L/C | 不可撤销信用证 |
| confirmed L/C | 保兑信用证 |
| unconfirmed L/C | 不保兑信用证 |
| non-transferable L/C | 不可转让信用证 |
| transferable L/C | 可转让信用证 |

| | |
|---|---|
| L/C without recourse | 无追索权信用证 |
| clean L/C | 光票信用证 |
| anticipatory L/C | 预支信用证 |
| clean payment L/C | 全部预支信用证 |
| partial anticipatory L/C | 部分预支信用证 |
| red clause L/C | 红条款信用证 |
| back to back L/C | 背对背信用证 |
| revolving L/C | 循环信用证 |
| automatic revolving L/C | 自动循环信用证 |
| non-automatic revolving L/C | 非自动循环信用证 |
| cumulative revolving L/C | 可积累循环信用证 |
| non-cumulative revolving L/C | 不可积累循环信用证 |
| standby L/C | 备用信用证 |
| usance credit payable at sight L/C | 假远期信用证 |
| UCP L/C | 600 跟单信用证统一惯例(600 号出版物) |
| trust receipt | 信托收据 |
| time/usance/term draft | 远期汇票 |

5. Insurance 保险

| | |
|---|---|
| actual total loss | 实际全损 |
| constructive total loss | 推定全损 |
| average | 海损 |
| general average | 共同海损 |
| particular average | 单独海损 |
| free from particular average（FPA） | 平安险 |
| with particular average（WPA）/ with average（WA） | 水渍险 |
| All Risks | 一切险,全险 |
| additional risks | 附加险 |
| China Insurance Clause（CIC） | 中国保险条款 |
| extraneous risks | 外来风险 |
| franchise | 相对免赔额 |
| Institute Cargo Clause（ICC） | 协会货物保险条款 |
| insurance | 保险 |
| insurer | 保险商,承保人 |

| the insured | 被保险人，投保人 |
| insurance agent | 保险代理人 |
| insurance broker | 保险经纪人 |
| insurance company | 保险公司 |
| insurance coverage | 投保范围 |
| insurance claim | 保险索赔 |
| insurance policy | 保险单 |
| insurance certificate | 保险凭证 |
| open policy | 预约保单 |
| Ocean Maritime Cargo Clauses | 海洋运输货物保险条款 |
| partial loss | 部分损失 |
| premium | 保险费 |
| People's Insurance Company of China（PICC） | 中国人民保险公司 |
| general additional risks | 一般附加险 |
| hook damage | 钩损险 |
| risk of odor | 串味险 |
| risk of rust | 锈损险 |
| risk of leakage | 渗漏险 |
| risk of clash and breakage | 破损破碎险 |
| risk of shortage | 短量险 |
| damage caused by heating and sweating | 受热受潮险 |
| salvage charges | 救助费用 |
| strikes，riots and civil commotions（SRCC） | 罢工暴动民变险 |
| special additional risks | 特殊附加险 |
| theft，pilferage and non-delivery（TPND） | 偷窃和提货不着险 |
| underwriter | 承保商 |
| war risk | 战争险 |
| warehouse to warehouse（W/W） | 仓至仓条款 |

## Ⅲ. Quality，Weight，Measurement，Packing，Marking，Transportation，Documents and Main Ports
### 质量、重量、尺码、包装、标记、运输、单据与世界主要港口

1. Quality，weight and measurement 质量、重量与尺码

| article number（Art No.） | 货号 |

| | |
|---|---|
| counter sample | 回样,对等样品 |
| conditional weight | 公量 |
| description of goods | 货物描述 |
| name of commodities | 品名 |
| detailed specifications | 详细的规格 |
| fair average quality（FAQ） | 大路货,良好平均品质 |
| grade of goods | 货物等级 |
| gross weight | 毛重 |
| net weight | 净重 |
| tare | 皮重 |
| gross for net | 以毛作净 |
| legal weight | 法定重量 |
| weight ton | 重量吨 |
| long ton | 长吨(1016 千克) |
| short ton | 短吨(907 千克) |
| metric ton（MT） | 公吨(1000 千克) |
| measurement ton | 尺码吨 |
| model/type number | 型号 |
| quality as per seller's sample | 质量以卖方样品为准 |
| quality as per buyer's sample | 质量以买方样品为准 |
| sale by descriptions and illustrations | 凭说明书和图样买卖 |
| pattern number | 型号 |
| sale by grade | 凭等级买卖 |
| sale by specification | 凭规格买卖 |
| sale by standard | 凭标准买卖 |
| specifications of goods | 货物的规格 |
| original sample | 原样 |
| duplicate sample | 复样 |
| counter sample | 对等样品 |
| sealed sample | 封样 |
| specification | 规格 |
| more or less clause | 溢短装条款 |
| quantity | 数量 |

2. Packing and markings 包装与标记

| | |
|---|---|
| commercial packing | 商业包装 |
| customary/usual packing | 常规包装 |
| designated packing | 指定包装 |
| export packing | 出口包装 |
| in bulk | 散装 |
| inner packing | 内包装 |
| marketing packing | 销售包装 |
| neutral packing | 中性包装 |
| nude packing | 裸包装 |
| outer packing | 外包装 |
| packing charges/expenses | 包装费 |
| packing material | 包装材料 |
| packing specifications | 包装规格 |
| transportation packing | 运输包装 |
| sales packing | 销售包装 |
| cargo in bulk | 散装货 |
| nude cargo | 裸装货 |
| brand designated by the buyer | 定牌 |
| marks and No.s | 标志与编号 |
| seaworthy packing | 适合海运包装 |
| waterproof packing | 防水包装 |
| stencil | 印制 |
| shipping marks | 运输标志,唛头 |
| indicative marks | 指示性标志 |
| warning mark | 警告性标志 |
| full container load（FCL） | 整箱货 |
| less than container load（LCL） | 拼箱货 |
| twenty-foot equivalent unit（TEU） | 标准集装箱,相当于 20 英尺集装箱单位 |
| case | 箱 |
| carton | 纸箱 |
| corrugated carton | 瓦楞纸箱 |
| wooden case | 木箱 |
| crate | 板条箱 |

| | |
|---|---|
| wooden crate | 木条箱 |
| cardboard box | 纸板盒 |
| plywood case | 胶合板箱 |
| 3-ply plywood case | 三层夹板箱 |
| wooden box | 木盒 |
| bag/sack | 袋 |
| gunny/jute bag | 麻袋 |
| nylon bag | 尼龙袋 |
| poly bag | 塑料袋 |
| poly-woven bag | 塑料编织袋 |
| 3-ply craft paper bag | 三层牛皮纸袋 |
| jumbo bag | 特大袋 |
| drum | 桶 |
| wooden cask | 木桶 |
| barrel | 粗腰桶 |
| straw bale | 草包 |
| pallet | 托盘 |
| press packed bale | 紧压包 |
| aluminum foil package | 铝箔包 |
| pot | 壶 |
| can | 罐 |
| tin | 听 |
| basket | 笼(篓,篮) |
| bamboo basket | 竹笼(篓,篮,筐) |
| wicker basket | 柳条筐 |
| container | 集装箱 |
| container terminal | 集装箱码头 |
| container bill of lading | 集装箱提单 |
| container service | 集装箱业务 |
| container-ship | 集装箱船 |
| auto container | 汽车集装箱 |
| dress hanger container | 挂衣集装箱 |
| dry cargo container | 干货集装箱 |
| flat rack container | 框架集装箱 |

| | |
|---|---|
| open top container | 开顶集装箱 |
| pen container | 牲畜集装箱 |
| platform container | 平台集装箱 |
| shipper-owned container | 货主自有集装箱 |
| specialty container | 特种集装箱 |
| refrigerator container | 冷藏集装箱 |
| tank container | 罐式集装箱 |
| ventilated container | 通风集装箱 |
| circle | 圆形 |
| square | 正方形 |
| triangle | 三角形 |
| rectangle | 长方形 |
| oval | 椭圆形 |
| heart | 心形 |
| downward triangle | 倒三角形 |
| pear-shaped | 葫芦形 |
| pentagon | 五边形 |
| hexagon | 六边形 |
| parallelogram | 平行四边形 |
| trapezoid | 梯形 |
| handle with care | 小心搬运 |
| this side up | 此面朝上 |
| not to be thrown down | 请勿抛掷 |
| not to be laid flat | 请勿平放 |
| no hooks | 请勿用钩 |
| keep upright | 勿倒置 |
| keep out of the direct sun | 避免日光直射 |
| guard against damp | 防潮 |
| keep cool | 保持冷藏 |
| keep away from cold | 请勿受冷 |
| keep away from heat | 请勿受热，远离热源 |
| keep dry | 防湿 |
| keep in a dry place | 保持干燥 |
| keep in a cool place | 在冷处保管 |

| | |
|---|---|
| keep away from boilers | 远离锅炉 |
| perishable goods | 易腐物品 |
| fragile | 易碎品 |
| corrosive | 腐蚀性物品 |
| dangerous goods | 危险品 |
| explosive | 爆炸品 |
| inflammable | 易燃品 |
| poison | 有毒物品 |
| poison gas | 毒气 |
| radioactive | 放射性物品 |

3. Transportation 运输

| | |
|---|---|
| liner transport | 班轮运输 |
| charter party（C/P） | 租船合同 |
| voyage charter party | 航次租船合同 |
| time charter party | 定期租船合同 |
| over-weight surcharge | 超重附加费 |
| port surcharge | 港口附加费 |
| port congestion surcharge | 港口拥塞附加费 |
| deviation surcharge | 绕航附加费 |
| direct additional | 直航附加费 |
| fumigation charge | 熏蒸费 |
| booking note | 托运单（订舱委托书） |
| shipping order（S/O） | 装货单（下货纸） |
| mates receipt | 收货单,大副收据 |
| loading list | 装货清单 |
| dock receipt | 场站收据 |
| rail transport | 铁路运输 |
| road transportation | 公路运输 |
| airway transport | 航空运输 |
| ocean/marine transport | 海洋运输 |
| inland water transportation | 内河航运 |
| international combined transport | 国际联运 |
| intermodal/multimodal transport | 多式联运 |
| consignment | 托运物,运输 |

| | |
|---|---|
| consignor/shipper | 发货人，托运人 |
| carrier | 承运人 |
| consignee | 收货人 |
| container transport | 集装箱运输 |
| calling port | 停靠港 |
| direct steamer | 直达船 |
| demurrage（money/fee/charge） | 滞期费 |
| dispatch money | 速遣费 |
| Chinese main ports（CMP） | 中国主要港口 |
| European main ports（EMP） | 欧洲主要港口 |
| estimated time of departure（ETD） | 预计起航时间 |
| estimated time of arrival（ETA） | 预计到达时间 |
| freight | 运费 |
| freight forwarder/forwarding agent | 货运代理人 |
| freight forwarding company | 货运代理公司 |
| freight to collect/be paid | 运费到付 |
| freight prepaid/paid | 运费已付 |
| land/continental bridge | 大陆桥 |
| lay time | 装卸时间 |
| notifying party | 通知方 |
| optional port | 选择港 |
| parcel post transport | 邮包运输 |
| port of destination | 目的港 |
| port of transshipment | 转运港 |
| port of loading/shipment | 装运港 |
| partial shipment | 分批装运 |
| shipping advice | 装运通知 |
| shipping instructions | 装运须知 |
| shipping space | 舱位 |
| shipping documents | 装运单据 |
| transshipment | 转运 |
| tramp | 不定期租船 |
| weather working days | 晴天工作日 |
| take delivery of | 提货 |

## 4. Documents 单据

| | |
|---|---|
| airway bill | 空运单 |
| bill of lading | 提单 |
| clean B/L | 清洁提单 |
| unclean B/L / foul B/L | 不清洁提单 |
| charter party B/L | 租船提单 |
| copy B/L | 副本提单 |
| direct B/L | 直航提单 |
| liner B/L | 班轮提单 |
| original B/L | 正本提单 |
| on deck B/L | 舱面提单 |
| shipped on board B/L / on board B/L / shipped B/L | 已装船提单 |
| received for shipment B/L | 收讫待运提单 |
| named B/L / straight B/L | 记名提单 |
| bearer B/L | 不记名提单 |
| order B/L | 指示提单 |
| transshipment B/L | 转船提单 |
| through B/L | 联运提单 |
| multi-modal transport B/L / combined transport B/L | 多式联运提单 |
| stale B/L | 过期提单 |
| advanced B/L | 预借提单 |
| anti-dated B/L | 倒签提单 |
| commercial documents | 商业单据 |
| transport documents | 运输单据 |
| insurance documents | 保险单据 |
| official documents | 官方文件 |
| commercial invoice | 商业发票 |
| cargo receipt | 货物收据 |
| consular invoice | 领事发票 |
| customs invoice | 海关发票 |
| manufacturer invoice | 制造商发票 |
| proforma invoice | 形式发票 |

| | |
|---|---|
| certificate of origin | 原产地证 |
| packing list | 装箱单 |
| railway bill | 铁路运单 |
| weight memo | 重量单 |
| certificate of origin | 产地证 |
| GSP Form A | 普惠制产地证 |
| in duplicate | 一式两份 |
| in triplicate | 一式三份 |
| in quadruplicate | 一式四份 |
| in quintuplicate | 一式五份 |
| in sextuplicate | 一式六份 |
| in septuplicate | 一式七份 |
| in octuplicate | 一式八份 |
| in nonuplicate | 一式九份 |
| in decuplicate | 一式十份 |

5. Main ports 世界主要港口

| 港口 | 中文译名 | 所在国家 |
|---|---|---|
| Aden | 亚丁 | 也门 |
| Alexandria | 亚历山大 | 埃及 |
| Amsterdam | 阿姆斯特丹 | 荷兰 |
| Antwerp | 安特卫普 | 比利时 |
| Auckland | 奥克兰 | 新西兰 |
| Baltimore | 巴尔的摩 | 美国 |
| Bankok | 曼谷 | 泰国 |
| Barcelona | 巴塞罗那 | 西班牙 |
| Beirut | 贝鲁特 | 黎巴嫩 |
| Bordeaux | 波尔多 | 法国 |
| Boston | 波士顿 | 美国 |
| Bremen | 不莱梅 | 德国 |
| Buenous Aires | 布宜诺斯艾利斯 | 阿根廷 |
| Calcutta | 加尔各答 | 印度 |
| Chittagong | 吉大港 | 孟加拉国 |
| Colombo | 科伦坡 | 斯里兰卡 |
| Gdansk | 格但斯克 | 波兰 |

| | | |
|---|---|---|
| Genoa | 热那亚 | 意大利 |
| Glasgow | 格拉斯哥 | 英国 |
| Hamburg | 汉堡 | 德国 |
| Hong Kong | 香港 | 中国 |
| Honolulu | 火奴鲁鲁（檀香山） | 美国 |
| Houston | 休斯敦 | 美国 |
| Istanbul | 伊斯坦布尔 | 土耳其 |
| Jeddah | 吉达 | 沙特阿拉伯 |
| Karachi | 卡拉奇 | 巴基斯坦 |
| Kobe | 神户 | 日本 |
| Lisbon | 里斯本 | 葡萄牙 |
| Liverpool | 利物浦 | 英国 |
| London | 伦敦 | 英国 |
| Los Angeles | 洛杉矶 | 美国 |
| Manila | 马尼拉 | 菲律宾 |
| Marseilles | 马赛 | 法国 |
| Melbourne | 墨尔本 | 澳大利亚 |
| Montreal | 蒙特利尔 | 加拿大 |
| Nagoya | 名古屋 | 日本 |
| Naples | 那不勒斯 | 意大利 |
| New Orleans | 新奥尔良 | 美国 |
| New York | 纽约 | 美国 |
| Osaka | 大阪 | 日本 |
| Philadelphia | 费城 | 美国 |
| Quebec | 魁北克 | 加拿大 |
| Rangoon | 仰光 | 缅甸 |
| Rijeka | 里耶卡 | 南斯拉夫 |
| Rio De Janeiro | 里约热内卢 | 巴西 |
| Rostock | 罗斯托克 | 德国 |
| Rotterdam | 鹿特丹 | 荷兰 |
| San Francisco | 旧金山 | 美国 |
| Singapore | 新加坡 | 新加坡 |
| Southampton | 南安普顿 | 英国 |
| Stockholm | 斯德哥尔摩 | 瑞典 |

| Sydney | 悉尼 | 澳大利亚 |
| Tokyo | 东京 | 日本 |
| Tripoli | 的黎波里 | 利比亚 |
| Valparaiso | 瓦尔帕来索 | 智利 |
| Vancouver | 温哥华 | 加拿大 |
| Venice | 威尼斯 | 意大利 |
| Wellington | 惠灵顿 | 新西兰 |
| Yokohama | 横滨 | 日本 |

## Ⅳ. Contract, Business Negotiation, Inspection, Claim and Arbitration
## 合同、业务洽谈、检验、索赔及仲裁

### 1. Contract 合同

| contract | 合同，订立合同 |
| contractor | 订约人，承包人 |
| sales contract | 销售合同 |
| sales confirmation | 销售确认书 |
| trade agreement | 贸易协议 |
| memorandum | 备忘录 |
| executor contract | 尚待执行的合同 |
| originals of the contract | 合同正本 |
| copies of the contract | 合同副本 |
| written contract | 书面合同 |
| agency contract | 代理合同 |
| barter contract | 易货合同 |
| binding contract | 有约束力合同 |
| commercial contract | 商业合同 |
| international trade contract | 国际贸易合同 |
| compensation trade contract | 补偿贸易合同 |
| cross license contract | 互换许可证合同 |
| exclusive license contract | 独家许可证合同 |
| export contract | 出口合同 |
| import contract | 进口合同 |
| formal contract | 正式合同 |
| forward contract | 期货合同 |

| | |
|---|---|
| illegal contract | 非法合同 |
| indirect contract | 间接合同 |
| installment contract | 分期合同 |
| know-how license contract | 专业技术许可合同 |
| patent license contract | 专利许可合同 |
| trade mark license contract | 商标合同 |
| transferable license contract | 转让许可合同 |
| non-transferable license contract | 不可转让许可合同 |
| service contract | 服务合同 |
| long-term contract | 长期合同 |
| short-term contract | 短期合同 |
| unilateral contract | 单方承担义务合同 |
| contract of affreightment | 包运合同，租船契约 |
| contract of employment/engagement | 雇佣合同 |
| contract of carriage | 运输合同 |
| contract of arbitration | 仲裁合同 |
| contract of insurance | 保险合同 |
| contract for future delivery | 远期交货合同 |
| contract for payment of goods by installment | 分期付款的买卖合同 |
| contract for purpose | 购货合同 |
| contract for service | 劳务合同 |
| contract for the delivery of goods by installment | 分期交货合同 |
| contract for goods | 订货合同 |
| amendment of contract | 修正合同 |
| cancellation of contract | 撤销合同 |
| expiration of contract | 合同期满 |
| renewal of contract | 合同续订 |
| interpretation of contract | 解释合同 |
| execution/performance of contract | 履行合同 |
| completion of contract | 完成合同 |
| contract price | 合约价格 |
| contract wages | 合同工资 |
| contract sales | 订约销售 |
| contract law | 合同法 |

| | |
|---|---|
| contract parties | 合同当事人 |
| make a contract / sign a contract / place/enter into a contract | 签订合同 |
| draw up a contract | 拟订合同 |
| draft a contract | 起草合同 |
| countersign a contract | 回签合同 |
| carry out/implement/execute/fulfill/perform a contract | 执行合同 |
| break a contract | 违约 |
| terminate a contract | 解除合同 |
| approve a contract | 审批合同 |
| honor a contract | 恪守合同 |
| alter a contract | 修改合同 |
| abide by/adhere to a contract | 遵守合同 |
| bring a contract into effect | 使合同生效 |
| go/come into effect | 生效 |
| cease to be in effect/force | 失效 |
| contractual | 合同的,契约的 |
| contractual practice/usage | 合同惯例 |
| contractual claim | 根据合同的债权 |
| contractual liability/obligation | 合同规定的义务 |
| contractual specification | 合同规定 |
| contractual income | 合同收入 |
| contractual terms and conditions | 合同条款和条件 |
| contractual guarantee | 合同担保 |
| contractual-joint-venture | 合作经营,契约式联合经营 |
| agreement | 协议 |
| loan agreement | 贷款协议 |
| bilateral trade agreement | 双边贸易协议 |
| multilateral trade agreement | 多边贸易协议 |
| commercial agreement | 商业协议 |
| compensation trade agreement | 补偿贸易协议 |
| distributorship agreement | 销售协议 |
| exclusive distributorship agreement | 独家销售协议 |
| guarantee agreement | 担保协议 |

| | |
|---|---|
| international trade agreement | 国际贸易协议 |
| joint venture agreement | 合营协议 |
| licensing agreement | 许可证协议 |
| management agreement | 经营管理协议 |
| operating agreement | 经营协议 |
| partnership agreement | 合伙协议 |
| supply agreement | 供货协议 |
| trade agreement | 贸易协议 |
| vessel sharing agreement | 公用舱位协议 |
| agreement on general terms and conditions on business | 一般经营交易条件的协议 |
| agreement on loan facilities up to a given amount | 商定借款协议 |
| agreement on import licensing procedure | 进口许可证手续协议 |
| agreement of fixing price | 共同定价协议 |
| agreement of reimbursement | 偿付协议 |
| agreement in writing | 书面协议 |
| agreement to resell | 转售协议 |

2. Business negotiation 业务洽谈

| | |
|---|---|
| acceptance | 接受 |
| late acceptance | 逾期接受 |
| quotation | 报价 |
| selling offer | 售货发盘 |
| buying offer | 购货发盘 |
| withdrawal | 撤回 |
| revocation | 撤销 |
| cut to the limit | 降到极限 |
| meet sb. half way | 折中,各让一半 |
| allowance | 折让,补贴 |
| bid | 出价,递盘 |
| bargain | 讨价还价 |
| counter offer | 还盘 |
| firm offer/definite offer | 实盘 |
| offer with engagement | 具约束力的报盘(实盘) |
| non-firm offer/indefinite offer | 虚盘 |
| offer without engagement | 不具约束力的报盘(虚盘) |

| | |
|---|---|
| inquiry/enquiry | 询价，询盘 |
| invitation to offer | 邀请发盘 |
| modification | （发盘的）修改 |
| offer | 报盘 |
| offerer/offeror | 发盘人 |
| offeree | 受盘人 |
| order | 订单 |
| initial order | 首次订单 |
| fresh order | 新订单 |
| trial order | 试订单 |
| repeat order | 续订单 |
| duplicate order | 重复订单 |
| outstanding/pending order | 未完成的订单 |
| place an order (with sb. for sth.) | （向某人）订购（某物） |
| accept an order | 接受订单 |
| execute/fulfill/carry out an order | 执行订单 |
| cancel an order | 取消订单 |
| withdraw an order | 撤销订单 |
| decline/turn down/refuse an order | 拒接订单 |
| confirm/take on/entertain an order | 接受订单 |
| hold up/suspend an order | 暂停执行订单 |
| product list | 货单 |
| price list | 价格单，价目表 |
| purchase note | 购货单 |
| quotation sheet | 报价单 |
| rebate | 回扣 |
| win-win concept | 双赢理念 |
| product negotiation | 产品谈判 |
| technology trade negotiation | 技术贸易谈判 |
| service trade negotiation | 服务贸易谈判 |
| international project negotiation | 国际工程谈判 |
| one-to-one negotiation | 一对一谈判 |
| team negotiation | 团组谈判 |
| multilateral negotiation | 多边谈判 |

| | |
|---|---|
| horizontal negotiation | 水平谈判 |
| vertical negotiation | 垂直谈判 |
| host-court negotiation | 主场谈判 |
| guest-court negotiation | 客场谈判 |
| changing-court negotiation | 场地轮流谈判 |
| third-place negotiation | 中立地谈判 |
| oral negotiation | 口头谈判 |
| written negotiation | 书面谈判 |
| excessively demanding | 先苦后甜,过分要求 |
| emotional outburst | 感情迸发 |
| tag-team tactic | 车轮战术 |
| divide and conquer | 分而治之 |
| create competition | 利用竞争 |
| use stick and carrot/red face and white face | 软硬兼施,胡萝卜大棒策略,红白脸策略 |
| reaching for a yard after getting an inch | 得寸进尺 |
| feint to the east and attack in the west | 声东击西 |
| take advantage of another's faults | 利用他人失误 |
| ultimatum/take it or leave it | 最后通牒 |
| restriction/limited authority | 限制策略 |
| no precedents | 没有先例 |
| fatiguing tactics | 疲劳战术 |
| adjournment | 休会 |
| retreat in order to advance | 以退为进 |
| show weakness for sympathy/seek commiseration | 示弱求怜 |
| show one's hand | (摊牌)先让步 |
| be tough and strong | 以攻对攻 |
| equal and voluntary participation | 平等自愿 |
| credibility first | 信誉至上 |
| mutual reciprocity and mutual benefits | 互惠互利 |
| maximize commonality and minimize difference | 求同存异 |
| speak on good ground | 有理有据 |
| separate the people from the problem | 人事分开,对人不对事 |

### 3. Inspection 检验

| | |
|---|---|
| Commodity Inspection Bureau | 商品检验局 |
| Inspection Certificate | 检验证书 |
| Disinfection Inspection Certificate | 消毒检验证书 |
| Inspection Certificate of Value | 价值检验证书 |
| Inspection Certificate of Quality | 质量检验证书 |
| Inspection Certificate of Health | 卫生检验证书 |
| Inspection Certificate of Origin | 原产地检验证书 |
| Inspection Certificate of Weight | 重量检验证书 |
| Inspection Certificate of Tank/Hold | 验舱证书 |
| Inspection Certificate of Loss or Damage | 残损证书 |
| Inspection Certificate of Damaged Cargo | 验残检验证书 |
| Inspection Certificate of Cargo Weight and Measurement | 货载衡量检验证书 |
| Inspection Certificate of Fumigation | 熏蒸证书 |
| Inspection Certificate of Temperature | 测温证书 |
| Veterinary Inspection Certificate | 兽医检验证书 |

### 4. Claim and arbitration 索赔与仲裁

| | |
|---|---|
| arbitration | 仲裁 |
| arbitral award | 仲裁裁决 |
| arbitration clause | 仲裁条款 |
| breach/violation of contract | 违反合同,违约 |
| breach/violation of condition | 违反要件 |
| claim | 索赔 |
| claim settlement | 理赔 |
| short delivery | 短交 |
| short unloaded | 短卸 |
| lost in transit | 短失 |
| damage report | 破损证明 |
| marine protest | 海难报告 |
| dispute | 争执,纠纷 |
| defendant | 被诉方 |
| plaintiff | 起诉方 |

| | |
|---|---|
| discrepancy and claim clause | 异议、索赔条款 |
| fundamental breach | 根本违约 |
| minor breach | 轻微违约 |
| material breach | 重大违约 |
| force majeure | 不可抗力 |
| lodge a claim against sb. | 向……提出索赔 |
| penalty | 罚金 |

## V. Simplified Words/Phrases and Abbreviations
## 简化字词及缩写

| | |
|---|---|
| ASAP | as soon as possible |
| FYI | for your information |
| ETD | estimated time of departure |
| ETA | estimated time of arrival |
| UOS | unless otherwise specified |
| EMP | European main ports |
| CMP | Chinese main ports |
| CCPIT | China Council for the Promotion of International Trade |
| COSCO | China Ocean Shipping Co. |
| ICC | International Chamber of Commerce |
| | Institute Cargo Clauses |
| ISO | International Standards Organization |
| S.R.C.C | Strikes，Riots and Civil Commotions |
| T.P.N.D | Theft，Pilferage and Non-Delivery Risks |
| SS，S/S | steamship |
| B/L | bill of lading |
| B/E | bill of exchange |
| CIF | cost，insurance and freight |
| CFR | cost and freight |
| CIFC | cost，insurance，freight and commission |
| FOB | free on board |
| COD | cash on delivery |
| D/P | documents against payment |
| D/A | documents against acceptance |

| | |
|---|---|
| TT | telegraphic transfer |
| CAD | cash against documents |
| USD | United States dollar |
| MT | metric ton |
| KG | kilogram |
| IRREV | irrevocable |
| ADJ | adjust |
| CERT | certificate |
| EXP | export |
| IMP | import |
| ADDS/ADS | address |
| ADDN | addition |
| ATTN | attention |
| ADV | advise/advice |
| LIC | licence |
| MAX | maximum |
| MIN | minimum |
| DOC | document |
| INV | invoice |
| SPEC | specification |
| CONDI | condition |
| MEMO | memorandum |
| NEGO | negotiate |
| APPROX | approximate |
| JAP | Japan |
| IMMED | immediate |
| MANUF | manufacture |
| AIRFRT | airfreight |
| CONSGNT | consignment |
| INSTRCTN | instruction |
| SHPMT | shipment |
| ACDG | according |
| APPLCTN | application |
| FM | from |

| | |
|---|---|
| YD | yard |
| QLTY | quality |
| QUTY | quantity |
| BTWN | between |
| RCVD | received |
| SMPL | sample |
| ABV | above |
| ABT | about |
| ACPT | accept |
| MSG | message |
| N | and |
| R | are |
| B | be |
| U | you |
| UR | your |
| OZWZ/OTHWS | otherwise |
| SHPG | shipping |
| SHPD | shipped |
| AMDT | amendment |
| CFMTN | confirmation |
| ACPTBL | acceptable |
| AGNST | against |
| AGRMT | agreement |
| ALRDY | already |
| CHN/CN | China |